Identity, Multilingualism and CALL

Advances in CALL Research and Practice
Series Editor: Greg Kessler, Ohio University

This series is published in cooperation with the Computer Assisted Language Instruction Consortium (CALICO). Each Spring just prior to the CALICO annual conference the series publishes one volume comprised of original studies on a specific topic.

Published:
2016
Landmarks in CALL Research
Looking Back to Prepare for the Future, 1995–2015
Edited by Greg Kessler

2017
Learner Autonomy and Web 2.0
Edited by Marco Cappellini, Tim Lewis, and Annick Rivens Mompean

2018
Assessment Across Online Language Education
Edited by Stephanie Link and Jinrong Li

2019
Engaging Language Learners through CALL
From Theory and Research to Informed Practice
Edited by Nike Arnold and Lara Ducate

2020
Understanding Attitude in Intercultural Virtual Communication
Edited by Ana Oskoz and Margarita Vinagre

2021
Project-Based Language Learning and CALL
From Virtual Exchange to Social Justice
Edited by Michael Thomas and Kasumi Yamazaki

Identity, Multilingualism and CALL

Responding to New Global Realities

Edited by Liudmila Klimanova

SHEFFIELD UK   BRISTOL CT

Published by Equinox Publishing Ltd.

UK Office 415, The Workstation, 15 Paternoster Row, Sheffield,
South Yorkshire S1 2BX
USA ISD, 70 Enterprise Drive, Bristol, CT 06010

www.equinoxpub.com

First published 2022

© Liudmila Klimanova and contributors 2022

All rights reserved. No part of this publication may be reproduced or transmitted in any form or by any means, electronic or mechanical, including photocopying, recording or any information storage or retrieval system, without prior permission in writing from the publishers.

British Library Cataloguing-in-Publication Data

A catalogue record for this book is available from the British Library.

ISBN-13 978 1 80050 079 2 (paperback)
978 1 80050 080 8 (ePDF)
978 1 80050 177 5 (ePub)

Library of Congress Cataloging-in-Publication Data

Names: Klimanova, Liudmila, 1976- editor.
Title: Identity, multilingualism and CALL : responding to new global realities / edited by Liudmila Klimanova.
Description: Sheffield, South Yorkshire ; Bristol, CT : Equinox Publishing Ltd, 2022. | Series: Advances in CALL research and practice | Includes bibliographical references and index. | Summary: "This volume focuses on a range of topics and studies that address the notion of plurilingualism and multilingual identity in computer-mediated language learning (CALL) spaces"-- Provided by publisher.
Identifiers: LCCN 2022010654 (print) | LCCN 2022010655 (ebook) | ISBN 9781800500792 (paperback) | ISBN 9781800500808 (ePDF) | ISBN 9781800501775 (ePub)
Subjects: LCSH: Language and languages--Computer-assisted instruction for foreign speakers. | Language and languages--Study and teaching--Technological innovations. | Group identity. | Multilingualism. | Multicultural education. | LCGFT: Essays.
Classification: LCC P53.28 .I34 2022 (print) | LCC P53.28 (ebook) | DDC 418.0078/5--dc23/eng/20220406
LC record available at https://lccn.loc.gov/2022010654
LC ebook record available at https://lccn.loc.gov/2022010655

Typeset by Sparks – www.sparkspublishing.com

Contents

1 Introduction to the Volume: On the State of Identity Research in CALL

Liudmila Klimanova

1 Identity and Language Learning

This volume is about *identity* and its relationship with language as it is learned and used in digitally mediated spaces. Addressing current research and scholarship on second language (L2) use and development, it aims to give readers a comprehensive overview of key themes, constructs, and contexts that have emerged from language learners' interactions with and in continuously shifting digital landscapes.

Identity is a fundamental research construct in applied linguistics that captures the individual and social complexities of language learning and the social hierarchy of power relations that give access to or restrict language learners from participating as legitimate speakers in particular types of discourses (Block, 2007). Identity is constituted in and through language (Norton, 2013). Furthermore, identity in language use extends beyond static social labels and roles and encompasses dynamic, ever-changing ways of being, the ways "a person understands his or her relationship to the world, how that relationship is constructed across time and space and how the person understands possibilities for the future" (Norton, 2013, p. 45). Identity performances are always closely tied to language use and can explain the choice of linguistic resources deployed by language learners in communicative spaces (Darvin, 2016; De Fina, 2016).

Since Firth and Wagner's 1997 seminal critique of the second language acquisition (SLA) science for conceptualizing language learners solely within the frames of cognitive science and linguistics, and for disregarding dynamic and diversified social contexts in which language learning takes place (Block, 2007; Firth & Wagner, 1997; Norton & De Costa, 2018), identity research has been growing exponentially. For SLA research, considering identity as a critical acquisition variable means uncovering the relationship of power, native speaker hegemonies reproduced from within social digital spaces as well as imposed by larger social and institutional structures. It is not surprising that the CALL scholarship has quickly embraced and operationalized this construct in relation to myriad digitally mediated contexts where L2 learners find themselves having to use and negotiate language and meaning in order to deploy and contest desired identities and subject positions (Thorne et al., 2015). This new trend reflects an ongoing diversification and liminalization of digital communication. Writing, speaking, formal and informal genres, and digital media merge in a variety of intricate ways, facilitating translingual and transcultural virtual encounters (Canagarajah, 2013), but also restricting and complexifying digital modes of interpersonal interaction producing uniquely digital interactional practices which require new epistemological theorizations and analytical approaches.

Globalization, 'internetization' or the empowerment of electronic connectivity, and technologization of human interaction have exerted new profound pressures on what it means to speak more than one language, and how to seek out and pursue L2 learning opportunities in digital communities (Douglas Fir Group, 2016). Digitally mediated interaction leads to new insights into how L2 learners use language to formulate ideas, create and articulate meanings, and enact identities (Darvin, 2016) as they straddle the borders of private and public online and offline worlds, and fluidly move across educational and non-institutional social media spaces. They enter and navigate multiple contexts of power, and continuously negotiate spaces where they can claim the right to speak. Just as in the offline world, online contexts may be inclusive and exclusive, reflecting existing power differentials and inequalities (Van Deursen & van Dijk, 2014). Learners need, along with demonstrating their language skills, to perform legitimate speaker identities to gain access to social resources available in digital spaces, and engage along the way their emotions, attitudes, and ideologies (Kramsch, 2009). The questions to pose for identity research in CALL are to ask how L2 learners position themselves and are positioned by others (participants and tools) in digital social spaces and technologized learning environments, and how these positions shape their language use (Klimanova & Dembovskaya, 2013), experience (Klimanova, 2020), and investment (Darvin & Norton, 2017; Norton, 2013) in the language and literacy practices of these diverse contexts. This introductory chapter presents a brief synthesis of the research on L2 identity in CALL, and more broadly in digitally mediated contexts, and addresses the following questions:

- How has identity research in CALL evolved over the past few decades?
- How does identity research in CALL intersect with digital multilingualism and multilingual users?
- What operational constructs and concepts are applied to researching identity in digital social spaces?
- What are the current approaches to investigating L2 identity in computer-mediated communication (CMC) and CALL?
- What new avenues of empirical inquiry emerge from the contributions to this volume in response to technological advancements in social digital communication?

By answering these questions, this chapter introduces important issues and trends and possible future avenues for L2 identity research in CALL for language acquisition specialists.

2 A Brief History of Identity Research in CALL

Identity research in CALL never existed in a vacuum, and its evolution was impacted by developments of socio-psychological approaches in CMC studies (Androutsopoulos, 2006) and language acquisition theory (Klimanova, 2021). Computer mediation opened new possibilities for second language learning and applied linguists began to examine digitally mediated language use and communication for evidence of L2 development first in educationally engineered communicative settings, and more recently in non-institutional digital environments and multilingual communities. Informed by a substantial body of language and identity-related research, CALL contexts quickly became a new medium in the exploration of digital affordances for the performance of various social identities.

Earlier research on computer-mediated learning environments recognized categorically stable social and cultural roles (e.g., nationality, occupation, first language, gender) that characterized L2 learners participating in computer-mediated, developmentally significant L2 interaction (e.g., Warschauer, 1997). These roles were used to establish the rationale for explaining differing learning outcomes and communication strategies in CMC. Online interaction was described as disembodied, artificial, and separated from the offline lives of language learners (Androutsopoulos, 2006). At the same time, computer mediation was found to have an equalizing effect on communication, leading to increased language production and active engagement in communicative strategies (Ortega, 1997), and offering reticent and shy learners ample opportunities to engage in communicative practice through building virtual identities that were different from 'real-life' personas (Chun, 1994). Although the majority of earlier CMC research in CALL was dominated by language-oriented paradigms (Klimanova, 2021), psychological factors, and the capacity of online platforms to liberate L2 learners by enabling agentive roles not readily available to them in physical classrooms (Kelm, 1996), brought about new understandings of individual factors in CALL research.

Following the social turn in applied linguistics (Block, 2003), and a post-structuralist re-conceptualization of L2 identity as dynamic, fluid, and dependent on social and ideological contexts of language use (Norton, 2000, 2013), a focus on identity performances gradually became one of the central themes in CALL research, suggesting a contextualized and holistic lens through which language use was examined in digitally mediated contexts, particularly in CMC studies (e.g., Nguyen & Kellogg, 2005; Warschauer et al., 2002). The increasing availability of online social networks and virtual affinity groups warranted a new body of research on non-educational, recreational, and professional online environments, or "the wilds" (Sauro & Zourou, 2019; Thorne, 2010). These unstructured digital contexts offered rich and novel data for examining the non-scripted use of L2 for purposes that extended beyond mere improvements in language and communication skills. Digital contexts quickly became secure outlets for multilingual literacy practices, and language socialization and were often examined through the prism of the socio-cultural theory of cognition (Basharina, 2007; Lantolf & Thorne, 2006) where language played a critical mediating role in regulating social relations and identity performances in a community of shared practice (e.g., Lam, 2000, 2004). Claims were made about a transformative role of digital social spaces in offering L2 learners various opportunities for socially balanced and egalitarian communication and for building a more positive and empowering L2 identity than the one enacted in educational settings (e.g., Freiermuth & Jarrell, 2006; Sauro & Zourou, 2019; Schreiber, 2015). These digital playspaces were seen as venues where intricate self-positioning strategies and role shifting resulted in full or partial (peripheral) social inclusion (Hanna & de Nooy, 2003).

As newly emerging digital spaces continued to diversify virtual interaction, CALL theory began to adopt more constructs from applied linguistics and CMC studies to explain a dynamic shifting of subject positions taking place in L2 learners' recreational and educational digital spaces. Increased vernacular uses of L2 helped introduce the notions of *transportable* and *situated* identity (Zimmerman, 1998) in digital communication research and bring into focus dynamic tensions between the person's online and offline lives. Situated identity performances were to explain how learners' offline transportable identities, represented by stable social roles and labels, frequently came into conflict with the identities they were eager to enact in digital spaces while self-positioning in response to a CMC genre and a specific social context in which they engaged. These tensions allowed for "an interplay between students' non-academic identities and the discursively constructed institutional roles of the classroom" (Thorne et al., 2015, p. 40).

The social considerations in the study of digital identity performances have gradually expanded to include more critical foci and issues, moving to the forefront a new body of research on the role of English in global networks, and its impact on CALL research (Pasfield-Neofitou, 2011; Sauro, 2016), online power hegemonies (Helm et al., 2012), linguistic multicompetence and code-switching (or use of multiple languages and sign systems in digital communication) (Androutsopoulos, 2013b). Following the multilingual turn in applied linguistics as an alternative to still dominant monolingual theories and pedagogies in language education (May, 2014), CALL research began to re-situate the notion of multilingualism and multilingual competence more centrally in digital identity research (Buendgens-Kosten & Elsner, 2018). The monolithic notion of *language learner* in CALL settings has been supplemented by a more nuanced and comprehensive understanding of *language users* with their complex linguistic repertoires and plurilingual performances in non-structured digital spaces, where subject positions and identity performances were examined within larger global, phenomenological, and critical scales (Kramsch, 2009; Schreiber, 2015). The merging of L2 learners' offline lives and their dynamic and ever-changing virtual social networks both in educational/professional and recreational/private domains brought about the phenomenon of *virtual subjectivity* and the focus on identity performances in connection to a multitude of personal histories, experiences, stances, and tensions surrounding L2 learners' past and present online and offline activities (Klimanova, 2020).

Recent CALL studies conceptualize identity work within learners' positioning systems (Sauro, 2004) where identity performances are understood to be subject to continuous negotiation and reaffirmation in response to various social contextual cues (Bucholtz & Hall, 2005; Wu, 2018). Participants of digital communities have been increasingly viewed as empowered, agentive, and invested, deploying agency as a driving force in language learning (Vandergriff, 2016). The new digital realities and technological contradictions have triggered a wave of identity studies at the intersection of the institutional and private uses of second languages in digitally mediated language learning contexts (Klimanova, 2021). Following the developments in SLA research, the CALL field has significantly expanded the scope of identity studies to include digital contexts where bi/multilingual users create, sustain, and adapt their linguistic identities while engaging with diverse digital communities in an increasingly multilingual fashion. In these spaces, increased presence and visibility of "big" and "small" languages provide greater levels of multilingual provision and linguistic differentiation, but also create new boundaries and delineations for multicompetent language users (Kelly-Holmes, 2019).

3 Researching Identity in CALL

In the past decades, CALL studies examined identity performance in two broad contexts: as an outcome of participation in institutional digital spaces or non-institutionally located online cultures, or as a design element of educational practice or digital platforms (Thorne et al., 2015). Identity research in computer-mediated communication is predominantly marked by a socio-constructivist paradigm that focuses on the micro-level of interaction and meaning-making (Darvin, 2018). In this regard, identity studies in CALL are typically situated within the qualitative domain of investigative inquiry and emerge from a close examination of online interactional records, which can be scripts of online chats or recorded messages. Transcripts of CMC data are analyzed using various types of textual analysis, including discourse analysis, critical discourse analysis (CDA), conversation analysis, and, more broadly, grounded theory approaches (Hadley, 2016; Thorne et al., 2015). The choice of methodological approach is driven by specific research questions and hypotheses the researcher poses for a given study of identity development in CMC. The object of such investigative inquiry is a dynamic use of linguistic and non-linguistic (e.g., multimodal) identity markers and enactment of L1/L2 situated and transportable identities (Zimmerman, 1998), but also learner lived experience in digital social contexts.

To ensure analytical rigor and adequately capture the phenomenological experience of learners, identity researchers employ a method of *data triangulation* (use of multiple data sources in a single, multi-layered analysis), supporting interactional analyses with empirical evidence obtained from interviews with learners, journals, and reflective narratives. The purpose of data triangulation is to obtain the most accurate depiction of learners' motivations, perspectives, and intentions associated with identity enactment in

CMC environments and a more holistic understanding of identity development. The challenge of identity research in digital spaces lies in the accurate description of the relationship between language use and self-positioning, which is complicated by a growing array of semiotic tools at the learner's disposal to construct a digital text. This complexity of digital communication explains a wide array of research paradigms and methodological approaches that account for various facets and dimensions of identity enactment in digital spaces, from multimodal, ethnographic (Domingo, 2016), and ethnomethodological to the critical (De Costa & Norton, 2016; Norton, 2013). Thus, Darvin (2018) outlines four prevalent methodologies in identity research in applied linguistics: case studies, narrative inquiry, conversation analysis, and critical discourse analyses. These methodologies are also typically used to examine identity construction in CMC contexts.

The *case study approach* focuses on individual experiences and provides a "contextualized profile of a person" or a focal group (Darvin, 2018, p. 779), examining linguistic, cultural, political, and social contexts that exert influence on the person's self-identification. The advantages of this approach lie in its attention to personal and socio-cultural aspects of lived experience and to the shifting identities of language learners in response to the change of communicative contexts and prevalent norms and ideologies (Duff, 2019). The most notable example of the case study approach in CMC research is the study of Lam (2000), who examined the construction and transformation of textual identities of an ethnic Chinese teenage schoolboy, Almon, who was engaged in synchronous and asynchronous CMC interactions with Japanese and Chinese students. To build a complete research case, Lam analyzed Almon's interactions with transatlantic peers over a period of six months, examined his website, and conducted semi-structured interviews. From these observations of Almon's digital texts and analysis of his interviews, Lam identified the motivations and strategies Almon used to articulate his online textual identity of a legitimate English speaker as he negotiated diverse discourses on the internet. In a later study, Lam (2004) again employed the case study approach to analyze the texts produced by two Cantonese girls in the United States who struggled in their ESL classroom at school but found a creative outlet for self-positioning as English writers in a Cantonese-English chatroom where their texts contained a mixture of English and Cantonese words, Romanized Chinese texts, and emoticons. Lam concluded that this code-switching strategy marked the girls as bilingual Chinese emigrants in a network of their peers. Their translingual CMC activity made them more confident and empowered English speakers at school.

Among the most cited limitations of the case study approach is a challenge of generalizability on a basis of an individual case, and an inherent bias associated with the researcher's preconceived ideas about the context and its impact on an individual participant (Darvin, 2016). At the epistemological level, case studies rely on the positivist assumption that social reality is independent of the researcher that observes it, and such observations are the basis of new knowledge (Duff, 2014, 2019). To account for the bias entails acknowledging that social reality, including digital reality, is not given but is dynamically constructed differently by different individuals.

Narrative analysis, another prevalent research paradigm in CALL identity research, is a systematic study of stories of life experiences (Chase, 2005) that relies on the power of storytelling to reveal individual ideologies, and the significance of big stories in understanding a person's identity and construction of *self* within specific institutional, organizational, discursive, and local cultural contexts (Bamberg, 2006). Stories are "privileged forms/structures/systems for making sense of *self* by bringing the coordinates of time, space, and personhood into a unitary frame so that the sources behind these representations (such as 'author', 'teller', and 'narrator') can be made empirically visible for further analytical scrutiny in the form of 'identity analysis'" (Bamberg & Georgakopoulou, 2008, p. 378). Narrative inquiry in CMC research begins with an assumption that through narration, study participants can explain the choices they make when they construct their online identities. This approach allows the researcher to understand underlying motives guiding learners in their choice of self-positioning in CMC contexts. Klimanova (2020), for example, used the multiple-case study approach to analyze the narratives of Aaron, Alina, and Andrew, three Russian L2 learners, about their lived experience positioning themselves as Russian speakers on a popular Russian social networking site. Their narratives were elicited via *phenomenological interviews* (Smith et al., 2009) and other qualitative instruments for evaluating personal constructs and lived experiences. The researcher found it essential to access the entirety of the learners' individual experience and understand each participant's voice – "the account of individual experience is inherently constrained by the voice of the 'experiencer', and by the pre-reflected first-hand acquaintance with a newly experienced reality and with the content of our action in it" (Klimanova, 2020, p. 289). The analysis demonstrated that Aaron's conception of his online identity was inseparable from this offline military persona. Alina's story revealed her hidden struggle with legitimizing her identity of a Russian heritage speaker in virtual encounters with her transatlantic Russian-speaking peers. Finally, Andrew's online identity construction was marked by his concealed efforts to come to terms with ideologies of genre-tool connections and reconcile his casual use of social networks with the formal context of teacher-controlled language-learning activity. These narratives unveiled distinct trajectories of lived experience for each participant which were shaped by a multitude of subjectivities and identities they assumed when constructing their online personas. Klimanova argued that L2 learners' personal histories, emotional insecurities, and prior experiences with the virtual world and digital tools are implicated in the digital texts they created in CMC contexts (Klimanova, 2020, p. 304).

Whereas the previous two methodologies described in this section rely on qualitative data to elicit learners' accounts of identity-building strategies, *conversation analysis (CA) of computer-mediated communication* focuses specifically on interactional dimensions of digital communication and its impact on language use and learning (Tudini & Liddicoat, 2017). CA derives its robust analytical tools from conversation analysis of natural human-to-human conversations and treats digital interaction records as the main data source for identifying unique interactional resources for identity construction available to users in digitally mediated contexts. While CA offers no theoretical framework that can explain *identity-in-digital interaction*, as, for example, the sociolinguistic theory of identity (Bucholtz & Hall, 2005), its analytical instruments rely on indexical, context-bound theorizations of identity enactment. Conversational analysts begin their inquiry with an assumption that social life is organized through talk and interaction, and identity is constructed in an unfolding conversation with other people – "as an oriented-to, recipient-designed accomplishment of interaction" (Benwell & Stokoe, 2016, p. 68). In other words, identity categories are derived from what interactants communicate to each other as they adopt social positions and claim language and cultural affiliations. For the CA of identity construction in digital contexts, it is critical to examine naturally occurring communication data to observe how identity markers are instantiated and resisted by L2 learners in online communication (Kasper & Wagner, 2014).

The CA approach offers identity researchers a robust methodological toolkit for scrutinizing natural online interaction and investigating ideological biases and assumptions of race, gender, language, country affiliation, and sexual orientation reproduced through language. Among its limitations are low generalizability (Kasper & Wagner, 2014), and its exclusive attention to the structural and semantic features of online interactions – "how the participants carry out the interaction" (González-Lloret, 2011, p. 318) – without considering an interactant's voice and internal motivations. To account for these factors in identity research in CMC contexts, CA is frequently combined with other qualitative methods and analytical frameworks. On the other hand, the longitudinal study of a person's online interactions or a comparison of a person's online interactions in distinct digital contexts allows identity researchers to identify distinct identity-building strategies employed over time. Klimanova and Dembovskaya (2013), for example, employed multiple layers of data including elements of CA combined with discourse analysis and semi-structured interviews to examine how Russian speaker identities are instantiated, accommodated, and transformed by American learners of Russian in two CMC contexts: online interactions with native-speaking peers guided by the course instructor, and in Russia-based virtual communities of common interest. The researchers used a line-by-line analysis of online interactions between learners and native speakers to identify special turns where participants engaged in the negotiation of identity. Their study demonstrated that one's presumed situational identity of a language learner in instructional CMC contexts does not always map onto one's desired transportable identity. In one instance, they observed how a native speaker corrected the use of an informal expression produced by a heritage speaker as inappropriate for an L2 learner, an identity that the heritage speaker deemed undesirable due to their heritage background.

Participant interviews are consistently used in CMC identity research to support conversational analyses and provide a layer of self-reported data from study participants. Thorne et al. (2015) identified three approaches to carrying out interviews in identity research: (1) semi-structured interviews are used to collect demographic data and/or obtain data on participants' attitudes and perceptions; (2) less structured interviews are used at the end of the study "to open the door for learners to volunteer information," (3) finally, interviews that allow the researcher to confirm what they observed in the interactional records by asking participants to comment ("stimulated recall") on specific elements in the interactional data. Thorne et al. (2015) argue that the latter approach helps overcome the challenge of interpreting the discursive dimensions of L2 identity enactment from the participant's viewpoint and validates the researcher's interpretations of the CMC data, as was the case in the Klimanova and Dembovskaya (2013) study.

The critical and social justice-oriented turns in applied linguistics have prompted a new body of identity research involving *critical discourse analysis* (Zotzmann & O'Regan, 2016) and *critical approaches to the study of online communication* (Helm, 2017) where identity projections in digital social spaces are examined in connection with existing power structures and unequal access to languages and language-learning opportunities in CALL settings. CDA allowed researchers to consider how online language identity performances and self-positioning are often implicated by larger-scale social practices and enacted in unequal ways (Ortega, 2017). This study of inequitable practices in institutional and informal CALL contexts leads to significant pedagogical implications for transformative action and social justice outcomes (Darvin, 2018). In addition to CMC studies of online interactions (e.g., Helm et al., 2012; Ortega & Zyzik, 2008), the critical dimension of identity research has prompted a discussion of language-learning apps and online platforms and their power to restrict language identity performances by providing access to a limited number of language interfaces and options, thus preventing opportunities for multilingual self-expression (Buendgens-Kosten, this volume).

4 Digital Multilingualism, Multilingual Identity, and CALL Research

In conjunction with the notion of digital identity, this volume focuses on multilingualism, multilingual contexts, and multilingual subjects (Kramsch, 2009). Our interest in multilingualism is two-fold. On the one hand, digital media have become increasingly ubiquitous and multilingual, promoting the exposure to and use of multiple languages. As an ecology of multilingual environments (Thorne et al., 2015), digital mediascapes are often characterized by the term *linguistic superdiversity* (Blommaert & Rampton, 2011). The result of this digital superdiversity is *hyperlingualism*, which became possible due to the growing technological affordances that increase the availability of multiple languages on the internet, and due to the emerging ideologies that underpin multilingual play in digital communication (Kelly-Holmes, 2019). On the other hand, users of technological spaces often find themselves in linguistically diverse social encounters, and multilingual practices conflict with the ideals of ideologically monolingual societies and monolingual L2 teaching pedagogies (Buendgens-Kosten, 2020; Trentman, 2019). Thus, Ortega (2017) points out that multilingualism thrives in digital worlds, taking various forms and manifestations from the growing availability of languages other than English (see also Danet & Herring, 2007). There are increased multilingual accommodations embedded in global social networks and public digital platforms (e.g., Facebook translation app, Google Translate) to the provision of spaces for the use of less-spoken and marginalized languages and their digital substitutes, and the encouragement of multilingual meaning-making through creative semiotic code-mixing and meshing. This global trend, however, is not fully reflected in the scope of current CALL research in the leading CALL journals where most published work focuses on English (Sauro, 2016).

In addition to the growing networked multilingualism (Androutsopoulos, 2013a) shaped by increased network-facilitated contact between speakers of multiple languages, the global digital mediascapes offer infinite access to rich multilingual and semiotic resources for the assembly of multimodal messages, engagement in multilingual plays, and translingual meaning-making (García & Wei, 2013; Li, 2018) – all of which lead to more nuanced and idiosyncratic ways of self-positioning and digital identity enactment. It is not surprising that interacting in multiple languages, code-mixing, and meshing are becoming progressively common practice among internet users, providing social space for translocal affinity groups whose members often share and exchange their diverse linguistic repertoires (Leppänen & Peuronen, 2012). Today's digital communication becomes more participatory and more reliant on crowdsourcing for linguistic localization by instant translation tools (Androutsopoulos, 2013b; see Kelly-Holmes, 2019, about how Facebook implemented crowdsourced translation mechanisms bypassing language professionals). Linguistic boundaries are not enforced, and non-prescriptive language use is easily tolerated. Consequently, the issues of language ownership, competence, and legitimacy in digital contexts are less of a concern in digital participation (Kelly-Holmes, 2019).

As more marginalized languages find their online outlets, some languages "get left behind" due to restrictive designs of apps and online platforms, and "the increasing tailoring and personalizing of online language provision" as a result of increased marketing for an individual user and mass linguistic customization (Kelly-Holmes, 2019, p. 33). In some contexts, digital platforms create an illusion of language choice, while in reality users' choice is limited to the algorithmic language filtering based on the geopolitical location of their IP address and linguistic settings available to them in the design of digital platforms and language-learning products (Buendgens-Kosten, 2020).

These inequitable multilingual practices also permeate CALL contexts. In instructional CALL, linguistic isolation is often an outcome of monolingual ideologies that pervade language teaching pedagogies and prescribe the use of the "target" language at the expense of the rich plurilingual repertoires and unique ways of thinking and viewing the world and moving effortlessly across languages and cultures that a multilingual learner brings into the classroom from non-institutional online and offline social contexts. Buendgens-Kosten (2020) proposes the term *monolingual bias* – "a deficit in considering the full range of pre-existing languages of a learner, of languages used in a setting, or of (plurilingual) skills in the design of and the research on CALL" (p. 307; see also Henry, 2017) – to explain a severe lack of published scholarship about CALL products and practices that support language learners in using their plurilingual skills. Although research on multilingual communication in digital spaces exists, the focus is often on networked multilingualism and informal CMC practices in non-institutional digital contexts (e.g., Schreiber, 2015). Multilingual CALL contexts and products, and the "multilinguality" of language learners and instructional materials remain on the margins in CALL research (Buendgens-Kosten and Elsner, 2018). In this regard, Ortega (2017) calls to acknowledge the limitations of the existing monolingual paradigms in language learning and recognize the need to address "the monolingual problem in CALL research" (Buendgens-Kosten, 2020) by generating more empirical studies on multilingual practices in instructional and informal digitally mediated language learning.

The multilingual turn in applied linguistics, discussed in the previous sections, urges us to also take a more critical look at *the CALL learner* as a multilingual subject with agency and a unique digitally mediated personal identity (Schulze & Smith, 2016). Increased multilingualism in offline and digital contexts creates new demands on the part of language learners who are now expected not only to be proficient in compartmentalized languages but also to show aptitude in navigating linguistic plurality in offline and online social and professional spheres (Council of Europe, 2018; Ortega, 2017). This consideration is particularly valid for the identity work for which multilingual users of digital spaces have to engage the full spectrum of their cultural and linguistic capital (Bourdieu, 1991; Duff, 2017).

Equally important are the considerations of technological affordances and CALL product designs in liberating or restricting users' identity performances (Buendgens-Kosten, this volume). In this respect, Kramsch (2009) points out that the computer and networked communication have offered the learner *self* the unlimited potential for distributed authorship and intersubjectivity, boundary-free language play, and creativity. In return, multilingual users of digital spaces must "reinvent perceptible boundaries" between their online and offline languages, experiences, and imagined scenarios – "the multilingual subject is not defined by its boundless freedom and agency, but, on the contrary, by the linguistic and discursive boundaries it abides by in order to, now and then, transgress them" (p. 183). Examining a digital language learner through this critical multilingual lens enables a more holistic understanding of their linguistic multicompetence and its critical role in determining their self-positioning and identity performance in digital contexts.

5 The Scope of this Volume

The chapters in this volume address a wide range of topics and issues related to identity research in educational and informal CALL. The volume is aimed at a diverse audience, including CALL specialists, graduate students, and teaching practitioners. The contributions bring together cutting-edge research at the intersection of identity, multilingualism, technology, and digitally mediated communication, highlight the key theoretical models underlying the studies of identity in applied linguistics and CALL, and outline new and exciting possibilities in researching identity in a variety of instructional and informal digitally mediated language-learning contexts.

The most fruitful area of CALL identity research concerns learner identity work in intercultural virtual exchanges, also known as telecollaboration projects, or the practices "of sustained, technology-enabled, people-to-people activities in which constructive communication and interaction take place between individuals or groups who are geographically separated and/or from different cultural backgrounds, with the support of educators or facilitators" (EVOLVE, 2019, para. 1). Intercultural virtual exchanges produce large amounts of data to evidence the complex nature of language choice and self-positioning in digitally mediated, cross-cultural encounters. In this volume, Sevilla-Pavón and Nicolaou (Chapter 10) and Izmailova (Chapter 12) examine participants' multilingual identity projections and individual experiences with classroom-based intercultural telecollaboration. Drawing on the conceptual framework of Appraisal Theory (Martin & White, 2005), Sevilla-Pavón and Nicolaou explore monoglossic and heteroglossic discourses in discussion posts and examine participants' efforts to create individual and common dialogic spaces for identity performances. In these efforts, heteroglossic language ideologies are connected to desired millennium hybrid multilingual and multicultural identities in the age of increased mobility and globalization. In Izmailova's study, multilingual telecollaboration created a rich space for expressing and resisting one's multilingual identity in response to the mainstream monolingual ideologies. The participants in this study portrayed themselves predominantly as monocultural Americans in a virtual exchange where students exchanged their language cultures through instructor-assigned monocultural identifications. At the same time, engagement in cultural comparisons contributed to participants' reorientation from strongly ethnocentric toward more ethnorelative intercultural stances (Bennett, 1993).

Klimanova (Chapter 11) examined systematic and intentional plurilingualism in synchronous multi-party video-based virtual exchange, involving a group of multilingual speakers. Drawing on the notion of *translanguaging*, a dynamic process in which multilingual speakers navigate complex social and cognitive demands through the deployment of multiple languages as an integrated communication system (Li, 2018), Klimanova proposes to consider systematic translingual practices as an integrated communicative micro-ecology (Kramsch & Whiteside, 2008) that leads to the building of dynamic *multilingual group identity* in a synchronous intercultural CMC video chat.

In the same line of inquiry, Lesoski's chapter (Chapter 3) underscores the plurilingual nature of telecollaboration and discusses how established monolingual stances negatively affect learners' perception of their linguistic identities. In this study, translanguaging and using multilingual repertoires in an intercultural virtual encounter is viewed by one heritage speaker of German as a sign of deficit rather than as a valued asset. Similarly, in another study, Kristine, a native English speaker, struggles with identifying herself and asserting her Korean heritage as she establishes her place in a virtual community of Korean-heritage speakers (Yang, Chapter 14). This deficit-based mindset, grounded in the negative beliefs about switching between linguistic repertoires, permeates language teaching practices.

Helm and Hauck (Chapter 2) address this concern more closely while examining existing ideologies of monolingualism that often inform the instructional design of virtual exchange partnerships and their impact on participants' identities and their positioning. In particular, they unfold historically grounded pedagogical assumptions and contradictions that underlie linguistic organizations (Kelly-Holmes, 2019) in two common formats of intercultural virtual exchange – E-Tandem and Online Facilitated Dialogue (OFD). Their analysis shows that monolingual prescriptivism and 'one-language-at-a-time' ideologies, which often characterize institutional virtual exchanges, fail to hold water when participants' interactions and positionings are closely examined through the lens of semiodiversity (Pennycook, 2008) and translingualism (Li, 2018). Following Ortega's (2017) call to adopt a social-justice perspective in CALL research, Helm and Hauck's mission is to problematize the exclusive nature of forced monolingual communication and advocate for the creation of inclusive and equitable multilingual and translingual spaces for performing identities in intercultural virtual education.

In this respect, another emergent theme in CALL-based identity research *is language teacher identity* (LTI). Teacher identity has long been a focus of scholarship in the field of applied linguistics and second/foreign language education (Kayi-Aydar, 2019; Varghese et al., 2016). Recent studies of teacher identity deployment in digitally mediated learning platforms, however, point to the growing role of digital contexts, experiences with digital technology, and online teaching in the validation of multilingual language teachers. Mannion and Leontas (Chapter 8) and Park (Chapter 9) examine the social and discursive nature of language teacher identity development. Mannion and Leontas' chapter reports on the study of the identity-related perceptions of doctoral students participating in a CALL teacher training program. Their findings suggest a critical connection between explicit and implicit declarations of doctoral students' own digital identities and their perceptions of the ideal technology-related teaching practices in language education. The authors argue for the importance of considering teacher identity at the intersection of perceived and imagined *language teacher* and *teacher-educator identities* collectively and dialogically constructed within a digitally mediated community of future teaching professionals. Their focus is on graduate students' reflections on perceived and apperceived (digital) identities, and their impact on CALL teacher identity building. In a similar vein, Park's study adopts a case-based approach to examine Korean as a foreign language (KFL) teachers' self-positioning in a digitally mediated teaching environment. Her study is framed in the context of COVID-19 pandemic-instigated online teaching practices where professional teacher identities were challenged by a novel and stress-provoking teaching situation. Park concludes that the identities of online language teachers are formed from a complex array of situated positionings, and sub-identities harmonized and co-constructed in the intricate layers of interactions among teachers, students, and the online teaching environment where learning is taking place.

By far one of the most intriguing and novel themes in CALL-based identity research is dynamic user-device interactions (Caws & Hamel, 2016) and their consequences on positioning strategies of users, and the linguistic repertoires from which they can draw when they engage in complex and intricate identity work in social digital spaces. This notion of "mutual shaping" describes a relationship between users and technology and recognizes that the digital medium is not passive or neutral (Quan-Haase, 2016). As a technology-oriented field, CALL cannot ignore the mediational role of technological tools in shaping human communication and self-positioning, often in restrictive ways. In this volume, Buendgens-Kosten (Chapter 6) rightly points out that most of the identity research in CALL has been almost exclusively centered on CMC contexts, leaving tool-user relationships severely underresearched. Meanwhile, tool-user interactions are often dependent upon specific design features of digital platforms and devices which shape user language identities in ways that can be concurrently liberating and constricting. Drawing from the conceptualizations of *the ideal L2 self* and *the ideal multilingual self* (Dörnyei, 2010), Buendgens-Kosten's chapter adopts an explicitly non-CMC perspective on identity research in CALL and examines how product design choices in multilingual non-CMC CALL products, privilege certain languages and linguistic identities at the expense of others, and how language-learning apps and platforms model their legitimate users and create a field of action in which users imagine themselves as speakers or learners of the languages they know or learn. Thus, Gaspar (Chapter 13) examines the technical capabilities of *HelloTalk*, a free language-exchange app, for constructing rich multimodal messages fueled by language learners' imagination. Imagination in this study is fluid and co-constructed by the participants through the creation of a new imaginable reality where physical distance and time difference are digitally mediated, and imagined co-presence is achieved through synchronous multimodal conversation and instantaneous imagined immersion in a language exchange partner's physical, linguistic, and cultural space. Multimodal expression, multisensory communication, and language play made possible by the app feed virtual experiences and contribute to the enactment of a *learner's imagined projected self* – a type of imagination in which participants imagine themselves living the actual (physical, linguistic, and cultural) reality of their native-speaking exchange partner.

In a similar pursuit to explore and uncover user-medium relations, Vandergriff (Chapter 4) explores the semiotic value of social hashtagging for performing a multilingual virtual self. As a linguistic feature of social networks at the intersection of text and metatext, hashtags contribute to establishing users' social presence and index users' identity through stance-marking (Zappavigna, 2015). The use of multilingual hashtags is linked to heteroglossic discourses and playful identity performances of multilinguals. Vandergriff argues that such uses of social media affordances constitute social media literacy – a form of symbolic competence of multilingual subjects (Kramsch, 2009; Kramsch & Whiteside, 2008).

Vazquez-Calvo, Shafirova, and Zhan (Chapter 5) examine the multimodal format of TikTok (a video-focused social networking service that hosts a variety of short-form user videos) for casual and collective language-learning practices, where plurilingual repertoires of TikTokers contribute to the building of interactive TikTok user identities. Similar to the use of social tagging on Instagram (Chapter 4), hashtagging in TikTok is a unique semiotic space for covert multilingual identity performances as TikTokers play with various identifications as native speakers, language learners, language experts, bi/multilingual influencers in their hashtag self-identification posts. While English is positioned by the TikTok platform as the main code of communication, creators of TikTok videos manage to mediate across rich semiotic assemblages to create multimodal configurations of multilingual practices in informal ('folk') language learning and teaching.

In formal institutional settings, access to multilingual resources was found to create opportunities for meaningful learning experiences for multilingual students. Jacob, Montoya, and Warschauer in this volume (Chapter 7) examine the computation thinking curriculum that accommodates multicompetence and multilingual ability, promotes inclusion, and cultivates students' computer science identity development, fostering their investment in the field of computer science. The authors conclude that the diversification of the school curriculum through embedding responsive materials from a variety of cultural and linguistic origins leverages students' existing linguistic, social, cultural, and semiotic resources and promotes more active participation and deeper engagement in computer science disciplinary practices.

The volume offers a wide array of perspectives on the study of multilingual identity in CALL and highlights newly emerging themes and avenues for exploration in the future research on identity enactment in digitally mediated educational and informal language learning contexts. It is my hope as editor that the volume will inspire its readers to engage in the fascinating study of identity in digital spaces.

References

Androutsopoulos, J. (2006). Introduction: Sociolinguistics and computer-mediated communication. *Journal of Sociolinguistics, 10*, 419–438. https://doi.org/10.1111/j.1467-9841.2006.00286.x

Androutsopoulos, J. (2013a). Networked multilingualism: Some language practices on Facebook and their implications. *The International Journal of Bilingualism: Cross-Disciplinary, Cross-Linguistic Studies of Language Behavior, 19*(2), 185–205. https://doi.org/10.1177/1367006913489198

Androutsopoulos, J. (2013b). Participatory culture and metalinguistic discourse: Performing and negotiating German dialects on YouTube. In D. Tannen, & A. Trester (Eds.), *Discourse 2.0* (pp. 47–73). Georgetown University Press.

Bamberg, M. (2006). Stories: Big or small: Why do we care? *Narrative Inquiry, 16*, 139–147.

Bamberg, M., & Georgakopoulou, A. (2008). Small stories as a new perspective in narrative and identity analysis. *Text & Talk, 28*(3), 377–396.

Basharina, O. K. (2007). An activity theory perspective on student-reported contradictions in international collaboration. *Language Learning & Technology, 11*(2), 82–103. http://dx.doi.org/10125/44105

Bennett, M. J. (1993). Towards ethnorelativism: A developmental model of intercultural sensitivity. In R. M. Paige (Ed.), *Education for the intercultural experience* (pp. 21–71). Intercultural Press.

Benwell, B., & Stokoe, E. (2016). Ethnomethodological and conversational analytic approaches to identity. In S. Preece (Ed.), *The Routledge handbook of language and identity* (pp. 66–82). Routledge.
Block, D. (2003). *The social turn in second language acquisition.* Georgetown University Press.
Block, D. (2007). The rise of identity in SLA research, post Firth and Wagner (1997). *The Modern Language Journal, 91*, 863–876. https://doi.org/10.1111/j.0026-7902.2007.00674.x
Blommaert, J., & Rampton, B. (2011). Language and superdiversity. *Diversities, 13*(2), 1–21.
Bourdieu, M. (1991). *Language and symbolic power.* Polity Press.
Bucholtz, M., & Hall, K. (2005). Identity and interaction: A sociocultural linguistic approach. *Discourse Studies*, *7*(4–5), 585–614.
Buendgens-Kosten, J. (2020). The monolingual problem of computer-assisted language learning. *ReCALL*, *32*(3), 307–322. https://doi.org/10.1017/S095834402000004X
Buendgens-Kosten, J., & Elsner, D. (2018). *Multilingual computer assisted language learning*. Multilingual Matters. https://doi.org/10.21832/9781788921497
Canagarajah, A. S. (2013). *Translingual practice: Global Englishes and cosmopolitan relations*. Routledge.
Caws, C., & Hamel, M.-J. (Eds.). (2016). *Language-learner computer interactions: Theory, methodology and CALL applications*. John Benjamins.
Chase, S. (2005). Narrative inquiry: Multiple lenses, approaches, voices. In N. Denzin & Y. Lincoln (Eds.), *The Sage handbook of qualitative research* (pp. 651–680). Sage.
Chun, D. M. (1994). Using computer networking to facilitate the acquisition of interactive competence. *System*, *22*(1), 17–31.
Council of Europe. (2018). *Common European framework of reference for languages: Learning, teaching, assessment: Companion volume with new descriptors*. https://rm.coe.int/cefr-companion-volume-with-new-descriptors-2018/1680787989
Danet, B., & Herring, S. C. (2007). *The multilingual internet: Language, culture, and communication online*. Oxford University Press. https://doi.org/10.1093/acprof:oso/9780195304794.001.0001
Darvin, R. (2016). Language and identity in the digital age. In S. Preece (Ed.), *The Routledge handbook of language and identity* (pp. 523–540). Routledge.
Darvin, R. (2018). Identity. In A. Phakiti, A., P. De Costa, L. Plonsky, & S. Starfield, (Eds.) *The Palgrave handbook of applied linguistics research methodology*. Palgrave Macmillan. https://doi.org/10.1057/978-1-137-59900-1_35
Darvin, R., & Norton, B. (2017). Language, identity, and investment in the twenty-first century. In T. L. McCarty and S. May (Eds.), *Language policy and political issues in education* (pp. 227–240). Springer International Publishing.

De Costa, P., & Norton, B. (2016). Identity in language learning and teaching: Research agendas for the future. In S. Preece (Ed.), *The Routledge handbook of language and identity* (pp. 586–601). Routledge.

De Fina, A. (2016). Linguistic practices and national identities. In S. Preece (Ed.), *The Routledge handbook of language and identity* (pp. 163–178). Routledge.

Domingo, M. (2016). Language and identity research in online environments: A multi-modal ethnographic perspective. In S. Preece (Ed.), *The Routledge handbook of language and identity* (pp. 541–557). Routledge.

Dörnyei, Z. (2010). The L2 motivational self system. In Z. Dörnyei & E. Ushioda (Eds.), *Motivation, language identity and the L2 self* (pp. 9–42). Multilingual Matters.

Douglas Fir Group. (2016). A transdisciplinary framework for SLA in a multilingual world. *Modern Language Journal*, *100*(Supplement 2016), 19–47.

Duff, P. (2014). Case study research on language learning and use. *Annual Review of Applied Linguistics*, *34*, 233–255.

Duff, P. (2017). Commentary: Motivation for learning languages other than English in an English-dominant world. *Modern Language Journal*, *101*(3), 597–607.

Duff, P. (2019). Case study research. Making language learning complexities visible. In J. McKinley & H. Rose, *The Routledge handbook of research methods in applied linguistics* (pp. 144–153). Routledge.

EVOLVE (2019). *What is virtual exchange?* https://evolve-erasmus.eu/about-evolve/what-is-virtual-exchange/

Firth, A., & Wagner, J. (1997). On discourse, communication, and (some) fundamental concepts in SLA research. *Modern Language Journal*, *91*(5), 757–772.

Freiermuth, M., & Jarrell, D. (2006). Willingness to communicate: Can online chat help. *International Journal of Applied Linguistics*, *162*, 190–213.

García, O., & Wei, L. (2013). *Translanguaging*. Palgrave. https://doi.org/10.1057/9781137385765

González-Lloret, M. (2011). Conversation analysis of computer-mediated communication. *CALICO Journal*, *28*(2), 308–325. http://citeseerx.ist.psu.edu/viewdoc/download?doi=10.1.1.456.8944&rep=rep1&type=pdf

Hadley, G. (2016). Grounded theory method. In S. Preece (Ed.), *Routledge handbook of research methods in applied linguistics* (pp. 264–275). Routledge.

Hanna, B., & de Nooy, J. (2003). A funny thing happened on the way to the forum: Electronic discussion and foreign language learning. *Language Learning & Technology*, *7*(1), 71–85. http://dx.doi.org/10125/25188

Helm, F. (2017). Critical approaches to online intercultural language education. In S. Thorne & S. May, *Language, education, and technology*. Springer.

Helm, F., Guth, S., & Farrah, M. (2012). Promoting dialogue or hegemonic practice? Power issues in telecollaboration. *Language Learning & Technology*, *16*(2), 103–127. http://dx.doi.org/10125/44289

Henry, A. (2017). L2 motivation and multilingual identities. *The Modern Language Journal*, *101*(3), 548–565. https://doi.org/10.1111/modl.12412

Kasper, G., & Wagner, J. (2014). Conversation analysis in applied linguistics. *Annual Review of Applied Linguistics*, *34*, 171–212.

Kayi-Aydar, H. (2019). Language teacher identity. *Language Teaching*, 52, 281–295. https://doi.org/10.1017/S0261444819000223

Kelly-Holmes, H. (2019). Multilingualism and technology: A review of developments in digital communication from monolingualism to idiolingualism. *Annual Review of Applied Linguistics*, *39*, 24–39. https://doi.org/10.1017/S0267190519000102

Kelm, O. (1996). The application of computer networking in foreign language education: Focusing on principles of second language acquisition. In M. Warschauer (Ed.), *Telecollaboration in foreign language learning* (pp. 19–28). University of Hawai'i Press.

Klimanova, L. (2020). The phenomenology of experiencing oneself online: Critical dimensions of identity and language use in virtual spaces. In Freiermuth, M., & Zarrinabadi, N. (Eds.), *Technology and the psychology of second language learners and users (New language learning and teaching environments)* (pp. 279–307). Palgrave-Macmillan.

Klimanova, L. (2021). The evolution of identity research in CALL: From scripted chatrooms to engaged construction of the digital self. *Language Learning & Technology*, *25*(3), 186–204. http://hdl.handle.net/10125/73455

Klimanova, L., & Dembovskaya, S. (2013). L2 identity, discourse, and social networking in Russian. *Language Learning & Technology*, *17*(1), 69–88. http://dx.doi.org/10125/24510

Kramsch, C. (2009). *The multilingual subject: What foreign language learners say about their experience and why it matters.* Oxford University Press. https://doi.org/10.1111/j.1473-4192.2006.00109.x

Kramsch, C., & Whiteside, A. (2008). Language ecology in multilingual settings. Towards a theory of symbolic competence. *Applied Linguistics*, *29*(4), 645–671. https://doi.org/10.1093/applin/amn022

Lam, W. S. (2000). L2 Literacy and the design of the self: A case study of a teenager writing on the internet. *TESOL Quarterly*, *34*(3), 457–482.

Lam, W. S. (2004). Second language socialization in a bilingual chat room: Global and local considerations. *Language Learning & Technology*, *8*(3), 44–65.

Lantolf, J., & Thorne, S. (2006). *Sociocultural theory and the genesis of second language development.* Oxford University Press.

Leppänen, S., & Peuronen, S. (2012). 'Multilingualism on the internet', in M. Martin-Jones, A. Blackledge & A. Creese (Eds.), *The Routledge handbook of multilingualism*. Routledge, 384–402.

Li, W. (2018). Translanguaging as a practical theory of language. *Applied Linguistics*, *39*(1), 9–30. https://doi.org/10.1093/applin/amx039

Martin, J. R., & White, P. R. (2005). *The language of evaluation. Appraisal in English.* Palgrave.

May, S. (Ed.) (2014). *The multilingual turn: Implications for SLA, TESOL, and bilingual education.* Routledge. https://doi.org/10.4324/9780203113493

Nguyen, H., & Kellogg, G. (2005). Emergent identities in on-line discussions for second language learning. *The Canadian Modern Language Review*, *62*(1), 111–136. https://doi.org/10.3138/cmlr.62.1.111

Norton, B. (2000). *Identity and language learning: Gender, ethnicity, and educational change*. Pearson Education Limited.

Norton, B. (2013). *Identity and language learning: Extending the conversation.* Multilingual Matters.

Norton, B., & De Costa, P. I. (2018). Research tasks on identity in language learning and teaching. *Language Teaching*, *51*(1), 90–112. https://doi.org/10.1017/S0261444817000325

Ortega, L. (1997). Processes and outcomes in networked classroom interaction: Defining the research agenda for L2 computer-assisted classroom discussion. *Language Learning & Technology*, *1*(1), 82–93. http://dx.doi.org/10125/25005

Ortega, L. (2017). New CALL-SLA research interfaces for the 21st century: Towards equitable multilingualism. *CALICO Journal*, *34*(3), 285–316.

Ortega, L., & Zyzik, E. (2008). Online interactions and L2 learning: Some ethical challenges for L2 researchers. In S. Magnan (Ed.), *Mediating discourse online* (pp. 331–355). John Benjamins.

Pasfield-Neofitou, S. (2011). Online domains of language use: Second language learners' experiences of virtual community and foreignness. *Language Learning & Technology*, *15*(2), 92–108. http://dx.doi.org/10125/44253

Pennycook, A. (2008). English as a language always in translation. *European Journal of English Studies*, *12*(1), 33–47.

Quan-Haase, A. (2016). *Technology and society: Inequality, power, and social networks* (2nd ed.). Oxford University Press.

Sauro, S. (2004). Cyberdiscursive tug-of-war: Learner repositioning in a multimodal CMC environment. *Working Papers in Educational Linguistics*, *19*(2), 55–72.

Sauro, S. (2016). Does CALL have an English problem? *Language Learning & Technology*, *20*(3), 1–8. Retrieved from http://llt.msu.edu/issues/october2016/sauro.pdf

Sauro, S., & Zourou, K. (2019). What are the digital wilds? *Language Learning & Technology*, *23*(1), 1–7.

Schreiber, B. R. (2015). "I am what I am": Multilingual identity and digital translanguaging. *Language, Learning & Technology*, *19*, 69–87.

Schulze, M., & Smith, B. (2016). The first L of CALL—Language. *CALICO Journal*, 33(3), i–iii. https://doi.org/10.1558/cj.v33i3.31602

Smith, J. A., Flowers, P., & Larkin, M. (2009). *Interpretative phenomenological analysis: Theory, method, and research*. Sage.

Thorne, S. L. (2010). The "intercultural turn" and language learning in the crucible of new media. In F. Helm & S. Guth (Eds.), *Telecollaboration 2.0 for language and intercultural learning* (pp. 139–164). Peter Lang.

Thorne, S. L., Sauro, S., & Smith, B. (2015). Technologies, identities, and expressive activity. *Annual Review of Applied Linguistics*, *35*, 215–233.

Trentman, E. (2019). Reframing monolingual ideologies in the language classroom: Evidence from Arabic study abroad and telecollaboration. In B. Dupuy & K. Michelson (Eds.), *Pathways to paradigm change: Critical examinations of prevailing discourses and ideologies in second language education* (pp. 108–132). Cengage Learning.
Tudini, V., & Liddicoat, A. (2017). Computer-mediated communication and conversation analysis. In S. Thorne & S. May, *Language, education, and technology*. Springer.
Van Deursen, & van Dijk, J. A. G. (2014). The digital divide shifts to differences in usage. *New Media & Society*, *16*(3), 507–526. https://doi.org/10.1177/1461444813487959
Vandergriff, I. (2016). *Second-language discourse in the digital world. Linguistic and social practices in and beyond the networked classroom*. John Benjamins. https://doi.org/10.1075/lllt.46
Varghese, M. M., Motha, S., Trent, J., Park, G., & Reeves, J. (guest eds.) (2016). Language teacher identity in multilingual settings (special issue). *TESOL Quarterly*, 3, 541–783.
Warschauer, M. (1997). Computer-mediated collaborative learning: Theory and practice. *Modern Language Journal*, *81*(4), 470–481.
Warschauer, M., Said, G. R. E., & Zohry, A. G. (2002). Language choice online: Globalization and identity in Egypt. *Journal of Computer-Mediated Communication*, *7*(4). https://doi.org/10.1111/j.1083-6101.2002.tb00157.x
Wu, Z. (2018). Positioning (mis)aligned: The (un)making of intercultural asynchronous computer-mediated communication. *Language Learning & Technology*, *22*(2), 75–94. https://doi.org/10125/44637
Zappavigna, M. (2015). Searchable talk: The linguistic functions of hashtags. *Social Semiotics*, *25*(3), 274–291. https://doi.org/10.1080/10350330.2014.996948
Zimmerman, D. H. (1998). Discoursal identities and social identities. In C. Antaki & S. Widdicombe (Eds.), *Identities in talk* (pp. 87–106). Sage.
Zotzmann, K., & O'Regan, J. (2016). Critical discourse analysis and identity. In S. Preece (Ed.), *Routledge handbook of language and identity* (pp. 113–127). Routledge.

About the Author

Liudmila Klimanova, Ph.D., is an Assistant Professor of Russian and Second Language Acquisition in the College of Humanities, University of Arizona, USA. Her research focuses on topics related to (critical) virtual exchange, task-based language learning, and identity deployment in digital spaces.

2 Language, Identity, and Positioning in Virtual Exchange

Francesca Helm and Mirjam Hauck

1 Introduction

Virtual exchange (VE), also known as "telecollaboration" (Belz, 2003), is "a practice, supported by research, that consists of sustained, technology-enabled, people-to-people education programs or activities in which constructive communication and interaction takes place between individuals or groups who are geographically separated and/or from different cultural backgrounds, with the support of educators or facilitators" (EVOLVE, 2019). It is a form of computer-assisted language learning (CALL) and has been hailed as an experiential learning opportunity that offers participants (semi) authentic language interactions with peers, mediated by technology. However, Ortega (2017) highlights the monolingual language ideologies that permeate CALL research, including VE. Considerations of 'authenticity' in VE, for example, are often rooted in monolingual ideologies assuming nation-state boundaries and interactions with 'native speakers'. Ortega (2017) identifies new CALL-SLA (second language acquisition) research interfaces pointing toward equitable multilingualism informed by the 'social justice turn' in SLA. Drawing on Piller (2016), she reminds us that "most multilinguals will experience injustice, discrimination, and oppression in part related to their learning, unlearning, and relearning of multiple languages over their lifespan" (Ortega, 2017, p. 286). She proposes a number of questions to be used by CALL-SLA scholars as a guide while planning their studies, more specifically for examining the potential of their research to promote multilingualism and social justice and thus to support equitable multilingualism as a field.

This conceptual contribution is inspired by Ortega's (2017) questions. In particular we consider how different language ideologies are reflected in VE designs, how they might impact on participant identities and on how participants position themselves during an exchange. We ask how we can gesture toward inclusive and equitable multilingual and translingual practices in VE in the spirit of the aforementioned social justice turn.

Another set of questions underlying our approach has been raised by Kelly-Holmes (2019), who defines the online organization of languages as "the ways in which languages are made available, supported, presented, represented, and managed in digital spaces" (p. 25). In exploring multilingualism and technology she asks (p. 25): how many languages are available? How much content is available in which particular languages? What is the role of English and other dominant languages? What hierarchies and orderings are present? What is available for people whose main or preferred language is not provided? Yet, here we are concerned not with the internet at large but with pedagogically designed online spaces such as those used for language and intercultural learning, i.e., VE. The organization of languages in VE is informed – explicitly or implicitly – by language ideologies, "self-evident ideas and objectives a group holds concerning roles of language in the social experiences of members as they contribute to the expression of the group" (Heath, 1989, p. 393). Canagarajah (2017) and other scholars (Flores & Rosa, 2015; Pennycook, 2008; Piller, 2016) draw our attention to language ideologies and their interconnections with language practices. This is what we seek to do in this chapter by discussing the implications for participant interactions and positioning of VE framing, VE configurations, and VE spaces.

To start with, we want to clarify our own 'locus of enunciation' as a way to localize and decolonize scholarly knowledge (Diniz de Figueiredo & Martinez, 2021). We are both white, female academics located in Europe who have lived and worked in Italy, Germany, the UK and the US. We have been practicing and researching VE both within and outside of language education in higher education in the Global North and have, only recently, begun to unpick some of the assumptions and ideologies in the discourses surrounding CALL – VE being one of them.

In recent years, several formats of VE have emerged, including dyads, triads, or small groups of learners, and adopting monolingual, bilingual, and – occasionally – also multilingual approaches to language use (Dooly & Vinagre, 2021). Here, we will limit ourselves to two models of VE – Tandem and online facilitated dialogue (OFD) – and explore their underlying language ideologies, their linguistic organization as well as the identity categorizations made salient through their design. These models were selected as, on the surface, they present two seemingly contrasting orientations to language organization in VE, that is, bilingual and monolingual, lingua franca. We examine the assumptions and contradictions embedded in these conceptualizations of language and language organization and how they can conceal and/or hinder translingual practices and thus equitable multilingualism.

After a brief introduction to the VE models in Section 2, we look at concepts such as multilingualism, translingual practice, identity, subjectivity and positioning (Section 3) and apply them to the chosen models, drawing on relevant literature (Sections 3.1 and 3.2). In the final section (Section 4) we consider the wider implications of our observations for theoretical approaches to VE and for VE practices that gesture toward social justice.

2 VE Models

VE happens in a variety of digital spaces, including social networking sites, institutional learning management systems (LMSs), and bespoke platforms such as the one used by the Soliya Connect program (see Figure 2.1). This is mirrored by a similar variety of VE formats, in foreign language education (FLE) in particular. Most well known are collaboratively designed and implemented exchanges, i.e., telecollaborative models, and Tandem-based exchanges. Recently another format of VEs has emerged, designed and implemented by non-governmental organizations (NGOs), whereby participants are organized into transnational groups and supported by specially trained

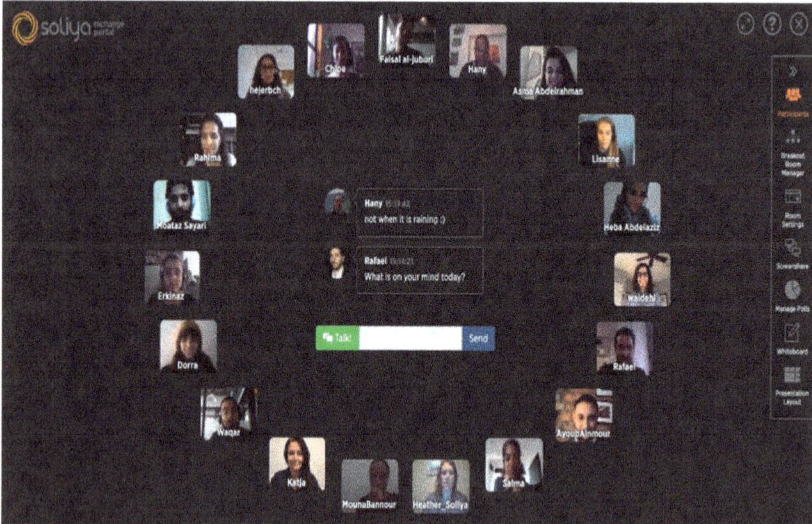

Figure 2.1. The Soliya Connect Program

facilitators and/or educators, also referred to as OFD (https://soliya.net/introduction-to-online-dialogue-facilitation). We will concentrate on Tandem-based exchanges and OFD and their languages organizations.

2.1 Tandem-Based Exchanges

Tandem is one of the longest-established forms of VE, based on the face-to-face Tandem language learning models which were established in 1979 when Jürgen Wolff developed the procedure for organizing individual Spanish-German Tandem partnerships in Madrid, which later became the basis for the TANDEM® Network. Tandem-based exchanges are generally bilingual since learners of different L1–L2 combinations come together in a pair with the aim of learning from each other (O'Rourke, 2007). They are based on the principles of learner autonomy (Little & Brammerts, 1996; Schwienhorst, 2004) and reciprocity: each student is responsible for their own and their partner's learning, having to support their partner as much as they wish to be supported themselves. Today Tandem is often integrated into classroom practices with more institutional partnerships and arrangements being developed.

2.2 Online Facilitated Dialogue (OFD)

A model of VE which has emerged outside of FLE is that of dialogue-based exchanges, designed and managed by specialist organisations such as Soliya or the Sharing Perspectives Foundation. OFD stems from the field of peace-building and conflict studies and is informed by theories of intergroup relations and dialogue (Himelfarb, 2014; Himelfarb & Idriss, 2011). Participants interact in small groups of 10–12 students from a wide range of national, cultural, and linguistic backgrounds using English as a lingua franca. They take part in regular two-hour synchronous sessions led by one or two facilitators trained to provide a safe and effective learning environment and to ensure that dialogue remains respectful and meaningful and that everyone is heard. The sessions are semi-structured, including facilitator-prepared activities and exchanges on topics chosen by the groups, such as youth aspirations, religion, poverty, migration, and media (Helm, 2018). OFD originally used a bespoke platform (see Figure 2.1) where participants are arranged in a campfire-style circle with a chat window at the center.

Both VE models, Tandem and OFD, are bounded spaces, intentionally designed to foster interactions for (language) learners and thus set the parameters within which participants can position themselves and "perform" their identities, including through the use of language(s) and other available semiotic resources. In Ortega's (2017) view, both bilingual Tandem and lingua franca VE bode well for equitable multilingualism. Yet, she wants to put the multilingual ethos of VE under the lens of research to establish whether these digital environments actually encourage translanguaging practices (see Section 3.1).

To this effect we will delineate relevant theoretical concepts and apply them to concrete examples from recent literature on Tandem exchanges and OFD.

3 Theoretical Backdrop

There are several theoretical concepts which are relevant to our observations. We have divided them into two groups according to their respective foci: language (Section 3.1) and identity (Section 3.2).

3.1 Multilingualism, Monolingualism, and Translingual Practices

The fields of Applied Linguistics and SLA have been witnessing a rich discussion around multilingualism (Duff & Byrnes, 2019; The Douglas Fir Group, 2016). It continues to be a subject of debate due to different understandings and conceptualizations of language. One of the enduring legacies of colonialism is the 'language myth' underpinning orthodox linguistics that perceives languages as discrete entities, which can be studied separately from context, history, and geography (Makoni & Pennycook, 2005). With the development of European nation-states in the eighteenth century, the notion of a common, named language as a requirement for national identity spread. It influenced the way people conceptualize language/s and has led to monolingual ideologies (Cenoz & Gorter, 2015). As a result, language continues to be viewed by many as a static, fixed code or system, governed by rules and structures which are defined by a homogeneous speech community. Unsurprisingly, language teaching is dominated by 'standard language' and raciolinguistic ideologies: the conceptualization of linguistic competence as the ability of idealized, white, monolingual native speakers of a national standard language (Flores & Rosa, 2015). Another consequence is 'native speakerism', i.e., a hegemonic power structure subordinating and marginalizing 'non-native speakers' (Kumaravadivelu, 2016).

The social turn in SLA (Block, 2003) led to increasing recognition of language as a social practice whereby learning a new language entails learning to participate in new communities and negotiate identities. It has challenged the deficit view of language learners who strive for native speaker competence and made concepts such as agency and identity (see Section 3.2) more relevant – the former being understood as an individual's socioculturally mediated capacity to act (Ahearn, 2001), often seen as dynamic, emerging and shaped in and by interaction with others (van Lier, 2008). According to Ortega (2017), the social turn has been completed but the bi/multilingual turn is still underway. Today it is generally acknowledged that the majority of the world's population is multilingual. Nonetheless, many societies are ideologically monolingual, and most multilinguals experience injustice and marginalization in relation to their learning throughout their lives (Makoni & Pennycook, 2012; Ortega, 2017; Piller, 2016). Monolingual ideologies also continue to dominate Western education systems (see Vallejo & Dooly, 2019 for a recent overview), perceiving of bi/plurilinguals' repertoires as the sum of 'parallel monolingualisms' (Heller, 1999) or 'two solitudes' (Cummins, 2008). In many classrooms 'one-language-only' and 'one-language-at-a-time' ideologies persist (Kelly, 2015; Llompart & Nussbaum, 2018; Pennycook, 1994/2017; Vallejo & Dooly, 2019). Monolingual ideologies also pervade CALL (Ortega, 2017), study abroad programs (Trentman, 2019), and VE (Ortega, 2017; Trentman, 2019). Trentman (2019), for example, analyzed the experiences of US learners of Arabic in both virtual and physical environments. She found that monolingual language ideologies led to expectations of monolingual immersion in both study abroad and VE, which contrasted with the plurilingual realities encountered in these spaces. This led to students not taking up some opportunities for language learning and relationship building – something a translingual approach would have encouraged.

Canagarajah (2015) proposes the concept of 'translingual practice' to capture phenomena such as 'code mixing', 'code meshing' and translanguaging. He is interested in the processes and orientations underlying these practices as they transcend individual languages and words and involve the use of diverse semiotic resources. Significantly, for Canagarajah (2015), translingual is different from multilingual. While the former is about the dynamic interactions between languages and communities – that is, when speakers of different sociolinguistic and sociocultural backgrounds come together – the latter conceives of the relationship between languages in an additive manner, i.e., 'whole' languages added on top of each other. Translingual practices are often considered a practice to be discouraged (Al-Bataineh & Gallagher, 2018), and provoke contrasting and often contradictory attitudes

(Erling & Moore, 2021; Palfreyman & Al-Bataineh, 2018). At the other end of the spectrum, they are seen as a normal and strategic practice within a plurilingual ideology (García & Li, 2014; Trentman, 2019) and as a form of inclusive multilingualism (Backus et al., 2013), akin to Ortega's (2017) equitable multilingualism.

The concept of "intersemiotic translanguaging" (Baynham et al., 2015, p. 19), i.e., shifting between modalities, including offline and online modes, oral and written and/or visual language, echoes Canagarajah's (2015) framing of the processes involved in translingual practice, namely the use of a variety of semiotic resources. Yet, such translingual practices have only started to be acknowledged and explored in VE (Canals, 2020; Griggio & Pittarello, 2020; Trentman, 2019; Walker, 2018). This is surprising as the possibilities VEs offer participants to communicate and "perform" their identities by drawing on multiple meaning-making modes, and thus on their full 'semiotic budget' (Hauck & Satar, 2018) to position themselves in relation to other VE participants, seem endless. An exception is the work of Satar and Hauck (2021), who illustrate the impact of a digital and semiotic skills gap on equitable online participation in learning communities such as those found in VE.

Next, we apply the concepts presented and discussed to Tandem and OFD, expanding on them as appropriate. As a reminder, the following questions raised by Kelly-Holmes (2019) guide our thinking in this section:

- How are languages organized in the chosen VE models?
- How many languages are available?
- How much content is available in which particular language/s?
- What is the role of English?
- What hierarchies and orderings are present?
- What measures are taken to promote inclusive and equitable multilingualism, if any?

3.1.1 Language Organization and Ideologies in Tandem-Based VEs

Tandem-based VEs are considered bilingual exchanges, but often reflect the monolingual ideologies described above. The principle of reciprocity underpinning them (see Section 2.1) has been used in a prescriptive way, that is by 'dictating' (Narcy-Combes et al., 2020) that partners benefit equally from the exchange which is often expressed in terms of time spent interacting in each language (Kötter, 2003). This prescriptive approach also prevails in online Tandem sites supporting students in finding partners and giving them advice on how to engage. The SEAGULL website, for example, gives the following advice:

> Each time you meet, speak in one language only and then switch to the other language at a previously arranged time. Don't give in to the temptation of staying with the language that both partners speak and understand best! To be fair, pay attention that both partners get about the same amount of speaking time in their target language (the language they want to learn), so that both partners can benefit equally from the meeting.[1]

The language ideology reflected in this extract indexes a monolingual approach, or, at best, parallel or separate bilingualism and thus the concept of 'two solitudes' (Cummins, 2008) whereby languages are seen as bounded entities as students are instructed to clearly distinguish between the use of the two 'target languages'. They are separated temporally, with 50% of the total time being dedicated to each language during interactions which are expected to be strictly monolingual.

Reciprocity has also been interpreted in a more descriptive fashion though, asking each partner to engage and facilitate the other's learning and translingual approaches have been endorsed. Walker (2018), for example, in a case study of bilingual learners of English and German involved in an online exchange, reports that information for participants stated the following:

> [...] the expectation for both languages to be used for mutual benefit. However, negotiation of language arrangements was left up to each group to negotiate, in line with the principle of collaborative autonomy. No hard and fast rules were set, but the teachers modelled translingual practices such as code switching or mixing woven into some of their contributions. (p. 21)

Drawing on Cook's (1996) notion of multicompetence and Swain's (2006) notion of languaging, Walker (2018) defines translanguaging as "a form of language-in-use during which speakers draw on their entire linguistic repertoires to make meaning" (p. 20). She uses the concept for examining interactive languaging practices in the context of a bilingual project task on globalization and localization, with learners working in small groups and exploring the topic from a social, cultural, environmental or economic perspective. She found that translanguaging was used not as a strategy to address lexical

[1] https://www.seagull-tandem.eu/tips para. 2 Language

gaps – reflecting the deficit view underpinning monolingual ideologies – but rather as an approach which afforded participants flexibility in language use and allowed them to create opportunities for learning which were beneficial to all group members. This mirrors Canagarajah's (2015) process-oriented view of translanguaging. Exploratory talk whereby students engaged with ideas and negotiated meanings was produced translingually, and in their synchronous discussions error correction was not present. Only in the first of their five synchronous meetings was the amount of time dedicated to each language equally distributed, while in the remaining meetings either English or German predominated. Long passages in German or English became interwoven into a meaningful whole, allowing the learners to navigate the complex demands of the project. In the participants' collective written productions on a wiki, the focus was on language and here students provided linguistic feedback and/or corrections.

Similar flexibility and explicit modeling of translingual practices are also present in Griggio and Pittarello's (2020) 'eTandem project'. This Tandem-inspired pre-mobility VE matches incoming international students with domestic students and future outgoing students and supports six languages: Italian, French, Spanish, Portuguese, German and English, i.e., the main 'named' European languages. The aims of the project are "to promote inclusive multilingualism and develop participants' digital and intercultural competences, critical thinking and interest in global issues as well as their language skills."[2]

Students engage in two configurations of communication: 'one-to-one' and 'many-to-many'. The former follows the prescriptive Tandem approach, "where the time should be equally split between Italian and other target languages, for both students to benefit from the language exchange" (Griggio & Pittarello, 2020, p. 130). The 'many-to-many' occurs in two modes: asynchronous e-communities on Facebook and Moodle and synchronous facilitated dialogue sessions in groups of 8–12 students. The different configurations are illustrated in Figure 2.2.

The community interactions are organized around themes and each week facilitators publish 2–3 posts relating to a specific topic. They could be said to have adopted "a co-languaging strategy" (van der Walt, 2013, p. 150), a multilingual approach where languages co-exist, with posts offering similar content in English and Italian or other languages spoken in the community, and thus reflecting the aforementioned additive conceptualization of languages in multilingualism (see Section 3.1). Links to online resources often

[2] http://cla.unipd.it/en/e-tandem/

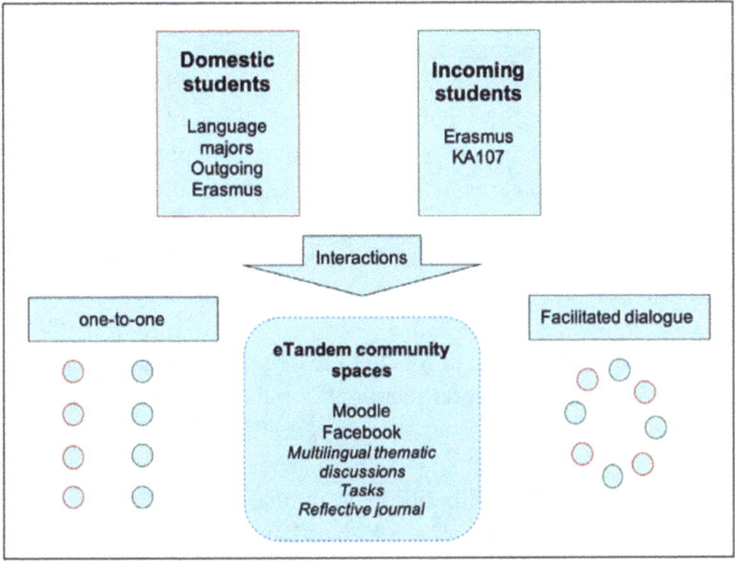

Figure 2.2. Configurations of Participants in the eTandem Project (Griggio & Pittarello, 2020, p. 130)

available in multiple languages are provided and participants are encouraged to use their full linguistic repertoires. The focus is on the content and interactions, and error correction is not advised.

The two examples presented above speak to the gradual emergence of translingual approaches in Tandem learning as reported in the recent literature (Narcy-Combes et al., 2020) and could be seen as initial steps in the direction of promoting equitable multilingualism in VE and as a contribution to the social justice turn in SLA. They do this by creating different spaces and activities in which multilingual or translingual practices are modelled and explicitly encouraged.

3.1.2 Language Organization and Ideologies in OFD Exchanges

OFD ostensibly follows a monolingual approach, drawing on a single shared language, usually English. Yet research suggests that exchanges can also gesture toward a translingual stance. Helm and van der Velden (2020), for example, report on the Erasmus+ VE project, a European Commission initiative in which several OFDs were run by the NGOs Sharing Perspectives Foundation and Soliya. The majority were carried out in English, but a small number took place in Arabic and French, i.e., in languages shared across several countries in the Euro-Mediterranean region. Though these OFDs were not designed as language learning programs, many students participated because they were introduced into their university curricula as elements of or an alternative to English language courses. Educators saw them as an authentic learning experience with transformative potential (Reynolds, 2020), providing opportunities for intercultural engagement and English language practice. They were particularly valued in those contexts where mobility and other opportunities are restricted for students for socio-economic and political reasons (see, for example, Al Mqadma & Al Karriri, 2020, in relation to Gaza).

The attitude toward English was not prescriptive in terms of orientations to standard varieties or error correction, but rather the focus was on engaging with fellow participants and sharing perspectives. While the main language was English, in fact many Englishes came together in these encounters – that is, participants with different regional accents and varying levels of proficiency. OFD facilitators are seen as key in creating an inclusive environment as they initiate sessions with ice-breaking activities, ask questions and prompt dialogue inviting all participants to speak. They provide a written summary of the interaction in the chat (see Figure 2.1), often using paraphrases to support understanding for those who may have difficulties (Helm, 2018; Helm & van der Velden, 2021).

In terms of language ideologies, OFD could be seen to embody an approach of English as "a language always in translation," bringing hundreds of people together in "the global traffic of meaning" (Pennycook, 2008, p. 33). This conceptualization of English suggests that although English is the main language used, meanings are diversified. Pennycook (2008) calls this 'semiodiversity' (diversity of meanings), a term capturing the fact that different social, cultural, and historic meanings are brought to the fore. In this type of exchange, i.e., between people who are not so-called 'native speakers', an increased "willingness to cooperate and accept unsolved situations and arbitrary solutions among participants" (Hua, 2015, p. 68) has been noted. They also allow learners to "take a more multilingual stance despite having been previously socialized into linguistic insecurity and perfectionism" (Ortega, 2017, p. 299). Helm and van der Velden (2021) describe this multilingual stance as a "collaborative ethos," reporting that OFD participants and facilitators helped one another in expressing themselves and making themselves understood through translation, using online tools to support themselves or each other, engaging in paraphrasing and explaining:

> We did not grow up expressing ourselves in English but, even if we are not expert users, we discussed about politics, poetry, economy and history in a successful way. When somebody did not know a specific term, others explained to him or her. Not being native speaker makes your behaviour modest, and you can feel free to ask for explanations. On the other hand, it is also true that this situation did not enable us to talk normally as we do in our mother tongue. However, it may prompt us to improve our English and to gain some confidence. (Female, 23, Italy)

Helm and Acconcia (2019) also found that OFD participants reported flexible language use in their exchanges and evidence of a translingual stance, though attitudes toward this were sometimes ambivalent, if not critical. For example, some interviewees reported instances where a language other than English was used among participants, and this was viewed as being negative.

This section has provided examples to illustrate different language ideologies that have been found to inform the two VE models in question – from the monolingual ideology and prescriptivism of bilingual Tandem exchanges to a more flexible translingual stance which can be found both in Tandem exchanges where multiple languages are explicitly called into play and in OFDs. The latter might, at first glance, appear to be monolingual VEs, but on closer analysis they indicate translingual practices by involving multiple meanings, and thus semiodiversity, through the use of English.

We now move on to the second set of concepts that has informed our observations.

3.2 Identity, Subjectivity, and Positioning

VE participants tend to be discursively constructed in terms of national languages, identities, and cultures (Messina Dahlberg & Bagga Gupta, 2015; Liddicoat & Scarino, 2013; Train, 2006), often represented as static and essentialist. As Train (2006) puts it, the field is characterized by "the assumption of one-nation-one-culture-one-self as the only desirable model of community, language, culture and identity" (p. 257). This has been confirmed by researchers such as Ortega and Zyzik (2008) and Ortega (2017), who mention the persistent identification of a fixed culture with "so-called native speakers as a homogeneous group" (Ortega, 2017, p. 341).

The potential for identity work in the context of VE has been recognized by scholars such as Block (2007/2014), Kramsch (2009), Norton (2000/2013), and Klimanova (2021), but has been little explored to date.

Most research on identity has happened in the field of second language learning and, in particular, immigrant learners (e.g., Norton, 2000/2013; Pavlenko & Blackledge, 2004), and in study abroad contexts (Diao & Trentman, 2021; Mori & Sanuth, 2018). Identity performance in digital contexts such as social networking and online gaming sites and fanfiction has recently also gained research interest (e.g., Thorne et al., 2015). However, this cannot be said in relation to VE and CALL (Ortega, 2017).

The interplay between language and identity has been recognized as being complex, multilayered, and in constant flux (Block, 2007/2014; Bucholtz & Hall, 2005; Norton, 2000/2013; Norton & Toohey, 2011). Focusing on the fluidity and co-construction of identity in interactions allows us to move away from static representations of culture and monolithic understandings of the intercultural. Through VE we can create opportunities for "identity work" with students engaging in identity construction and negotiation based on meaning-focused intercultural interactions with geographically distant peers.

In contrast to the aforementioned essentialist view of identity, "subjectivity" as introduced by Weedon (1987/1997) is "precarious, contradictory and in process, constantly reconstituted in discourse each time we think or speak" (p. 32). Thus, subjectivity relates to the way subjects position themselves and/or are positioned through discourse, and is socially and historically embedded. Like identity, positionality is dynamic and changes over time and space (Lineham & McCarthy, 2000). If identity and subjectivity are understood as discursively constructed and reconstituted every time we engage in interaction and (re)position ourselves, it becomes clear how contexts and practices can limit opportunities for language learners to engage in language use. However, the opposite also applies: contexts and practices can be designed specifically to offer learners enhanced opportunities for social interaction and positioning through the way they use language and other semiotic resources available to them. VEs are a case in point as they provide contexts orchestrated by educators with the aim of increasing opportunities for language and, we would argue, identity work. The fact that these opportunities are mediated by technology adds another dimension to identity performance and positionality. Hence, mediated identities along with situated and relational identities warrant further consideration with regard to identity work in VE.

3.2.1 Situated, Mediated, and Relational Identities

According to Zimmerman (1998), situated identities are those local, ethnographically-specific cultural positions which are institutionally existent, such as teachers and students, doctors and patients. They tend to be associated with expectations as to how identities play out in these contexts, more specifically the discourse identities the individuals align to. In the classroom, for example, teachers initiate interactions and students respond to teacher prompts and the teacher provides feedback (Richards, 2006). Many online language classrooms tend to reproduce the situated identities we find in face-to-face learning and teaching. This also holds true for VEs, which are, as we have seen, intentionally designed by educators or VE organizations, which not only specify the language organization but also how (in dyads, triads, small groups), where (in forums, on social media, an LMS, via videoconferencing, etc.), and sometimes when participants are to interact.

At the same time, technology mediation radically transforms communication and other social processes, including those in VE (Kern, 2014, 2015). The modalities and configurations of interaction that VE designers establish, the conventions for communication within the exchange environment, and the affordances of the tools used influence the interactions, identity work, and positionality of the participants. Whether an asynchronous forum is used for interaction, or a synchronous videoconferencing tool, will have a significant impact on how participants play out their identities. Asynchronous communication offers time to think and reflect, and to carefully compose messages and create and curate one's identity. In addition, many asynchronous tools now allow the integration of other media such as emoticons, images, and hyperlinks. The COVID-19 pandemic, however, has led to the large-scale adoption of synchronous videoconferencing in educational contexts, almost normalizing this form of mediated communication. A growing body of VE research reports on the added benefits and challenges of videoconferencing. Satar (2020), for example, illustrates how semiotic resources other than language can trigger, signal, or augment translingual practices, and how these assist learners in projecting themselves socially and emotionally into their online interactions. She concludes that "it is desirable for participants to engage fully by employing all aspects of their communicative repertoire and all aspects of their multiple identities, one of which is their L1 identity" (p. 149).

Finally, while identity is often conceived of as an inherently individual, psychological trait, Bucholtz and Hall (2005) remind us that "identities are never autonomous or independent but always acquire social meaning in relation to other available identity positions and other social actors" (p. 598).

Hanna and de Nooy (2009) highlight the relevance of relational identity in their study of online discussion forums: "forum discussion […] is not a game of solitaire where one's strategies can be adopted without reference to other players but rather a game where self-positioning also depends on that of the other participants in the debate" (p. 154).

How do these concepts apply to Tandem exchanges (Section 3.3) and OFD (Section 3.4)? What is the impact of these VE models on participants' identity work, more specifically on how they position themselves in the exchanges?

3.3 Identity Work and Positioning in Tandem-Based VEs

Tandem casts participants into the category of "autonomous language learners" (see Section 2.1) who understand their language needs and are expected to negotiate these with their partners. This VE model also brings to the fore the relational dimension of identity as the students are also partners expected to support one another in their language learning. In the metadiscourse of Tandem learning, partners are represented in various ways: as "conversation partners, not language teachers,"[3] "informal linguistic tutors […] providing feedback on their use of the target language" (O'Dowd, 2021, p. 2). They are expected to alternate between the "language expert" – often framed as "native speaker" – and "language learner," and there are expectations as to how these identities are to play out. Thus, error correction is an established practice (Lewis, 2020) and advice as to how this should be done is often provided.

Increasingly, when Tandem learning occurs in institutional contexts, other spaces for interaction are created, which provide opportunities for different positionings and allow for different forms of relational identities to emerge, such as members of a group or community (Griggio & Pittarello, 2020; Walker, 2018; Yang, 2018; Yang & Chen, 2014). In these spaces, different norms or expectations for interaction and relations are established. Griggio and Pittarello (2020), for example, specify that in the community space, error correction is not expected, and focus should be on meaning making in whatever language(s) the students choose to use. In their case study (see Section 3.1.1), aspects of the participants' transportable identities are made relevant, such as their status as university students in a European context. Their future or imagined identities as mobile students, living in a new context and speaking multiple languages, also come to the fore, as well

[3] https://www.seagull-tandem.eu/tips/

as knowledge of their local/national education contexts which may be relevant for other group members. This plurilingual, transnational community space and engagement in translingual practices may better prepare students for the plurilingual nature of their study abroad experience, in contrast to the expectations of immersion in a homogeneous language community shaped by monolingual ideologies of language (Trentman, 2019). In terms of mediated identities, the authors specify that community spaces were created in Moodle and Facebook (see Figure 2.2). Students who choose Facebook already have accounts and may be characterized as skilled "semantic traders" (Hampel & Hauck, 2006) – experienced in the realization of the affordances of a variety of modes and able to make efficient use of multiple modalities. As a result, they can position themselves as "networked cosmopolitans," flexibly using different European languages in a multilingual, multimodal community. They are familiar with Facebook's "cultures of use" (Thorne, 2003) – its culturally-specific communicative norms and modes – and share an interest in foreign languages, cultures, and travel.

3.4 Identity Work and Positioning in OFD

The situated identities relevant in OFDs are those of "group member" and "facilitator" (Helm, 2018). As mentioned before, groups consist of 10–12 participants and diversity in terms of gender and sociocultural backgrounds is the guiding principle for group formation. In the context of the Erasmus+ VE project, the cultural fault line was that between European and South Mediterranean countries and the exchanges addressed issues such as migration, gender, and media including social media, and relations between Western and predominantly Muslim societies. They positioned participants as youth in specific sociocultural contexts, and as active citizens in linguistically and culturally diverse, globalized societies. Group members appeared to orient to these positionings. The following quote from an Italian participant who positions herself as a Western woman testifies to this effect:

> In Western countries the main problem is violence against women, gap in wages, abortion stigma. They say that in the West we achieved more rights, and we overcame all problems, but we mentioned that there are still problems. They were surprised that there are still problems regarding women. (Helm & van der Velden, 2020, p. 42)

Being a member of the group became part of a new shared identity participants acquired through the exchange, which contributed to their learning experience and their sense of being active citizens:

> Hearing some realistic sharing feels like I have already been with these people in those situations. Thanks to the group's stories, I can see the world from a deeper perspective out of the box I live in. I felt involved in world issues and responsible to be part of the change. (Female, 22, Tunisia, in Helm & van der Velden, 2020, p. 41)

The group members authenticate one another as speakers of English, with their criteria being the extent to which they can convey their stories and perspectives, not the accuracy or "correctness" of their speech. The participants' identity work is clearly mediated by the technology used. The videoconferencing platform (see Figure 2.1) allows them to see each other. Hence, visual markers of identity are present and index aspects of their transportable identities, such as gender, ethnicity, and in some cases religion.

Now, what is the takeaway from our observations in relation to language, identity, and positioning in VE?

4 Concluding Thoughts

As language educators and VE scholars grounded in European traditions of telecollaboration and VE, writing this chapter has given us an opportunity to critically reflect on our own positionalities, beliefs, and approaches, and our complicity in reinforcing dominant ideologies in our research and practice. Inspired by Canagarajah (2017), who advocates for a more systematic exploration of the interconnection between language ideologies and language practices, and Ortega (2017), who advocates for equitable multilingualism in CALL, we have focused on the language ideologies underpinning two bespoke types of VE. We have illustrated how Tandem-based VEs are generally considered to be bilingual but in their prescriptive instantiations reflect a monolingual "one-language-at-a-time" ideology, based on a temporal separation of named languages and a deficit attitude toward translingual practices. Walker's (2018) study of multimodal translingual practices supports the work of other researchers exploring translingual approaches, such as Yang (2018), who found that the use of L1 allowed for the exploration of ideas in greater depth. In Griggio and Pittarello's (2020) eTandem project, the separation of languages and error correction were advised for dyadic interactions, but additional spaces were created for many-to-many communication where inclusive multilingualism was modeled and endorsed. The OFD model of VE was also explored, and though at first sight it appears to be a monolingual exchange and to endorse the hegemony of English, it gestures toward the equitable multilingualism Ortega (2017) calls for. The fact that English is not the main language of most participants, support of trained facilitators, emergence of a group identity, and a collaborative ethos allowed individuals with varying levels of competence to participate and overcome linguistic insecurities. However, research by Helm and Acconcia (2019) also found that attitudes to translingual practices were ambivalent and at times contradictory.

Thus the pervasiveness of monolingual ideologies underscores the need to raise awareness and model translingual practices, intentionally building them into VE design as part of the social justice turn in SLA. In the case of OFD this could be addressed in the professional development of facilitators through translations via the text chat at the center of the OFD interface (see Figure 2.1), and through interpreting, for example, to extend the modest translingual practices already in place and to foster inclusive multilingualism.

Li (2018) advocates for translanguaging as a practical theory of language for the 21st century, arguing that it "creates a social space for the language user by bringing together different dimensions of their personal history, experience, and environment; their attitude, belief, and ideology; their cognitive and physical capacity, into one coordinated and meaningful performance" (p. 23). Expanding on the idea that the interplay between language and identity is in constant flux (see Section 3.2), he points to the transformative power of the "translanguaging space" which is continuously evolving and allows new identities, values, and practices to emerge. Trentman (2019) reminds us that plurilingual pedagogies explicitly acknowledge when individuals draw creatively from their full linguistics repertoire to participate in transformative translanguaging spaces. She also highlights how this allows them to "develop a critical awareness of connections between language and structures of power in the world (García & Li, 2014; Piccardo, 2017)" (p. 127).

VEs offer the potential to be such a translanguaging space where "teachers and students can go between and beyond socially constructed language and educational systems, structures and practices to engage diverse multiple meaning-making systems and subjectivities, to generate new configurations of language and education practices, and to challenge and transform old understandings and structures" (Li, 2018, p. 24) and in this way promote social justice.

However, current instantiations of VE, particularly their language organizations, steer learners to normative behaviors and meanings and shape how they position themselves and how they "perform" identities. Hence, there is a need for educators and learners to understand how languages and technologies are used in situated and enculturated ways and how they can reinforce dominant ideologies and limit the identities and positionings available to VE participants. There is also a need to imagine how languages and technologies might be used in VE and beyond to challenge these ideologies.

As CALL practitioners we need to critically reflect on our beliefs and practices, and on our complicity in reinforcing dominant language ideologies as they are likely to influence learner agency, identity work and language, and intercultural learning, including in VE contexts.

We should model inclusive multilingualism and translingual practices and create spaces and opportunities not only for learners' linguistic repertoires to be celebrated and further enriched but also to understand the historic and political structures which perpetuate injustices originating in European colonialist monolingual ideologies and the problematic links made between nation, language, and culture.

Acknowledgments

The authors would like to thank the blind reviewers for their critical advice to improve this chapter.

References

Ahearn, L. M. (2001). Language and agency. *Annual Review of Anthropology*, 30, 109–137.

Al-Bataineh, A., & Gallagher, K. (2018). Attitudes towards translanguaging: How future teachers perceive the meshing of Arabic and English in children's storybooks. *International Journal of Bilingual Education and Bilingualism*, 4(3), 386–400. https://www.researchgate.net/deref/https%3A%2F%2Fdoi.org%2F10.1080%2F13670050.2018.1471039

Al Mqadma, A., & Al Karriri, A. (2020). Erasmus+ Virtual Exchange for internationalisation in besieged areas: A case study of the Islamic University of Gaza. In F. Helm & A. Beaven (Eds.), *Designing and implementing virtual exchange – a collection of case studie*s (pp. 167–178). Research-publishing.net. https://doi.org/10.14705/rpnet.2020.45.9782490057726

Backus, A., Gorter, D., Knapp, K., Schjerve-Rindler, R., Swanenberg, J., ten Thije, J. D., & Vetter, E. (2013). Inclusive multilingualism: Concept, modes and implications. *European Journal of Applied Linguistics* 1(2), 1–37.

Baynham, M., Bradley, J., Callaghan, J., Hanusova, J., & Simpson, J. (2015). Language, business and superdiversity in Leeds. *Working Papers in Translanguaging and Translation* (Working Paper No. 4). http://www.birmingham.ac.uk/generic/tlang/index.aspx_

Belz, J. (2003). Linguistic perspectives on the development of intercultural competence in telecollaboration. *Language Learning and Technology*, 7(2), 68–117.

Block, D. (2003). *The social turn in second language acquisition*. Washington, DC: Georgetown University Press.

Block, D. (2007/2014). *Second language identities*. Continuum.

Bucholtz, M., & Hall, K. (2005). Identity and interaction: A socio-cultural linguistic approach. *Discourse Studies*, 7(4–5), 585–614.

Canagarajah, S. (2015). Clarifying the relationship between translingual practice and L2 writing: Addressing learner identities. *Applied Linguistics Review*, 6(4), 415–440. https://doi.org/10.1515/applirev-2015-0020

Canagarajah, S. (2017). *Translingual practices and neoliberal policies*. Springer.

Canals, L. (2020). Multimodality and translanguaging in negotiation of meaning. *Foreign Language Annals*, 1–24. https://doi-org.libezproxy.open.ac.uk/10.1111/flan.12547

Cenoz, J., & Gorter, D. (2015). *Multilingual education: Between language learning and translanguaging*. Cambridge University Press.

Cook, V. (1996). Competence and multi-competence. In G. Brown, K. Malmkjaer, & J. Williams (Eds.), *Performance and competence in second language acquisition* (pp. 57–69). Cambridge University Press.

Cummins, J. (2008). Teaching for transfer: Challenging the two solitudes assumption in bilingual education. *Encyclopedia of Language and Education* (vol. 5: Bilingual Education). Springer Science+Business Media.

Diao, W., & Trentman, E. (Eds.). (2021). *Language learning in study abroad: The multilingual turn*. Multilingual Matters.

Diniz de Figueiredo, E. H., & Martinez, J. (2021). The locus of enunciation as a way to confront epistemological racism and decolonize scholarly knowledge. *Applied Linguistics*, 42(2), 355–359.

Dooly, M., & Vinagre, M. (2021). Research into practice: Virtual exchange in language teaching and learning. *Language Teaching*, 1–15. https://doi.org/10.1017/S0261444821000069

Duff, P., & Byrnes, H. (2019). SLA across disciplinary borders: Introduction to the Special Issue. *The Modern Language Journal*, 103(Supplement 2019), 3–5.

Erling, E. J., & Moore, E. (2021). Socially just plurilingual education in Europe: Shifting subjectivities and practices through research and action. *International Journal of Multilingualism*. https://doi.org/10.1080/14790718.2021.1913171

EVOLVE (2019). *What is Virtual Exchange?* https://evolve-erasmus.eu/about-evolve/what-is-virtual-exchange/_

Flores, N., & Rosa, J. (2015). Undoing appropriateness: Raciolinguistic ideologies and language diversity in education. *Harvard Educational Review*, 85, 149–171.

García, O., & Li, W. (2014). *Translanguaging: Language, bilingualism and education*. Palgrave Macmillan.

Griggio, L., & Pittarello, S. (2020). How a multilingual project can foster and enhance international mobility. In F. Helm & A. Beaven (Eds.), *Designing and implementing virtual exchange – a collection of case studies* (pp. 127–139). Research-publishing.net. https://doi.org/10.14705/rpnet.2020.45.1121

Hampel, R., & Hauck, M. (2006). Computer-mediated language learning: Making meaning in multimodal virtual learning spaces. *JALT CALL Journal*, 2(2), 3–18.

Hanna B. E., & de Nooy, J. (2009). *Learning language and culture via public Internet discussion forums*. Palgrave Macmillan.

Hauck, M., & Satar, M. (2018). Conceptualizing participatory literacy: New approaches to building and sustaining co-presence in situated learning communities. In R. Kern & C. Develotte (Eds.), *Online multimodal communication and intercultural encounters* (pp. 133–157). Routledge.

Heath, S. B. (1989). Language ideology. In E. Barnouw (Ed.), *International encyclopedia of communications* (vol. 2) (pp. 393–395). Oxford University Press.

Heller, M. (1999). *Linguistic minorities and modernity: A sociolinguistic ethnography*. Longman.

Helm, F. (2018). *Emerging identities in virtual exchange*. Research-publishing.net. https://doi.org/10.14705/rpnet.2018.25.9782490057191

Helm, F., & Acconcia, G. (2019). Interculturality and language in Erasmus+ Virtual Exchange. *European Journal of Language Policy*, 11(2), 211–233.

Helm, F., & van der Velden, B. (2021). *Erasmus+ Virtual Exchange: 2020 Impact Report*. Luxembourg: Publications Office of the European Union. https://europa.eu/youth/sites/default/files/eyp/eve/attachments/ec-01-21-404-en-n_final.pdf

Helm, F., & van der Velden, B. (2020). *Erasmus+ Virtual Exchange: 2019 Impact Report*. https://op.europa.eu/en/publication-detail/-/publication/0ee233d5-cbc6-11ea-adf7-01aa75ed71a1/language-en

Himelfarb, S. (2014). The real eHarmony: How young people meeting on the Internet might help build peace in some of the world's most volatile regions. *Foreign Policy*. https://foreignpolicy.com/2014/01/02/the-real-eharmony/

Himelfarb, S., & Idriss, S. (2011). *Exchange 2.0* (Special Report). U.S. Institute of Peace. http://www.usip.org/sites/default/files/Exchange2.0.pdf

Hua, Z. (2015). Negotiation as the way of engagement in intercultural and lingua franca communication: Frames of reference and interculturality. *Journal of English as Lingua Franca*, 4(1), 63–90.

Kelly, M. (2015). Challenges to multilingual language teaching: Towards a transnational approach. *European Journal of Language Policy*, 7(1), 65–83. https://doi.org/10.3828/ejlp.2015.5

Kelly-Holmes, H. (2019). Multilingualism and technology: A review of developments in digital communication from monolingualism to idiolingualism. *Annual Review of Applied Linguistics*, 39, 24–39.

Kern, R. (2014). Technology as pharmakon: The promise and perils of the internet for foreign language education. *The Modern Language Journal*, 98(1), 340–357.

Kern, R. (2015). *Language, literacy and technology*. Cambridge University Press.

Klimanova, L. (2021). The evolution of identity research in CALL: From scripted chatrooms to engaged construction of the digital self. *Language Learning & Technology*, 25(3), 186–204. http://hdl.handle.net/10125/73455

Kötter, M. (2003). Negotiation of meaning and codeswitching in online tandems. *Language Learning & Technology*, 7(2), 145–172. https://doi.org/10125/25203

Kramsch, C. (2009). *The multilingual subject: What foreign language learners say about their experience and why it matters*. Oxford University Press.

Kumaravadivelu, B. (2016). The decolonial option in English teaching: Can the subaltern act? *TESOL Quarterly*, 50(1), 66–85.

Lewis, T. (2020). From Tandem learning to e-Tandem learning: How languages are learnt in Tandem exchanges. In S. Gola, M. Pierrard, E. Tops, & D. Van Raemdonck (Eds.), *Enseigner et apprendre les langues au XXIe siècle. Méthodes alternatives et nouveaux dispositifs d'accompagnement*. Peter Lang.

Li, W. (2018). Translanguaging as a practical theory of language. *Applied Linguistics*, 39(1), 9–30.

Liddicoat, A. J., & Scarino, A. (2013). *Intercultural language teaching and learning*. Wiley.

Lineham, C., & McCarthy, J. (2000). Positioning in practice: Understanding participation in the social world. *Journal for the Theory of Social Behaviour*, 30(4), 435–453.

Little, D., & Brammerts, H. (Eds.). (1996). *A guide to language learning in Tandem via the Internet* [CLCS Occasional Paper No. 46]. Trinity College.

Llompart, J., & Nussbaum, L. (2018). Doing plurilingualism at school: Key concepts and perspectives. In S. Melo-Pfeifer & C. Helmchen (Eds.), *Plurilingual literacy practices at school and in teacher education* (pp. 15–29). Peter Lang.

Makoni, S., & Pennycook, A. (2005). Disinvesting and (re)constituting languages. *Critical Inquiry in Language Studies*, 2, 137–156.

Makoni, S., & Pennycook, A. (2012). Disinventing multilingualism. In M. Martin-Jones, A. Blackledge, & A. Creese (Eds.), *The Routledge handbook of multilingualism* (pp. 439–453). Routledge.

Messina Dahlberg, G., & Bagga Gupta, S. (2015). Learning on-the-go in institutional telecollaboration: Anthropological perspectives on the boundaries of digital spaces. In E. Dixon & M. Thomas (Eds.), *Researching language learner interaction online: From social media to MOOCs*. CALICO Monograph Series (vol. 13). CALICO.

Mori, J., & Sanuth, K. K. (2018). Navigating between a monolingual utopia and translingual realities: Experiences of American learners of Yorùbá as an additional language. *Applied Linguistics*, 39, 78–98.

Narcy-Combes, M. N., Narcy-Combes, J. P., McAllister, J., & Leclere, M. (2020). *Language learning and teaching in a multilingual world (new perspectives on language and education)*. Multilingual Matters.

Norton, B. (2000/2013). *Identity and language learning: Gender, ethnicity and educational change*. Pearson Education/Longman.

Norton, B., & Toohey, K. (2011). Identity, language learning, and social change. *Language Teaching*, 44(4), 412–446.

O'Dowd, R. (2021). What do students learn in virtual exchange? A qualitative content analysis of learning outcomes across multiple exchanges. *International Journal of Educational Research*, 109. https://doi.org/10.1016/j.ijer.2021.101804

O'Rourke, B. (2007). Models of telecollaboration (1): eTandem. In R. O'Dowd (Ed.), *Online intercultural exchange*. Multilingual Matters.

Ortega, L. (2017). New CALL-SLA research interfaces for the 21st century: Towards equitable multilingualism, *CALICO Journal*, 34(3), 285–316.

Ortega, L., & Zyzik, E. (2008). Online interactions and L2 learning: Some ethical challenges for L2 researchers. In S. Magnan (Ed.), *Mediating discourse online* (pp. 331–355). John Benjamins.

Palfreyman, D. M., & Al-Bataineh A. (2018). This is my life style, Arabic and English: Students' attitudes to (trans)languaging in a bilingual university context. *Language Awareness*, 27(1–2), 79–95.

Pavlenko, A., & Blackledge, A. (Eds.). (2004). *Negotiation of identities in multilingual contexts*. Multilingual Matters.

Pennycook, A. (2008). English as a language always in translation. *European Journal of English Studies*, 12(1), 33–47.

Pennycook, A. (1994/2017). *The cultural politics of English as an international language*. Routledge.

Piccardo, E. (2017). Plurilingualism as a catalyst for creativity in superdiverse societies: A systemic analysis. *Frontiers in Psychology*, 8, 2169.

Piller, I. (2016). *Linguistic diversity and social justice: An introduction to Applied Sociolinguistics*. Oxford University Press.

Reynolds, A. (2020). Erasmus virtual exchange as an authentic learner experience. In M. Hauck & A. Müller-Hartmann (Eds.), *Virtual exchange and 21st century teacher education: Short papers from the 2019 EVALUATE conference* (pp. 85–99). Research-publishing.net. https://doi.org/10.14705/rpnet.2020.46.1135

Richards, K. (2006). "Being the teacher": Identity and classroom conversation. *Applied Linguistics*, 27(1), 51–77.

Satar, M. (2020). L1 for social presence in videoconferencing: A social semiotic account. *Language Learning and Technology*, 24(1), 129–153. https://www.lltjournal.org/item/3137

Satar, M., & Hauck, M. (2021). Exploring digital equity in online learning communities (Virtual Exchange). In A. de Medeiros & D. Kelly (Eds.),

Language debates – theory and reality in language learning, teaching and research. Language acts and worldmaking, 2 (pp. 270–290). John Murray Press.

Schwienhorst, K. (2004). Native-speaker/non-native-speaker discourse in the MOO: Topic negotiation and initiation in a synchronous text-based environment. *Computer Assisted Language Learning*, 17(1), 35–50.

Swain, M. (2006). Languaging, agency and collaboration in advanced second language proficiency. In H. Byrnes (Ed.), *Advanced language learning: The contribution of Halliday and Vygotsky* (pp. 95–108). Continuum.

The Douglas Fir Group. (2016). A transdisciplinary framework for SLA in a multilingual world. *The Modern Language Journal*, 100(S1), 19–47. https://doi.org/10.1111/modl.12301

Thorne, S. L. (2003). Artifacts and cultures-of-use in intercultural communication. *Language Learning & Technology*, 7(2), 38–67.

Thorne, S. L., Sauro, S., & Smith, B. (2015). Technologies, identities, and expressive activity. *Annual Review of Applied Linguistics*, 35, 215–233.

Train, R. (2006). A critical look at technologies and ideologies in internet-mediated intercultural foreign language education. In J. A. Belz & S. L. Thorne (Eds.), *Internet-mediated intercultural foreign language education* (pp. 247–284). Thomson Heinle.

Trentman, E. (2019). Reframing monolingual ideologies in the language classroom: Evidence from Arabic study abroad and telecollaboration. In B. Dupuy & K. Michelson (Eds.), *Pathways to paradigm change: Critical examinations of prevailing discourses and ideologies in second language education* (pp. 108–132). Cengage Learning.

Vallejo, C., & Dooly, M. (2019). Plurilingualism and translanguaging: Emergent approaches and shared concerns. Introduction to the Special Issue. *International Journal of Bilingual Education and Bilingualism*, 23(1), 1–16. https://doi.org/10.1080/13670050.2019.1600469

van der Walt, C. (2013). *Multilingual higher education. Beyond English medium orientations*. Multilingual Matters.

van Lier, L. (2008). Agency in the classroom. In J. P. Lantolf & M. E. Poehner (Eds.), *Sociocultural theory and the teaching of second languages* (pp. 163–186). Equinox.

Walker, U. (2018). Translanguaging: Affordances for collaborative language learning. *New Zealand Studies in Applied Linguistics*, 24(1), 18–40.

Weedon, C. (1987/1997). *Feminist practice and poststructuralist theory* (2nd ed.). Blackwell.

Yang, S. J. (2018). Language learners' perceptions of having two interactional contexts in eTandem. *Language Learning & Technology*, 22(1), 42–51. https://scholarspace.manoa.hawaii.edu/bitstream/10125/44577/1/22_01_yang.pdf

Yang, S. C., & Chen, J. J. (2014). Fostering foreign language learning through technology enhanced intercultural projects. *Language Learning & Technology*, 18(1), 57–75. http://llt.msu.edu/issues/february2014/yangchen.pdf

Zimmerman, D. H. (1998). Discoursal identities and social identities. In C. Antaki & S. Widdicombe (Eds.), *Identities in talk* (pp. 87–106). Sage.

About the Authors

Dr. Francesca Helm is Assistant Professor of English Language at the Department of Political Science, Law and International Studies at the University of Padova, Italy. She is chair of the Education Innovation working group of the Coimbra Group, a European network of universities, and founding member of the association UNICollaboration. Her research and recent publications focus on intercultural dialogue, virtual exchange and internationalisation of higher education. She was a member of the team responsible for monitoring and evaluation of the Erasmus+ Virtual Exchange pilot project.

Dr. Mirjam Hauck is Associate Head for Internationalisation, Equality, Diversity and Inclusion in the School of Languages and Applied Linguistics at the Open University, UK, President of the European Association for Computer Assisted Language Learning (EUROCALL) and founding member of UNICollaboration. She has published widely on the use of technologies for the learning and teaching of languages and cultures in virtual exchange contexts. Her scholarly work focuses on intercultural communicative competence and critical digital literacy. She is a regular speaker at international conferences, Associate Editor of the *CALL Journal* and an editorial board member of *ReCALL* and *LLT*.

3 Multilingual Identities and Intercultural Education during Telecollaboration: A Heritage Language Learner Case Study

Carly M. Lesoski

1 Introduction

As language classrooms have increasingly become digitally connected, alternative opportunities to engage in intercultural education have become more accessible to many learners, although this access is inequitable (Ortega, 2017). Telecollaboration is one such opportunity that has gained favor as a practice for connecting students to members of target language and culture communities. Researchers in computer-assisted language learning (CALL) have focused heavily on telecollaboration, especially with an interest in how the practices affect the experiences of monolingual students learning a foreign language (Ortega, 2017).

Any attempt to understand how identity functions in a multilingual language learning landscape must consider the impact that multilingualism and learners' identities have on their intercultural education. Vollmer Rivera and Teske (2018) state that telecollaboration research, much like classroom practices, tends to focus on the dichotomy between native and non-native language speakers, a practice that leaves learners with backgrounds outside of these presumed norms out of the discussion. Such learners include heritage language learners (HLLs), who enter our classrooms with personal experience with the target language and culture.

The goal of the present case study is to describe an HLL's telecollaboration experiences and identify potential strategies to mitigate impeding factors, focusing on HLL identity as it relates to the languages they speak. The current case study centers on Lilly and her identities as a multilingual speaker of German, English, and Spanish, as well as the ways these identities fluctuate and are situationally interrelated within the telecollaboration context.

This study shows that telecollaboration can allow HLLs to negotiate their plurilingual identities. Lilly often described a sense of being between languages and cultures, as she was positioned as German by her American peers and as American by her German peers. Her own perceived language deficits added to the perception of lack of belonging. Lilly took control of her identity by positioning herself as a native speaker of German within minutes of the first interaction beginning. Although Lilly was a native English speaker, a heritage German speaker, and had learned Spanish for years, she focused heavily on her perceived language deficits. Much of her deficit-based mindset was related to her negative views toward translanguaging, often describing the switching between languages as a sign of her lack of proficiency.

To begin this chapter, I outline research relating to HLLs and telecollaboration, with an emphasis on the experiences of multilingual learners. I define identities and present research on the identities of HLLs, followed by a discussion of the ways that telecollaboration, identity, and HLLs interact and intersect. The context of the current study and the background to the case study subject are both detailed, including the process for data collection and results. I give the results of the analysis, beginning with overall identities, before transitioning to how these identities relate to Lilly's three languages, and concluding with changes and relationships between identities. This chapter ends with lessons learned and future directions for praxis and research.

2 Telecollaboration and Heritage Language Learners

Over the past decade, CALL research has more fully begun to examine heritage language learner identity (Leeman et al., 2011). However, research has yet to address the myriad challenges multilingual HLLs may face during telecollaboration, particularly in their identity negotiation. This section addresses prior research on telecollaboration, HLLs, identity, as well as the intersections between these three concepts.

2.1 Telecollaboration

The terminology surrounding this particular pedagogical approach is in flux, with terms in use that include virtual exchange, teletandem, telecollaboration, and others (see Dooly & O'Dowd, 2018 and O'Dowd, 2018 for detailed discussions). As this assignment was described to the learners as telecollaboration, and it followed the goals and structure of telecollaboration at the time, I will use this term throughout this chapter. Telecollaboration is a digital communicative exchange between learners of different linguistic and cultural backgrounds, typically to improve language proficiency and/or intercultural competence (O'Dowd, 2013; Schenker, 2015; Telles, 2015), which often occur between language learners in formal educational settings. Telecollaboration has a core goal of advancing learners' intercultural competence through interaction in often multilingual, digital environments (Schenker, 2015; Telles, 2015), although it is worth noting that the goals and structures of telecollaboration are diverse (Dooly & O'Dowd, 2018; O'Dowd, 2018).

Research has shown that telecollaboration is an effective pedagogical practice for various aspects of language learning (Helm, 2015), such as increasing oral proficiency (Akiyama & Saito, 2016; Canto et al., 2013), development of intercultural competence (Belz, 2002; Chun, 2011; Schenker, 2012a, 2012b), and providing opportunities for incidental learning (Kabata & Edasawa, 2011), in addition to a variety of other benefits. Dooly (2011) described telecollaboration as a multilingual practice. In her study, students worked together to create a monolingual product and passed through various stages of target language usage. Learners' usage of multiple languages increased their ability to work collaboratively to create a monolingual product (Dooly, 2011).

2.1.1 Telecollaboration as Intercultural and Plurilingual Education

Recent scholars have argued for the efficacy of telecollaboration as a form of intercultural education, with Lee and Song (2019) finding that the outcomes of telecollaboration concerning affective and behavioral aspects of intercultural communicative competence are comparable to those of education abroad. They argue that telecollaboration may be a cost-effective alternative to education abroad programs for some learners; they emphasize that education abroad can have a greater impact on cultural knowledge while noting that affective development may have a greater role in prejudice reduction. This is particularly important within the American higher education system, as telecollaboration may allow learners in a variety of programs to experience a type of intercultural education without having to take on greater student debt or extend their time to degree. As Goertler and Schenker (2021) note, only 10% of US undergraduates are able to take part in an education abroad program, leaving room for the expansion of various forms of intercultural and international education.

While there are similarities between telecollaboration and education abroad in some aspects of intercultural communicative competence (ICC) development, the majority of researchers advise using telecollaboration as a complement to or preparation for education abroad (Jeanneau & Giralt, 2016) or as a follow-up to continue connection to the target language and culture (Lee, 2017). Trentman (2021) describes telecollaboration as "virtual mobility" (p. 108), framing it as a complement to physical avenues to authentic language interaction. In fact, telecollaboration in many ways requires the crossing of virtual borders to communicate with others whom students may not meet in their day-to-day digital media usage. This virtual border crossing allows for greater access to intercultural education and authentic communication.

Research on telecollaboration as an avenue for intercultural education is abundant. As O'Dowd and Dooly (2020) explain, telecollaboration or virtual exchange supports language learners in developing pragmatic competence and in building an understanding of the relative nature of culture and values. Bohinski and Leventhal (2015) reported that telecollaboration made learners more aware of gaps in their cultural knowledge. Schenker (2012a) used Byram's model of ICC to examine the experience of university students during a telecollaborative exchange and found that development in several aspects of ICC was apparent. Yet, challenges remain, such as the development of appropriate tools and measures for assessing ICC (Goertler et al., 2018.)

In an increasingly connected world in which multilingualism is the norm rather than the exception, telecollaboration is, in and of itself, a plurilingual and pluricultural experience in which students can engage. With a critical lens, Helm (2015) describes an ideology of native-speakerism, which focuses on the native speaker as the ideal language speaker and is common in telecollaboration practice and research. Trentman (2021) pointed out that most existing research on telecollaboration was on monolingual learners of a foreign language in a classroom setting, a context that she describes as inherently plurilingual. This is particularly true of the US, where the gold standard guidelines set forth by ACTFL discourage the use of translanguaging in the language classroom in favor of 90% or higher target language use (ACTFL, n.d.). In contrast, the CEFR guidelines highlight the importance of plurilingual and pluricultural competence (Council of Europe, 2018). These guidelines emphasize the importance of plurilingual and pluricultural classrooms in developing awareness of similarities and differences. In fact, the Council of Europe (2018) notes, "In the reality of today's increasingly diverse societies, the construction of meaning may take place across languages and draw upon user/learners' plurilingual and pluricultural repertoires" (p. 27).

Plurilingual environments encourage utilizing the affordances that translanguaging can offer language learners in an increasingly connected plurilingual world.

> [Translanguaging] posits that rather than possessing two or more autonomous language systems, as has been traditionally thought, bilinguals, multilinguals, and indeed, all users of language, select and deploy particular features from a unitary linguistic repertoire to make meaning and to negotiate particular communicative contexts (Vogel & García, 2017, Summary).

In a telecollaborative setting, translanguaging would be using resources from multiple languages to convey an idea.

2.2 Heritage Language Learners

The term HLL encompasses a grouping of language learners with widely varied cultural and linguistic knowledge (Teske & Vollmer Rivera, 2018; Valdés & Kibler, 2012). Leeman (2015) emphasizes that there is not a single definition nor a clear set of criteria for what constitutes a true HLL. Some HLLs are working to develop their language abilities while others focus on the maintenance of their heritage language (He, 2006). He (2006) considers heritage language learning a vertical process in that it occurs across generations and locations, in contrast to the horizontal process of foreign language learning that occurs within a classroom at a specific time. He (2010) points out that an HLL's social status within their heritage communities is often tenuous and complicated. HLLs are often excluded by systems and practices that perpetuate monolingualism as a norm (Teske & Vollmer Rivera, 2018).

Klimanova and Dembovskaya (2013) report findings from their research on L2 identities during a telecollaborative exchange on a Russian social networking site. They describe the unique experiences of HLLs in a telecollaborative exchange as a "test of their heritage speaker privileges" (p. 82). They reported that the HLLs shared their heritage in the first interaction as a way to legitimize themselves and to elevate their status to be equal to that of their Russian native-speaker partners. As participants in the telecollaboration, HLLs were able to "rework their identities as American students and intersubjectively reconstruct their Russian speaker identities" (Klimanova & Dembovskaya, 2013, p. 82). By engaging in identity exploration during the telecollaboration, the HLLs were able to negotiate their American and Russian identities, as well as their conceptualization of what defines native speakers of a language. Similarly, in their study of an HLL's experiences in an extracurricular telecollaboration project, Yang and Yi (2017) conclude that the partnership and membership in the telecollaborative community created a "safe space where they were able to negotiate, perform, or contest multiple identities" (p. 111).

2.3 Identity

Identity describes the way people view their relationship to the world around them, how this relationship is structured throughout time and space, as well as how one views their possibilities for the future (Norton, 2013). Researchers who use frameworks of identity push back against essentialist categories often ascribed to learners, such as motivated versus unmotivated or non-native speaker versus native speaker (Norton, 2013; Norton & McKinney, 2011). Identity researchers seek to uncover the ways learners view themselves and how these perceptions affect the process of learning a language.

The construct of identity attempts to encapsulate a set of ever-changing characteristics of learners, making it difficult to operationalize (Thorne et al., 2015). Importantly, Norton (2013) emphasizes that identity is a site of struggle where learners work to reconcile their conceptions of self with their experiences into a clear understanding of who they are and where their capabilities lie. Thorne et al. (2015) point out that learning and identity exist in a reciprocal relationship, informing and influencing the development of the other, which creates a dynamic tension.

In a study on monolingual ideologies in telecollaboration and study abroad environments, Trentman (2021) echoed this sentiment, highlighting the potentially hindering nature of positioning learners as two monolinguals in one brain, which uses a multilingual perspective versus a plurilingual perspective that views language repertoires as whole, united systems. Trentman (2021) found that while

> participants expressed monolingual ideologies of language, which shaped their expectations for language learning in the contexts of study abroad and telecollaboration... their linguistic practices were consistently plurilingual, across a wide variety of social contexts. (p. 114)

In this particular passage, Trentman highlights the reality that even learners who express a belief in the importance of monolingual communication for language acquisition tended to participate in multilingual interactions. The choice to participate multilingually served a variety of functions, including assisting learners in acquiring lexical knowledge, thus supporting their language development.

Yang and Yi (2017) point out that the very nature of telecollaboration necessitates that participants play roles as both the expert and novice, which may affect how learners view themselves as part of the target language-speaking world. Their study also found that telecollaboration offered learners a space in which to perform and experiment with a variety of identities, particularly for the HLL participant they examined. Yang and Yi (2017) describe language learning as a process in which the learner is inherently attempting to position their self within a global context. Furthermore, Ushioda (2011) urges educators to focus on the multiple identities their students bring into the language classroom rather than positioning students as mere language learners (see also Chen, 2013). This gives learners the space to negotiate their identities and imagined futures without expectations placed upon them by their instructor (Ushioda, 2011).

2.4 Telecollaboration, Identity, and HLLs

While research into HLL identity has been a topic for quite some time, researchers only more recently have begun studying telecollaboration through an identity lens. HLLs bring especially complex networks of identities to their language learning experience due to their experiences existing within and between different linguistic and cultural communities. These identities can be fraught with contradictions that make telecollaborative exchanges with native speakers more complex. Many HLLs exist in a space between being a native speaker and a language learner. Several factors dictate their experience navigating this space between the two: their level of language proficiency, cultural connections, and how native speakers of their languages view them (Leeman et al., 2011). For HLLs in formal classroom settings, communication with native speakers of their heritage language can lead to shifts in and challenges to HLL identities (Klimanova & Dembovskaya, 2013; Yang & Yi, 2017).

Klimanova and Dembovskaya (2013) noted that HLLs were quick to assert their HLL identities in their telecollaborative exchanges, which served to position them on an even playing field with their Russian native-speaker partners. The HLLs were able to co-construct their identities as Americans and as speakers of Russian (Klimanova & Dembovskaya, 2013). Yang and Yi (2017) focused on an extracurricular eTandem project with an adult HLL of Korean,

Kristine. Kristine began the project with low proficiency but soon realized grammatical perfection was not necessary for successful communication. She was able to connect on a deeper level with her Korean heritage while still expressing a sense of being neither fully Korean nor fully American.

HLLs' experiences differ from those of their monolingual peers in that they come to interactions in the target language with a variety of "real world" experiences with the language, as well as unique connections to the culture. This complex and at times fraught reality leads to the negotiation of HLLs' identities as members of language speaking and learning communities, as well as of their identities as members of multiple cultures. As other researchers have pointed out, very few studies in CALL address the experiences of learners outside the native speaker–non-native speaker dichotomy (Ortega, 2017; Teske & Vollmer Rivera, 2018). The studies cited here show evidence of growing research interest in the HLL experience in traditional foreign language learning environments.

3 Methodology

This section presents the study context, including the parameters of the telecollaboration project. Following this, I introduce the case study participant, Lilly. To conclude this section, I provide relevant details of the coding and analysis of the data.

3.1 Case Study Context and Subject

The present case study data came from data collected as part of a larger research project on learners' language and intercultural competence development during telecollaboration (see Goertler et al., 2018; Lesoski, 2019) with the addition of a follow-up interview. In the interview, I gathered information on Lilly's life since telecollaboration, including whether she was communicating with her partner and what her study abroad plans were, as well as doing a stimulated recall with two short segments of the telecollaboration recordings. The participants in this project were students in an upper-level German course at a Midwestern university in the US. The students in the American context communicated with students enrolled in a teacher-training course at a partner university in Germany. It is important to note that in US-American German programs HLLs are often included in the same courses as their non-heritage language learning peers, as there are fewer German HLLs than Spanish HLLs, who are more likely to have options for HLL-focused courses at many larger universities.

Participants spent seven weeks communicating with their partners who were students in an English-medium course for future educators at a German university. For each of the seven weeks, students were required to answer a set of questions that bridged the content and learning outcomes for the two courses with their partners. Overall, the project focused both implicitly and explicitly on ICC development. While the tasks were not specifically designed to focus on students' identities, the discussions often centered on participants' individual experiences and perceptions. In turn, this led to explicit and implicit discussions of identities. Briefly, the topics of the seven interactions were as follows (see Appendix A for a sample task):

1. Introduction: Who am I?
2. Stereotypes and Cultural Diversity
3. Teaching and Learning Other Languages
4. Technology-mediated Communication and Learning
5. The US vs Germany
6. Reflection
7. My Future and My Language of Study

For purposes of learner autonomy and scheduling challenge mitigation, students could choose their platform for communication, although the instructional team recommended video chats because of our observations of the quality of interactions from the previous semester. Lilly, the case study subject, and her partner, Claudia, heeded this advice and communicated using Skype video chat. Participants were required to communicate using 50% German and 50% English and were allowed to determine how to allot time to each language. The assignment for their course required them to submit proof of their interaction. They submitted the audio recordings of their interactions that served as the data used for subsequent analysis. The dataset is described in further detail following an introduction to Lilly.

3.1.1 Case Study Participant: Lilly

The case study subject, Lilly, was a German-American student at a US university. Lilly explained that she studied "education, German, Spanish" and Teaching English to Speakers of Other Languages (TESOL). Her goal was to become a high school German teacher either in the US or on an American military base in Germany. Her ideal future location changed frequently throughout her discussions with Claudia, her German telecollaboration partner. Lilly acknowledged her uncertainty about where, geographically, she wanted to land in the future. Of the available participants, I chose Lilly because of her relatively high language proficiency and her background as an HLL, the combination of which made her unique.

Lilly often described her experiences speaking German with her family. She claimed she spoke German with her father, although decreasingly so since starting her university studies. They bonded by watching German-language cooking shows and cooking German dishes together. Lilly also spoke German with her sister, who was planning to participate in the same year-long study abroad program. According to Lilly, her mother, an American, spoke German very poorly. While growing up in Germany, Lilly attended a German-medium elementary school where she found herself struggling academically. Her mother's lack of German proficiency, and therefore her inability to help Lilly with schoolwork, led to the decision to move Lilly to an English-medium school on the military base where her family lived.

Initially, Lilly had planned to study abroad in Germany during the following German academic year (September to July). In the follow-up interview (described in Section 3.2), she claimed that this particular program was a major factor in her decision to attend the university at which she studied. Yet, she did not study abroad with her intended program. She cited financial reasons for her inability to participate in the year-long program, while her sister was still able to participate. At the time of the interview, she did plan to spend a semester at a German university.

3.2 Data and Analysis

This chapter utilizes data collected as part of a larger research project (see Goertler et al., 2018; Lesoski, 2019). The data utilized for this analysis include 1) audio recordings of interactions that took place via videoconferencing, 2) course blog posts, and 3) a follow-up interview that occurred approximately one year after the end of the telecollaboration project. Lilly and her peers submitted the audio recordings of their interactions as part of the telecollaboration assignment in their fourth-year German course. Weekly course blog posts reflected on the material for a given week, occasionally including the telecollaborative exchanges. These posts were copied from the course blog and saved in files by week. For the follow-up interview, I met with Lilly and gathered updates on her academic progress and her interactions with Claudia, in addition to completing a short, stimulated recall with two selections from the exchanges. This interview was audio-recorded and later transcribed.

For previous studies, I transcribed the spoken interactions between Lilly and her partner using an audio player and a Google Doc for each of the seven tasks. The use of German and English made it impossible to use automatic transcription software, yet the process of transcribing allowed me to begin pre-coding and commenting on the data. Following this, I coded the data in NVivo, a qualitative coding and data visualization software, using a rubric to parse out students' work with identity and other aspects of their experience. I developed the rubric for a pilot study and tested it on a single case study using the three main concepts of investment – identity, capital, and ideology (Darvin & Norton, 2015) – before it was ultimately applied to examine several participants' interactions in previous analyses (Lesoski, 2019). Following this, I refined the coding scheme to be more specific by utilizing gerunds to emphasize the active nature of identity negotiation. For example, the pilot rubric included the term "identity," and for the final version of the rubric I refined this code to differentiate between describing identity and accepting or rejecting a position. For the current analysis, I utilized data coded under the category *describing identity* and focused specifically on utterances in which Lilly mentioned her languages (see Appendix B for the full rubric). This category encompassed data in which a person describes their relationship to the world, broadly construing the concept of identity.

4 Results

This section begins with a description of Lilly's multiple identities, pointing to specific portions of her interactions with Claudia and highlighting how each of these excerpts exhibits important parts of Lilly's identities, especially as they relate to her multilingual identities. Finally, I present how her language identities relate to and interface with one another. Throughout the coming sections, I present excerpts of the data in their original language with my translations for the interactions that took place in German.

4.1 Overall Identities

In Task 1, students discussed answers to a set of questions about themselves that they had been given, which included a general, open question, "Who am I?", and more specific prompts, such as describing their language learning biographies (see Appendix A for Task 1 description). Lilly started the interaction by describing the complexities of navigating growing up in a bilingual and bicultural household. She described existing between cultures and not necessarily feeling a sense of belonging in either context. She told Claudia,

> So, I put German American and that's because, like, my mom is American and my dad is German. So, I've kind of lived in both worlds. I wouldn't say that I am just American, and I wouldn't say that I am just German. Like, I'm a mix of both, so I don't really belong to either country so... so like that's probably a really big part of my culture.

She positioned herself as an outsider in both contexts and acknowledged the importance of this reality to her sense of cultural belonging. Later in their discussion, Claudia asked how Lilly felt about life in a bicultural household. Lilly admitted that she found it difficult but claimed that it was overall very rewarding. During the stimulated recall portion of the interview, Lilly listened to this interaction and shared that she still felt much the same way. She also mentioned that she did not know when to use the pronouns *we* versus *they* when describing members of American or German culture as she struggled with whether she was within or outside of each group.

4.2 Identities in Relation to Lilly's Three Languages

In the first task, Lilly mentioned to Claudia that she grew up speaking German, which was the reason she stated she had no preference for which language they would begin using during the telecollaborative exchange. Claudia expressed surprise that Lilly grew up speaking German and Lilly replied,

> My English is much better than my German because I only went to German school until fourth grade and then after that I went to American school and then I stopped speaking German. So, like my... my German ability kind of came to a halt and I mean it's still good but it's not nearly as good as my English. My English is much better.

She made this assertion only minutes into their first interaction. Here Lilly shared her background with German and the struggles that she had encountered in maintaining her German proficiency, especially after switching to the American school on the military base where her family was living. She evaluated her German proficiency as being lower than her English proficiency but shared that she could still speak German well.

In some of her interactions, Lilly considered herself as having spoken poor English as a child, while in others she claimed she simply lacked the ability to read and write in English. In Task 3, Lilly explained that when she started attending the American school on the military base where her family lived in Germany, she was unable to read or write in English and that she had spoken with a strong German accent. Later in Task 3, she said, "German is different. I started learning English. Well, I already knew English. I already knew how to speak English. I didn't know how to read or write in Germany in third grade." This area of focus for her came from conflicting memories and contributed to the struggle between her identities.

In addition to German and English, Lilly was learning Spanish. She regarded learning languages as a way of expanding her cultural identity and repeatedly mentioned her Spanish proficiency as being lacking, despite taking upper-level Spanish courses. While talking about places they had traveled for Task 1, Lilly told her partner that she had never been to a Spanish-speaking country even though she spoke "a little Spanish." Her partner expressed surprise that she characterized it as a little Spanish despite her studies. Lilly went on, "Well yeah, it's a little more. I don't know. Honestly, I... my Spanish is not as good as I'd like it to be." Here she revealed her conflicted identities as both a learner and speaker of Spanish.

Then, Lilly recalled a conversation with a friend who was a Spanish major, "I said, come to Germany and I'll teach you German and we'll go travel Germany and I'll go to Spain with you and you teach me more about Spanish." In this interaction, Lilly positioned herself as being an expert speaker of German, capable of teaching someone else German, while also describing her Spanish proficiency as needing improvement. This excerpt highlights Lilly's views toward two of her languages, as well as the relationship she has conceptualized between them. She could use her German skills and proficiency as currency to help her gain further Spanish skills.

4.3 Changes and Relationships Between Identities

A complex, changing relationship Lilly had with her HLL identity emerged from the data. This became evident, for example, when she mentioned her experiences of learning English "like a second language" and of learning Spanish as a foreign language with other non-native speaker peers. She often mentioned how poor she perceived her Spanish proficiency to be, especially compared with her German proficiency. During the interview, I asked Lilly about her oral proficiency interview (OPI) scores, which are required for language teaching certification in the state where Lilly lived. She had only taken the OPI for German and said she was not planning to take the one for Spanish yet, as she was not comfortable enough with her language abilities to be ready to teach Spanish.

Lilly frequently described the complex and challenging relationship between her German and English speaker identities. This contentious relationship began early for Lilly as she navigated the German-medium and English-medium educational landscapes in Germany. In Task 3, Lilly expressed the lack of motivation she had while learning to read in English at the American school. This was particularly salient for her, as she had already learned to read and write in German at her German-medium elementary school. She shared an anecdote with her partner about her first day in American school on base. According to Lilly, she could barely read or write English and spoke with a terrible German accent.

> Da war ich und das war ich glaub in der vierten Klasse. Und sie wollten, dass ich Ice Cream buchstabiere. Und dann habe ich... dann habe ich gedacht, “Ok, wie hört sich das in meinem Kopf an?” Weil ich muss das schreiben, das E-I-S und dann und dann C-R-E-M-E. Und dann haben sie die Lehrerinnen haben sich so angeschaut... da habe ich überhaupt nicht kapiert, dass auf Englisch so viele unbetonte Buchstaben gibt. Sie sind total nutzlos. Dann habe ich gedacht, dass Englisch die dümmste Sprache auf der ganzen Welt war. [*There I was and that was I think fourth grade and they wanted me to spell “ice cream.” And then I... then I thought, “Ok, how does that sound in my head?” Because I needed to write it, the I-C-E and then and then C-R-E-A-M. And then they, the teachers, just looked at me, because I didn’t understand that English has unstressed letters. They’re totally useless. Then I thought that English was the dumbest language on the entire planet.*]

In this example, Lilly shared what she found to be a particularly significant moment in her English language learning experience. She continued to portray her shock at the correct spelling, shock that stemmed from her experience having learned to write in German first.

Lilly’s negative feelings toward the English language stemmed from her inability to use her previous German linguistic knowledge to spell English words correctly. This is notable, as Lilly chose to recount her background learning her current dominant language instead of recalling her experiences in German or Spanish courses. In doing so, Lilly distanced herself from her identity as an English native speaker to contrast her experiences learning German and

English. Lilly made this decision to legitimize herself as a competent German speaker by delegitimizing her positionality as a native English speaker.

While sharing her language learning biography in Task 1 (Appendix A), including the reason for learning each of her languages, Lilly categorized Spanish as being the only language she had truly learned by choice. German and English were the languages she had acquired throughout her childhood.

> Well, for German I didn't really have a choice, right. Neither for English. But for Spanish, I don't think it was one specific moment but I oh I also love music... when I listen to Spanish music every... every time... like it motivates me to do it more.

She stated that she found music to be a major motivating factor in her choice to learn Spanish. In other interactions, Lilly highlighted her enjoyment of Spanish-language television shows as well. This stood in contrast to statements she made in Task 4 about her general distaste for German music and film. She discussed her tendency to listen to more English and Spanish music than music in German. According to Lilly, the trouble she had with German-language media, in general, was due to her lack of ability to understand the media. She shared the problems she faced in watching German-language news.

> ...the *Tagesschau* whatever *100 Sekunden* thing, it's so fast. I have a lot of trouble. I usually watch… because I just want to see what's going on in general, but even then, they talk really, really fast and I don't understand a lot of the words that they're using, so I get like the general picture, but I don't understand all of the details.

Despite her reported difficulties with the vocabulary, she shared that she still watched the *Tagesschau in 100 Sekunden* to stay informed about current events. In contrast, she credited her inability to understand German films to the films themselves being confusing.

> Ich finde es leichter Filme auf Englisch zu verstehen, weil die Filme besser sind. Ich weiß nicht. Deutsche Filme machen nicht immer Sinn. Sie sind überall für mich, glaube ich. Es gibt schon gute Deutsche Filme, aber ich schaue lieber Englische Filme. [*I find it easier to understand movies in English because the movies are better. I don't know. German movies don't always make sense. They're all over the place to me, I think. There are good German films, but I prefer to watch movies in English.*]

She hedged her statement that German movies are all over the place and softened her statements by saying there are German films she enjoys. The only times she expressed enjoying German television or movies was concerning the quality time she spent with her father, a native German speaker. In contrast, Lilly spoke excitedly about her love for Spanish-language music and television shows. This is particularly interesting when one considers the way she had characterized her experiences with both languages. While she was generally more critical of her Spanish-language abilities, she ultimately enjoyed using the language for pleasure more than German.

Lilly's complex relationship between the identities associated with the three languages she spoke extended into her classroom experiences as well. Lilly described being able to use her explicit knowledge of Spanish to bolster her explicit knowledge of German, despite her assessment that her Spanish proficiency was lower than her German proficiency.

> It's actually helpful to know Spanish because I would say there's more commonalities between German and Spanish than there are between Spanish and English. You know, like *kennen* and *wissen* are the same thing as in Spanish. It's to know someone... and to know something, but it's two different words, *saber* and *conocer*. So, it's just like little things like that, they have a lot in common with German.

In this interaction, Lilly created a relationship between Spanish and German, showing how her lower proficiency in Spanish is still enough to help her better understand German vocabulary. This is especially interesting because Lilly focused on the way her understanding of Spanish lexical items supports her understanding of German vocabulary, despite having spoken German much longer.

In the course blog, Lilly shared that she would ask her non-HLL classmates to explain German grammar to her because she had not had the experience of learning German grammar explicitly. She wrote, "Weil ich bilingual aufgewachsen bin, ist Deutsche Grammatik schwer für mich zu verstehen weil ich sie nie lehrnen mußte" [*Because I was raised bilingually, German grammar is hard for me to understand because I never had to learn it.*] In this instance, Lilly labeled her German HLL experiences as being less advantageous than her non-HLL peers' language learning experiences because she perceived her explicit understanding of German grammar to be less than that of her peers; she attached a great deal of importance to grammatical knowledge.

The relationship she saw between the two languages she was learning in classroom settings also included her experiences of translanguaging using Spanish and German. In one such example during Task 7, the final telecollaboration interaction, Lilly described translanguaging when she was unable to produce sentences in Spanish.

> I like all my other Spanish classes, but I hate this one because my professor talks really fast and I don't understand anything and it's really frustrating. And like, it's funny because every time he says something and I don't know what to say, I'll like start to speak and I'll like start to say German words because I don't know what to say in Spanish and then I'll start speaking in German.

Lilly drew a connection between her perceived lack of Spanish-language proficiency and her German-language ability. The way she described the phenomenon conceptualized the languages as two distinctly separate systems rather than viewing them as a plurilingual repertoire on which she drew to communicate (see Trentman, 2021). This is reflective of the negative attitudes toward translanguaging common in many language classrooms.

Lilly began the interview by explaining that she was studying German with minors in TESOL and Spanish with the goal of getting her Secondary Education Certification, the same subjects she had been studying during the telecollaboration. She shared that she was studying German because she grew up there and already spoke the language.

> I study Spanish because I already knew German and I wanted somewhat of a challenge and then I decided to add on ESL... because I used to be an ESL as well so I felt like something that I kind of connected with and I could be good at.

In this excerpt, Lilly expressed feeling a connection to English as a Second Language (ESL) learners because, according to her, she had been in their situation before. It is worth noting that technically Lilly would have been in an English as a Foreign Language (EFL) context before she began learning English with the other Americans at the school on the base.

5 Telecollaboration and HLL Identities

Lilly used her language-related identities and experiences to inform one another. For example, she used her knowledge of Spanish to inform her understanding of German. She used knowledge of Spanish grammatical forms to scaffold her understanding of German grammar because, according to her, she only learned German grammar implicitly, not explicitly. In terms of her identities, Lilly situated herself at the intersection of expert German speaker, proficient heritage-language learner, and lacking non-native speaker.

As Klimanova and Dembovskaya (2013) have found in their research, the identities of HLLs can be fraught to begin with and further complicated by the experience of telecollaboration while telecollaboration also allows them a space to negotiate their multiple identities. Lilly entered the telecollaboration fairly confident in her German-language abilities and she expressed a firm identity of being a proficient German speaker. Similar to observations made by Klimanova and Dembovskaya (2013), Lilly was quick to establish her status as an HLL in the first interaction with Claudia. Lilly's communications with Claudia revealed the uncertainty surrounding her multiple language speaker identities. Lilly tended to lean on her connections to her other languages when experiencing or describing challenges she faced in the other languages.

The results of this study show that telecollaboration can be a fruitful if not challenging and complex practice for HLLs to negotiate their plurilingual identities. Lilly often described a sense of being between languages and cultures. Her experiences as a German American living in Germany and the US left her with the sense that she did not belong to either culture, as she was positioned as German by her American peers and as American by her German peers. One way that Lilly took control of her identity was by immediately positioning herself as a native or heritage speaker of German at the beginning of her interactions with Claudia. Despite her high proficiency in German and English and years of Spanish studies, she described her language proficiencies from a deficit perspective. Much of her deficit-based mindset was related to her negative views toward translanguaging; she viewed her need to switch between her linguistic repertoires as a sign of her lack of proficiency.

5.1 Limitations

The present case study has several limitations that should be noted. This study is not generalizable in the traditional (quantitative) sense to the experiences of any larger population due to its sample size of one. Tracy (2010) explains that the aim of qualitative research, including case studies, tends not to focus on generating significance in a statistical sense and therefore excludes generalizability as a possibility. Rather, qualitative researchers aim for transferability and naturalistic generalization (Tracy, 2010). Tracy defines transferability as a study's power to be relatable to readers' circumstances and experiences. Naturalistic generalizability refers to the extent to which readers can learn vicariously from the lessons shared in a given report and apply those lessons to their teaching context (Tracy, 2010).

Additionally, I was not an instructor in the classroom at the time of the study, therefore I was unable to take fieldnotes or build rapport with participants, an important part of many qualitative researchers' methods (see Saldaña, 2011). However, my absence from the classroom does mitigate any concern of teacher bias. A lack of video recordings could also be considered a limitation, as this removes many important context clues from the dataset, including gestures and facial expressions.

5.2 Lessons Learned for Identity, Multilingualism, and CALL

By gaining deeper insights into the ways that multilingual students, in particular HLLs, may negotiate and form often-conflicting identities in the telecollaborative environment, CALL researchers can begin to understand the impacts this has on such learners' intercultural education. While the current study did not examine how instructors can get past the challenges of designing telecollaborative exchanges to meet the needs of typical language learners and HLLs, several strategies are worth exploring based on the evidence presented here. The strategies offered in this report are to increase instructor presence in telecollaboration, restructure tasks to be welcoming to multilingual identities and communication, and adopt plurilingual pedagogical practices.

Researchers have suggested that instructors' engagement throughout the process may play a key role in the success of telecollaborative exchanges (Schenker, 2012;a Schaefer, 2020). In addition to being the most concrete of the suggestions offered here, this strategy has support in research going back a decade. Schenker (2012a) highlighted the importance of instructor presence in telecollaboration to reduce confusion and mitigate potential conflicts. Instructors can consider reviewing the interactions regularly and incorporating reflections and discussions within the classroom context. Creating space for students to discuss successes and challenges, as well as the ways they are expressing or performing certain identities, can help learners to process their experiences.

These types of reflections are supported by Ushioda's (2011) assertion that it is key for language educators to consider and engage the identities of the student as a whole rather than focusing solely on their identity as language learners. By increasing our understanding of the identities that students may bring into the language classroom, CALL practitioners and researchers may be able to develop effective strategies to reduce the impact of any complicating factors that may impede intercultural and multilingual education. Naturally, it cannot be expected that instructors know what multiple identities and configurations thereof will be represented in any given cohort of students, therefore activities that let learners express and process their identity shifts are key to creating an affirming plurilingual learning environment, such as that encouraged by the Council of Europe (2018).

Moving out from a specific practice to a larger-scale paradigm shift, Trentman (2021) suggested more generally that language instructors adopt "pedagogies informed by plurilingual language ideologies in language classrooms" (p. 108). One such practice may be to encourage students to use their entire linguistic repertoire to communicate with their partners during telecollaboration. In the results of the study, Trentman (2021) highlighted that

> learners were able to leverage their existing linguistic resources to gain access to new ones, although they did not necessarily view it this way. In the telecollaboration environment, the most common example was the students' reliance on their partners' knowledge of English to learn new vocabulary. (p. 120)

Rather than viewing their use of English as a means to access lexical knowledge, participants viewed switching to English as a failure and proof of their lack of proficiency. Lilly demonstrated this same viewpoint in her exchanges with Claudia when she mentioned switching to German while speaking Spanish or English. Instead of valuing the ways her plurilingual repertoire gave her access to communicative opportunities, she marked these instances as negative.

As part of creating a plurilingual environment, language instructors could expand the previously mentioned opportunities for students to engage with their own telecollaboration data and to analyze their interactions. Students could learn about translanguaging and examine particular interactions where translanguaging has occurred. Instructors should be careful to avoid framing translanguaging as negative and rather highlight its efficacy as a learning support and reality of multilingual environments. This negative characterization could potentially lead learners to have a negative view of the linguistic repertoires, as evidenced by Lilly's deficit-based mindset toward the three languages she spoke. As Trentman (2021) pointed out, translingual pedagogies require a focal shift "from *which* language is being used to *how* students and teachers are using language to expand our linguistic repertoires" (p. 127, emphasis in original). Celic and Seltzer (2013) offer a variety of recommendations for implementing translanguaging pedagogies in the language classroom, such as student collaboration with multilingual partners. The telecollaborative project described in this chapter did not explicitly require students to stay in one language or another, but students were required to use 50% English and 50% German. This may have discounted students' other linguistic resources and the roles those repertoires may play in increasing the quality of interaction for students.

In thematizing translanguaging explicitly with our students, language instructors can highlight a variety of important points. For example, using English lexical items while speaking is not inherently a failure or invitation to drop the target language completely in interactions. It is simply a tool to increase the fluency of the conversation and to ensure both sides are on the same page. In fact, this practice has been shown to allow students to continue using the target language and to potentially expand their resources through follow-up and clarification with their partners (Trentman, 2021). Social justice can be tied into education on translanguaging as well. Trentman (2021) emphasized that conversations with students around translanguaging in the classroom can be coupled with discussions of colonialism, the basis for the concept of multilingualism. Additionally, English loan words are part of many languages, such as German, and the effects of language contact can be meaningfully integrated into the language classroom. Much like the promotion of ICC in the language classroom, promoting plurilingual competence can offer a variety of benefits to students (Celic & Seltzer, 2013).

While these practices may be useful for a specific subset of learners, being HLLs in this case, they have the potential to help other learners as well. By valuing the entire linguistic repertoires our students possess, we value their identities as speakers of these languages and as members of other cultural groups. This could serve to create more welcoming spaces for international students learning their third or fourth language in our classroom by creating a space in which they can use their first language to support their language development.

5.3 Future Directions

The present study highlights the importance of developing and testing strategies for creating telecollaboration environments designed for a broader range of student experiences, such as those of students with prior real-world experience with the language. The question remains as to the best methods for language instructors to consider multiple student identities when they are designing intercultural and international experiences like telecollaboration. Further study is needed to evaluate practices related to strategies for effectively creating plurilingual telecollaborative environments that meet the needs of a broader student population, including the recommendations made in this chapter. Future research on how multilingual students leverage their translanguaging abilities while negotiating identities could support the development of more inclusive telecollaborative environments and practices.

References

ACTFL. (n.d.). Facilitating target language use. https://www.actfl.org/resources/guiding-principles-language-learning/target-language

Akiyama, Y., & Saito, K. (2016). Development of comprehensibility and its linguistic correlates: A longitudinal study of video-mediated telecollaboration. The Modern Language Journal, 100(3), 585–609. https://doi.org/10.1111/modl.12338

Belz, J. (2002). Social dimensions of telecollaborative foreign language study. Language Learning & Technology, 6(1), 60–81. http://dx.doi.org/10125/25143

Bohinski, C. A., & Leventhal, Y. (2015). Rethinking the ICC framework: Transformation and telecollaboration. Foreign Language Annals, 48(3), 521–534. https://doi.org/10.1111/flan.12149

Canto, S., Jauregi, K., & van den Bergh, H. (2013). Integrating cross-cultural interaction through video-communication and virtual worlds in foreign language teaching programs: Is there an added value? ReCALL, 25(1), 105–121. https://doi.org/10.1017/S0958344012000274

Celic, C., & Seltzer, K. (2013). Translanguaging: A CUNY-NYSIEB guide for educators. CUNY-NYSIEB. Retrieved from http://www.cuny-nysieb.org/wp-content/uploads/2016/04/Translanguaging-Guide-March-2013.pdf

Chen, H. (2013). Identity practices of multilingual writers in social networking spaces. Language Learning & Technology, 17(2), 143–170. http://dx.doi.org/10125/44328

Chun, D. (2011). Developing intercultural communicative competence through online exchanges. CALICO Journal, 28(2), 392–419. http://www.jstor.org/stable/calicojournal.28.2.392

Council of Europe. (2018). Common European Framework of Reference for Languages: Learning, Teaching, Assessment. Companion Volume with New Descriptors. https://rm.coe.int/cefr-companion-volume-with-new-descriptors-2018/1680787989

Darvin, R., & Norton, B. (2015). Identity and a model of investment in applied linguistics. Annual Review of Applied Linguistics, 35, 36–56. https://doi.org/10.1017/S0267190514000191

Dooly, M. (2011). Divergent perceptions of telecollaborative language learning tasks: Task-as-workplan vs. task-as-process. Language Learning & Technology, 15(2), 69–91. http://dx.doi.org/10125/44252

Dooly, M., & O'Dowd, R. (2018). Telecollaboration in the foreign language classroom: A review of its origins and its application to language teaching practice. In M. Dooly & R. O'Dowd (Eds.), In this together: Teachers' experiences with transnational, telecollaborative language learning projects (pp. 11–34). Peter Lang. https://doi.org/10.3726/b14311

Goertler, S., & Schenker, T. (2021). From study abroad to education abroad: Language proficiency, intercultural competence, and diversity. Routledge.

Goertler, S., Schenker, T., Lesoski, C., & Brunsmeier, S. (2018). Assessing language and intercultural learning during telecollaboration. Assessment Across Online Language Education, 21–48.

He, A. W. (2006). Toward an identity theory of the development of Chinese as a heritage language. Heritage Language Journal, 4(1), 1–28. https://doi.org/10.46538/hlj.4.1.1

He, A. W. (2010). The heart of heritage: Sociocultural dimensions of heritage language learning. Annual Review of Applied Linguistics, 30, 66–82. https://doi.org/10.1017/S0267190510000073

Helm, F. (2015). The practices and challenges of telecollaboration in higher education in Europe. Language Learning & Technology, 19(2), 197–217. http://dx.doi.org/10125/44424

Jeanneau, C., & Giralt, M. (2016). Preparing higher education language students for their period abroad through telecollaboration: The I-TELL Project. All Ireland Journal of Higher Education, 8(2). http://hdl.handle.net/10344/6280

Kabata, K., & Edasawa, Y. (2011). An ethnographic study of a key-pal project: Learning a foreign language through bilingual communication. Computer Assisted Language Learning, 20(3), 189–207. https://doi.org/10.1080/09588220701489473

Klimanova, L., & Dembovskaya, S. (2013). L2 identity, discourse, and social networking in Russian. Language Learning & Technology, 17(1), 69–88. http://dx.doi.org/10125/24510

Lee, L. (2017). Employing telecollaborative exchange to extend intercultural learning after study abroad. In J. Jackson & S. Oguro (Eds.), Intercultural interventions in study abroad (pp. 137–154). Routledge.

Lee, J., & Song, J. (2019). Developing intercultural competence through study abroad, telecollaboration, and on-campus language study. Language Learning & Technology, 23(3), 178–198. http://hdl.handle.net/10125/44702

Leeman, J. (2015). Heritage language education and identity in the United States. Annual Review of Applied Linguistics, 35, 100–119. https://doi.org/10.1017/s0267190514000245

Leeman, J., Rabin, L., & Román-Mendoza, E. (2011). Identity and activism in heritage language education. The Modern Language Journal, 95(4), 481–495. https://doi.org/10.1111/j.1540-4781.2011.01237.x
Lesoski, C. M. (2019). Identity and capital during telecollaboration in the German language classroom (doctoral dissertation). Retrieved from https://doi.org/10.25335/ncz1-0e23
Norton, B. (2013). Identity and language learning: Extending the conversation (2nd ed.). Multilingual Matters. https://doi.org/10.21832/9781783090563
Norton, B., & McKinney, C. (2011). An identity approach to second language acquisition. In D. Atkinson (Ed.), Alternative approaches to second language acquisition (pp. 85–106). Routledge. https://doi.org/10.4324/9780203830932
O'Dowd, R. (2013). Telecollaboration and CALL. In M. Thomas, H. Reindeers, & M. Warschauer (Eds.), Contemporary computer-assisted language learning (pp. 123–141). Bloomsbury Academic.
O'Dowd, R. (2018). From telecollaboration to virtual exchange: State-of-the-art and the role of UNICollaboration in moving forward. Journal of Virtual Exchange, 1, 1–23. https://doi.org/10.14705/rpnet.2018.jve.1
O'Dowd, R., & Dooly, M. (2020). Intercultural communicative competence development through telecollaboration and virtual exchange. The Routledge handbook of language and intercultural communication (2nd ed., pp. 361–375). Routledge.
Ortega, L. (2017). New CALL-SLA research interfaces for the 21st century: Towards equitable multilingualism. CALICO Journal, 34(3), 285–316. https://doi.org/10.1558/cj.33855
Saldaña, J. (2011). Fundamentals of qualitative research. Oxford University Press.
Schaefer, R. (2020). Facilitating the co-construction of interculturality in teletandem through pedagogical mediation. DELTA: Documentação de Estudos em Lingüística Teórica e Aplicada, 36. https://doi.org/10.1590/1678-460X2020360410
Schenker, T. (2012a). Intercultural competence and cultural learning through telecollaboration. CALICO Journal, 29(3), 449–470. https://www.jstor.org/stable/10.2307/calicojournal.29.3.449
Schenker, T. (2012b). The effects of a virtual exchange on language skills and intercultural competence (doctoral dissertation). Retrieved from https://d.lib.msu.edu/islandora/object/etd:442/datastream/OBJ/download/
Schenker, T. (2015). Telecollaboration for novice language learners – negotiation of meaning in text chats between non-native and native speakers. In E. Dixon & M. Thomas (Eds.), Researching language learner interactions online: From social media to MOOCs, CALICO Monograph Series, 13, 237–257.
Telles, J. A. (2015). Teletandem and performativity. Revista Brasileira de Linguística Aplicada, 15(1), 1–30. https://doi.org/10.1590/1984-639820155536
Teske, K., & Vollmer Rivera, A. V. (2018). A critical exploration of heritage language learners' identities within Hellotalk. Revista do GEL, 15(3), 279–301. https://doi.org/10.21165/gel.v15i3.2399

Thorne, S., Sauro, S., & Smith, B. (2015). Technologies, identities and expressive activity. Annual Review of Applied Linguistics, 35, 215–233. https://doi.org/10.1017/S0267190514000257

Tracy, S. J. (2010). Qualitative quality: Eight "Big-Tent" criteria for excellent qualitative research. Qualitative Inquiry, 16(10), 837–851. https://doi.org/10.1177/1077800410383121

Trentman, E. (2021). Reframing monolingual ideologies in the language classroom: Evidence from Arabic study abroad and telecollaboration. In Dupuy, B. and Mitchelson, K. (Eds.), Pathways to paradigm change: Critical examinations of prevailing discourses and ideologies in second language education. Cengage Learning.

Ushioda, E. (2011). Language learning motivation, self and identity: Current theoretical perspectives. Computer Assisted Language Learning, 24(3), 199–210. https://doi.org/10.1080/09588221.2010.538701

Valdés, G., & Kibler, A. (2012). Heritage language teaching. In C. A. Chapelle (Ed.), The encyclopedia of applied linguistics, 1–4. Blackwell Publishing Ltd. https://doi.org/10.1002/9781405198431.wbeal0498

Vogel, S., & García, O. (2017). Translanguaging. In G. Noblit & L. Moll (Eds.), Oxford research encyclopedia of education. Oxford University Press. https://doi.org/10.1093/acrefore/9780190264093.013.181

Vollmer Rivera, A. V., & Teske, K. (2018). The critical intersection of heritage language learning and eTandem learning environments. IALLT Journal of Language Learning Technologies, 48, 97–112. https://doi.org/10.17161/iallt.v48i0.8580

Yang, S. J., & Yi, Y. (2017). Negotiating multiple identities through eTandem learning experiences. CALICO Journal, 34(1), 97–114. https://doi.org/10.1558/cj.29586

About the Author

Carly M. Lesoski is a Learning Innovations Program Manager at Dartmouth College and is the e-Learning Explaing columnist for the National Teaching and Learning Forum. She has published on language learner identity and telecollaboration, and her continuing research interests include student and instructor identities and experiences with accessibility practices.

Appendix A: Task 1

1. Who am I?
2. Introduce yourselves (e.g., What is your name? What are you studying? What are your hobbies? What languages do you speak at home or with your family?). Share your language learning biographies (e.g., Which language(s) are you learning?).
3. When did you feel most motivated to learn a world language and why? What language learning experiences have you had (e.g., at home/in community programs/in school/in university)?
4. Talk about stay(s) abroad (e.g., Have you been abroad? Where? What was the purpose of your stay abroad? What was your most influential experience (positive and negative)?).
5. Explain if and how you use the language you're learning in this course in your everyday life. (Who do you communicate with and how (in person, on the phone, video chat, etc.)? Do you watch or listen to any media in the language you're learning? How often do you engage in these activities?)

Appendix B: Coding Rubric

Code	Definition
Describing identity	Person describes their relationship to the world
Accepting position	Person agrees with position ascribed to them by partner
Rejecting position	Person disagrees with position ascribed to them by partner
Imagining communities/future	Person describes their perceived possibilities for the future
Possessing economic capital	Describing money or financial affordances one has
Needing economic capital	Describing money or financial affordances one needs
Possessing cultural capital	Describing resources one possesses that help them to understand their cultures and other cultures
Needing cultural capital	Describing resources one needs to help them to understand their cultures and other cultures
Possessing linguistic capital	Describing verbal and written language skills one has
Needing linguistic capital	Describing verbal and written language skills one needs
Possessing social capital	Describing networks that give the person power or access
Needing social capital	Describing networks that one needs to gain power or access

4 #multilingualself: Hashtagging as a Resource for Performing a Multilingual Identity

Ilona Vandergriff

1 Introduction

Research on SLA and identity has long recognized that L2 learners are socially motivated agents (Drummond & Schleef, 2016), who use their linguistic resources for their own social positioning. L2 identity does not develop in isolation but is shaped instead by the social context, including the structures, resources, and practices in which the learner uses the L2 (Norton, 2013). This important insight allows for theorizing L2 identity in extramural L2 practices. As "sites of self presentation and identity negotiation" (Papacharissi, 2011, p. 304), social networking services (SNSs), in particular, promise to offer insights into the multilingual self. This chapter explores L2 identity on a social media platform as it looks at hashtags as a semiotic resource in performing a multilingual virtual self (Kramsch, 2009).

Among the many different ways in which social actors index their identity, discursive construction of identity through stance-taking is predominant (Bucholtz & Hall, 2005; Du Bois, 2007). Over time, as stances accumulate, a social identity emerges. Though stance-taking is pervasive across all contexts, "stance-rich" environments (Barton & Lee, 2013, p. 31) like SNSs facilitate stance-taking through digital affordances. Moreover, the research record on social media shows that social networks play a key role in the presentation of the self (e.g., Fullwood & Attrill-Smith, 2018; Lee-Won et al., 2014; Rui & Stefanone, 2013a,b). Social media users typically engage in positive self-presentation with the intent to create positive impressions and to gain social approval, e.g., by posting about accomplishments. At the same time, users engage in protective self-presentation to avoid negative impressions (Arkin, 1981; Casale et al., 2015; Lee-Won et al., 2014, p. 414;

Rui & Stefanone, 2013b, p. 111). Self-presentation in social media is thus a highly strategic activity for the virtual self (Lee-Won et al., 2014; Rui & Stefanone, 2013a,b).

Among the major SNSs, Instagram, a popular photo-sharing app that allows users to take photos and post them online, is particularly interesting in its affordances and constraints for self-presentation. First, Instagram provides key affordances for the strategic promotion and marketing of the self, such as filters that allow users to modify photos. Second, digital practice research suggests that users do take up these affordances: by and large, Instagram users focus more on forms of individual self-promotion such as selfie posting than on community-oriented behavior (Hu et al., 2014; Sheldon & Bryant, 2016; see also Dumas et al., 2017). At the same time there is some evidence that community norms, though they differ across communities (e.g., Meese et al., 2015; Rui & Stefanone, 2013a,b), discourage excessive self-promotion. In short, both digital features and norms embedded within online communities affect self-presentation in different ways.

In this chapter, I explore how one multilingual user takes up affordances of social tagging. Hashtags, originally designed to link related content in the fast-moving, "noisy" Twitter environment, are a linguistic feature of text-based digital communication and a particularly interesting tool for self-presentation. First, they allow for self-promotion by enabling posts to be seen by large audiences who are not followers of the Instagram accounts in question (Dumas et al., 2017). Second, hashtags have also been found to index identity through stance-marking (Matley, 2018; Zappavigna, 2015), but the strategic use of hashtags for the discursive construction of identity remains underexplored, especially in multilingual contexts.

This chapter reports on an empirical analysis of social tagging in Instagram in a naturalistic setting. The data will show how the competent, clever, and playful use of trilingual hashtagging serves a key role in a carefully calibrated self-presentation. It is hoped that the results might inspire future empirical analyses of extramural L2 digital practices and thus contribute to the larger effort of developing a better understanding of naturally occurring L2 digital discourse.

2 Research Overview

2.1 Stance

My analysis of multilingual virtual self-presentation draws on discourse-analytic frameworks, in particular Stance Theory and Appraisal Theory, to explore the functions of multilingual social tagging in a multimodal context. It is difficult to overstate the importance of stance in performing identity. In online and offline interaction, stance-taking is the predominant way of indexing a social identity (Bucholtz & Hall, 2005). The subject (Subject$_1$) evaluates something (Object) and thereby positions themselves, aligning or disaligning with Subject$_2$ (Du Bois, 2007). Evaluating something is thus an important resource not only for presenting the self but also for construing solidarity (Bednarek & Martin, 2010). When taking stances, people index identity not only through *what* they say but also through *how* they say it. In other words, users of language perform their identity within uses of language as they rely on different languages and/or different registers, styles, and genres of the same language. These uses of language in turn depend on (situational and textual) context.

As stances accumulate over time, a social identity emerges. Online personal accounts on Instagram present such an accumulation of stances, allowing a virtual identity to sediment in the feed (see Bucholtz, 2007). In terms of its affordances and constraints for self-presentation, Instagram has attracted much attention in psychological research (e.g., Halpern et al., 2017; Hendrickse et al., 2017; Moon et al., 2016; Slater et al., 2017). With some notable exceptions (Lee & Chau, 2018; Matley, 2018), Instagram remains underexplored in linguistic studies.

2.2 Multilingual and Heteroglossic Resources

Social media users draw on a wide range of multimodal resources to present and negotiate a virtual self. Several studies (Androutsopoulos, 2014; Leppänen et al., 2009; Pérez & Cassany, 2018, among others) have shown that multilingual practices play a key role in the presentation and negotiation of local, global, and translocal identities. In his analysis of the strategic language choices of young multilinguals on Facebook, Androutsopoulos (2014) finds that users make strategic language choices to maximize or partition audiences. Leppänen et al. (2009) analyze the use of linguistic resources among multilingual Finns in virtual forums and video games. Their research underscores that a narrow focus on language choice obscures a larger and more complex picture. Users draw on their entire linguistic and textual repertoire, which includes the resources different languages provide but also a range of genres and registers in each (Leppänen et al., 2009). This particular form of language use is known as "heteroglossia," a type of codeswitching. It differs from other types of codeswitching in that it is a deliberate style choice language users make (Bakhtin, 1981). Heteroglossia or double-voicing (Bakhtin, 1981) is performance through language use, "fabricated by social actors who have woven voices of society into their discourse" (Androutsopoulos, 2011, p. 282).

Exploiting heteroglossia not only within one language but within their entire linguistic repertoire, multilinguals use different registers and styles as well as different languages to voice competing attitudes. The juxtaposition of various codes *is* the juxtaposition of various stances, in that each code comes with its own resonances. Leppänen et al. (2009) underscore that different voices are not unified, contradictions not synthesized. Instead heteroglossia is the "coexistence, combination, alternation, and juxtaposition of ways of using the communicative and expressive resources language/s offer us" (Leppänen et al., 2009, p. 1082). Combining and recombining linguistic material from various languages and codes is often a form of ludic play that is very common in all genres, especially in digital discourse (Androutsopoulos, 2011; for ludic play in social media see Deumert, 2014; for ludic play in language learning see Cook, 2000; LaScotte & Tarone, 2019).

2.3 Social Tagging

Hashtags are user-generated metadata tags preceded by a hash (#) that serve to cross-reference content in social media, such as Twitter, Instagram, or Facebook. Originally used as metadata for the sole purpose of categorizing web content to enable searchability, hashtags have taken on additional functions, including commenting on or evaluating people, ideas, concepts (#kamala,[1] #blacklivesmatter), promoting events (#olympics) and brands (#mcdonalds). Existing research on social tagging draws heavily on Twitter data (e.g., Giaxoglou, 2018; Gleason, 2018; Scott, 2015; Zappavigna & Martin, 2018). By contrast, relatively fewer studies have focused on the practice and functions of tagging on other platforms, e.g., on Flickr (Barton, 2018), Instagram (Lee & Chau, 2018; Matley, 2018) and Tumblr (Bourlai, 2018). As the internet is increasingly multilingual, the tags associated with a given post are often in more than one language (e.g., Giaxoglou, 2018; Lee & Chau, 2018). This is hardly surprising because hashtags are an important tool for users to improve findability. From this perspective, tags are additive in bringing multiple audiences to the post. At the same time, side-by-side texts in different languages are often not exact translations of each other (e.g.,

[1] Hashtags are not case-sensitive – #KAMALA, #Kamala and #kamala, e.g., are used interchangeably.

Barton & Lee, 2013), suggesting that multilingual tagging does more than allow for multilingual access.

Straddling everyday communication and computer code, hashtags are located at the intersection of text and metatext. Beyond serving as metadata that allow users to link related content, hashtags have been associated with stance-taking. Whereas the two functions are distinct, they often merge into a single form. A single hashtag, e.g., #badmother, is both topic-marking and stance-marking (Zappavigna, 2014). Like other stance markers, stance-marking hashtags allow people to position themselves. In his study of impoliteness in Instagram, Matley (2018, p. 72) shows that hashtags play a key role in self-presentation:

> The hashtag allows for a balancing act of strategies regarding inappropriate content in terms of both audience management and self-presentation. It allows posters to perform different forms of face work to multiple audiences, mitigating or aggravating face threat depending on the importance of the audience for the poster. The hashtag equally allows for both protective self-presentation [...] as well as acquisitive self-presentation.

In discussing the strategic role of stance-marking hashtags, Matley (2018) underscores the interpersonal function of self-presentation. Along the same lines, Zappavigna (2014) investigates how hashtags promote "ambient affiliation" in an online community. She finds that slightly self-deprecating hashtags, e.g., mildly self-critical tags that accompany the description of a minor mishap or mistake, promote audience alignment because they propose a shared bond to the audience:

> While this post does function at one level to inform the ambient audience about a minor event in the microblogger's domestic life, it also interpersonally aligns the ambient audience around a humorous shared experience of parental inadequacy. This interpersonal function is marked by the self-deprecating hashtag '#badmother'. The hashtag playfully classifies the microblogger as failing to live up to a parenting ideal by acting as a kind of conversational aside that connects this post with a putative collective of other inept parents. (Zappavigna, 2014, p. 212)

Based on her analysis, Zappavigna (2014) argues that audiences are more likely to align with stances they can relate to. Taking an evaluative stance people might affiliate with, users therefore construe attitudes about ideation (including people, things, or ideas). In SNSs, users often bond around significant issues such as political developments but also around quotidian issues (Knight, 2010), e.g., love of coffee or parenting (Zappavigna, 2015). As stances are negotiated and shared in networked interaction they accumulate, fusing ideational and interpersonal meanings into shared bonds. According to Knight (2010, p. 43), "we discursively negotiate our communal identities through bonds that we can share, and these bonds make up the value sets of our communities and culture, but they are not stable and fixed." Taking stances that others can align with is thus an integral part of building community.

3 Data and Methodology

3.1 Data Collection

This study draws on a small, specialized corpus collected by capturing the Instagram stream of a single user ("Maaria"[2]). Instagram is a social media platform for sharing images and video. The data collection relied on a combination of different sampling criteria, namely "theme," "individual," and "convenience" (see also Androutsopoulos, 2013; Herring, 2004). Maaria's Instagram stream was initially observed as part of a larger netnography on extramural L2 online interaction (Vandergriff, 2016). Guided by Herring's (2004) data sampling recommendations, I initially sampled Instagram by theme, specifically via the hashtag #learngerman. I then selected Maaria's Instagram stream – her account was public at the time of data collection – because the posts consistently drew on more than one language. At that time, I did not have any direct contact with Maaria. I observed her stream but did not engage with her Instagram account. I neither "followed" her account nor did I post any replies. In short, my role as researcher was more "lurker" than "participant."

Permission to use these data was obtained after initial data selection. I keep all names confidential. The screenshots of posts included in the analysis do not show human subjects. Given the lack of uniquely identifying data, I believe I have taken every possible step to minimize any potential harm to the participants in this study and that my data collection and reporting are in line with best practices as laid out in the 2020 Association of Internet Researchers' report (Franzke et al., 2020).

---

[2] To protect privacy, all screen names have been anonymized.

The resulting corpus allows for systematic observation of textual data with the goal of gaining insights into multilingual practices (see also Androutsopoulos, 2008). The present analysis of hashtag use is limited to a subset of data, spanning roughly three and a half years (February 8, 2014 to May 25, 2017). Maaria is a trilingual in her 20s, who lives in Finland. At the point of data collection, her account had 168 followers. With posts about food, travel, and music, the vast majority of Maaria's microblogging can be described as selective self-disclosures that make her quotidian activities and experiences, such as baking a cake or studying for an exam, visible for others (Oulasvirta et al., 2010). All but a handful of her posts draw on more than one language, namely Finnish, English, and German.[3]

3.2 Methodology

Grounded in discourse-analytic frameworks, I explore the patterns that emerge in multilingual hashtag use. Specifically, this study uses a metafunctional approach including Stance Theory (Du Bois, 2007), Bucholtz and Hall's (2005) analytic framework for the discursive construction of identity, and Appraisal Theory (Martin & White, 2005; see also Zappavigna, 2015). The first part provides an overview of the data with a focus on language choice. Distinguishing between content tagging and stance-marking functions of hashtags, I then focus the analysis on stance-marking tags in order to understand how Maaria performs her identities within uses of multiple languages and how she invites alignment with audiences.

My study thus addresses the following questions:

1. How do multilingual hashtags enact a multilingual identity?
2. How do multilingual hashtags create alignment with audiences?

Ultimately, this chapter aims to contribute to a better understanding of hashtags as a semiotic resource of the digital age.

---

[3] Finland has a relatively high rate of multilingualism. Finnish is spoken by more than 94% of the population as a first language (Van Parys, 2012) and nearly 45% of people in Finland speak English as a foreign language. Approximately 30% speak Swedish and about 13% speak German as a foreign language.

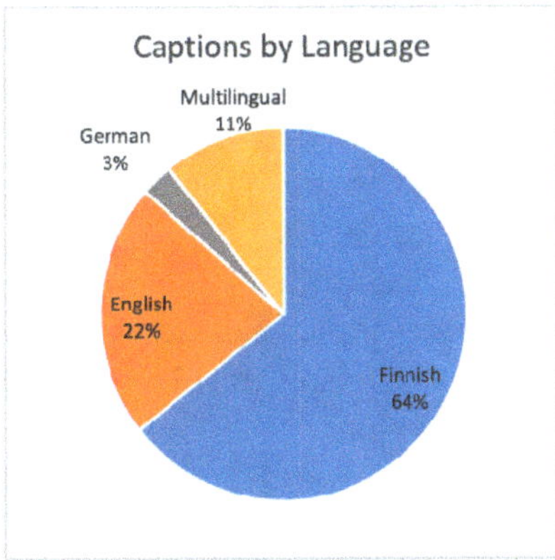

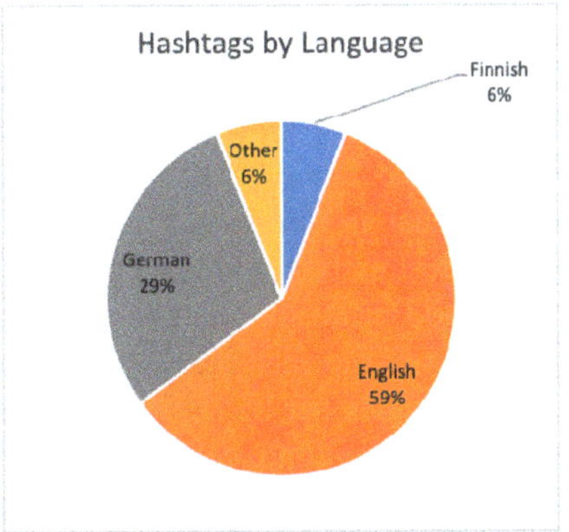

Figure 4.1. Captions and Hashtags by Language

4 Analysis

4.1 Classifying Hashtags by Language

With a total of 7759 hashtags in 329 Instagram posts, the data appear to be particularly rich in social tagging.[4] All 329 posts have multilingual captions and/or multilingual hashtags in Finnish, Maaria's L1, as well as in English and German, her additional languages.[5] Figure 4.1 shows that at 64%, the vast majority of captions are in Finnish, 22% are in English, and 3% are in German. Hashtags, by contrast, are predominantly in English (59%) and German (29%) whereas Finnish hashtags make up only 6% of the total number in the data.

In the present context of the quantitative analysis, suffice it to say that Maaria draws on her multilingual resources in distinctly different ways in tagging as opposed to captioning. In the next section, I take a closer look at the hashtags in their contexts.

4.2 Content Analysis

By and large, the posts are acts of selective self-disclosure of mundane activities or experiences. The data fall into thematic clusters, with 45% food-related

[4] The data show an average of 23.6 tags per post; Instagram limits the number of hashtags to 30.

[5] The analysis will leave aside the two Swedish and two Spanish hashtags found in the data.

content, 21% of the posts about music and/or faith, 12% related to travel, 8% to studies, 5% to watching sports, and 5% to family and friends. This classification is not unproblematic because the clusters frequently overlap. For example, food- and travel-related content overlaps in a post about eating döner kebab in Berlin. Across these thematic clusters, Maaria's posts show her interest in the German language and the German-speaking cultures. She travels to Berlin, she roots for the German soccer team, she listens to Austrian music, she eats German food, she studies German verbs. In this way, the posts index her L2 identity across content domains.

At the same time, certain thematic clusters show a stronger correlation with hashtag language. Food-related content, for example, shows 35% German tagging (compared with 29% across all content domains). When filtering all food-related content to baking-related posts, German hashtags even make up 40% of all hashtags. The quantitative analysis suggests that Maaria draws on particular elements of her multilingual repertoire for particular tagging purposes. To explore these functions of tagging further, I analyze two sample posts. The first, *Maaria the Baker*, exemplifies food-related content, the largest thematic cluster in the data (see Figure 4.2).

Figure 4.2. Post 1 *Maaria the Baker*

> ‘I baked something. Not sure what it is. But it’s gooooooood.
> #marianne #mochabit (baked good) #orsomethinglikethatperhaps
> #goodshit #tastyshit #unhealthyshit #lovethisshit #nam
> #mums #baking #foodlove #foodishappiness #bakingtime
> #bakingisfun #chocolate #coffee #cake #mintchocolate
> #chocolateisgoodforthesoul #icecream #chocolate #coffee #baking
> #bakingislove #cake #icecream
> #nomnomnom’

> I baked something. Not sure what it is. But it’s gooooooood.
> #marianne #mokkapala
> #taijotainsinnepäinehkä #goodshit
> #tastyshit #unhealthyshit #lovethisshit
> #nam #mums #baking #foodlove
> #foodishappiness #bakingtime #bakingisfun #chocolate
> #coffee #cake #mintchocolate
> #chocolateisgoodforthesoul #icecream
> #schokolade #kaffee #backen
> #backenistliebe #kuchen #eis
> #nomnomnom

Post 1 can be described as a multimodal post on baking. The caption accompanying the picture of a chocolate dessert with sprinkles is in English, followed by 27 hashtags in Finnish, English, and German.

The second post, illustrative of studies-related content, is about learning German (see Figure 4.3).

> Beginnen, beginnt, begann, hat begonnen. Bringen, bringt, brachte, hat gebracht. Ein/steigen, steigt ein, stieg ein, ist eingestiegen. En opi nättä ikinä!
> Saipahan ainakin päänsäyn, jos en muuta...
> #epätoivo #feelingstupid #too #difficult #studying #german #verbs
> #iwillneverrememberthese #reading #book #atwork #working
> #summerjob
> #work #arbeit #lernen #lesen #studieren #deutschbuch #deutsch
> #ichliebediesesprache #deutschesprache #deutschlernen
> #schweirig #scheiße #verben #turkulainenhumanisti #tasche

> ‘To begin, begins, began, has begun. To bring, brings, brought, has brought. To get on, gets on, got on, has got on. I will never learn these.
> If I don’t stop, I’ll get a headache…

Figure 4.3. Post 2 *Maaria the Student*

> #despair #feelingstupid #too #difficult #studying #german #verbs #iwillneverrememberthese #reading #book #atwork #working #summerjob #work #work #learn #read #study #germanbook #german
> #ilovethislanguage #germanlanguage #learngerman #difficult #shit #verbs #turkuliberalartsstudent #bag'

Maaria's caption in Post 2 lists three irregular German verb paradigms next to the photo of a German textbook, along with 20 hashtags in three languages: Finnish, English, and German.

These two posts exemplify the type of post found throughout the corpus. As a group, Maaria's 329 posts largely represent positive self-presentations by highlighting an accomplishment (or an effort), they are rich in stance-marking, and tend toward self-deprecating humor. They also show how digital affordances allow users to perform identity within an identity repertoire (Baxter, 2016).

As a first step in the analysis, I consider to what extent the multilingual tags are direct translations of each other. With some exceptions such as English #work and German #arbeit, the hashtags in the different languages are *not* simply translations of each other.

4.3 Stance-marking Tags: Appraisal

In Post 1 content tags include #chocolate and #schokolade (chocolate) as well as #cake and #kuchen (cake). The vast majority of the hashtags evidenced in the data set are *not* primarily category labels that classify content to enhance the posts' searchability. Other hashtags, e.g., #tastyshit and #backenistliebe (#baking is love) foreground the stance-taker's evaluation and prioritize a commentary function rather than a categorizing function, but the two functions of hashtags are not mutually exclusive and often overlap. #tastyshit, for example, has the categorizing function "food" alongside the stance-marking function "tasty." And #backenistliebe (baking is love) categorizes the post as baking-relating content but also conveys an emotive stance toward it. For the purpose of this analysis, neutral referential hashtags that show no evaluation such as #cake were coded as "no appraisal" and excluded from the Appraisal analysis.

Following Zappavigna (2015), I apply Martin and White's (2005) appraisal model from systemic-functional linguistics to online discourse, which allows for a detailed analysis of the discourse semantics of hashtags. In this framework, stances are described as attitudes, then categorized into affect (expressing emotion), judgment (assessing people and behaviors), and appreciation (evaluating things/entities). In addition, the Appraisal model considers explicitness by differentiating between explicitly judgmental ("inscribed") and more neutral (where judgment is "invoked"). Finally, it allows the analyst to code for valence, differentiating between "positive" and "negative." What follows is an Appraisal analysis of Posts 1 and 2, cited here in translation only, which results in some duplicates. In Post 2, for example, the hashtags in lines 14 and 15 both read "#work" whereas the original read "#work #arbeit." A final note on Tables 4.1 and 4.2: captions and hashtags not containing Appraisal are marked by "–."

The analysis shows a large number of stance-marking hashtags; they set up oppositional contrasts, which stand side by side and remain unresolved: bad appearance, good taste; good taste, bad for health. The contrasting attitudes find expression in different voices, i.e., they draw on various sets of linguistic resources such as different registers and languages. For example, the neutral content tags "#chocolate" or "#coffee" contrast sharply with the concatenated phrase #orsomethinglikethatperhaps, which – in its vagueness – playfully flouts hashtagging norms for humorous effect. Another example is the play with registers, as in popular slang "#goodshit" in contrast to the somewhat corny advertising slogan "#backenistliebe" (#bakingislove).

Table 4.1. Appraisal Analysis of Post 1 (Maaria the Baker)

	Caption	Appraisal
1)	I baked something.	–
2)	Not sure what it is.	[ideation: appearance; appreciation negative, invoked]*
3)	But it's gooooooood.	[ideation: taste; appreciation positive, inscribed: expressive]
	Hashtag	**Appraisal**
1)	#marianne	–
2)	#mochabit (or baked good)	–
3)	#orsomethinglikethatperhaps	[ideation: appearance; appreciation negative, invoked]
4)	#goodshit	[ideation: taste; appreciation positive, inscribed]
5)	#tastyshit	[ideation: taste; appreciation positive, inscribed]
6)	#unhealthyshit	[ideation: nutrition value; appreciation negative, inscribed]
7)	#lovethisshit	[ideation: taste; appreciation positive, inscribed]
8)	#nam	[ideation: taste; appreciation positive, expressive]
9)	#foodlove	[ideation: food; affect positive, inscribed]
10)	#foodishappiness	[ideation: food; affect positive, inscribed]
11)	#bakingisfun	[ideation: baking; affect positive, inscribed]
12)	#chocolateisgoodforthesoul	[ideation: chocolate; appreciation positive, inscribed]
13)	#bakingislove	[ideation: baking; affect positive, inscribed]
14)	#nomnomnom	[ideation: taste; appreciation positive, inscribed: expressive]

*The square brackets stand for an "and" relation. For example, as shown in 3), "gooooooood" is coded as "appreciation" that is "positive" and "inscribed: expressive."

The mix of registers and languages illustrates Maaria's heteroglossic tagging practice, which I discuss in Section 4.4.

Post 2 also reveals playful heteroglossic tagging, as shown in the Appraisal analysis in Table 4.2.

Like Post 1, Post 2 shows double-voiced tagging, e.g., with three hashtags (line 1 "#epätoivo" "#despair," line 21 "#ichliebediesesprache" "#ilovethislanguage," and line 25 #shit) drawing on three languages and different

Table 4.2. Appraisal Analysis of Post 2 (Maaria the Student)

	Caption	Appraisal
1)	To begin, begins, began, has begun. To bring, brings, brought, has brought. To get on, gets on, got on, has got on.	–
2)	I will never learn these.	[Ideation: self as German learner; affect negative, invoked]
3)	If I don't stop, I'll get a headache…	[ideation: self as German learner; affect negative, invoked]

	Hashtag	Appraisal
1)	#despair	[ideation: self as German learner; affect negative, inscribed]
2)	#feelingstupid	[ideation: self as German learner; affect negative, inscribed]
3)	#too*	
4)	#difficult	[ideation: learning German; affect negative, invoked]
5)	#studying	–
6)	#german	–
7)	#verbs	–
8)	#iwillneverrememberthese	[ideation: self as German learner; affect negative, invoked]
9)	#reading	–
10)	#book	–
11)	#atwork	–
12)	#working	–
13)	#summerjob	–
14)	#work	–
15)	#work	–
16)	#learn	–
17)	#read	–
18)	#study	–
19)	#germanbook	–
20)	#german	–
21)	#ilovethislanguage	[ideation: self as German learner; affect positive, inscribed]
22)	#germanlanguage	–
23)	#learngerman	–
24)	#difficult	[ideation: learning German; affect negative, invoked]
25)	#shit	[ideation: learning German; affect negative, inscribed]
26)	#verbs	–
27)	#turkuliberalartsstudent	[ideation: self as Turku Liberal Arts student; affect positive, invoked]
28)	#bag	–

*Hashtags 3 and 4 taken together represent an Appraisal; their separation is a playful flouting of tagging norms.

registers to express what appear to be competing high-affect stances, which I discuss further in the next section.

It is important to underscore what "affect" means in the Appraisal model. The analytic lens is strictly textual and leaves aside Maaria's emotional state. For example, the hashtags #epätoivo (#despair) or #feelingstupid, though they refer to affective states, are *communication devices*. Emotive communication is thus a form of self-presentation, and as such "it is inherently strategic, persuasive, interactional, and other-directed by its very nature" (Caffi & Janney, 1994, p. 329; cf. Parret, 1984; Robinson, 1986; Arndt & Janney, 1991). Viewing stance-marking hashtags as devices of communication rather than as expressions of emotions allows for an analytic focus on textual data rather than affective states.

4.4 Heteroglossic Tagging

The analysis shows that the same content is associated with positive and negative affect, suggesting a tension between competing points of view (e.g., in Post 1 hashtag lines 4, 5, 7, 8, 9, 10, and 11 show positive affect whereas hashtag lines 3 and 6 show negative affect). The different affects result from viewing the stance object through different lenses, as it were. In other words, a slight shift from one attitudinal target to another on the content, e.g., from appearance to taste (Post 1) or from learning German to the German language (Post 2), changes the polarity of the evaluation. These different stances find expression not just in the content of the tags but also in the code that expresses this content. In other words, tagging draws on semiotic resources *within* a language and *across* languages.

The analysis of attitudinal meaning in the two posts shows that both captions and hashtags mark stances, raising the question why hashtags, whose original function is content tagging, are used for stance-marking at all. In other words, why not restrict stance-taking to captions? In Post 1, for example, hashtag line 3 largely serves the same Appraisal function as caption line 2. Similarly, in Post 2, hashtag line 8 largely has the same Appraisal function as caption line 2. In other words, what advantages do hashtags as a textual form have over captions? I argue that hashtagging is a particularly good fit for heteroglossic posts. My contention is based on the differences between hashtag clusters and caption texts as evidenced in the data collection. Hashtag clusters differ from caption texts in that the tags appear in random order.[6] Whereas in captions the ordering of elements generally fol-

[6] This study did not specifically focus on hashtag ordering.

lows genre conventions and grammatical rules, there are no constraints on the ordering of hashtags within a hashtag cluster. Moreover, hashtag clusters are not "woven" together, unlike texts, which include grammatical cohesive ties that provide continuity, e.g., through pronominal substitution (I baked **something**. Not sure what **it** is. But **it**'s gooooooood.). Whereas caption texts generally use conjunctive elements that systematically connect different units, hashtag clusters typically do not mark semantic relationship between hashtags. This is not to say that hashtag clusters do not show cohesive markers. Lexical cohesion is pervasive: in Post 1 #marianne, #mochabit, #orsomethinglikethatperhaps, #goodshit, #tastyshit, for example, have identical references. Other hashtags collocate, that is they often co-occur in the same context, e.g., #foodlove and #nonnomnom. In short, hashtags largely rely on lexical cohesion rather than conjunctive elements or grammatical cohesion.

Hashtag clusters are exceptionally well suited to double-voiced posts because hashtags seem suspended next to each other. In the larger context of the multimodal posts, hashtag clusters in the data create the impression that Maaria is dialoguing with herself, vacillating between a positive and negative appreciation of the object. In this way, heteroglossic hashtags allow the poster to comment on her own emotional state, to create an extra layer, or to undercut her own voice, all of which serve in strategic self-presentation. They allow Maaria to operate in multiple registers and in multiple languages at once. For example, #taijotainsinnepäinehkä "orsomethinglikethatperhaps" (Post 1) tags the mochabit but does so in a way that conveys a negative Appraisal. One such hashtag can change the meaning of the entire post, especially when that hashtag signals irony. In the data, tags relate in complex ways, more or less directly, underscoring, contextualizing, undercutting, or reframing content. Captions, by contrast, are associated with a single voice. Even if the user is wavering, apparent contradictions are synthesized into a single authorial voice. This can be seen in Post 1 where the caption marks the contrast between appearance (Not sure what it is.) and taste (**But** it's gooooooood.) explicitly with adversative "but" with the effect that hashtags stand side by side without being synthesized into a single voice.

Compared with captioning, tagging compresses a lot of illocutionary force into a series of a short string of signs. In context, such heteroglossic tagging generates humor effects because the register, style, or genre it evokes is incongruous with other elements of the post. The advertising slogan #backenistliebe "#bakingislove" (Post 1, hashtag line 13), for example, is funny in the context of the lightly self-deprecating post. #epätoivo

"#despair" (Post 2, hashtag line 1), for example, is funny only in the context of Maaria's temporary frustration with German verb paradigms.

4.5 Indexing a Multilingual Identity

In her hashtagging practice, Maaria draws more heavily on her English (59%) and German (29%) than on her L1, Finnish (6%), as shown in Figure 4.1. This is particularly interesting because in the captions Finnish is dominant (Figure 4.1). The finding suggests that non-L1 linguistic resources may especially lend themselves to heteroglossic tagging, at least in particular online contexts. The specific linguistic registers, genres, and styles Maaria draws on in her multilingual heteroglossing hashtagging allow her to index her identity in another way. Using certain hashtags is a way for someone to convey that they are part of a certain scene. #backenistliebe "bakingislove" or #tastyshit, for example, shows that the user is in the know in terms of digital media use. The analysis of the data suggests that multilingual hashtagging may be motivated, at least in part, by what Androutsopoulos (2013) has called networked multilingualism, shaped by two interrelated processes: being networked (i.e., digitally connected to other individuals and groups) and being in the network (i.e., embedded in the global web). More specifically, being in the network implies access to slang like #tastyshit and access to advertising slogans such as "Backen ist Liebe," popularized by a margarine brand.

Multilingual tagging is a rich semiotic resource that does not require a high level of proficiency in the L2/foreign language because the same hashtags can be used over and over again, especially because users tend to stick to particular content domains. In addition, Web 2.0 makes available a host of tools that facilitate the use of existing tags, for example by suggesting tags to users. Digital culture celebrates the recombination of existing resources in the creation of new content, a norm that aligns well with the needs of novice language learners, who learn to recombine language "chunks."

In sum, multilingual hashtags are an important linguistic resource not only in content tagging but, importantly, in acts of positioning, a type of stance-taking that evaluates objects primarily in order to position the subject. The data illustrate how hashtags communicate stances, including contradictory stances. This is important because hashtags allow the juxtaposed stances to alternate or stand side by side, giving the impression that the user is dialoguing with themselves within a single post (see also Evans, 2016). In fact, tagging appears to be uniquely suited to heteroglossia, allowing multilinguals to construct complex meanings.

4.6 Aligning with Others

Maaria takes stances to index identity and present a virtual self but stance-taking is first and foremost a social action. As conceptualized in Du Bois' (2007) stance triangle, a speaker's stance allows for calibrating alignment with others. In fact, it is primarily through verbal stance-taking that relationships develop. By offering the audience stances to align with, Maaria's stance-marking hashtags promote rapport as well as build and maintain community. This is not to say that hashtags whose sole function is to categorize posts do not have a community-building effect. They very well may, e.g., when users search for content and end up interacting with like-minded users.

Widely shared stances, or bonds, are prevalent in the dataset. In Post 1 and elsewhere in the data, Maaria evokes the chocolate-is-love bond, for example. Another is the feeding-is-love bond, realized in the data as #backenistliebe "#bakingislove" (Post 1). Although they are widely shared and closely associated with online communities, bonds are negotiable. In networked interaction, this negotiation can take different forms. Bonds can be rallied around or rejected, or they can be laughed at, e.g., in the chocolate-addiction bond evoked in some of her food-related posts (see Post 1, for example) or the German-is-difficult bond in Post 2. Maaria's stances invite solidarity not because she *rallies* around these bonds but because she *proposes* them as a laughing affiliation to her followers (see Zappavigna, 2015). In laughing at her own weaknesses and inviting her followers to join her, Maaria is simultaneously proposing a self-deprecation bond. Both posts exemplified in this chapter propose a self-deprecation bond to Maaria's followers that invites them to laugh with her at her inadequacies. In Post 2, this self-deprecation bond is marked explicitly in hashtag 2) "#feelingstupid." However, more often than not, the self-deprecation bond is not *explicitly* marked in the data. In Post 1, for example, self-deprecation is implicit. It is evoked through the image of imperfect food and stances that playfully resist labeling the baked product (e.g., #orsomethinglikethatperhaps). Bonds can be marked explicitly by hashtag or not.

Self-disclosure that includes negative aspects of self projects authenticity while self-deprecating humor serves as politeness strategy for maintaining face (Brown & Levinson, 1987) where uninhibited positive self-presentation could appear as bragging. At the same time, any negative self-disclosure can be risky, especially in an SNS context that is biased toward positivity (e.g., Reinecke & Trepte, 2014). In the data, self-disclosure is highly selective and largely limited to content related to quotidian actions and experiences where negative revelations are unlikely to undermine a positive self-presentation

– 51% of Maaria's posts in the dataset feature food-related content[7] sharing mundane actions and experiences around eating, baking, and cooking. In the data, food-related content features prominently, even in posts that are primarily travel-related.

Even though content is focused on the user, Maaria's self-disclosure is not navel-gazing because it primarily serves an interpersonal function. That is because identities are social even as they are personal (Bucholtz & Hall, 2005; Zimmerman, 1998) and stance-taking is critical to building and maintaining rapport with others. In her work on social tagging, Zappavigna (2015) refers back to Firth (1964) to highlight the key role of affiliation in discursive interaction. Firth (1964, p. 12) suggested that the "promotion, establishment, and maintenance of communion of feeling is perhaps four-fifths of all talk." If interactional speaking is even more important than transactional speaking, sharing attitudinal meaning is central to both fostering social interaction and positioning the self. Zappavigna (2014, p. 212) argues that a Firthian perspective on online interaction "sensitizes us to the ways in which microblogging texts propose social 'bonds' to their ambient audience in order to invite such communion of feeling." Building on Firth (1964), a robust research record has underscored the importance or even prevalence of social talk in discursive interaction, e.g., through work on "phatic communion" (Malinowski, 1972) or "small talk" (Coupland, 2000). Through this lens, digital tools including hashtags are a rich resource for affiliating with others.

The link between rapport and humor is so strong that humor in discursive interaction is often perceived as indexing a good social relationship. Because identity is taken to be co-constructed and emergent (e.g., Archakis & Tsakona, 2005), discourse, in general, and humorous discourse, in particular, play important roles in a range of social functions, including self-representation, group-building, and attaining relational goals in online contexts (e.g., Vásquez, 2019; Yus, 2018). The data yield evidence of different types of humor and play, including ludic play with language forms and genre conventions. Post 1 illustrates Maaria's playful approach. First, the image itself produces humor effects. On Instagram where digital affordances such as filters encourage the "aestheticization of everyday life" (Ibrahim, 2015, p. 42), the picture of the chocolate product in "Maaria the Baker" (Post 1) flouts genre norms. Second, Maaria plays with elements of the language. Aside from playful nonstandard spellings, e.g., the vocal spelling of "gooooooood" in Post 1 or lexical surrogates as in #nomnomnom (Post 1), the dataset contains

---

[7] This percentage includes baking-related content.

many examples of play with hashtagging norms. Concatenated-phrase tags such as #taijotainsinnepäinehkä (#orsomethinglikethatperhaps) play with the function of tagging. Ostensibly, the tag aims to label what the image shows, but the product defies labeling; the humor effect is largely due to the tag's norm-flouting opaqueness that plays with genre conventions. Hashtagging #too and #difficult (Post 2) separately rather than as one concatenated-phrase tag (#toodifficult) also subverts tagging norms in that hashtags do not have syntax and are normatively independent of each other. Moreover, the abundance of hashtags in the data, with an average 23.5 hashtags per post, suggests ludic play. Above all, humor effects arise from heteroglossic tagging as humor is created by the perception of incongruity (Attardo, 1994). Followers may perceive incongruities but they will find them funny only if they appreciate the resonances of the various codes (Kramsch & Whiteside, 2008). Shared humor creates an online social connection through shared enjoyment, a phenomenon researchers have explored as "ambient affiliation" (Zappavigna, 2011, 2014) and "conviviality" (Varis & Blommaert, 2015). Given the social benefits of humor, the abundance of humor and play in the tagging data is not surprising.

Appraisal has mostly been considered with respect to language use but Martin and White (2005) suggest that the model might also be used for studying language users. Viewed as a group, the content analysis of the data collection suggests what Martin and White have labeled an "Appraisal signature," i.e., "the idiolectal reconfigurations of meaning-making potential by which individual authors achieve a recognizable personal style" (Martin & White, 2005, p. 208). Based on my analysis, Maaria's style can be described with respect to ideation as highly selective, slightly self-deprecating self-disclosures of quotidian actions and experiences (related primarily to food, study, and music) that use heteroglossic stance-marking hashtags to propose laughing affiliations to followers. Because identity sediments over time (Bucholtz & Hall, 2005), Appraisal can provide an analytic framework for the emergence of a virtual L2 or multilingual self.

5 Summary and Conclusion

Hashtags have emerged as a rich semiotic resource. First, the present analysis documented and described hashtags in their multifunctionality. In line with previous research (including Evans, 2016; Zappavigna, 2014, 2015; Zappavigna & Martin, 2018), the data showed that in addition to serving as metadata for content tagging (e.g., #chocolate), hashtags mark user stance.

These two functions of hashtags are distinct but not mutually exclusive (see Section 4.3). Just as there is no unique function associated with hashtags, the function of stance-marking is not limited to hashtags: Stances are marked in both hashtags and captions (see Section 4.3).

The present analysis was concerned with multilingual hashtagging in particular. Many of the Finnish, English, and German hashtags the data yielded are not direct translations of each other, a finding that aligns with prior research (e.g., Barton & Lee, 2013; Lee & Chau, 2018). To be sure, Maaria's trilingual hashtagging may maximize audience by providing multilingual access, but it does much more. First, it indexes Maaria's multilingual virtual self. More importantly, multilingual resources offer enhanced stance-marking affordances. Maaria's rich heteroglossic repertoire allows her to draw on linguistic resources from different registers, styles, or genres in more than one language. Because each code evokes its own meaning, the juxtaposition of voices *is* the juxtaposition of stances. In the data, multilingual hashtag clusters yielded heteroglossic tagging, i.e., juxtaposed or alternating voices that give expression to contradictory stances (see also Leppänen et al., 2009) (see Sections 4.3 and 4.4). That hashtagging seems to be particularly well suited to heteroglossia is a promising preliminary finding that warrants further research into the extent to which the affordance is taken up in multilingual practice.

In posts that center around selective self-disclosures, double-voiced discourse allows for playful identity performance. Heteroglossic tags, in particular, allow users to dialogue with themselves within a single post (see also Evans, 2016). In her self-presentation Maaria positions herself as a baker, a German student, a tourist, a daughter, among other roles. Avoiding the pitfalls associated with unmitigated positive self-disclosures (see e.g., Arkin, 1981; Casale et al., 2015; Lee-Won et al., 2014; Rui & Stefanone, 2013a, b), the posts tend to orient to minor mishaps, imperfections, or inadequacies with self-deprecating humor. In this way, both the selection of self-disclosures and the stances taken play a key role in the carefully calibrated presentation of the multilingual virtual self. This insight raises the question as to whether the presentation of the virtual self is actually worth all the effort users like Maaria put into it. While the "cost" may be high, so are the stakes, especially because in social networks, stances accumulate as posts accumulate. This accumulation of stances allows for a virtual identity to sediment (see Bucholtz, 2007) in two ways: posts appear one at a time in a follower's Instagram feed and also in the online archive that is a user's Instagram grid. Because accumulated stances persist in social networks, the stakes may be higher than in other contexts where stances are more ephemeral.

Because stance-taking is primarily a social action, stance-marking hashtags are an important resource not only for presenting the self but also for building and maintaining solidarity. Maaria's stances on quotidian experiences around baking, studying, traveling, for example, propose a shared bond to the audience. The humorous, slightly self-deprecating hashtags that accompany the description of a minor baking mishap or her difficulty memorizing German verb paradigms promote audience alignment or what Zappavigna (2014) has called "ambient affiliation." Audiences can relate through the chocolate-addiction and the German-grammar-is-hard bonds. It is difficult to overstate that the function of these posts is not to reveal affective states. Rather, heteroglossic tagging is intentional semiotic action, marking stances that others can align with.

To what extent, if any, the findings of this study are generalizable is unclear. The most significant limitation is that all data were generated by one user. Even if Maaria's use of multilingual hashtags resembles a more widely shared practice, participant characteristics, including education levels, gender, and age, are likely to play a role, as does the topic or theme (Herring, 2004). Future research will have to take a closer look at different factors to see how individual factors or their combinations and interactions affect hashtagging practices, in general, and heteroglossic hashtagging in particular.

I conclude with two important points that link extramural digital practice to language education. As a digital practice, heteroglossic hashtagging has important implications for language learning. Double-voiced discourse requires linguistic expertise. As a form of symbolic competence – defined as a user's "acute ability to play with various linguistic codes and with the various spatial and temporary resonances of these codes" (Kramsch & Whiteside, 2008, p. 664) – social media literacy including hashtagging is central to language use in the 21st century and should therefore play a bigger role in language learning. Even though more and more classrooms are beginning to offer learners structured opportunities for developing multiliteracy, current classroom practice does not accurately reflect the heterogeneity of authentic multimodal digitally mediated discourse. The findings of the present analysis exemplify how important hashtags are to multilingual social networking, especially because they appear to play a key role in the presentation of a multilingual virtual identity.

In documenting multilingual practice in naturalistic digital discourse, this study points to the divergence between classroom and extramural digital L2 practices when it comes to the use of more than one language. Whereas most classrooms that advocate for maximizing target language use actively discourage multilingual practices (e.g., Macaro, 2005), such practices are very common in L2 digital discourse (e.g., Androutsopoulos 2004, 2007a,b; Tsiplakou, 2009; Vandergriff, 2016). When interacting with other multilinguals, drawing on more than one language appears to be the norm rather than the exception. Classroom practice should encourage rather than discourage learners to leverage multilingual resources as they contribute to the development of a multilingual virtual self (e.g., Kramsch, 2009; Pérez & Cassany, 2018).

References

Androutsopoulos, J. (2004). Non-native English and sub-cultural identities in media discourse. In H. Sandøy (Ed.), *Den fleirspråklege utfordringa/The multilingual challenge* (pp. 83–98). Novus.

Androutsopoulos, J. (2007a). Language choice and code-switching in German-based diasporic web forums. In B. Danet & S. C. Herring (Eds.), *The multilingual Internet: Language, culture, and communication online* (pp. 340–361). Oxford University Press. https://doi.org/10.1093/acprof:oso/9780195304794.003.0015

Androutsopoulos, J. (2007b). Bilingualism in the mass media and on the Internet. In M. Heller (Ed.), *Bilingualism: A social approach* (pp. 207–230). Palgrave Macmillan. https://doi.org/10.1057/9780230596047_10

Androutsopoulos, J. (2008). Potentials and limitations of discourse-centered online ethnography. *Language@Internet*, 5, article 8. urn:nbn:de:0009-7-16100

Androutsopoulos, J. (2011). From variation to heteroglossia in the study of computer-mediated discourse. In C. Thurlow & K. Mroczek (Eds.), *Digital discourse: Language in the new media* (pp. 277–298). Oxford University Press. https://doi.org/10.1093/acprof:oso/9780199795437.003.0013

Androutsopoulos, J. (2013). Online data collection. In C. Mallinson, B. Childs, & G. Van Herk (Eds.), *Data collection in sociolinguistics: Methods and applications* (pp. 236–249). Routledge. https://doi.org/10.4324/9780203136065

Androutsopoulos, J. (2014). Language when contexts collapse: Audience design in social networking. *Discourse, Context & Media*, 4–5, 62–73. https://doi.org/10.1016/j.dcm.2014.08.006

Archakis, A., & Tsakona, V. (2005). Analyzing conversational data in GTVH terms: A new approach to the issue of identity construction via humor. *Humor*, 18(1), 41–68. https://doi.org/10.1515/humr.2005.18.1.41

Arkin, R. M. (1981). Self-presentation styles. In J. T. Tedeschi (Ed.), *Impression management theory and social psychological research* (pp. 311–333). Academic Press. https://doi.org/10.1016/B978-0-12-685180-9.50020-8

Arndt, H., & Janney, R. W. (1991). Verbal, prosodic, and kinesic emotive contrasts in speech. *Journal of Pragmatics*, 15(6), 521–549. https://doi.org/10.1016/0378-2166(91)90110-J

Attardo, S. (1994). *Linguistic theories of humor*. Mouton de Gruyter. https://doi.org/10.1515/9783110219029

Bakhtin, M. M. (1981). *The dialogic imagination: Four essays* (M. Holquist, Ed.). University of Texas Press.

Barton, D. (2018). The roles of tagging in the online curation of photographs. *Discourse, Context & Media*, 22, 39–45. https://doi.org/10.1016/j.dcm.2017.06.001

Barton, D., & Lee, C. (2013). *Language online: Investigating digital texts and practices*. Routledge. https://doi.org/10.4324/9780203552308

Baxter, J. (2016). Positioning language and identity. In S. Preece (Ed.), *The Routledge handbook of language and identity* (pp. 34–49). Routledge. https://doi.org/10.4324/9781315669816

Bourlai, E. E. (2018). 'Comments in tags, please!': Tagging practices on Tumblr. *Discourse, Context & Media*, *22*, 46–56. https://doi.org/10.1016/j.dcm.2017.08.003

Brown, P., & Levinson, S. C. (1987). *Politeness: Some universals in language usage* (Vol. 4). Cambridge University Press.

Bucholtz, M. (2007). Shop talk: Branding, consumption, and gender in American middle-class youth interaction. In B. S. McElhinny (Ed.), *Words, worlds, and material girls: Language, gender, globalization* (pp. 371–402). Mouton de Gruyter. https://escholarship.org/uc/item/9pg070r7

Bucholtz, M., & Hall, K. (2005). Identity and interaction: A sociocultural linguistic approach. *Discourse Studies, 7*(4–5), 585–614. https://doi.org/10.1177/1461445605054407

Caffi, C., & Janney, R. W. (1994). Toward a pragmatics of emotive communication. *Journal of Pragmatics*, *22*(3–4), 325–373. https://doi.org/10.1016/0378-2166(94)90115-5

Casale, S., Fioravanti, G., Flett, G. L., & Hewitt, P. L. (2015). Self-presentation styles and problematic use of internet communicative services: The role of the concerns over behavioral displays of imperfection. *Personality and Individual Differences*, 76, 187–192. https://doi.org/10.1016/j.paid.2014.12.021

Cook, G. (2000). *Language play, language learning*. Oxford University Press.

Coupland, J. (2000). *Small talk*. Routledge.

Deumert, A. (2014). The performance of a ludic self on social network(ing) sites. In P. Seargeant & P. Tagg (Eds.), *The language of social media* (pp. 23–45). Palgrave Macmillan. https://doi.org/10.1057/9781137029317_2

Drummond, R., & Schleef, E. (2016). Identity in variationist sociolinguistics. In S. Preece (Ed.), *The Routledge handbook of language and identity* (pp. 50–65). Routledge.

Du Bois, J. W. (2007). The stance triangle. In R. Englebretson (Ed.), *Stancetaking in discourse: Subjectivity, evaluation, interaction* (pp. 139–182). John Benjamins. https://doi.org/10.1075/pbns.164.07du

Dumas, T. M., Maxwell-Smith, M., Davis, J. P., & Giulietti, P. A. (2017). Lying or longing for likes? Narcissism, peer belonging, loneliness and normative versus deceptive like-seeking on Instagram in emerging adulthood. *Computers in Human Behavior*, 71, 1–10. https://doi.org/10.1016/j.chb.2017.01.037

Evans, A. (2016). Stance and identity in Twitter hashtags. *Language@Internet*, 13, article 1. Urn:nbn:de:0009-0-54947 https://www.languageatinternet.org/articles/2016/evans/

Firth, J. R. (1964). *Papers in linguistics*. Oxford University Press.

Franzke, A. S., Bechmann, A., Zimmer, M., & Ess, C. and the Association of Internet Researchers (2020). *Internet Research: Ethical Guidelines 3.0*. https://aoir.org/reports/ethics3.pdf

Fullwood, C., & Attrill-Smith, A. (2018). Special issue on 'constructing the self online'. *Cyberpsychology, Behavior and Social Networking*, 21(1), 3–4. https://doi.org/10.1089/cyber.2017.29096.cfu

Giaxoglou, K. (2018). #JeSuisCharlie? Hashtags as narrative resources in contexts of ecstatic sharing. *Discourse, Context & Media*, 22, 13–20. https://doi.org/10.1016/j.dcm.2017.07.006

Gleason, B. (2018). Thinking in hashtags: Exploring teenagers' new literacies practices on Twitter. *Learning, Media and Technology*, 43(2), 165–180. https://doi.org/10.1080/17439884.2018.1462207

Halpern, D., Katz, J. E., & Carril, C. (2017). The online ideal persona vs. the jealousy effect: Two explanations of why selfies are associated with lower-quality romantic relationships. *Telematics and Informatics*, 34(1), 114–123. https://doi.org/10.1016/j.tele.2016.04.014

Hendrickse, J., Arpan, L. M., Clayton, R. B., & Ridgway, J. L. (2017). Instagram and college women's body image: Investigating the roles of appearance-related comparisons and intrasexual competition. *Computers in Human Behavior*, 74, 92–100. https://doi.org/10.1016/j.chb.2017.04.027

Herring, S. (2004). Computer-mediated discourse analysis: An approach to researching online behavior. In S. A. Barab, R. Kling, & J. H. Gray, J. H. (Eds.). *Designing for virtual communities in the service of learning* (pp. 338–376). Cambridge University Press. https://doi.org/10.1017/CBO9780511805080.016

Hu, Y., Manikonda, L., & Kambhampati, S. (2014, May). What we Instagram: A first analysis of Instagram photo content and user types. In *Proceedings of the 8th International Conference on Weblogs and Social Media, ICWSM 2014* (pp. 595–598). The AAAI Press.

Ibrahim, Y. (2015). Instagramming life: Banal imaging and the poetics of the everyday. *Journal of Media Practice*, 16(1), 42–54. https://doi.org/10.1080/14682753.2015.1015800

Knight, N. K. (2010). Laughing our bonds off: Conversational humor in relation to affiliation. Unpublished Ph.D. dissertation, University of Sydney. https://ses.library.usyd.edu.au/handle/2123/6656

Kramsch, C. (2009). *The multilingual subject: What foreign language learners say about their experience and why it matters.* Oxford University Press. https://doi.org/10.1111/j.1473-4192.2006.00109.x

Kramsch, C., & Whiteside, A. (2008). Language ecology in multilingual settings. Towards a theory of symbolic competence. *Applied Linguistics*, 29(4), 645–671. https://doi.org/10.1093/applin/amn022

LaScotte, D., & Tarone, E. (2019). Heteroglossia and constructed dialogue in SLA. *The Modern Language Journal*, 103, 95–112. https://doi.org/10.1111/modl.12533

Lee, C., & Chau, D. (2018). Language as pride, love, and hate: Archiving emotions through multilingual Instagram hashtags. *Discourse, Context & Media*, 22, 21–29. https://doi.org/10.1016/j.dcm.2017.06.002

Lee-Won, R. J., Shim, M., Joo, Y. K., & Park, S. G. (2014). Who puts the best 'face' forward on Facebook?: Positive self-presentation in online social networking and the role of self-consciousness, actual-to-total Friends ratio, and culture. *Computers in Human Behavior*, 39, 413–423. https://doi.org/10.1016/j.chb.2014.08.007

Leppänen, S., Pitkänen-Huhta, A., Piirainen-Marsh, A., Nikula, T., & Peuronen, S. (2009). Young people's translocal new media uses: A multiperspective analysis of language choice and heteroglossia. *Journal of Computer-Mediated Communication*, 14(4), 1080–1107. https://doi.org/10.1111/j.1083-6101.2009.01482.x

Macaro, E. (2005). Codeswitching in the L2 classroom: A communication and learning strategy. In E. Llurda (Ed.), *Non-native language teachers: Perceptions, challenges, and contributions to the professions* (pp. 63–84). Springer. http://dx.doi.org/10.1007/0-387-24565-0_5

Malinowski, B. (1972). Phatic communion. In J. Laver & S. Hutcheson (Eds.), *Communication in face-to-face interaction* (pp. 146–152). Penguin.

Bednarek, M., & Martin, J. R. (2010). *New discourse on language: Functional perspectives on multimodality, identity, and affiliation.* Continuum.

Martin, J. R., & White, P. R. (2005). *The language of evaluation.* London: Palgrave Macmillan. https://doi.org/10.1057/9780230511910

Matley, D. (2018). 'Let's see how many of you mother fuckers unfollow me for this': The pragmatic function of the hashtag #sorrynotsorry in non-apologetic Instagram posts. *Journal of Pragmatics*, 133, 66–78. https://doi.org/10.1016/j.pragma.2018.06.003

Meese, J., Gibbs, M., Carter, M., Arnold, M., Nansen, B., & Kohn, T. (2015). Selfies at funerals: Mourning and presencing on social media platforms. *International Journal of Communication*, 9, 1818–1831. https://ijoc.org/index.php/ijoc/article/download/3154/1402

Moon, J. H., Lee, E., Lee, J. A., Choi, T. R., & Sung, Y. (2016). The role of narcissism in self-promotion on Instagram. *Personality and Individual Differences*, 101, 22–25. http://dx.doi.org/10.1016/j.paid.2016.05.042

Norton, B. (2013). *Identity and language learning: Extending the conversation.* Multilingual Matters. https://doi.org/10.21832/9781783090563

Oulasvirta, A., Lehtonen, E., Kurvinen, E., & Raento, M. (2010). Making the ordinary visible in microblogs. *Personal and Ubiquitous Computing*, 14(3), 237–249. https://doi.org/10.1007/s00779-009-0259-y

Papacharissi, Z. (2011). Conclusion: A networked self. In Z. Papacharissi (Ed.), *Networked*

self: Identity, community and culture on social network sites (pp. 304–318). Routledge.

Parret, H. (1984). Regularities, rules and strategies. *Journal of Pragmatics*, 8(4), 569–592. https://doi.org/10.1016/0378-2166(84)90043-2

Pérez, M., & Cassany, D. (2018). Writing and sharing: Teenagers' writing practices and identity on Instagram. *Aula de Encuentro*, 20(2), 75–94. https://doi.org/10.17561/ae.v20i2.5

Reinecke, L., & Trepte, S. (2014). Authenticity and well-being on social network sites: A two-wave longitudinal study on the effects of online authenticity and the positivity bias in SNS communication. *Computers in Human Behavior*, 30, 95–102.

https://doi.org/10.1016/j.chb.2013.07.030

Robinson, D. (1986). Metapragmatics and its discontents. *Journal of Pragmatics*, 10(6), 651–671. https://doi.org/10.1016/0378-2166(86)90145-1

Rui, J., & Stefanone, M. A. (2013a). Strategic self-presentation online: A cross-cultural study. *Computers in Human Behavior*, 29(1), 110–118. https://doi.org/10.1016/j.chb.2012.07.022

Rui, J. R., & Stefanone, M. A. (2013b). Strategic image management online: Self-presentation, self-esteem and social network perspectives. *Information, Communication & Society*, 16(8), 1286–1305. https://doi.org/10.1080/1369118X.2013.763834

Scott, K. (2015). The pragmatics of hashtags: Inference and conversational style on Twitter. *Journal of Pragmatics*, 81, 8–20. https://doi.org/10.1016/j.pragma.2015.03.015

Sheldon, P., & Bryant, K. (2016). Instagram: Motives for its use and relationship to narcissism and contextual age. *Computers in Human Behavior*, 58, 89–97. https://doi.org/10.1016/j.chb.2015.12.059

Slater, A., Varsani, N., & Diedrichs, P. C. (2017). #fitspo or #loveyourself? The impact of fitspiration and self-compassion Instagram images on women's body image, self-compassion, and mood. *Body Image*, 22, 87–96. https://doi.org/10.1016/j.bodyim.2017.06.004

Tsiplakou, S. (2009). Doing (bi)lingualism: Language alternation as performative construction of online identities. *Pragmatics*, 19(3), 361–391. https://doi.org/10.1075/prag.19.3.04tsi

Van Parys, J. (2012). Languages in Finland. https://languageknowledge.eu/countries/finland

Vandergriff, I. (2016). *Second-language discourse in the digital world: Linguistic and social practices in and beyond the networked classroom*. Benjamins. https://doi.org/10.1075/lllt.46

Varis, P., & Blommaert, J. (2015). Conviviality and collectives on social media: Virality, memes, and new social structures. *Multilingual Margins: A Journal of Multilingualism from the Periphery*, 2(1), 31–31. https://doi.org/10.14426/mm.v2i1.55

Vásquez, C. (2019). *Language, creativity and humor online*. Routledge. https://doi.org/10.4324/9781315159027

Yus, F. (2018). Identity-related issues in meme communication. *Internet Pragmatics*, 1(1), 113–133. https://doi.org/10.1075/ip.00006.yus

Zappavigna, M. (2011). Ambient affiliation: A linguistic perspective on Twitter. *New Media & Society*, 13(5), 788–806. https://doi.org/10.1177/1461444810385097

Zappavigna, M. (2014). Enacting identity in microblogging through ambient affiliation. *Discourse & Communication*, 8(2), 209–228. https://doi.org/10.1177/1750481313510816

Zappavigna, M. (2015). Searchable talk: The linguistic functions of hashtags. *Social Semiotics*, 25(3), 274–291. https://doi.org/10.1080/10350330.2014.996948

Zappavigna, M., & Martin, J. R. (2018). #Communing affiliation: Social tagging as a resource for aligning around values in social media. *Discourse, Context & Media*, 22, 4–12. https://doi.org/10.1016/j.dcm.2017.08.001

Zimmerman, D. H. (1998). Identity, context and interaction. In C. Antaki & S. Widdicombe (Eds.), *Identities in talk* (pp. 87–106). Sage Publications Ltd. http://dx.doi.org/10.4135/9781446216958.n6

About the Author

Ilona Vandergriff is a professor of German at San Francisco State University. She holds a Ph.D. in German linguistics from UC Berkeley. Her main research interest is in discursive, practice-driven approaches to foreign- and second-language use in technology-mediated environments that begin with what L2 users do when they connect with others online. She is the author of *Second-language Discourse in the Digital World. Linguistic and social practices in and beyond the networked classroom* (2016).

5 Language Learning Hashtags on TikTok in Chinese, Italian, and Russian

Boris Vazquez-Calvo, Liudmila Shafirova, and Leticia-Tian Zhang

1 Introduction

Interest in how social media users learn language keeps growing. For instance, in a revision on the use of social networking sites for language learning, Reinhardt (2019b) concludes that there is "evidence that social media used informally can afford the development of intercultural, socio-pragmatic, and audience awareness, language learner and user identities, and particular literacies (p. 31)." Let us also emphasize two aspects from Reinhardt's words: (1) the increasing prominence of the *informal* aspect of language learning (Benson, 2011), and (2) the correlation between more digitally mediated opportunities for social interaction and the subsequent informal language learning. We refer to language learning informally and online as *language learning in the digital wilds*.

Language learning in the digital wilds (Sauro & Zourou, 2019; Thorne et al., 2015) makes use of an unusual metaphor – *digital wilds* – accentuating the informal and digital components of this type of learning under four premises: (1) it happens outside the classroom, (2) the learner's actions originate the learning, (3) learning or teaching is not the main or sole purpose of the digital context or community in which the learning takes place (often interlocked with entertainment), and (4) learning is not mediated or directed by curriculum, teacher guidelines, or any other document or policy (Sauro & Zourou, 2019, pp. 2–3). Our exploration of TikTok falls within this emerging approach in CALL. Terms related to language learning in the digital wilds include *extramural language learning* (Sundqvist, 2019; Sylvén & Sundqvist, 2012), *online informal language learning* (Sockett, 2014), or *language learning beyond the classroom* (Benson, 2011), among others. While terminological profusion reflects diverse nuanced approaches to an emerging subfield in CALL, it also shows the vitality of ongoing research targeting how digitization and social media influence language learning in multiple ways.

Novel social media emerge and propagate at great speed, and consequently provide new and alter past communicative affordances with uncharted potential for language learning and identity building. In doing so, *language learning in the digital wilds* and related approaches become the spearhead of a collection of studies in CALL trying to keep up with the erratic and often unpredictable nature of digital technologies and social media. Because of their novelty, latest social media, such as TikTok, have attracted less attention in CALL. In a recent commentary, Chik and Benson (2020, n.p.) highlighted:

> "The school-based online learning is also primarily text-based with a lot less consideration for the visual mode of communication. Schools have not caught on to Instagram and they certainly have not considered TikTok. Now that schools are online, literacy practices are still being taught according to the genre theory of the late 1990s."

Growing parallel to its Chinese sister app Douyin, TikTok is a social network based on micro *video-blogging* – sharing and commenting on short videos of normally 60 seconds at the maximum (TikTok is currently experimenting with up to three-minute videos). In 2020, TikTok had become one of the most popular social media platforms for young people, surpassing 2 billion downloads (Kaye et al., 2020). Communicative affordances of TikTok include opportunities for users to upload, watch, share, and comment on videos about TikTokers' daily activities, to express their thoughts and opinions on (current) topics of diverse nature, and collectivize other practices that go locally or globally "viral" in representation of some shared symbolism or just for fun (social dances, challenges, etc.).

Our initial exploration of TikTok hashtags for language learning is opportune because it connects (1) the growing relevance of informal language learning, including identity manifestations, through social media, and (2) the evolving nature of social media and their affordances for language learning. Let us explore in more detail prior research at the intersection of social media, language learning, and identification.

2 Literature Review

In a recent literature review, Reinhardt (2020) scoped historical trends to study social media in language learning, which he categorized into four metaphors: (1) social media as *windows*, (2) social media as *mirrors*, (3) social media as *doorways*, and (4) social media as *playgrounds*. Reinhardt's proposal is reminiscent of the metaphors often used to explicate the role of CALL as tutors, tools, and ecologies for language learning/teaching, and tries to incorporate social media into the mapping of CALL.

1. *Social media as windows*. L2 users/learners can watch or observe practices in the target language, which can be more naturalistic or metalinguistic. Twitter users are exposed to meme use and circulation daily, yet there are spaces online where more discussion "about language learning" happens, as found by Isbell (2018) in his exploration of subreddit interest-driven groups about the Korean language.
2. *Social media as mirrors*. L2 users/learners can potentially present themselves in some identity work and play or reflect on what others portray as part of a purposefully reflective repertoire to "be online" as an add-on to or part of their complex identities. An example can be analyzing selfies online or other semiotic choices on YouTube videos, introductory posts on Facebook, or, more advanced, how author identity interplays in fanfiction writing (Chang and Chang, 2019; Vazquez-Calvo et al., 2020; Shafirova et al., 2020a).
3. *Social media as doorways*. L2 users/learners can participate in communities and practices in the target language and culture or in intercultural, hybrid contexts. Nanako is a fitting example of using social media as a doorway or passage to participating in the target language community (Black, 2006). Chinese-speaking Nanako moved to Canada with her family when she was 11. As she became part of a new linguistic community, she used fanfiction sites to develop written fluency, accuracy, and self-confidence. She found her own voice and peer validation as an English-L2 speaker online.

   Another interlinguistically and interculturally intensive example is fan translation, where fan translators strive to mediate between cultures to produce cultural products available to local communities, often including minoritized languages like Catalan (Vazquez-Calvo, 2020) or off-stream cultural practices like playing retro video games (Vazquez-Calvo, 2018; Vazquez-Calvo et al., 2019). Other examples include watching and commenting on TV series with subsequent subject positioning in relation to other cultures. For instance, Zhang and Cassany (2019a,b) studied online interactions of Chinese fans in the Spanish TV Series *El Ministerio del Tiempo*. Fans' talk through onscreen *danmu*[1] comments induced distinctive subject positioning and meaning negotiation of several topics related to Spanish language and culture.

4. *Social media as playgrounds*. L2 users/learners can construe social media as safe, bounded spaces for play and autonomous and gameful learning. Social media are an extension to powerful, situated practices of language learning through video games (Reinhardt, 2019a) and other popular culture-infused practices. In doing so, paratextual practices in social media become texts worth exploring, analyzing, and learning (Consalvo, 2017), such as creating, editing, and publishing TikTok videos or creating, posting, and circulating memes (Yus, 2018).

While looking at things online, presenting themselves, participating in communities, or playfully learning, social media users leave traceable marks. They may push a *like* button, post a comment on Facebook, retweet a meme, or upload a video on TikTok. With every interaction online, there is a record of users' interests, beliefs, routines, and ideologies. This record of traceable marks online allows us to hypothesize how social media users, including L2 learners, portray and identify themselves. This is in specific reference to social media as *mirrors*. An interesting example is that of Aleksandar, a Serbian hip-hop singer who purposefully motivates code meshing and translingual practices (part English, part Serbian, specific hip-hop signs of meaning, links, etc.) to create an easily recognizable online persona on Facebook (Schreiber, 2015). While Aleksandar shows a fluid, descriptive approach to (trans)languaging, online identity work can also unearth prescriptive language uses and ideologies, as seen by Song's exploration of a Korean blog (Song, 2019). Song identified how Korean bloggers' metacommentaries on language opposed to translanguaging on the grounds that (1) Korean speakers who mix English were negatively perceived as "show-offs," and (2) investing time and effort to distinguish L1 and L2 codes and proper spelling was positively valued as a sign of national, patriotic, and potentially anti-imperialist values.

[1] Literally, "bullet screen," *danmu* (or *danmaku* in Japanese) refers to a commentary technology originated in Japan, which superimposes comments onto the video frame, creating a visual effect of barrage comments.

The two examples above offer detailed analyses on interest-driven linguistic practices and identity work in framed contexts (semi-professionalization efforts of a hip-hop artist on Facebook; investment in language learning which surfaced linguistic ideologies on a forum). However, TikTok complexifies the context of analysis (micro videos, often edited videos with multiple signs and symbols [gifs, superimposed text, etc.], open commentary), both for analyzing the language learning potential of TikTok and for analyzing identity work and performance through such special micro video sharing. Given the lack of prior studies, we will try to produce a preliminary exploration of what happens on TikTok in relation to language learning and especially identification. We propose an exploration of three hashtags (#learnchinese, #learnitalian, #learnrussian) in hopes of answering two research questions:

- RQ1. What type of video content do TikTokers upload in language learning-related hashtags?
- RQ2. How do TikTokers identify linguistically and culturally through their videos?

Our two domains of interest (TikTok as a space for language and potential metalinguistic practice, and identification) lead us to try to clarify what we mean by *online discourse* and *identification*, especially in online contexts as these concepts will act as our conceptual framework.

3 Conceptual Framework: Identification in Online Discourse

To study how TikTok video content affects language learning and identification, we depart from a dialogical conception of discourse and identity (Bakhtin, 1986), focusing on specific uses and choices of content, language, and multimodal resources where subject positioning becomes more salient. Here we understand the interrelation of discourse and identification from a sociocultural linguistic perspective (Ivanič, 2006). Identity can be construed as "a relational and sociocultural phenomenon that emerges and circulates in local discourse contexts of interaction rather than as a stable structure located primarily in the individual psyche or in fixed social categories" (Bucholtz & Hall, 2005, pp. 585–586).

From this interactional and sociocultural interpretation of identification, for practical analysis, we draw on Gee (1999), who also sees identification as a dynamic, multilayered process materialized through social interaction and discourse. Gee (1999) divides the notion of discourse into (1) *the "big D" Discourses* – the broader picture of a social situation, the trajectory one must follow to be identified in a certain way – and (2) *the "little d" discourses* – specific language/discourse practices in situated social interactions yielding nuanced details about the developing self. Consequently, individuals can exhibit, assume, or respond to rather prescribed identities (*"big D" Discourses*), such as national or ethnic identity. Individuals can also develop singular, operational, and negotiated identity ramifications (*"little d" discourses*), which can be aligned with, reinforce, or oppose the *"big D" Discourse* identification. In our inductive approach, we look at the "little d" discourses to make sense and (re-)frame the larger identification of individuals.

This interactional conceptualization of "identity as discourse" is practical in a digitally hybrid context, too. Past accounts could connect the "identity as discourse" framework to the evolving identification practices of adolescent YouTubers from Catalonia (Vazquez-Calvo et al., 2020) or from Russia (Shafirova et al., 2020a). Furthermore, the increasingly fluid nature of identity, particularly in online and hybrid contexts of social interaction, highlight the complexity of identifying with fixed top-down categories, such as ethnicity or nationality. Digitization turns identification into a process of appropriating diverse multimodal, linguistic, and cultural resources (Higgins, 2011; Pennycook, 2007; Shafirova et al., 2020b). For instance, Chang and Chang (2019) challenge the idea of prescribed national identities as they saw how Taiwanese YouTubers opted to oppose their prescribed identities as "foreigners/L2 speakers" by negotiating transnational identities. In other words, they did not align themselves with people who lack knowledge about the local culture or language, but they put themselves in a position of power by showing their knowledge about the country and positioning themselves as cultural mediators while introducing cultural practices from their home countries or showing valuable information about Taiwan to travelers from different countries.

As we see "identity as discourse," we also see "discourse as identity." In the dialogical process of subject positioning and social interaction, TikTok users make use of TikTok's multiple affordances for meaning making, thus appropriating a given discourse practice, shaping the discourse genre of *tiktoking* and the subgenre of *tiktoking for language learning*. Users' multifarious choices hint at ways of performing the discourse practice of tiktoking with varying interaction with others. Upon choosing what to tell and how (the purposeful choice of semiotic resources), concomitant portions of the TikTokers' and other interlocutors' identities emerge as part of the publication and interaction with an open audience. In other words, what they do and say through TikTok reveals portions of who TikTok producers and consumers are (or might be). An operational categorization here can be (1) *self-identity*, (2) *interactive identity*, and (3) *collective identity*, which helps to contextualize and analyze discourse performativity in shaping identity (Yus, 2016). In relation to self-identity, how you choose to present yourself (video image with self-concept, username), how you announce yourself to others (identity announcement), or how you are placed or seen by others (identity placement) may co-occur when posting a TikTok video. In relation to interactive identity, users negotiate within videos and with commenters the video content or derived content prompted by any aspect within video or external to the video itself but potentially close to the imaginary shared cognitive frame of all TikTok users. In relation to collective identity, discourse markers help indicate some sort of affiliation or membership to broader collectivities or communities.

In our study, we will try to connect self-, interactive, and collective identities of TikTokers to explicate the big and small discourses around the practice of tiktoking for language learning.

4 Methodology

This is a qualitative-interpretative study. It is a preliminary exploration of TikTok as a space for informal language learning and identity work. Hence, this exploratory study aims to open a new context of study and check further research possibilities. The study is inspired by features of ethnographic/autoethnographic research (Heigham & Sakui, 2009) and applies content and thematic analysis (Saldaña, 2015). The methodological approach is explained below in (1) TikTok as the context of study, (2) our role as researchers, (3) the fieldwork, data instruments, and final corpus of data – implementing online data collection techniques (Androutsopoulos, 2013) – (4) the analysis and validity of data (see the eight steps in 4.4), and (5) the ethical standards of the study. Our goal is to simulate TikTok users when accessing hashtags for language learning to give plausible, close-to-reality answers to the proposed RQs.

4.1 Context: TikTok Hashtags

TikTok is our context of study, and three popular hashtags represent our field in the online observation. The inclusion/exclusion criteria were that hashtags had to (1) refer to language learning, (2) be identical or similar to one another, and (3) feature a minimum of 10 million views. After an initial exploration in September 2020, we agreed that the most relevant hashtags for our ethnographic approach to TikTok were (1) Chinese: #learnchinese, 109.7 million views, (2) Italian: #learnitalian, 14.2 million views, and (3) Russian: #learnrussian, 10.5 million views.

4.2 Role of Researchers

We like to think of ourselves as *scavengers of the digital wilds*. We try to search for and collect online oddities, normally in the form of linguistic practices, which frequently receive little or no attention in research but which, we believe, are potential sources of inspiration for Applied Linguistics studies from several perspectives and for language learning.

On this occasion, given the prominence of TikTok as a social media for self and collective expression during confined periods, producing an exploratory study on how TikTok promotes language learning and related aspects like identity seemed relevant. Such a study can be taken up by other scholars to further research and conceptualize (or discard) micro vlogging as a language learning practice.

In this study, we conducted a participant observation with an emic approach. We used TikTok in a way potential TikTok users would, adopting the consumer's point of view. In other words, inserting ourselves into this learning situation helped us to approach the possible experience language learners encounter while using TikTok. It meant that we imagined ourselves and acted as TikTok users who would search for hashtags with the following formulation #learn*[language]*.

Each author-researcher chose an unfamiliar language. Author 1 (competent in Italian) followed the hashtag #learnrussian, author 2 (competent in Russian) followed #learnchinese, and author 3 (competent in Chinese) followed #learnitalian. All three authors share equivalent competence in English and Spanish. The researchers' linguistic repertoire is meaningful for triangulation and internal validation (see Section 4.4) because after the observation, each author-researcher could contrast their experience with another author-researcher competent in the target language.

Table 5.1. Corpus of Data

	#learnchinese	#learnitalian	#learnrussian	Total
Diary (words)	3,724	3,041	3,966	10,731
Videos (watched and stored)	50	53	62	165
Comments (stored)	250	265	310	825
Screenshots	203	153	128	484

4.3 Data Collection and Corpus

The data were collected from 4th to 11th of September. Every researcher spent 30 minutes a day watching videos on TikTok. After each daily exposure to TikTok, the researchers made immediate fieldnotes on the videos with perceptions and learning experiences. The final corpus of data is summarized in Table 5.1.

While our exposure to TikTok was limited timewise, it allowed us to build a considerable corpus of data with an average ($\bar{x}$) of 3,577 words in the diaries, 55 videos per hashtag, 275 comments per video watched, and 161 screenshots taken during the observation. In what follows we explain how we built our corpus and analyzed the data we collected.

4.4 Phases and Analysis

1. Each researcher was exposed to a hashtag of a language new to them (first author, #learnrussian; second author, #learnchinese; third author, #learnitalian) during 7 days for approximately 30 minutes daily.
2. Before the observation, each researcher noted the start time of the exposure.
3. During the observation, each researcher recorded identification and numerical data for each video (number of the video observed; publication date; number of likes; comments and shares; author, title, and main content). At this time, each researcher also stored each available video and took screenshots of what seemed interesting, such as comments that reinforced or contradicted the content in the videos.
4. After the observation, each researcher noted the finish time of the exposure and immediately wrote a reflection entry in the diary with open-ended guiding questions such as "What did I watch that caught

my attention?" or "What did I learn of the Chinese/Italian/Russian language or culture?".

5. Once the field diary was completed, a researcher with competence in the language of the hashtag (first author, Italian; second author, Russian; third author, Chinese) checked the corresponding diary drafted by the other researcher. After this verification, each checking researcher built a preliminary categorization of each diary.
6. In a verification meeting, all three researchers collectively agreed on a common categorization for the three diaries.
7. With the agreed categorization, each initial researcher could return to their initial hashtag, diaries, videos, and comments to code and categorize data. For the purposes of this chapter, two categorization analyses were made in relation to (1) language-related content on the TikTok videos observed, and (2) specific instances of identification, especially linguistic and cultural identification, in videos or comments.
8. Upon this individual analysis, all researchers collectively compared the categorized videos for emerging, inter-hashtag themes, and to ensure the internal validity of the analyses via ongoing triangulation *inter pares*.

4.5 Ethics

While content on TikTok is publicly available, we understand potential concerns about the "sense of privacy" when actively participating in social media. In keeping with the principles of the Association of Internet Researchers (AoIR) (Markham & Buchanan, 2012), we strived to safeguard the immediate identification of TikTok users analyzed here via anonymization and photo editing.

5 Findings

The findings section is organized to answer the two RQs regarding the typology of language learning video content on TikTok and derived identity work. Section 5.1 includes a categorization of the collected TikTok videos, explaining predominant topics in relation to language learning. Section 5.2 describes TikTokers' identity negotiation, including how they self-present (Section 5.2.1), how they choose strategies to reach wider audiences leaving traces of cultural and linguistic identification (Section 5.2.2), or how the comments section affords interactional and collective cultural identity negotiation (Section 5.2.3).

5.1 Language Learning-related Content on TikTok Videos

Table 5.2 shows the main themes identified in the videos in our dataset.

First, a predominant number of videos are centered on linguistic features of the target language. Twelve videos introduced basic notions on writing, including the alphabet and specific uses of punctuation. This category is particularly evident in #learnrussian videos, as the Cyrillic script proves distant and unfamiliar to the English-speaking audience on TikTok. For instance, using a whiteboard, a TikToker contrasted letters with those in the Latin alphabet, distinguishing homographs and homophones in Russian and English, to emphasize the aesthetics of writing, while another TikToker showed original calligraphy of individual letters.

Second, the most frequent subcategory – containing more than 90 videos – is focused on lexical knowledge, including basic phrases for daily interaction (greetings, self-introduction), common objects (numbers, colors), and idiosyncratic expressions or proverbs. Besides, some distinct topics emerged in each hashtag, such as phrases for relationships and flirting in #learnchinese videos (how to say "can I kiss you"), gastronomy in #learnitalian videos (*place an order and pay the bill*, *pasta names explained*), and swear words in #learnrussian videos. Vocabulary suggesting cross-linguistic

Table 5.2. Topics Discussed in Language Learning Videos on TikTok

Video content	Topic	Examples	Videos (*n*)
Language-focused	Alphabet, punctuation	RusD1V5 *How to write and read the Russian alphabet*	127
	Vocabulary, collocations, expressions	ChiD2V1 *Numbers in Chinese*	
	Pronunciation, speech	ItaD3V4 *Quick tips to sound like an Italian*	
	Grammar	RusD7V7 *Verb conjugation in Russian*	
Culture-focused	Cultural practices and beliefs	ChiD7V3 *Social expectations for Chinese women*	28
Learner experience	TikToker as language learner	ItaD2V4 *A Chinese girl trying to pronounce rr*	10

influence, loanwords, or shared etymology was also a popular topic (*Words you didn't know came from Italy, English words popular in Russian*). It is noteworthy how TikTokers drew on multimodal aids (songs, subtitles, authentic settings, colors, emojis) to help viewers' comprehension. For example, a common way of presenting new vocabulary was direct translation. Through direct translation, the TikToker utters a word or phrase in the target language, which they follow with a close translation in English (or in the reverse order), accompanied by bilingual or multi-alphabetic transcriptions (original language, English translation, Romanized transliteration for Chinese and Russian).

Third, more than 20 videos were related to pronunciation and speech. This is a recurrent theme in #learnitalian videos, where video topics ranged from pronunciation tips (pronounce words as they are written; roll your "r"s; be loud), the humorous imitation of the Italian accent when speaking English, to the (mis)pronunciation of Italian loanwords (pizza, cheese, pasta) in American English or the comparison of Italian and Spanish accents. In terms of Chinese, TikTokers made fun with the tones and tongue twisters, while #learnrussian videos stressed the normative pronunciation (intonation, soft/hard sound) with special attention on homophones, with English as a comparison point most of the time. Finally, three #learnrussian videos featured grammatical rules as a main topic (grammatical gender, adjective agreement, verb conjugation).

In the dataset, nearly 40 videos went beyond micro-linguistic features to discuss culture-related topics or share language learning experience. This subset of videos is closely related to RQ2 on TikTokers' linguistic and cultural identification through their videos. Let us explore some common identities and practices.

5.2 Identity Negotiation Through TikTok Videos and Comments

TikTokers presented themselves in the videos and thus prompted opportunities for identity negotiation with the TikTok community, in relation to the target languages and cultures. Their self-presentation falls well under "self-identity," and the more culture-related videos foregrounded interactive and collective identity development and negotiation. We could locate interactive and collective accounts of identification through the strategies implemented by TikTokers to grab viewers' attention. Our findings in this section are: (1) self-identification and presentation, (2) strategies in language learning hashtags on TikTok, and (3) interactive and collective identification.

5.2.1 Self-identification and Presentation

An interesting finding is that self-identity often relates to the linguistic repertoire of the TikToker. Explicitly or implicitly, each TikToker referred to the target language in the hashtag as their L1 or L2 or to themselves as bilingual/bicultural speakers. All TikTokers are plurilingual and use different languages (at least, English as an intermediary language and the target language). However, they explicitly or implicitly identify as L1, L2 or bilingual speakers to signal expertise and advanced knowledge in the target language (L1 speakers), intercultural competence (bicultural speaker), or minimize potential criticism as developing L2 learners who show progress in their linguistic development and some expertise, too, in the language they learn.

1. L1 TikTokers

Across our dataset related to the hashtags in Chinese, Italian, and Russian, most TikTokers were L1 speakers who often presented themselves as teachers/experts of the target language and culture (see Figure 5.1).

In Figure 5.1, all three hashtags represent the prominent tendency of influencers who are L1 speakers and present themselves as teachers/experts in the language. The self-presentation of being an L1 expert speaker is negotiated through the intention of the video – to show some basic vocabulary with multimodal and multilingual aids for comprehension, such as writing in Chinese and Cyrillic characters, transliteration into Latin alphabets (Romanization), or translation into English as a lingua franca. Also, these plurilingual L1-TikTokers would normally repeat the utterances they teach, transcribe,

#learnchinese

#learnitalian

#learnrussian

Figure 5.1. Self-positioning of TikTokers as L1 Expert Speakers

transliterate, and translate. Repetition often occurs at slower and faster paces to facilitate comprehension for viewers.

2. L2 TikTokers

With 7 out of 53 videos, L2 speakers who talked about their experience of learning or showed and/or taught some bits of the target language were most frequent in #learnitalian. Fewer examples (2) were seen in #learnrussian and in #learnchinese (1). In this #learnchinese, an L2 speaker who taught how to curse in Chinese was heavily criticized in the comments for mispronunciation.

In #learnrussian, one of the videos included a dramatization of imaginary thoughts of a Russian L2 learner by @milena. Here the TikToker does not talk, only shows letter correspondences between the Latin and Cyrillic alphabets and the complexity of the Cyrillic alphabet with letters which have no clear correspondence to the Latin counterpart. She purposefully selected the background song (*Human* by Christina Perri) and orchestrated the overlapping of lyrics so that, at the end of her playful dramatization, she could mimic and sing along with the chorus of the song, "But I am only human," to signal the complexity of learning a new alphabet which leaves her "hand-gesturing" in awe (Figure 5.2).

The appropriation of the song's lyrics, the purposeful use of graphic affordances in TikTok video editing, and the playful dramatization enhanced by both multimodal resources produced a humorous video that tries to connect emotionally with other language learners worldwide (@milena deliberately chose only English hashtags as an access point to a global audience) who go through similar trans-alphabetic experiences.

One of the most viewed #learnitalian video showed a Chinese girl introducing herself with the utterance "Io mi chiamo Azzurra" [*My name is Azzurra*]. In Figure 5.3, she tries to pronounce her chosen Western name, mispronouncing the /r/ as /l/. After several unfruitful attempts forcing herself to pronounce the /r/ in Azzurra, she alters her name and provides alternative nicknames by producing the following deliberate translanguaged utterance (Li, 2018): "Va bene, mi chiamo Blu or just call me Bella" [*Alright, my name is Blue or just call me Bella*]. Note that *azzurra* and *blu* in Italian both mean "blue," and *bella* means "beautiful."

With mispronunciation, translanguaging, and providing three alternative names for her (Azzurra, Blu, Bella), the TikToker masters self-deprecating humor with problematic phonetic realizations such as the rolled "r" for Chinese/Asian people learning Italian as a foreign language, negotiating her identity as a language learner and ensuring potential interlocutors' attention

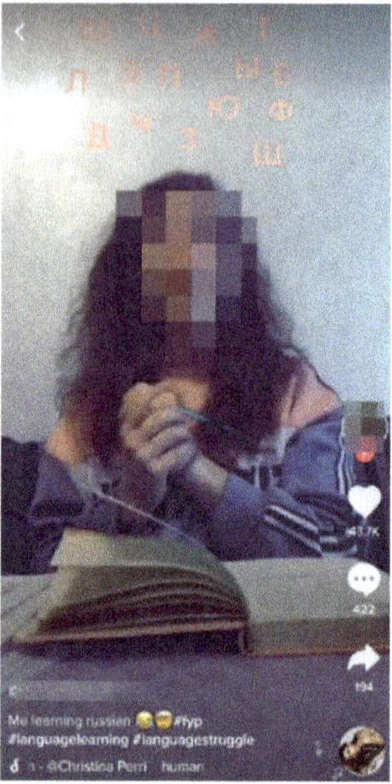

Figure 5.2. #learnrussian L2 TikToker

Figure 5.3. #learnitalian L2 TikToker

and comprehension: if potential interlocutors do not understand "Azzurra" in the first utterances, they will understand "Blu," and even if they do not make the direct semantic connection between a mispronounced Azzurra and Blu, they can simply call the TikToker "Bella," that is, beautiful.

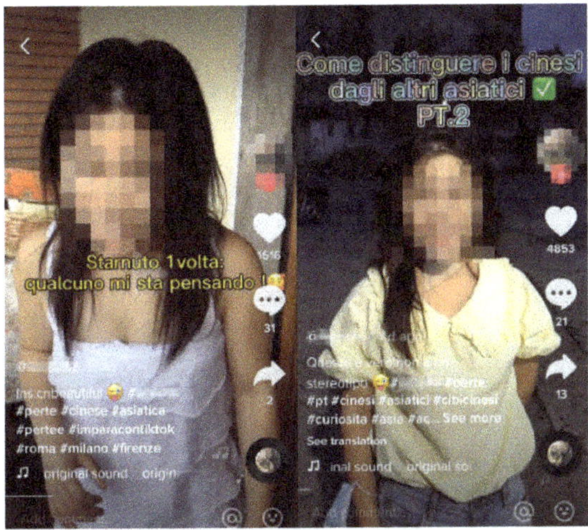

Figure 5.4. #learnitalian Videos of L2 Speakers

Through the hashtag, we accessed more of her videos sharing her experience living in Italy, as well as customs and traditions of her home country. In those videos, she presented herself as an expert in Chinese culture and shared her knowledge with her Italian followers. In Figure 5.4, she explained superstitions associated with sneezing in China (left) and showed how to distinguish Chinese from other Asians as the former prefer hot water (right). We can see that the other hashtags she uses are written in Italian, such as #perte, #cinese, #asiatici, and are clearly directed at Italian-speaking viewers interested in videos of people from China living in Italy, learning Italian, and experiencing the Italian culture. With these hashtags, the TikToker also positions herself according to her prescribed identity as a foreigner or migrant. Similar to the study on Taiwanese YouTubers (Chang & Chang, 2019), Azzurra negotiated her identity as a foreigner and L2 speaker from a position of power – of expertise in source culture traditions and knowledge of Italian as a target language.

3. Bilingual TikTokers

TikTokers who self-identified as bilinguals were found only in *#learnrussian* videos, with 10 out of 62 videos (9 of which were made by TikToker @Alina). These videos were made by heritage Russian speakers in the US and focused on experiences growing up in a Russian-speaking family, and on Russian traditions, culture, and language in contrast with American English.

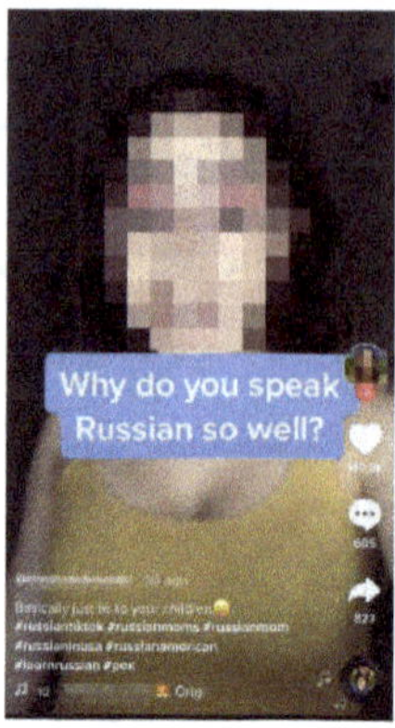

Figure 5.5. Russian–English Bilinguals in the US

In the example in Figure 5.5, @Alina comically describes her personal experience of growing up as a bilingual speaker in the US while impersonating her mother lying to her about not speaking English. She quickly switches from English to Russian and vice versa, creating a comical effect. Apart from teaching Russian, @Alina presents herself as a cultural broker, showing her US viewers glimpses of her upbringing as an ethnic minority and as a bilingual in the US. Like the previous TikToker (Figures 5.3 and 5.4), she negotiates her prescribed identity of a minority from a position of power of her expertise as a cultural broker between two cultural systems (US-North American, Russian) and as a TikTok "teacher" or rather "presenter/commentator" of the Russian language.

5.2.2 Strategies as Influencers on TikTok

Once we were able to explore how TikTokers self-identified, we moved on to their strategies to capture viewers' attention. These strategies provided us with an access point to more interactional and collective identities.

Most videos are selfie-like video commentary in our video dataset from the three hashtags. TikTokers often record themselves with the selfie option on their phones and later edit the video with TikTok and/or other video-editing options. Following this selfie approach, content selection was prominent in how they tried to catch viewers' attention. We identified three main strategies: (1) classroom simulation, (2) flirting and sexualization, and (3) comedy content.

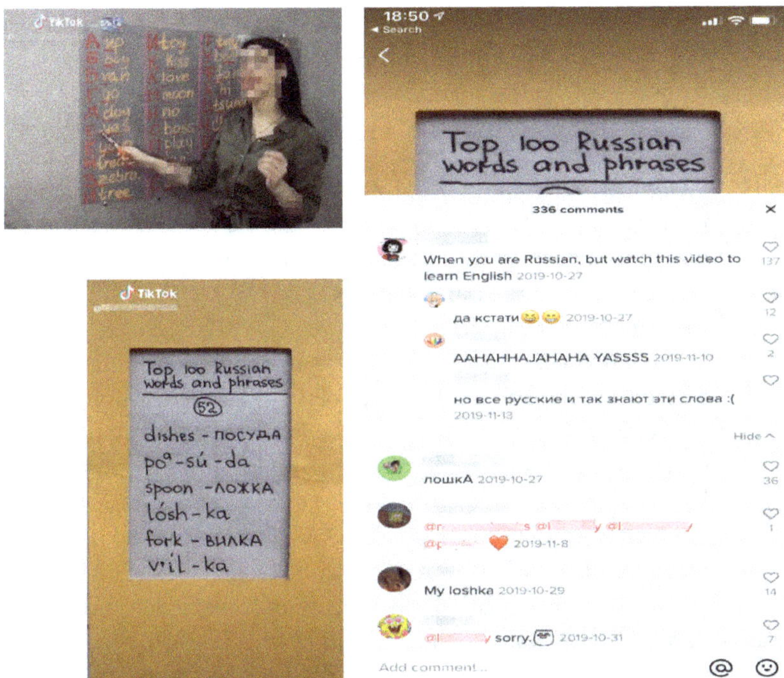

Figure 5.6. TikTokers in #learnrussian Simulating a Physical Classroom Session (Top) and a One-to-One Session with Handwritten Notes (Bottom)

1. *Classroom simulation.* Some TikTokers, especially in #learnrussian, identified as language teachers, which manifested in the disposition and arrangement of videos. These TikTokers tried to replicate a classroom setting with whiteboards or a typical one-on-one language teaching explanation aided by notes. These videos represent that more formal language learning opportunities are available on TikTok in the form of *learning pills* or formalized micro-teaching sessions. In Figure 5.6, we see instances of this classroom simulation in two formats: whiteboard disposition and a one-on-one lesson with a notebook. Here the material and multimodal conditions of TikTok are not appropriated (for instance, captioning and other video-editing techniques), instead it is used as a platform to engage with audiences.
2. *Flirting and sexualization.* Drenten et al. (2020) found that sexualization is common among female influencers on Instagram for

marketing and widespread attention. Similarly, on TikTok hashtags #learnrussian and #learnchinese, female TikTokers often drew on flirting vocabulary, revealing clothes, or beautifying filters ("Can I kiss you" in #learnchinese or "I am yours" in #learnrussian). Figure 5.1 exemplifies flirting and sexualization as a strategy for influencer identification, where the TikToker teaches how to say "You are pretty" in Chinese. Such TikTokers also present themselves as language teachers, so they rely on both sources (knowledge and a flirtatious demeanor) to attract more viewers.

3. *Comedy content.* Prominent in most videos was comedy content. TikTokers for language learning aspire to entertain while teaching a language, in similar ways to generic influencers (Gross & Wangenheim, 2018). Including comedic language and content through several strategies allows TikTok users to lower the learning anxiety level and construe TikTok as a space to have fun while accompanying their language learning efforts. As an example, we can use the video discussed in the previous section (Figure 5.5). @Alina gives a comedic impersonation of a mother and a daughter in a Russian-heritage household in the US. Mother and daughter negotiated the home language, either Russian or English. The dramatization ended up with Alina's statement in a written comment that heritage languages should be preserved.
4. Additional comedic instances included using stereotypical cultural comparisons (dramatization of Italians' hand gestures, obsession with certain gastronomic habits in Italy, stereotypical comments and behaviors received by students of Russian ancestry in US classrooms), learning situations (self-deprecating videos complaining about or stating the complexity of languages or comparing the linguistic diasystems, funny moments in the language classroom in #learnrussian), or discussion of learners' mistakes (mispronunciation in #learnchinese).

Next, we will discuss these strategies in connection with opportunities for developing interactive and collective linguistic and cultural identities.

5.2.3 Interactive and Collective Cultural Identification

We identified instances of identity negotiation through interactions with the followers in the comment section and how TikTok allowed for collective identification in terms of membership or allegiance to ethnic, national, linguistic, or cultural groupings.

Some of the L1, L2, and bilingual TikTokers created content around cultural traditions, customs, or rituals of their target language. The TikTokers presented themselves as experts in the target culture, playing the role of cultural brokers or mediators. Nevertheless, sometimes such cultural interpretations led to cultural generalizations and the reinforcement of stereotypes, which even if used humorously, provide a restrictive vision of the target culture.

In #learnchinese videos, there were only two videos tagged as overgeneralizations. In the example presented in Figure 5.7, the TikToker relates her personal experience of being raised as a girl in China; however, she presents with the overgeneralizing phrase "As a girl growing up in China, your Chinese mom be like...." She describes what behaviors, norms, and ideas a stereotypical Chinese mother embodies towards girls (no interaction with boys in school, marrying soon after university). She also wears a traditional Chinese dress and earrings, underlining her collective identification as a native Chinese speaker and a cultural expert. Also, similar to the comedic content mentioned above, it is possible that the cultural overgeneralization and presentation are part of the marketing strategy to attract an audience.

Figure 5.7. #learnchinese Collective and Interactional Identification

Interestingly, in the comments section (Figure 5.7), the video was not perceived as a cultural generalization but as a space to discuss similarities of female upbringing in different countries. Even though the commenters did not completely agree with this cultural generalization being attributed only to Chinese mothers ("I'm not Chinese tho"), they feel encouraged to share their individual experiences of the similar gender-centered restrictions and expectations. In the excerpt, the TikToker validates all comments without focusing on the contradictions spotted in the comments; hence, she continues negotiating her interactive identity as an expert in Chinese culture together with her gender identity.

In #learnitalian videos, a popular trend was the exaggerated performance of Italian stereotypes to make funny videos. An example is produced by the couple of Italian TikTokers shown in Figure 5.8.

In Figure 5.8 (left), Italian TikTokers present three steps on being Italian: (1) dress well, (2) use your hands, and (3) be loud. Similar to the #learnchinese example, their national collective identification as Italians is clearly pronounced with the use of Italian flags and the topic of the video. This cultural generalization is also discussed in the comments, in which commenters

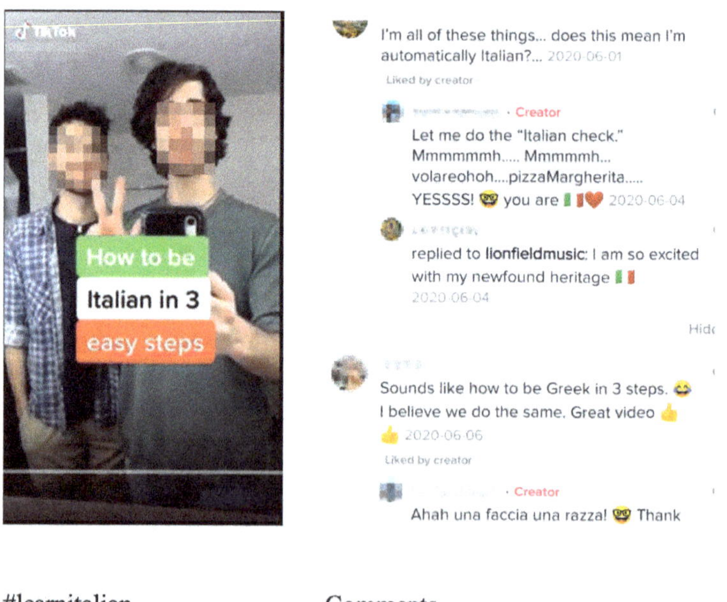

Figure 5.8. #learnitalian Collective and Interactive Identification

do not always agree with the generalization but do not challenge the expertise of the TikTokers in any way. In the first comment in Figure 5.8, the commenter ironically asks the TikTokers whether he is automatically Italian as he is all those things mentioned in the video, which challenges the cultural overgeneralization. The TikTokers respond with a funny comment that of course he is Italian. In this case, "being Italian" is presented as something desirable and something other people want to identify with. The discourse in the comments seems part of the video's entertainment and reiterates its entertaining purpose. Interactively these TikTokers present themselves as experts on the Italian culture as well as entertainers.

In #learnrussian videos, collective identification was also frequently presented by cultural generalizations. The TikToker who identifies as a Russian teacher makes a comparison between how Russians count numbers and how Americans count numbers on the palm of their hand (Figure 5.9).

In this comparison, she identifies herself collectively with Russian nation using the hashtag #Russian girl. She also presents herself as an expert in both US and Russian cultures. However, her audience disagree with her information. In the first comment in Figure 5.9 (left), we can see how a user with Russian-American heritage does not count in either way presented in

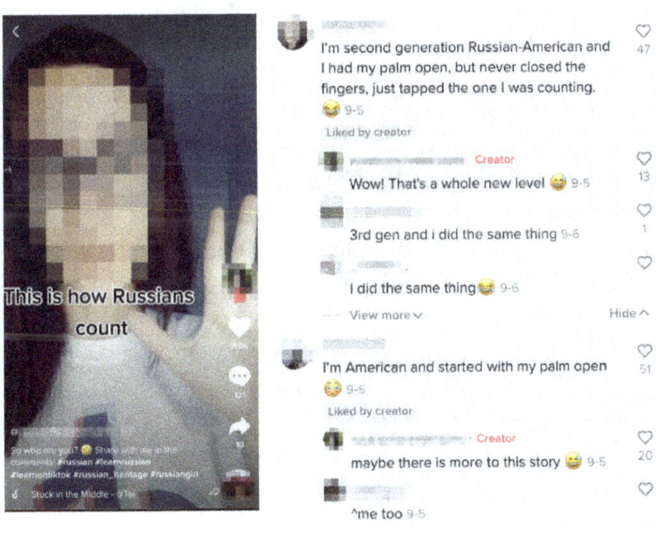

#learnrussian Comments

Figure 5.9. #learnrussian Collective and Interactional Identification

the video, not fitting into the duality of the comparison just between Russians and Americans. In the second comment, users from the US also debunk the counting system proposed by the TikToker, which she accepts, responding to the comment, "Maybe there is more to this story." Here her identity as an expert in Russian culture is being challenged in the comments, while the discourse of cultural generalization is partially debunked.

The common denominator here is for the TikTokers to use signs of collective identification with the country of their target language in the form of flags, clothes, and cultural generalizations. Cultural generalizations are often challenged in the comments, as the videos about cultural differences seem to encourage other users to talk and discuss their firsthand experiences, which frequently are contradictory to the TikTokers' generalizations.

6 Discussion and Conclusion

Through our shared exploration on TikTok, we have navigated three linguistic and culturally diverse hashtags: #learnchinese, #learnitalian, and #learnrussian. Overall, TikTok proved to be an active medium and platform for conveying language learning-related content in relation to multiple domains: (1) linguistic features (alphabet, vocabulary, pronunciation, grammar), (2) cultural practices and beliefs (customs, traditions), and (3) learner experiences (difficulties, humorous interpretation) (RQ1). More than half of the videos were focused on lexical and phraseological content, constituting by far the most frequent category. The selection of topics varied, and many seemed to be directed at attracting viewers' attention (flirting, cursing) or displayed cultural generalizations (pasta, vodka). Learner experiences also stood out as a particular category, where some TikTokers adopted a self-deprecating position (Lee, 2013) and downplayed their own sophisticated translanguaging capabilities (Figure 5.3).

Consistent with the platform positioning, English was the main language for communication and point of comparison, and many TikTokers provided cross-linguistic and cultural reflections, and animated such discussions in the comments (Figures 5.7 and 5.8). Prolific user-generated and authentic language content exemplifies the view of *folk linguistics* (Jaworski et al., 2004). In other words, lay people participate in metalinguistic talk, engaging in the representation and evaluation of language. Metalanguage on TikTok was not always accurate, nor linguistically informed (Figure 5.9), but these videos provide a fertile ground for extramural participation and informal learning through discussion of real-world language uses. That participation allowed us to discover contextual and textual practices that challenge a traditional, restrictive notion of multilingualism that construes languages as concrete, segmented, and separate entities even when in contact (see Canagarajah, 2011, Kelly-Holmes, 2019, or Li, 2018 for more dynamic accounts on multilingualism and related concepts). The findings on TikTok for language learning supersede such a restricted view on multilingualism by highlighting fluid dynamics of L1/L2 interaction and translingual practices.

Code meshing as the "materialization of translanguaging in texts" (Canagarajah, 2011, p. 403) was commonplace in all TikTok videos and comment sections, signifying the nature of digitally mediated communication that (1) blurs distinctions between L1 and L2 languages and (2) promotes spaces prone to mediating and intercultural skills. For example, as we accessed hashtags with the English formulation #learn[*language*], the intermediate lingua franca was mostly English. However, all TikTokers mediated across different languages and varieties with verbal (their utterance, superimposed text on videos such as captions or explanations, transliterations, translations), paralinguistic (emoticons), and non-verbal resources (mimicking, hand gestures, gazes) to configure a coherent polysemiotic assemblage (Canagarajah, 2018; Li, 2018). Some videos and/or comments included other linguistic systems as points of comparison because they were part of the proximate environment and serve a purpose to display distinction and genuineness (Italian versus Spanish or Russian versus Cyrillic). Translingual practices and the multimodal orchestration in most TikTok videos reinforce the idea that to educate in translanguaging, understood as "the general communicative competence of multilinguals" (Canagarajah, 2011, p. 403), educators ought to shy away from a "lingual bias" (Block, 2014, p. 54) that treats words as the primary analytical focus deserving attention in communication. In fact, many videos were carefully designed with multimodal aids and dynamic configurations (changing color, moving subtitles), revealing a surprising level of *multimodal literacies* (Eisenlauer, 2020) by TikTokers from the younger generation. The most evident drawback for language learning we discovered was probably the video's length, which limited in-depth description and contextualization of the content, thus complicating learners' comprehension or memorization – TikTok normally affords 60-second videos although it is now experimenting with videos up to 3 minutes.

On TikTok as a space where translingual practice flourished through language learning hashtags, we identified three main identities TikTokers associated with: L1 speakers, L2 speakers, or bilingual speakers (RQ2). Regardless of their identities explicitly mentioned or implicitly ascribed, all TikTokers showed plurilingual, transcultural and fluid abilities to move across languages and varieties (Pennycook, 2007). TikTokers modulated and negotiated their identities through their linguistic and semiotic choices, purposes, and contexts (Higgins, 2011). The common denominator among L1, L2, and bilingual TikTokers has been interlinguistic/intercultural mediation and influencer strategies for attracting viewers.

Interlinguistic/intercultural mediation meant that almost every TikToker put themselves into the position of the expert of some cultural reality relatively unknown to viewers. The most frequent group of TikTokers, L1 speakers with a multilingual repertoire, presented themselves as experts of the culture/language they were raised in; meanwhile, L2 speakers often showed the reality of being a foreigner in the target country in a similar fashion to L2 YouTubers in Taiwan (Chang & Chang, 2019). The last group were bilingual/bicultural individuals of heritage homes who shared the reality of being raised as an ethnic/linguistic minority. Such mediation was more comedic and less linguistically intensive, and a less formalized way of approaching cultural distance than that found in fan translation contexts (Shafirova et al., 2020b; Vazquez-Calvo et al., 2019).

Video categorization of popular TikTokers may be relevant for language educators as it indicates what language learners seek outside the classroom. Cultural aspects of language learning are among the most popular themes. Almost every TikToker in the dataset described their cultural experiences of upbringing or living in a territory/community where the L2 in hashtags is used. Through those experiences as L1, L2, or bilingual speakers, they offer a transcultural account for individuals online. TikTokers' stories and struggles seem to be of interest to language learners, and such experiences are rarely presented in traditional language curricula and materials, as many aspects in relation to emotivity or identity.

Nevertheless, TikTokers also presented some cultural generalizations. Mostly based on individual experiences or traits, these generalizations referred to social segments in the home context/country (Chinese mothers are controlling – Figure 5.7), or to a unitary set of population (every Italian is loud – Figure 5.8). Such generalizations presented the target culture in connection to the nation-state rather than fluid countries/territories. Culture was frequently presented as univocal rather than exploring minority, ethnic, gender, or class intersectionalities. In other words, culture was unified to work as a marketing strategy, simplified and presented in headlines, hashtags, and emojis. Such a compartmented view of culture was part of the jocosity of videos. However, these videos incited responses from TikTok viewers, who occasionally opposed the monotonal perspective. TikTokers also supported alternative views and encouraged people to share their experiences. Such an amicable disposition created a space of trust and afforded intercultural identity negotiation. Hence it would be interesting to explore the possibility of the use of such short videos in the classroom to promote intercultural and metalinguistic discussion.

The intercultural mediation on TikTok may serve as an inspiring point of departure for more complex mediating activities where language learners in formal education engage in the real practice of mediating between their cultures/languages and the target culture/language with a real TikTok audience in mind (Council of Europe, 2020).

Among the multiple influencer strategies, let us stress one that might be relevant for language educators: L2 TikTokers' appropriation of comedic content. TikTokers frequently used self-deprecating humor while sharing the difficulty of learning a foreign language, such as trans-alphabetic learning (Figure 5.2) or complex phonetic realizations, /r/ (Figure 5.3). These TikTokers negotiated their identities as learners and foreigners, which attracted other language learners in similar situations. The collective identification as learners who share their emotions in language learning and point at difficult linguistic features or aspects in relation to the language system and L2 literacy (for instance, acquiring trans-alphabetic literacy) might be an indicator of TikTok being a space not only for language learning but for safe, emotional support for L2 learners' practice. Sharing emotions and struggles in the language-learning process seldom forms part of language curricula, though it is relevant in the language learning for the digital wilds.

Our contribution pushes the boundaries of past research in social media for language learning and identity development, since it considers a novel discourse practice: tiktoking with brief, humorous and multimodally rich videos and direct response messages. Tiktoking might not be as prone to accuracy as other practices in the digital wilds such as fanfiction or fan translation, and so is to be used with caution by beginners. The practice of tiktoking foregrounds a fecund field of socialization opportunities to (1) lower the affective filter of L2 learning (Krashen, 1982), (2) develop an enhanced intercultural identity (by analyzing and exploring stereotyping and cultural generalizations through humor or challenging biased preconceptions about the target language and culture), and (3) practice and develop multimodal and translingual literacy practices.

While our exposure to TikTok was limited, we could depict a panoramic snapshot of language learning through the social sharing of micro video. The dataset still bears potential to focus on related topics such as specific linguistic ideologies and language awareness in connection with the different linguistic domains explored in videos. For example, a further exploration of data may lead to analyses of folk linguistic perceptions around linguistic complexity, language distance, linguistic purism, or pan-cultural feelings around linguistic features. Future directions also include focusing on the multimodal orchestration of TikTok videos and plausible ties with L2/plurilingual identification, as with prior research on Flickr-mediated language learning (Lee, 2013). More broadly, future studies may want to theorize how informal language learning changes as textualization and meaning-making practices decenter traditional conceptions of writing/language, and whether and how formal language education settings resist or appropriate such changes. Despite our limitations and the numerous avenues yet unexplored with TikTok and analogous social media, the fact that multimodally intensive social media are influencing language learning continues to be a major topic in CALL and language learning in the digital wilds (Sauro & Zourou, 2019).

Acknowledgments

The study was partly supported by the publicly funded research project *ForVid: Video as a language learning format in and outside the classroom* (RT2018-100790-B-100; 2019–2021), "Research Challenges" R+D+i Projects, Ministry of Science and Innovation, Spain. Liudmila Shafirova received financial support from National Funds through FCT – Fundação para a Ciência e a Tecnologia, I.P., under the project UIDB/00194/2020 (CIDTFF) and of the postdoctoral research grant with the reference 9651/BIPD/CIDTFF/2021, Portugal. Leticia-Tian Zhang also received support for this study from the Fundamental Research Funds for the Central Universities (2020QD036), China.

References

Androutsopoulos, J. (2013). Online data collection. In C. Mallinson, B. Childs, & G. Van-Kerk (Eds.), *Data collection in sociolinguistics* (pp. 236–250). Routledge.

Bakhtin, M. (1986). *Speech genres and other late essays*. University of Texas.

Benson, P. (2011). Language learning and teaching beyond the classroom: An introduction to the field. In P. Benson & H. Reinders (Eds.), *Beyond the language classroom* (pp. 7–17). Palgrave Macmillan.

Black, R. W. (2006). Language, culture, and identity in online fanfiction. *E-Learning and Digital Media*, *3*(2), 170–184. https://doi.org/10.2304/elea.2006.3.2.170

Block, D. (2014). Moving beyond "lingualism": Multilingual embodiment and multimodality in SLA. In S. May (Ed.), *The multilingual turn: Implications for SLA, TESOL, and bilingual education* (pp. 54–77). Routledge.

Bucholtz, M., & Hall, K. (2005). Identity and interaction: A sociocultural linguistic approach. *Discourse Studies*, *7*(4–5), 585–614. https://doi.org/10.1177/1461445605054407

Canagarajah, S. (2011). Codemeshing in academic writing: Identifying teachable strategies of translanguaging. *Modern Language Journal*, *95*(3), 401–417. https://doi.org/10.1111/j.1540-4781.2011.01207.x

Canagarajah, S. (2018). Translingual practice as spatial repertoires: Expanding the paradigm beyond structuralist orientations. *Applied Linguistics*, *39*(1), 31–54. https://doi.org/10.1093/applin/amx041

Chang, Y. C., & Chang, Y. J. (2019). Identity negotiation in the third space: An analysis of YouTube channels hosted by expatriates in Taiwan. *Language and Intercultural Communication*, *19*(1), 77–92. https://doi.org/10.1080/14708477.2018.1450878

Chik, A., & Benson, P. (2020). Commentary: Digital language and learning in the time of coronavirus. *Linguistics and Education*, 100873. https://doi.org/10.1016/j.linged.2020.100873

Consalvo, M. (2017). When paratexts become texts: De-centering the game-as-text. *Critical Studies in Media Communication*, *34*(2), 177–183. https://doi.org/10.1080/15295036.2017.1304648

Council of Europe. (2020). *Common European Framework of Reference for Languages: Learning, teaching, assessment – Companion volume*. Council of Europe Publishing. www.coe.int/lang-cefr

Drenten, J., Gurrieri, L., & Tyler, M. (2020). Sexualized labour in digital culture: Instagram influencers, porn chic and the monetization of attention. *Gender, Work & Organization*, *27*(1), 41–66. https://doi.org/10.1111/gwao.12354

Eisenlauer, V. (2020). The EFL-YouTube remix: Empowering multimodal and computational literacies for EFL purposes. *Journal of Visual Literacy*, *0*(0), 1–18. https://doi.org/10.1080/1051144X.2020.1826220

Gee, J. P. (1999). *An introduction to discourse analysis*. Routledge.

Gross, J., & Wangenheim, F. V. (2018). The big four of influencer marketing. A typology of influencers. *Marketing Review St. Gallen*, *2*, 30–38.

Heigham, J., & Sakui, K. (2009). Ethnography. In J. Heigham & R. A. Croker (Eds.), *Qualitative research in applied linguistics: A practical introduction* (pp. 91–111). Palgrave Macmillan.

Higgins, C. (2011). *Identity formation in globalized contexts: Language learning in the new millennium*. Mouton de Gruyter.

Isbell, D. R. (2018). Online informal language learning: Insights from a Korean learning community. *Language Learning & Technology*, *22*(3), 82–102. https://doi.org/10125/44658

Ivanič, R. (2006). Language, learning and identification. In R. Kiely, G. Clibbon, P. Rea-Dickens, & H. Woodfield (Eds.), *Language, culture and identity in applied linguistics* (pp. 7–29). Equinox.

Jaworski, A., Coupland, N., & Galasinski, D. (Eds.) (2004). *Metalanguage: Social and ideological perspectives*. Mouton de Gruyter. https://doi.org/10.1515/9783110907377

Kaye, D. B. V., Chen, X., & Zeng, J. (2020). The co-evolution of two Chinese mobile short video apps: Parallel platformization of Douyin and TikTok. *Mobile Media & Communication*. https://doi.org/10.1177/2050157920952120

Kelly-Holmes, H. (2019). Multilingualism and technology: A review of developments in digital communication from monolingualism to idiolingualism. *Annual Review of Applied Linguistics*, *39*(December), 24–39. https://doi.org/10.1017/S0267190519000102

Krashen, S. D. (1982). *Principles and practice in second language acquisition*. Pergamon.

Lee, C. (2013). "My English is so poor ... so I take photos." Metalinguistic discourses about English on FlickR. In T. Deborah & A. M. Trester (Eds.), *Discourse 2.0: Language and new media* (pp. 73–84). Georgetown University Press.

Li, W. (2018). Translanguaging as a practical theory of language. *Applied Linguistics*, *39*(1). https://doi.org/10.1093/applin/amx039

Markham, A., & Buchanan, E. (2012). *Ethical decision-making and Internet research: Recommendations from the AoIR ethics working committee (version 2.0)*. Retrieved from http://aoir.org/reports/ethics2.pdf

Pennycook, A. (2007). *Global Englishes and transcultural flows*. Routledge.

Reinhardt, J. (2019a). *Gameful second and foreign language teaching and learning: Theory, research, and practice*. Palgrave Macmillan.

Reinhardt, J. (2019b). Social media in second and foreign language teaching and learning: Blogs, wikis, and social networking. *Language Teaching*, *52*(01), 1–39. https://doi.org/10.1017/S0261444818000356

Reinhardt, J. (2020). Metaphors for social media-enhanced foreign language teaching and learning. *Foreign Language Annals*, (May), 234–242. https://doi.org/10.1111/flan.12462

Saldaña, J. (2015). *The coding manual for qualitative researchers*. Sage.

Sauro, S., & Zourou, K. (2019). What are the digital wilds? *Language Learning & Technology*, *23*(1), 1–7. https://doi.org/10125/44666

Schreiber, B. R. (2015). "I am what I am": Multilingual identity and digital translanguaging. *Language Learning & Technology*, *19*(3), 69–87.

Shafirova, L., Cassany, D., & Bach, C. (2020a). From "newbie" to professional: Identity building and literacies in an online affinity space. *Learning, Culture and Social Interaction*, *24*(February 2019), 100370. https://doi.org/10.1016/j.lcsi.2019.100370

Shafirova, L., Cassany, D., & Bach, C. (2020b). Transcultural literacies in online collaboration: A case study of fanfiction translation from Russian into English.

Language and Intercultural Communication, *20*(6), 531–545. https://doi.org/10.1080/14708477.2020.1812621

Sockett, G. (2014). *The online informal learning of English*. Palgrave.

Song, R. (2019). "This may create a zero-lingual state": Critical examination of language ideologies in an English learning blog. *CALICO Journal*, *36*(1), 59–76. https://doi.org/10.1558/cj.35113

Sundqvist, P. (2019). COTS games in the digital wild and L2 learner vocabulary. *Language Learning & Technology*, *23*(1), 87–113.

Sylvén, L. K., & Sundqvist, P. (2012). Gaming as extramural English L2 learning and L2 proficiency among young learners. *ReCALL*, *24*, 302–321. https://doi.org/10.1017/s095834401200016x

Thorne, S. L., Sauro, S., & Smith, B. (2015). Technologies, identities, and expressive activity. *Annual Review of Applied Linguistics*, *35*, 215–233. https://doi.org/10.1017/S0267190514000257

Vazquez-Calvo, B. (2018). The online ecology of literacy and language practices of a gamer. *Educational Technology & Society*, *21*(3), 199–212. https://hdl.handle.net/10630/22509

Vazquez-Calvo, B. (2020). Guerrilla fan translation, language learning, and metalinguistic discussion in a Catalan-speaking community of gamers. *ReCALL*, 1–18. https://doi.org/10.1017/S095834402000021X

Vazquez-Calvo, B., Elf, N., & Gewerc, A. (2020). Catalan teenagers' identity, literacy and language practices on YouTube. In M. Freiermuth & N. Zarrinabadi (Eds.), *Technology and the psychology of second language learners and users* (pp. 251–278). Springer International Publishing. https://doi.org/10.1007/978-3-030-34212-8_10

Vazquez-Calvo, B., García-Roca, A., & López-Báez, C. (2020). Domesticar la "selva digital": el fanfiction a examen a través de la mirada de una fanfictioner. *Edmetic*, *9*(1), 21–51. https://doi.org/10.21071/edmetic.v9i1.12239

Vazquez-Calvo, B., Zhang, L. T., Pascual, M., & Cassany, D. (2019). Fan translation of games, anime and fanfiction. *Language Learning & Technology*, *23*(1), 49–71. https://doi.org/10125/44672

Yus, F. (2016). Discourse, contextualization and identity shaping the case of social networking sites and virtual worlds. In M. Carrió-Pastor (Ed.), *Technology implementation in second language teaching and translation studies* (pp. 71–88). Springer. https://doi.org/10.1007/978-981-10-0572-5_5

Yus, F. (2018). Identity-related issues in meme communication. *Internet Pragmatics*, *1*(1), 113–133. https://doi.org/10.1075/ip.00006.yus

Zhang, L. T., & Cassany, D. (2019a). "Is it always so fast?": Chinese perceptions of Spanish through danmu video comments. *Spanish in Context*, *16*(2), 217–242. https://doi.org/10.1075/sic.00035.zha

Zhang, L. T., & Cassany, D. (2019b). The "danmu" phenomenon and media participation: Intercultural understanding and language learning through "The Ministry of Time." *Comunicar*, *27*(58). https://doi.org/10.3916/C58-2019-02

About the Authors

Boris Vazquez-Calvo is an assistant professor at the Department of Language Education at the School of Education at the University of Málaga, Spain, where he teaches foreign language education to pre-service teachers of English. His research interests include formal and informal language learning, technology-mediated language learning, digital discourse and new literacies, and fandom communities. His most recent publications appear in *CALL*, *ReCALL*, *Language Learning & Technology*, and *Educational Technology & Society*.

Liudmila Shafirova is a postdoctoral researcher at the research center CI-DTFF, University of Aveiro, Portugal. Her research interests include informal language learning (Russian, English), multilingual computer-mediated interactions, and multiliteracies. Her recent publications on informal language learning appear in journals such as *Language Learning & Technology*, *Learning, Culture and Social Interaction*, and *Language and Intercultural Communication*.

Leticia-Tian Zhang is a lecturer at the Department of Hispanic and Portuguese Studies at Beijing Foreign Studies University, China, where she teaches Spanish. She is interested in digital discourse, especially novel genres such as *danmu* commenting and vlogging, and language learning in the fandom. Her recent publications appear in journals including *Discourse Studies*, *Multilingua*, and *Comunicar*.

6 Multilingualism in a Box? Identity in Non-CMC CALL

Judith Buendgens-Kosten

1 Introduction

Imagine two learners studying English as a foreign language. A teacher instructs both of them to practice English using a specific app. Student A quickly registers for the app, entering their age, gender, and native language. Student B hesitates for a moment when they realize that "native language" is a drop-down menu and only accepts a single response. Student A is pleasantly surprised that the app contains not only his L1 but also French, which he is studying at school. Student B wonders why none of the languages spoken in their family is part of the app. When reading a text in the app about the benefits of multilingualism for work, academic study, travel, and tourism, Student A is reminded of his recent vacation, while Student B finds their daily experience of living with and through several languages not reflected in the text.

One (fictional) app, two completely different sets of experiences in using it. In this chapter, I will examine how the design of language learning apps can harmonize with or conflict with self-concept and relevant self-guides of learners, or can create a space in which learners can vividly imagine their ideal self, or even extend what, to them, constitutes their ideal self. I do this by looking at a range of multilingual language learning apps, describing their designs and discussing potential effects these might have on diverse users.

1.1 Identity and Language Learning

This chapter uses identity in the sense of "the way a person understands his or her relationship to the world, how that relationship is constructed across time and space, and how the person understands possibilities for the future" (Norton, 2013, p. 4), and as such as multifaceted, changeable, and actively co-created. Identity is relevant for the (physical or metaphorical) classroom for a range of utilitarian reasons (cf., e.g., investment [Norton, 2013], or motivation [Dörnyei & Ushioda, 2010]), but also for ethical reasons: creating a setting for learning in which students feel seen and accepted contributes not only to language learning but also to the wellbeing of the individual student. Equally, language learning material that actively contributes to marginalization and other exclusionary processes has negative effects beyond the realm of language learning and teaching.

The discussion of identity in this chapter uses the Multilingual Computer-Assisted Language Learning (MCALL; Buendgens-Kosten & Elsner, 2018) lens: a perspective on CALL that tries to avoid the monolingual problem of CALL (Buendgens-Kosten, 2020a) by "actively and consciously work[s](ing) on the interstices of multilingualism and CALL" (Buendgens-Kosten & Elsner, 2018, p. xvii). It takes a plurilingual approach on language and language learning:

> The plurilingual approach emphasises the fact that as an individual person's experience of language in its cultural contexts expands, from the language of the home to that of society at large and then to the languages of other peoples (whether learnt at school or college, or by direct experience), he or she does not keep these languages and cultures in strictly separated mental compartments, but rather builds up a communicative competence to which all knowledge and experience of language contributes and in which languages interrelate and interact. (Council of Europe, 2001, p. 4)

The plurilingual approach recognizes the value of all language competences, including low-proficiency skills, receptive skills, or skills building on more than one language at the same time (e.g., intercomprehension or codeswitching). Instead of following an "ideal native speaker" model, it suggests a new aim for language education: "to develop a linguistic repertory, in which all linguistic abilities have a place" (Council of Europe, 2001, p. 5).

1.2 Identity and Non-CMC CALL

Identity plays an important role in CALL research, especially in the context of computer-mediated communication (CMC). This can be demonstrated by a quick search of the four topmost CALL journals for papers with *identity/identities* in their title. At the point of writing, there were four articles with *identity* in their title available on the *Computer Assisted Language Learning Journal* website (Alonso-Belmonte & Vinagre, 2017; del Rosal et al., 2017;

Kohn & Hoffstaedter, 2017; Ushioda, 2011),[1] four articles in *CALICO Journal* (Kitade, 2014; van Deusen-Scholl, 2018; Wildner-Bassett, 2013; Yang & Yi, 2017), four articles in *Language Learning & Technology* (Chen, 2013; Fong et al., 2016; Klimanova & Dembovskaya, 2013; Schreiber, 2015), as well as one article in *ReCALL* (Petersen et al., 2008).[2] From the 13 articles in CALL journals with *identity/identities* in their titles listed above, only one paper (Ushioda, 2011) did not have a clear CMC focus. This overwhelming focus on CMC in discussions of identity in CALL is also reflected in two recent special issues on identity, in *Computer Assisted Language Learning Journal*'s 2017 special issue entitled "Interculturality and identity in computer-mediated communication: Findings from L2 teaching contexts" and *ALSIC*'s 2017 special issue on "Identity Construction in Social Media."

Yet even though research on identity in CALL focuses nearly exclusively on CMC contexts, the example of the two learners presented at the beginning of the chapter illustrates how even in non-CMC products, design decisions can interact with learner identity, and impact learner identity, in beneficial or in harmful ways. Apps and software are cultural artefacts. Using them, accepting them, rejecting them, altering them makes up part of the experience of identity, identity expression, and identity negotiation. An app is not a human being, but it is the result of human meaning-making, and the effect of an app requiring you to indicate a native language, and only allowing one native language per person (Buendgens-Kosten, 2014), is similar, in some regards, to having one's linguistic background and profile (i.e., parts of one's self-concept) casually disregarded in everyday life. Also, digital language learning products may allow you to act using language, for example through play or simulations. This allows a learner to make experiences that might impact their Ideal L2 Self or Ideal Multilingual Self (see discussion below).

Therefore, this chapter takes an explicitly non-CMC perspective on identity in CALL. Instead of looking at social media, chat communication, communication in MMORPGs (Massively Multiplayer Online Role-Playing Games), in virtual and augmented reality, or as part of virtual exchanges, it will instead look at CALL "from a box": specific tools such as apps or games which are used by single users and require neither synchronous nor asynchronous communication with human beings.

---

[1] The three 2017 papers are from the same special issue on "Interculturality and identity in computer-mediated communication: Findings from L2 teaching contexts" (one editorial, two research papers).

[2] Interestingly, Gillespie (2020) does not identify identity as one of the trends of current CALL research.

1.3 The L2 Motivational Self System

A key foundation of this paper is the L2 Motivational Self System as suggested by Dörnyei. Dörnyei's (2010) psychological model includes three components: the "Ideal L2 Self," the "Ought-to L2 Self," and the "L2 Learning Experience." Ideal L2 Self and Ought-to-L2 Self constitute self-guides, i.e., "self-directed standards or acquired guides for being" (Higgins, 1987, p. 321), or, more simply speaking, elements of the self-regulatory system that represent a person's wishes, hopes, sense of obligation, etc. (Higgins et al., 1994, p. 276). The Ideal L2 Self is the first of the relevant self-guides and reflects "the person we would like to become" (Dörnyei, 2010, p. 29). The Ought-to L2 Self is the second of the relevant self-guides and "concerns the attributes that one believes one *ought to* possess to meet expectations and to *avoid* possible negative outcomes" (Dörnyei, 2010, p. 29). Finally, the L2 Learning Experience "concerns situated, 'executive' motives related to the immediate learning environment and experience (e.g., the impact of the teacher, the curriculum, the peer group, the experience of success)" (Dörnyei, 2010, p. 29).

Dörnyei states explicitly that this model is "centred around identity and identification" (Dörnyei, 2010, pp. 29–30). Self-guides can match or differ from a learner's self-concept (a learner's "actual/own attributes" (Higgins, 1987, p. 322) or, in other words, a person's "self-perceived attributes" (Higgins, 1987, p. 332). Higgins's self-discrepancy theory "postulates that we are motivated to reach a condition where our self-concept matches our personally relevant self-guides" (Higgins, 1987, p. 321). This can take the shape of desiring a certain state, or wishing to avoid a certain state:

> Ideal self-guides have a *promotion* focus, concerned with hopes, aspirations, advancements, growth and accomplishments; whereas ought self-guides have a *prevention* focus, regulating the absence or presence of negative outcomes associated with failing to live up to various responsibilities and obligations (Dörnyei, 2010, p. 18).

Dörnyei suggests that certain conditions have to be met for the L2 Motivational Self System to impact behavior and discusses how far instructional design and teacher behavior can impact these. He lists a total of six conditions: (1) "availability of an elaborate and vivid future self-image", (2) "perceived plausibility", (3) "harmony between the ideal and ought selves", (4) "necessary activation/priming", (5) "accompanying procedural strategies", and (6) the offsetting impact of a feared self (Dörnyei, 2010, pp. 19–21).

Ushioda (2011) argues that "how we engage our students' social identities in their L2 interactions within and beyond the classroom now would seem to have important consequences for how they visualize themselves as users of the L2 in the future" (p. 203). In this, Ushioda argues, the internet can play an important role as it provides opportunities "for trying out new and alternative identities and modes of self-presentation," which give learners the opportunity to engage in learning and communicating in exploratory and creative ways "without posing a threat to students' real-world identities and private selves" (Ushioda, 2011, p. 207).

Even non-CMC CALL can give learners the opportunity to use their target language in meaningful ways that tie in with their self-guides. For example, Barab et al. (2010) discuss how digital games, unlike non-interactive media, can "create a setting that learners can act upon (and change) in personally valued and socially significant ways" (p. 525). They coined the term "transformational play" to describe "taking on the role of a protagonist who must employ conceptual understandings to transform a problem-based fictional context and transform the player as well." They point out that "in a game, failure is tolerated and risk taking is encouraged; players can experiment with conceptual understandings and learn from the impact of unproductive choices" (Barab et al., 2010, p. 526). Similarly, in ludic, gameful (Reinhardt, 2019) CALL, it must be assumed, language learners can play around with language and language use, and experience themselves as somebody who uses language(s) for specific communicative or non-communicative goals, achieving outcomes within the game world, and potentially altering their self-concept and/or self-guides.

The L2 Motivational Self System focuses – as the name states – on the L2 only. Henry (2017) suggests extending this model to better cover multilingual settings. He suggests that "for people learning two or more additional languages, processes of emergence produce multilingual self-guides. These self-guides can be conceptualized as constituents of a higher-level multilingual motivational self-system" (Henry, 2017, p. 556) In other words, in addition to self-guides for the L2 and the L3, other self-guides can emerge that reflect the person as an (emergent) multilingual. Henry (2017) argues:

> [F]or people who develop an ideal multilingual self, motivation to learn the Ly can be greatly enhanced in that developing TL competence becomes part of a larger identity project. However, at the same time, it is also clear that the image of an ideal multilingual self is likely to lack detail and elaboration" (Henry, 2017, p. 557).

Henry also points out that we need to consider the effects of multiple non-L1 Self Systems interacting – for example when studying multiple foreign languages.

1.4 Purpose and Approach of This Chapter

The purpose of this chapter is to deepen the understanding of how design choices in multilingual non-CMC CALL products relate to questions of identity, viewed from the theoretical background of Dörnyei's L2 Motivational Self System, with multilingual extensions based on Henry (2017).

I will look at three language learning products that, at the surface level, include more than one language. The products selected are Romanica, a game on Romance intercomprehension; Duolingo, a translation-heavy language-learning app; and MElang-E, a serious game[3] that requires users to navigate multilingual dialogue trees. I will focus on aspects of the design that are relevant when talking about identity. For each product, I provide a focused description, based on a mix of experience using these apps and supplementary resources.[4] In a second step, I take a more interpretative stance and discuss implications of the design related to language(s) and multilingualism. Finally, in the conclusion, I combine the description and analysis of the three products and draw on connections between the design of the apps and Dörnyei's L2 Motivational Self System, focusing on two aspects of the design: representation of the user, and the inclusion and use of more than one language.

[3] Some authors use *serious game* in a very broad sense to refer to any game designed for learning purposes. Here, I am using the more narrow sense, of games that take up "serious" topics, such as mental health (Depression Quest) or the American War of Independence (For Crown and Colony?). In other words, serious games are educational games beyond the behavioristic "drill and kill" game types.

[4] Before beginning analysis, I had extensively used Duolingo (different languages, different app versions), and had spent time playing Romanica. I had been involved in the development of MElang-E, and drew on my knowledge of the development process as well as on my experience playtesting it. In the description and analysis, I draw on the product (in the case of Romanica and Duolingo: the Android phone app version, August 2020) itself, as well as on additional resources, such as descriptions in app stores, official websites, promotional videos. For the analysis, I also draw on published research on these products.

2 Description and Analysis

2.1 Romanica: Description and Analysis

Romanica (https://play.google.com/store/apps/details?id=com.CCCP.Romanica) is an app for the training of Romance intercomprehension, published by France's Ministère de la Culture. The game has a similar look to established commercial casual games such as Candy Crush Saga. The player travels along a map. At each station along the way, the player needs to pass one level of the game to be able to continue. These levels consist of different variants of the same intercomprehension mini-game: words or phrases in different languages "rain" from the top of the screen. The player needs to move them into the correct "buckets." These "buckets" can either be content-based (e.g., "agreement" or "disagreement") or language based (sorting each expression into the right language bucket). Different levels include different languages. According to published game material, the game offers French, Romanian, Italian, Spanish, Portuguese, Catalan, Occitan, and Corsican.

Linked from the app (cogwheel, "À propos") is a website by the Ministère de la Culture of France, explaining the storyline of the game:

> Le monde de *Romanica* se meurt. Depuis que l'on n'y parle plus qu'une seule langue, tous les habitants s'ennuient, se renferment sur eux-mêmes, fuient et abandonnent leurs cités, en passe de disparaître à jamais sous un épais manteau de nuages.
>
> Vous seuls pouvez ramener la vie et la lumière dans le monde de *Romanica*! Laissez de côté vos préjugés et vos doutes et faites renaître la diversité des langues de *Romanica* pour y ramener la joie et la vie avec tous ses habitants![5]

The app is available with a French and a Romanian interface and explanations. The default version after installation[6] was in French. The user can change the language at any time (except while playing one of the word-sorting mini-games) through the language menu (accessed by tapping a

[5] Translation: The world of Romanica is dying. Since people speak only a single language anymore, all the inhabitants are bored, withdrawn, escape from and leave behind their cities, which are in the process of disappearing forever under a thick cloud cover. Only you can return life and light to the world of Romanica! Leave aside your prejudices and your doubts and revive the languages of Romanica to bring back happiness and life to all its inhabitants!

[6] Default settings can depend on factors such as the language setting of the operating system, and might vary between users.

cogwheel in the upper right corner). The interface languages are presented by their names in their languages, for example "Română" and "Français." The project website explains the role of Romanian: "Ce jeu a été imaginé à l'occasion de la saison culturelle croisée France-Roumanie, qui s'étend jusqu'en 2019, et il est disponible en français et en roumain."[7] The eight languages in the game appear in a set order. In other words, players cannot choose to focus on a specific language or language combination but will encounter all eight languages over time (e.g., Romanian and French at station 1, Italian and Romanian at station 2, etc.).

For a certain number of "stars" earned (the stars reflect the number of mini-games played and the degree of success with which they were played), the player gets access to a "postcard" with a picture and a text providing intercultural or language-related trivia – the first postcard, for example, discusses "Bonjur" as a loanword from French used in Romanian, its history, and its cultural associations. The text of these postcards is always bilingual, in French and Romanian.

Romanica avoids making statements about the language status of players. Players need to be able to read French or Romanian to be able to play the game, but they are never required to identify themselves as native speakers/speakers/users/learners of any of the languages in the game.

The fantasy setting removes the languages from their usual contexts. In addition, the language material appears completely decontextualized, as single words or phrases raining from the top of the screen. The player is not a speaker but a manipulator of language(s)-as-objects. Language is the object of this game. Players move words and short phrases, sorting them rather than communicating through them.

The overarching plot, though not emphasized during actual gameplay, posits individual and societal monolingualism as a dangerous aberration: since the inhabitants of Romanica have become monolingual, the city has begun to die. In doing this, it sets up multi/plurilingualism as a norm. At the same time, "Laissez de côté vos préjugés et vos doutes"[8] can also be understood as prejudices and doubts regarding plurilingualism and/or the different languages in the game, which a player may hold but has to overcome to rescue Romanica.

---

[7] Translation: This game has been conceived on the occasion of the French-Romanian cross-season which runs until 2019, and is available in French and Romanian.

[8] Translation: Leave aside your prejudices and your doubts.

The languages included in the game are all Romance languages, reflecting its focus on Romance intercomprehension. French, Spanish, Italian, and, to a lesser degree, Portuguese are traditional 'Modern Foreign Languages', i.e., of internationally high status. Several of the languages included (French, Spanish, Portuguese) are clearly world languages spoken broadly across the globe and have official status in several countries. Other languages are national languages that are less frequently taught internationally (Romanian), or are regional and/or minority languages (Catalan, Corsican, Occitan). All languages included are languages spoken in Europe. Creoles (e.g., Haitian Creole) or constructed languages (e.g., Esperanto) are not included. The languages included are treated fairly equally, though the fact that the interface is available in French and Romanian, and that these languages are included first in the game, demonstrates a certain preference for these languages.

2.2 Duolingo: Description and Analysis

Duolingo[9] (cf., e.g., Chik, 2020; Falk & Götz, 2016; Loewen et al., 2019) is a language-learning app focusing on vocabulary and translation drills, as well as dictations.

When starting the app, learners can choose which language they wish to study – and through which language. As my interface language was set to German (automatically, based on the device's language setting), I was first offered "Englisch," "Spanisch," "Französisch" (through the medium of German). By clicking on "Mehr" [more], all options became visible. Regardless of the interface language, learners are offered the full range of language combinations available. In other words, a learner can study Klingon through English, and Italian through French at the same time. Not all languages are offered through all other languages, though. Nearly all target languages (except English itself, Catalan, and Guarani) are offered through English, with varying numbers of target languages for the other mediums of instruction. Some languages are offered as target languages, but never as mediums of instruction. English as target language is offered through the largest number of other languages. In the list, all language options are listed in the instructional language, so that, for example, German through Dutch is listed as "Duits vanuit Nederlands." The target languages are symbolized by abstract,

[9] https://play.google.com/store/apps/details?id=com.duolingo&hl

simplified flags, for example a simplified US flag for English and the flag of Paraguay for Guarani.[10]

On clicking a language combination that does not match the device's default language setting, a warning pops up: "Du wechselst gleich zur französischen App Version. Du solltest die Option nur nutzen, wenn du schon Französisch sprechen kannst."[11] Choosing a language combination with a new medium of instruction switches the user interface of the app to that instructional language.

It is possible to do several courses for the same target language, using different mediums of instruction (e.g., English through French, through Dutch, and through German). These function as independent courses, though. As a consequence, it is not possible to achieve a certain level in English through French and then to continue at this level in English through Dutch.

During registration the platform does not require information about languages spoken or about language status. Likewise, the user profile includes no fields for native language, languages spoken, etc., though it does include auto-generated information about language learning progress on the app. Flags (see discussion above) symbolize the languages studied. If one clicks on these, one gets additional information (which language is used as medium of instruction, how many experience points have been earned in each course).

Within the courses, Duolingo uses decontextualized words and phrases. That is, for most languages, Duolingo does not include dialogues, stories, or factual texts in its app.[12]

Duolingo avoids ascriptions such as "native speaker." As Duolingo works in a grammar-translation mode, a language beyond the target language is always needed. This language is framed as the means through which the target

---

[10] In most cases, these were national flags. This association between (exactly) one country and (exactly) one language is problematic for polycentric languages (like English) and for multilingual countries (like Paraguay). For a few languages, other – not national – flags were used (e.g., the League of Arab States for Arabic, Tino Rangatiratanga (the Māori sovereignty flag) for Māori), though these can bring their own sets of challenges when used to represent a specific language.

[11] Translation: You are switching to the French App version. You should use this option only if you can already speak French.

[12] For some target languages, Duolingo "stories" are available from the Duolingo website and also integrated in later app versions. These present language material embedded in dialogues. Duolingo podcasts with interviews in the target language and summaries in English are available as well but are not embedded in the app.

language is studied. Learners retain their freedom to use many instructional languages, either for different or for the same target language.

Chik (2020) describes a practice called "reverse tree" (in reference to the "skill tree" structure of the Duolingo language course). Learners who have completed one skill tree (e.g., Italian through English) then do the reverse tree (e.g., English through Italian). This is not done in order to learn the reverse tree target language (here: English) but the reverse tree medium of instruction (here: Italian). Chik observed: "As I started to assume a new linguistic identity as an Italian speaker learning English, I felt that I had a new level of control over a restrictive learning platform" (Chik, 2020, p. 23). She continues:

> Of course, the decision to do a reverse tree also means taking on a new linguistic identity; namely, becoming a "native" speaker of one's target language on Duolingo. To be motivated in language learning, maybe it is important to imagine a new linguistic self. The reverse tree provides possible space for learners to practice (not just imagine) their Ideal L2 self, and actually be officially treated as members of the target language. (Chik, 2020, p. 23)

As the app itself does not associate using a medium of instruction with being a native speaker of that language, other interpretations by learners engaging in reverse trees (including interpretations related to the Ideal Multilingual Self, or to one's identity as a resourceful language learner) might be possible.

The ability to *use* the language is stressed in promotional material, but the app itself (which does not provide easy access to the forums discussed by Chik, or to other features, such as Duolingo "Events"; https://events.duolingo.com/) focuses on *studying* the language. Success is measured in experience points and crowns (for units completed). Badges celebrate study successes and study habits. The focus of the Duolingo design[13] lies on *the user as learner* rather than the user as *language user*.

2.3 MElang-E: Description and Analysis

MElang-E (Multilingual Exploration of Languages in Europe, eudoit.eu/melang-e) is a single-player serious game in which the player takes up the role of Mali, a young adult from England who needs to travel across Europe

[13] Fear of the wrath (or tears) of Duo, the owl mascot of Duolingo, when one fails to keep up good study habits has long become an internet meme (cf. https://knowyourmeme.com/memes/evil-duolingo-owl).

to reunite his former teen band for a band contest (Buendgens-Kosten et al., 2019). The player navigates the game by selecting interlocutors and clicking through dialogue trees. In other words, the player plays by deciding what Mali says at specific points in the game, selecting from pre-scripted options. These options vary regarding content (for example, when the player decides whether Mali takes a single room or a shared room at the hostel), pragmatic features (e.g., different degrees of formality), and the language they are in. While English is always an option, specific dialogues also enable the use of Urdu (one of Mali's L1s), German, or French (languages Mali studied at school for a year). The dialogues continue differently based on the choices the player made.

In addition, Mali's interlocutors speak a range of other languages with which the player is confronted. The pre-scripted dialogue options allow the player to, for example, make Mali draw on intercomprehension,[14] or instead on mediation by a non-player character. Multilingual practices such as codeswitching are modelled by several bi- and multilingual non-player characters in the game. While Mali is positioned as a bilingual native speaker of English (and Urdu), the game features a large number of non-native-speaker non-player characters. These encompass both highly proficient speakers and less proficient speakers of English, with a broad range of accents. It also includes highly successful communicators with limited English proficiency, such as hostel manager Jürgen, whose English deviates from native-speaker norms in many regards but who is clearly comfortable communicating in English and playfully includes multiple other languages in his speech.

In MElang-E, players experience a trip across Europe through the perspective of Mali. Mali is, by default, a multilingual character, speaking English and Urdu as native languages, and having basic knowledge (around A1) of French and German. Playing as Mali via dialogue trees, they can vary the number and amounts of languages used, playing Mali either as very open to languages and happy to experiment with languages, using even very basic language skills, or as more reticent, depending mostly on English for communication. This provides potential for transformational play (Barab et al., 2010), just that instead of using conceptual understandings through the protagonist, they use linguistic resources to transform (i.e., effect outcomes in) the fictional context. The player can experience themselves as a plurilingual actor, as a person communicating successfully with a wide range of people.

[14] Doyé defines intercomprehension as "a form of communication in which each person uses his or her own language and understands that of the other" (2005, p. 7).

At the same time, the large number of non-player characters in the game represent the many types of being non-monolingual in Europe, be it as speaker of a regional/minority language, experienced user of English as a lingua franca, student of foreign languages, heritage speaker, occasional tourist, or globetrotter. Characters from all walks of life and of all levels of proficiency use English to communicate, to help Mali, or to make jokes at his expense. This provides learners with many multilingual, English-using role models.

Still, the player character of Mali means that the dominant character in the game is a (bilingual) native speaker of English, speaking a high-status variety of English. Players can make choices within the game regarding how Mali will act (such as whether he greets somebody in French or in English, if he chooses a polite or blunt way of phrasing something), but not who Mali is – a UK-born, male, middle-class, bilingual, non-disabled person of color.[15]

3 Conclusion

In this section, I will draw together observations and interpretations of features of the three programs discussed above, connecting these with Dörnyei's L2 Motivational Self System. I will cluster them across two dimensions: those that relate to the user and those that relate to the languages/the language material included and excluded in these programs.

3.1 Representing the User

The way the player is represented in these products is of relevance from an "L2 Motivational Self System" perspective. The relevant question becomes how the positionings implied by the products harmonize with existing self-guides or might inspire the development of beneficial self-guides.

3.1.1 Representing the User: Language Status

In Buendgens-Kosten (2014), I discussed how language-learning platforms collect information on or represent language status of the user, and which effects this has on affordances and, potentially, user experience. In none of the

[15] In a follow-up project to MElange-E, called EU·DO·IT, learners are offered three "profiles" of language learners, represented by three avatars with different linguistic profiles, but also different genders, ethnic backgrounds, interests, etc. Cf. also Buendgens-Kosten et al. (2019). This increases the choices of the player, and also allows some more targeted language transfer support.

three products discussed here are users asked to indicate of which language(s) they are native speakers, or which level of proficiency they have in which language. In the case of MElang-E, learners take up the role of Mali, and act through Mali (and his linguistic profile). In the case of Romanica, learners get to choose the interface language, but the fantasy world they engage with does not require any additional information on their linguistic profile, nor does it supply information on the linguistic profile of the player character. Similarly, on Duolingo, the choice of the medium-of-instruction language is phrased without any reference to speaker status, though, as Chik (2020) described, some users may read this as related to native-speaker status. In short, all three products avoid the pitfalls associated with building a product on fixed (sometimes even presumed monolingual) language identities. They avoid positioning a learner as native speaker of any specific language(s).

On the one hand, this is beneficial, as the absence of positioning a person as, for example, a monolingual native speaker reduces the probability of a conflict with the self-concept of the user. If a potential user is alienated from using the app by positionings they perceive as hostile (e.g., denying their self-concept as native speaker of a specific combination of L1s), the app cannot have a positive effect on the Ideal or Ought-to L2 Self. On the other hand, it also means that the learner's specific linguistic background can become invisible.[16]

3.1.2 Representing the User: Language Learner, Language User

Language-learning products can focus on the process of learning, or on the process of using a language. In short, they can create a field of action in which the user can imagine themselves as a user or learner of the language. In MElang-E, the player takes up the role of Mali and experiences themselves in that role as traveling, communicating, negotiating, joking, etc. in multiple languages. The focus of MElang-E is very much on the language user.[17] Many players of MElang-E would be able to imagine undertaking a

[16] From a more practical perspective, that means learning-supporting features of their linguistic profiles cannot be registered and used by the software. For example, in Duolingo, a bilingual learner can use the "German from English" and "Duits vanuit Nederlands" tracks in parallel, but there is no opportunity to blend, to mix and match, these. The learner, in short, has to decide which path to use or repeat content haphazardly by picking several paths. This, though, is more of a practical challenge than an identity-related one, and just adding a field "native language" in the user profile would not solve this problem.

[17] In the teaching material accompanying MElang-E, this is reversed. This material has been developed for use in the EFL classroom, where the user is very much in the role

trip similar to Mali's, using languages in comparable contexts. This way, the game can contribute to an "elaborate and vivid future self image" or provide "necessary activation/priming" for an existing self-image (Dörnyei, 2010, p. 19).

Romanica spins a fantasy story about a person rescuing a community by wielding the power of multilingualism. Within Romanica's many mini-games, though, the focus is very much on form-focused intercomprehension activities. The player may use the power of multilingualism to save a dying world – but they do it by sorting words into categories, not by reading a newspaper to learn about current events. The player experiences themselves as a language learner or, possibly, as a language analyzer.

Duolingo, finally, is all about language learning. While, depending on the app version, some interaction in the target language can be possible (and is always possible using the web-version forums), the "core" of Duolingo, which is available consistently from version to version, is about *learning* the language, not *using* it. Duolingo is heavily gamified and the gamification features (leader boards in the form of leagues, crowns and XP, badges) are connected to learning, not to use. To illustrate this further: Duolingo badge achievements include the "Strategist," earned by reading a tip (with metalinguistic information), "Wildfire," for completing a multi-day streak, or "Weekend Warrior," for completing lessons on the weekend. For contrast, one may compare this to the "Secret Agent's Language Challenges" app, which sets challenges such as "Triple agent" which encompasses "Greet 2 people in their own language (which is different from your first language)!", or "Eurovision," requiring the player to "Listen to 5 songs in different languages!" (Buendgens-Kosten, 2020b).

Dörnyei (2010, p. 29) defines the Ideal L2 Self as "the L2-specific facet of one's 'ideal self'." In principle, many things could characterize these L2-specific aspects, but the example provided by Dörnyei suggests an ideal self that *speaks* the L2. Dörnyei also distinguishes the L2 Learning Experience from the Ideal L2 Self and the Ought-to L2 Self. In other words, "'executive' motives related to the immediate learning environment and experience (e.g., the impact of the teacher, the curriculum, the peer group, the experience of success)" do not fall under Ideal L2 Self but under L2 Learning Experience (Dörnyei, 2010, p. 29). As neither Duolingo nor Romanica tap into

---

of a learner while filling out worksheets, discussing questions with a partner, or doing role plays. See also the MElang-E teaching material (http://eudoit.eu/wp-cc829-content/uploads/2019/04/MElang-E_Teacher-Material-II_Classroom-Activities.pdf) and Elsner & Lohe (2021).

visions of a future self as language user, one might argue they have nothing to contribute to a learner's developing Ideal L2 Self. Yet, the pride that users demonstrate in their app usage patterns and successes might hint at a close link between their identity and being a successful Duolingo learner, including, for example, being a person who completed a learning path or a user with a >100-day streak. A language user, one could argue, is not exclusively a person who *speaks* the language or *uses* the language for communication purposes but also a person who invests in the language by *playing* with the language, by *manipulating* the language, by formally *studying* the language. In that sense, the distinction between "Ideal L2 Self" and "L2 Learning Experience" blurs. For players who take Duolingo very seriously, a similar argument can be extended to the Ought-to Self, where studying is seen as necessary to avoid the undesirable outcome of losing a streak or dropping to a lower-level league.

3.2 Available Languages

When we discuss which languages and language varieties are included in different language-learning products, we do not only ask which languages can be studied through them but also who is modeled in these programs as a legitimate participant, a successful learner/user, or as having a right to speak (Norton, 2013). From an L2 Motivational Self System perspective, good design in this regard can contribute to the development of a vivid, detailed Ideal (L2/Multilingual) Self, and to the activation of that Ideal (L2/Multilingual) Self. Design can also, though, strengthen conflicts between self-guides or self-guides and self-concept.

3.2.1 Available Languages: What Is Available, What Is Missing?

All programs presented here include some languages and exclude others; privilege some languages, but not others. Romanica, for example, focuses on Romance languages and includes a wide range of Romance languages but excludes Romance creoles and Romance constructed languages. Still, within the selection made, there is a wide variety of Romance languages, from different (European) countries, with differing legal and social statuses – far beyond the selection one has come to expect from language-learning apps.

On Duolingo, English currently dominates, both as language of instruction and as target language. It is followed in dominance by the traditional modern foreign languages: German, French, Spanish, Italian. Overall, Indo-European languages (23 out of 39 languages) clearly dominate the list, with 8 Romance, 6 Germanic, 4 Slavic, and 3 Celtic languages (among others). While the representation of languages is clearly skewed, it must be acknowledged that the selection of options within Duolingo is quite broad, and likely to further improve over time through community engagement, as Duolingo creates new courses using volunteers (Duolingo, n.d.–b). At the point at which I am writing this (September, 2020), courses for Māori, Haitian Creole, Yucatec, Yiddish, and many other languages are under development. Also, existing target languages are being extended to new medium-of-instruction languages, such as English through Telugu, or Swedish through Russian (Duolingo, n.d.–a). This is, on the one hand, a powerful tool to extend the breadth of languages on offer, but might, on the other hand, lead to other types of bias, as sufficient numbers of bilingual and biliterate speakers who have the resources (time, internet access) to contribute to such a project are needed to add new courses. Languages not traditionally written (including, among others, many sign languages[18]), languages with few bilingual (or biliterate) speakers, languages spoken predominantly by individuals who lack such resources, will remain underrepresented.

In practice, this means that if Duolingo is recommended to learners as part of their out-of-class practice, some players may be able to access a course that allows them to study the target language through (one of) their L1(s) or (one of) their dominant language(s) and others will not have this opportunity – even if, admittedly, the choices are already broader than those which can be found in most other language-learning apps. As argued above, this may alienate some learners.

The range of languages in MElang-E is broad and reflects the languages spoken in the six locations within the game (Oxford, Frankfurt, Barcelona, Luxembourg, Tallinn, Istanbul). The absolute majority of languages are Indo-European, especially Indo-European languages frequently spoken in Europe. While many languages *appear* in the game, only a few languages are *substantially* included in the game: English, German, French, Spanish, Catalan, and Urdu. Languages related to migration tend to be underrepresented (e.g., Turkish in Frankfurt), but not completely absent (e.g., Russian in Tallinn). But MElang-E, through its large number of non-player characters, includes multiple varieties of several languages, such as different regionally influenced varieties of German[19] or different Englishes. Even with the

[18] Sign languages are not included in any of the apps or games discussed.

[19] It is rare for language-learning products to include different varieties, even in the case of pluricentric languages such as Spanish, German, or French. One notable exception is the "Frantasique" French course, which includes multiple Frenchs, and signals whenever

inclusion of regional minority language and dialectal variation, though, the game's focus on major international cities might fail to represent the daily linguistic experiences of learners living in more rural settings.

3.2.2 Available Languages: All Equal?

Among the languages that are included in these programs, some are "more equal than others." For example, in the case of Romanica, a range of languages is included in the game, but only two of these languages (French and Romanian) are also available as interface languages. In the case of MElang-E, English clearly dominates the gameplay. In the case of Duolingo, nearly every language is available through English, and English is available through the largest number of languages. The only exceptions to this are Guarani and Catalan, which are taught only through Spanish and, of course, English itself.

Such imbalances are not necessarily a problem. For example, MElang-E has been designed as a language-learning game for English in a multilingual Europe. In other words, while there are opportunities to practice German and French and to encounter, in more limited ways, other languages used in Europe, the game itself does not aim to be a fully developed course for Luxembourgish. Instead, it is a serious game that primarily supports the development of English language skills in a European setting, i.e., a setting in which English plays an important role as lingua franca but which is also characterized by the daily use of a wealth of other languages. The decisive point is not whether all languages are included on an equal footing but the *effects* of any imbalances: whether existing imbalances are perceived by learners as a slight to their own languages and linguistic profiles.

3.2.3 Available Languages: Monolingual or Plurilingual Outlook?

If multiple languages are included in a product, they can still be included in a way reminiscent of the monolingual habitus (Gogolin, 2008). A game might feature a range of monolingual speakers of different languages, or it may feature bilingual speakers who are featured exclusively in a "monolingual language mode" (Grosjean, 2012). A language-learning product might not be measured only against the presence and absence of languages but also against how their use reflects a wide range of non-monolingual practices.

Romanica uses languages in a very decontextualized way. The sorting of words into categories does not reflect daily linguistic practices in any way.

---

a variety is a non-France French. Like MElang-E, it utilizes multiple characters to represent the breadth of Frenchs (e.g., a Quebecois elevator).

The overarching purpose – fostering Romance intercomprehension, arousing interest in other Romance languages – is very much in harmony with a plurilingual outlook on language learning (CEFR 2001, 2018), but this is achieved without actually showing how people use intercomprehension in their lives. Still, it is not impossible that the playful engagement with forms supports learners in extending their Ideal L2 Self/Ideal Multilingual Self related to intercomprehension skills and intercomprehension use.

As discussed above, Duolingo allows learners to learn through different medium-of-instruction language paths but does not allow learners to connect them. Translation is an essential activity in all Duolingo courses, but always takes a traditional format (translation of decontextualized sentences from language a to language b, or vice versa). The contextualization customary in mediation activities that might encourage a learner to see themselves as a "language broker" (Norton, 2013, 111), as a builder of linguistic bridges between people and communities, is absent.

Having plurilingual language models may have an effect on the Ought-to L2 Self. Learners influenced by the monolingual habitus at school may have internalized a "two solitudes" (Cummins, 2008) perspective on L2 use, i.e., a perspective that assumes that languages already acquired and those currently studied should be kept strictly separate. Including plurilingual models might contribute, for example, to a normalization of transfer effects and non-native-speaker pronunciations. A teacher recommending MElang-E sends the message that intercomprehension or codeswitching are perfectly acceptable strategies for communication. A teacher encouraging apps that build on the learners' previously learned/acquired languages counters discourses that might limit a learner in tapping into their whole repertoire for purposes of language learning.

Henry (2017) has suggested that learners of multiple target languages can perceive conflict between those languages ("contentedly bilingual self") and that a "feared bilingual self" ("challenging the self-conception of being someone comfortable in only speaking their L1 and English and triggering a sense of discomfort associated with being a person who, in a globalized world and (possibly) a local multilingual school context, only speaks their L1 and English" [p. 561]) might be an antidote. I would suggest, as an alternative, giving learners the opportunity to develop vivid, detailed images of being multilingual that include, for example, smoothly adapting to the language needs of the interlocutor, using one's full repertoire to make connections with a broad range of people, drawing on multiple languages for humor or for other stylistic effects. Products like MElang-E, which allow learners to see many versions of (simulated) multilingual communication in action, might contribute to this.

3.3 Limitations of This Chapter and Suggestions for Further Research

Any conclusions must be drawn with a caveat. This chapter analyzes options language learners have when using Duolingo, Romanica, and MElang-E. How they *respond* to these options is beyond the scope of this chapter.

When looking at how learners respond to language-learning apps and games, concepts as used by Norton (2013) become increasingly important. In addition to looking at self-concept and relevant self-guides, as well as conflicts between them, we need to extend our perspective to encompass learner agency: the learner as the person resisting positionings, or working toward gaining the right to speak.

In this context, a more intersectional perspective that looks not only at the language(s) used but also at details of visual and acoustic representation becomes important, as discrimination and marginalization can occur at intersections of, for example, ethnicity and language status, or gender identity and language status. Who has the "right to speak" in an app? Whose English is put up as the model to be emulated? Who is framed as the ideal language learner?

Finally, language learning – like Macaroni and Cheese – may stem from a box but is "rehydrated," so to speak, in the actual context of use, such as a language-learning classroom. The classroom can be a place of critique, a place of contextualization, a place at which a broader range of perspectives is added to the "boxed" product. Looking at the product only – like looking at the "game" without looking at the "Game," to use Gee's terminology (2008, p. 24) – can never provide a full picture.[20]

Acknowledgments

MElang-E was created in a cooperation between Goethe University Frankfurt, Tallinna Ulikool, Lycée Michel Lucius Luxembourg, Université du Luxembourg, Istanbul University-Cerrahpasa, Universitat Ramon Llull,

[20] Cf. also deHaan's (2020) critique of research on game-based language learning/teaching that focuses only on the learner, to the exclusion of looking at the teacher and how they support the learning process.

Universitat Pompeu Fabras, Wöhlerschule, and Secció d'Institut de Canet de Mar, co-funded by the Erasmus+ Programme of the European Union. The author was a member of the design team (for the full credit list, see http://eudoit.eu/melang-e-credit-list). As this is a non-commercial product and the project has been concluded, there is no conflict of interest.

References

Alonso-Belmonte, I., & Vinagre, M. (2017). Interculturality and identity in computer-mediated communication: Findings from L2 teaching contexts. *Computer Assisted Language Learning*, 30(5), 343–350. https://doi.org/10.1080/09588221.2017.1321329

Barab, S. A., Gresalfi, M., & Ingram-Goble, A. (2010). Transformational play: Using games to position person, content, and context. *Educational Researcher*, 39(7), 525–536.

Buendgens-Kosten, J. (2014). The effects and functions of speaker status in CALL-oriented communities. In S. Jager, L. Bradley, E. J. Meima, & S. Thouësny (Eds.), *CALL design: Principles and practice; Proceedings of the 2014 EUROCALL Conference, Groningen, The Netherlands* (pp. 29–34). Research-publishing.net. https://doi.org/10.14705/rpnet.2014.000190

Buendgens-Kosten, J. (2020a). The monolingual problem of computer-assisted language learning. *ReCALL*, 32(3), 307–322. https://doi.org/10.1017/S095834402000004X

Buendgens-Kosten, J. (2020b). Review of "The secret agent's language challenges" app. *Studies in Self-Access Learning*, 12(4), 370–373. https://doi.org/10.37237/110405

Buendgens-Kosten, J., & Elsner, D. (2018). Multilingual CALL: Introduction. In J. Buendgens-Kosten & D. Elsner (Eds.), *Multilingual computer assisted language learning*. Multilingual Matters.

Buendgens-Kosten, J., Lohe, V., & Elsner, D. (2019). Beyond the monolingual habitus in game-based language learning: The MElang-E and EU·DO·IT projects in the interstices between linguistics, pedagogy and technology. *Journal of Gaming & Virtual Worlds*, 11(1), 67–83. https://doi.org/10.1386/jgvw.11.1.67_1

Chen, H.-I. (2013). Identity practices of multilingual writers in social networking spaces. *Language Learning & Technology*, 17(2), 143–170.

Chik, A. (2020). Motivation and informal language learning. In M. Dressman & R. Sadler (Eds.), *Blackwell handbooks in linguistics: [40]. The handbook of informal language learning* (pp. 13–26). Wiley-Blackwell. https://doi.org/10.1002/9781119472384.ch1

Council of Europe. (2001). *Common European Framework of Reference for Languages: Learning, teaching, assessment*. https://rm.coe.int/1680459f97

Council of Europe. (2018). *Common European Framework of Reference for Languages: Learning, teaching, assessment: Companion volume with new descriptors*. https://rm.coe.int/cefr-companion-volume-with-new-descriptors-2018/1680787989

Cummins, J. (2008). Teaching for transfer: Challenging the two solitudes assumption in bilingual education. In J. Cummins & N. H. Hornberger (Eds.), *Encyclopedia of language and education: Volume 5: Bilingual education* (2nd ed., pp. 65–75). Springer.

deHaan, J. (2020). Game-based language teaching is vaporware (Part 1 of 2): Examination of research reports. *Ludic Language Pedagogy*, 2, 115–139.

del Rosal, K., Conry, J., & Wu, S. (2017). Exploring the fluid online identities of language teachers and adolescent language learners. *Computer Assisted Language Learning*, 30(5), 390–408. https://doi.org/10.1080/09588221.2017.1307855

Dörnyei, Z. (2010). The L2 Motivational Self System. In Z. Dörnyei & E. Ushioda (Eds.), *Motivation, language identity and the L2 self* (pp. 9–42). Multilingual Matters.

Dörnyei, Z., & Ushioda, E. (Eds.). (2010). *Motivation, language identity and the L2 self*. Multilingual Matters.

Doyé, P. (2005). *Intercomprehension: Guide for the development of language education policies in Europe: From linguistic diversity to plurilingual education: Reference study*. Strasbourg. Council of Europe, Language Policy Division. http://rm.coe.int/intercomprehension/1680874594

Duolingo. (n.d.–a). *Help us build languages: The Incubator is where volunteers give life to new Duolingo courses.* https://incubator.duolingo.com/

Duolingo. (n.d.–b). *How can I suggest a new language course?* https://support.duolingo.com/hc/en-us/articles/204979660-How-can-I-suggest-a-new-language-course-

Elsner, D., & Lohe, V. (2021). A multilingual trip through Europe: Interkomprehensionsstrategien im Computerspiel MElang-E nutzen. *Der Fremdsprachliche Unterricht Englisch*, 55(171), 26–31.

Falk, S., & Götz, S. (2016). Interactivity in language learning applications: A case study based on Duolingo. In T. Zeyer, S. Stuhlmann, & R. D. Jones (Eds.), *Giessener Beiträge zur Fremdsprachendidaktik. Interaktivität beim Fremdsprachenlehren und -lernen mit digitalen Medien: Hit oder Hype?* (pp. 238–258). Narr Francke Attempto.

Fong, C. J., Lin, S., & Engle, R. A. (2016). Positioning identity in computer-mediated discourse among ESOL learners. *Language Learning & Technology*, 20(3), 142–158.

Gee, J. P. (2008). Learning and games. In K. Salen (Ed.), *The ecology of games: Connecting youth, games, and learning* (pp. 21–40). The MIT Press.

Gillespie, J. (2020). CALL research: Where are we now? *ReCALL*, 32(2), 127–144. https://doi.org/10.1017/S0958344020000051

Gogolin, I. (2008). *Der monolinguale Habitus der multilingualen Schule* (2nd ed.). Waxmann.

Grosjean, F. (2012). Bilingual and monolingual language modes. In C. A. Chapelle (Ed.), *The encyclopedia of applied linguistics* (pp. 1–9). Blackwell Publishing Ltd. https://doi.org/10.1002/9781405198431.wbeal0090

Henry, A. (2017). L2 motivation and multilingual identities. *The Modern Language Journal*, 101(3), 548–565. https://doi.org/10.1111/modl.12412

Higgins, E. T. (1987). Self-discrepancy: A theory relating self and affect. *Psychological Review*, 94(3), 319–340. https://doi.org/10.1037/0033-295X.94.3.319

Higgins, E. T., Roney, C. J. R., Crowe, E., & Hymes, C. (1994). Ideal versus ought predilections for approach and avoidance distinct self-regulatory systems. *Journal of Personality and Social Psychology*, 66(2), 276–286. https://doi.org/10.1037/0022-3514.66.2.276

Kitade, K. (2014). Second language teachers' identity development through online collaboration with L2 learners. *CALICO Journal*, 31(1), 57–77. https://doi.org/10.11139/cj.31.1.57-77

Klimanova, L., & Dembovskaya, S. (2013). L2 identity, discourse, and social networking in Russian. *Language Learning & Technology*, 17(1), 69–88.

Kohn, K., & Hoffstaedter, P. (2017). Learner agency and non-native speaker identity in pedagogical lingua franca conversations: Insights from intercultural telecollaboration in foreign language education. *Computer Assisted Language Learning*, 30(5), 351–367. https://doi.org/10.1080/09588221.2017.1304966

Loewen, S., Crowther, D., Isbell, D. R., Kim, K. M., Maloney, J., Miller, Z. F., & Rawal, H. (2019). Mobile-assisted language learning: A Duolingo case study. *ReCALL*, 20, 1–19. https://doi.org/10.1017/S0958344019000065

Norton, B. (2013). *Identity and language learning: Extending the conversation* (2nd ed.). Multilingual Matters.

Petersen, S. A., Divitini, M., & Chabert, G. (2008). Identity, sense of community and connectedness in a community of mobile language learners. *ReCALL*, 20(03), 361–379. https://doi.org/10.1017/S0958344008000839

Reinhardt, J. (2019). *Gameful second and foreign language teaching and learning: Theory, research, and practice*. Palgrave Macmillan. https://doi.org/10.1007/978-3-030-04729-0

Schreiber, B. R. (2015). "I Am What I Am": Multilingual identity and digital translanguaging. *Language Learning & Technology*, 19(3), 69–87.

Ushioda, E. (2011). Language learning motivation, self and identity: Current theoretical perspectives. *Computer Assisted Language Learning*, 24(3), 199–210.

van Deusen-Scholl, N. (2018). The negotiation of multilingual heritage identity in a distance environment: HLA and the Plurilingual Turn. *CALICO Journal*, 35(3), 235–256. https://doi.org/10.1558/cj.36723

Wildner-Bassett, M. E. (2013). CMC as written conversation: A critical social-constructivist view of multiple identities and cultural positioning in the L2/C2 classroom. *CALICO Journal*, 22(3), 635–656. https://doi.org/10.1558/cj.v22i3.635-656

Yang, S. J., & Yi, Y. (2017). Negotiating multiple identities through eTandem learning experiences. *CALICO Journal*, 34(1), 97–114. https://doi.org/10.1558/cj.29586

About the Author

Judith Buendgens-Kosten is a postdoctoral researcher and teacher educator at Goethe University Frankfurt. They hold an MA in Online and Distance Education from the Open University, UK, and a doctorate degree in English Linguistics from RWTH Aachen University, Germany. Their research interests encompass multilingual computer-assisted language learning and inclusive education in the EFL classroom.

7 Examining Identity Performance of Multilingual Students in Computer Science Education: A Narrative Case Study

Sharin Jacob, Jonathan Montoya, and Mark Warschauer

1 Introduction

Research to date indicates that multilingual students with diverse social, cultural, and linguistic needs benefit from responsive instructional materials and approaches that facilitate learners' positive disciplinary identification. Effective instructional approaches for developing computational thinking are those that leverage students' existing resources to engage them in discipline-specific practices (Lee, 2005; Moje et al., 2004). Within this context, there is a well-established body of research specifically targeting multilingual student engagement in Computer Assisted Language Learning (Canagarajah, 2013). Furthermore, there is a growing body of work on increasing identification with the field of computer science (CS) for diverse learners (James DiSalvo et al., 2011; Pinkard et al., 2017; Shaw & Kafai, 2020). However, what has been less well studied is how multilingual students construct computer science identities (for more information, see Jacob et al., 2020a, 2020b).

CS education opens up several opportunities for culturally and linguistically diverse students. As computing technologies are ubiquitous and permeate all aspects of our daily lives, computational competencies have become increasingly necessary for full participation in today's society (Wing, 2006). In fact, there is a $500 billion opportunity for CS graduates due to a projected 1.4 million job vacancies by 2026 (Bureau of Labor Statistics, 2015). However, developing CS knowledge is not only important for CS job preparation. The kind of thinking processes involved in computing prepare students to access a broad array of jobs in other fields -- and these are the jobs that are overwhelmingly concentrating not only salaries but also power, prestige, and influence in a knowledge economy (Bransford et al., 2000). To this end, CS education fosters innovative approaches to problem solving that can help solve a wide array of pressing problems across multiple domains of the human experience. As students develop as computational thinkers, they are able to actively identify and solve local problems in their communities, becoming computational actors for the social good (Tissenbaum et al., 2019). Finally, creativity represents a principal dimension of computing. As students use programming languages as a medium to use their imagination, creativity supports the main goal of CSforAll, which proposes students become developers and not just consumers of technology (Smith, 2016).

Studies on multicompetence indicate that multilingual students are at an advantage compared with their monolingual counterparts as they are able to learn both language and content at the same time (Cook, 1991, 2003). To this end, CS education brings its own linguistic opportunities as multilingual students simultaneously acquire text-based programming languages that contain abstract vocabulary, language, and syntax while mastering discipline-specific concepts, practices, and perspectives (Jacob et al., 2018). For example, students are expected to distinguish between the language specific to programming and common-usage counterparts (e.g., event, loops). Additionally, the tasks of inquiry-based learning in CS, including data interpretation, solution proposal, and presentation, provide rich learning opportunities for multilingual students when structured properly (Jacob et al., 2020a). However, to maximize these learning opportunities, concerted effort needs to be dedicated to uncovering the ways in which students' interest and participation in computer science can be fostered.

The purpose of this chapter is to examine how a computational thinking curriculum is implemented to develop multilingual students' computer science identities. A narrative case study design will be used to analyze student and teacher interviews and students' computational artifacts. From these data, we examine how the computational thinking curriculum is implemented to cultivate multilingual students' identity development and investment in the field of computer science.

We address the following research questions:

1. How do multilingual students invest in computer science while participating in a year-long computational thinking curriculum designed to meet their linguistic and sociocultural needs?
2. What are possible explanations for student investment in computer science? How is multilingual students' investment in the curriculum shaped by linguistic and sociocultural factors?

2 Review of the Literature

Media-rich programming environments such as Scratch (Resnick et al., 2009) provide a variety of affordances for the teaching of computer science to multilingual students. The relatively unrestricted platform of such programming environments allows students to express themselves in new and creative ways. Open-ended design possibilities support the integration of culturally responsive materials and pedagogies that draw on students' conceptual and linguistic resources. As students increasingly identify as academically and technologically competent designers, they incorporate this fluency into their identities, opening new avenues for their future engagement with technology. As these goal-oriented successes come into focus, students begin envisioning their possible selves (Dörnyei, 2009) in the field of computer science and CS careers.

Engaging marginalized, linguistically diverse students in the creative use of new media in after-school settings such as the Computer Clubhouse Network can leverage students' cultural and linguistic capital (Bourdieu, 1991; Darvin & Norton, 2017) to develop both their literacy and programmatic logic. The Computer Clubhouse Network consists of more than 100 after-school clubs in 21 countries that serve marginalized and low-income youth. Peppler and Warschauer (2011) conducted a case study on Brandy, a child with intellectual disabilities who participated in the Computer Clubhouse Network, which is located in South Los Angeles and a part of the larger Computer Clubhouse Network. Due to the wide range of modalities and skills involved in digital media creation, Brandy was able to identify with the learning opportunities presented in the clubhouse, which fostered both her literacy development and robust identity as a technologically competent designer (Peppler & Warschauer, 2011). Brandy entered the clubhouse as a pre-literate student with little to no experience with technology and emerged as one of the strongest programmers and designers at the clubhouse. For example, Brandy's most esteemed creation, her "star milk" animation, was described as "successful," "amazing" and "compelling" by a blind review of external professional media artists who had no background or demographic knowledge of the students in the clubhouse (Peppler & Warschauer, 2011, pp. 32–33). Once a sidelined member of the after-school community, Brandy developed her metalinguistic awareness, reading and writing skills, and self-efficacy to become a talented and respected multimedia artist (Peppler & Warschauer, 2011). When students are given multiple opportunities to create multimodal artifacts that connect to their lives, cultures, and communities, they leverage their resources to develop a sense of competence with academic and technical content.

In addition to promoting identification with computer science at the individual level, leveraging students' linguistic and cultural capital promotes identity development at the social level. Culturally responsive computing draws upon existing cultural practices and traditions to reveal the mathematical and computational concepts already utilized by particular communities. Kafai et al. (2014) connect the traditions of sewing and decorative beading already present in indigenous communities to engineering and computing practices through the utilization of electronic textiles (e-textiles). E-textiles blend crafting practices such as sewing and weaving with microprocessors, light bulbs, and sensors to explore science and engineering principles such as electricity and circuits in culturally responsive ways. Students use materials such as felt, conductive thread, and Velcro to create wearable items that are equipped with myriad creative technologies. Howell et al. (2016) piloted an e-textiles science unit with a classroom containing 30% of students designated as English learners. Researchers observed a marked increase in participation of multilingual students compared with classes that taught electricity and circuits through traditional means.

As with e-textiles, culturally responsive computing is often achieved through diversification of curricula to attract students from culturally diverse backgrounds. Eglash et al. (2013) developed culturally responsive simulations that utilize "heritage algorithms" to simulate diverse cultural artifacts. For example, they applied iterative logic on Cartesian lattices to simulate beadwork created by indigenous communities, and used fractal patterns to simulate traditional African arts and architecture. Overall, these tools significantly improved mathematics and computational thinking outcomes for secondary students, compared with a control group (Eglash et al., 2013). Furthermore, students responded positively to these tools regardless of whether their cultural backgrounds corresponded to the cultural origin of the historical artifact. Diversifying the curriculum through the utilization of such tools has great potential to attract multilingual students to computing by leveraging their interest in responsive materials from a variety of cultural origins.

The projects described above produced positive attitudes toward computing for multilingual and other marginalized students. These positive outcomes can be attributed to the bridging of out-of-school and in-school learning environments by leveraging students' linguistic and cultural capital to solidify their computer science identities (Darvin & Norton, 2017), creating a "third space" for student participation (Moje et al., 2004). A "third space" disrupts the traditional roles between students and teachers to create more horizontal, symmetrical spaces in which teachers and students co-navigate their official and informal identities. In doing so, students begin to see the parallels between their existing skills and practices and the curricula, which increases their identification with the discipline. Future research can focus on the utilization of these projects with language learners, with a focus on how these projects draw on their funds of knowledge to promote identification with CS fields.

3 Theoretical Frameworks

3.1 Investment

Our study draws from the Norton (2013) and the Darvin and Norton (2017) model of investment, grounded in studies of linguistic and cultural capital including the work of Bourdieu (1991) and Weedon (1997). The investment model identifies three factors influencing language learners' engagement in classroom learning: 1) the construction and negotiation of formal and informal identities, 2) the accumulation of linguistic and cultural capital, and 3) the formulation of ideologies that are reproduced by institutional and hegemonic practices (Darvin & Norton, 2017).

Norton's model assumes a strong association between technological advancement and identity development as a method for addressing the realities of a knowledge economy (see Figure 7.1). Within this context, Darvin

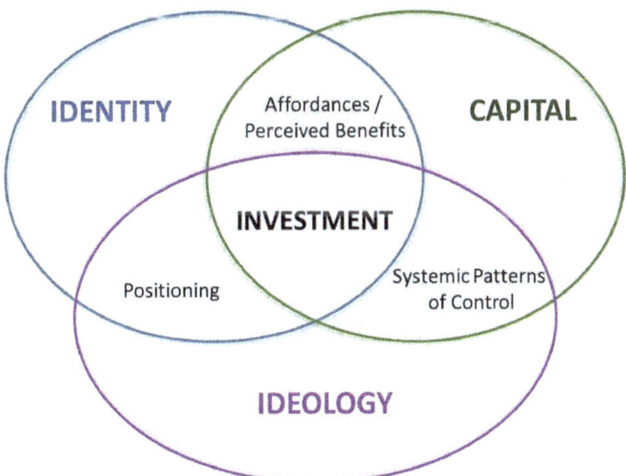

Figure 7.1. Darvin and Norton's 2017 Model of Investment

and Norton (2017) situate identity construction not only in the classroom but within the broader community, nation, and world. Darvin and Norton (2017) define investment as "complex, multiple identities, changing across time and space, and reproduced in social interaction" (p. 285).

To accommodate technological advancement, the investment model postulates that a person's ideologies transcend time and space through online spaces that operate outside the confines of these spatiotemporal boundaries. This affords language learners the opportunities to position themselves in multiple ways to accommodate these fluid spaces. At the same time, institutional and hegemonic patterns of control also contribute to shaping dominant narratives around what constitutes valuable linguistic and cultural capital within technological spaces. These in turn influence the perceived affordances and benefits that a student might acquire by participating in specific communities, such as the classroom. Therefore, when a teacher recognizes students' linguistic or cultural capital as legitimate, students will invest more heavily in classroom practices.

Finally, identity represents the site of struggle in which a language learner competes with conflicting ideologies and imagined future selves to develop durable dispositions toward specific learning contexts (Darvin & Norton, 2017). As a result, the investment model makes predictions about individuals' learning attitudes. For example, engaging experiences with learning lead to eventual beliefs that learning is worthwhile. Over time, attitudes grow more positive for avid learners, resulting in symbiotic relationships between learning and identity development. The inverse also applies: negative learning experiences and practices can adversely impact attitudes about learning, which in turn leads to disidentification with formal learning environments. To this end, students are imbued with agency by choosing to participate in what they perceive will provide affordances for their budding identities, and may engage or disengage from linguistic and discipline-specific practices in concert with their beliefs.

3.2 L2 Motivational System

Traditional research on L2 motivation studies focuses on psychology that explores how attributions are shared between individuals and cultural groups (Ricento, 2005). These attributions are examined under the model of *integrativeness*, or the process of modifying one's individual characteristics to more closely match target cultural norms (Gardner & Lambert, 1959). In light of globalization and the rise of English as an international language, scholars began to challenge the theory of integrativeness, focusing on the bicultural identity in which one roots themselves in local culture while assuming a globalized identity (Arnett, 2002). Csizér and Dörnyei (2005) conducted surveys on more than 13,000 L2 learners using structural equation modeling and to test the following constructs related to integrativeness: 1) instrumentality, 2) direct contact with L2 speakers, 3) cultural interest, 4) vitality of L2 community, 5) milieu, and 6) linguistic self-confidence. Instrumentality refers to the utility value inherent to learning, which is related to career enhancement and the benefits afforded by learning a new language or subject. A second key to L2 motivation involves the quality of contact that a learner has to other L2 speakers, which forms the basis of their attitudes toward these speakers and the tasks at hand. Cultural interest involves the appreciation of cultural practices associated with the media of the target language, including films, music, and television. The vitality of the L2 community refers to the perceived value that students assign to the cultural and linguistic practices associated with that community, such as perceptions of community wealth. Students are also motivated by their perception of language and subject matter, or milieu, as enacted in formal learning environments such as the classroom, as well as informal learning contexts involving parents, friends, and community. Finally, linguistic self-confidence refers to students' ability to master the language or subject matter at hand.

Findings from the structural equation model found instrumentality and attitudes toward members of the L2 community to be antecedents to integrativeness. One of the main impacts of the 2006 study was underscoring the importance of classroom dynamics in constructing L2 motivational systems, which resulted in the L2 Motivational Self System, comprising the following three components: ideal L2 self, ought-to L2 self, and L2 learning experience. The L2 ideal self parallels Norton's imagined communities insofar as it represents what the L2 learner envisions themselves becoming with respect to their current selves. The ought-to self refers to the extrinsic factors that cause L2 learners to act in specific ways to avoid negative outcomes. Finally, the L2 learning experience includes the ways in which components of the learning environment (teacher, curriculum, peer group, experience of success) affect student motivation. We expand our view of the L2 Motivational Self System to include the integrated nature of language and content instruction (Brinton et al., 2003; Schleppegrell et al., 2004) and to guide our understanding of both language and content learning as it relates to identity development.

3.3 Opposition and Resistance

The above theoretical frameworks outline the factors that contribute to building multilingual students' identities within specific education domains. However, there are also factors that contribute to opposition and resistance to identity development. We borrow heavily from Hand (2010) to discuss these factors. Well-established research has identified several factors that lead to student opposition in the classroom, including achievement-focused views (McLeod, 1987; Willis, 1977), classroom power dynamics (D'Amato, 1996; Leander, 2002; McFarland, 2001), and pervasive racial stereotyping (Fordham & Ogbu, 1986; Fryer, 2006; Stinson, 2006). Opposition that has been observed in the classroom has been described as an unfolding social drama that is driven by instructional practices and social ties (McFarland, 2001, 2004). This drama arises as participants frame their peers and teachers in particular ways that are reified through time and experience and begin to assume dramatic qualities. In particular, discussion-based collaborative activities have the potential to foster these social dramas (Hand, 2010). Within these scenarios, certain students may assume dominant roles and accrue social capital through participation, yet their participation may not be recognized as legitimate in their formal learning environments. Experiences such as these lead to opposition, resistance, and ultimately disidentification from formal instruction.

4 Methods

4.1 Overview of the Curriculum Intervention

Researchers worked collaboratively with teachers to adapt an existing grades 3–5 curriculum created by a path-breaking initiative that seeks to normalize computer science education in a large urban school district from PreK–12. The computational thinking curriculum was chosen by stakeholders due to its alignment with the Computer Science Teaching Association K-12 Computer Science Standards, and then adapted to meet the needs of the district's culturally and linguistically diverse students. Design-based implementation research was used to design, test, and refine the curriculum for further scaling and implementation.

The curriculum was grounded in effective practices for engaging multilingual students in STEM as outlined by a report conducted by the National Academies of Sciences, Engineering, and Medicine (NASEM, 2018).

According to this report, effective practices for teaching multilingual students STEM include: 1) engaging students in disciplinary practices, 2) encouraging rich classroom discourse, 3) building on students' multiple meaning-making resources, 4) encouraging students to use multiple registers and modalities, 5) providing explicit focus on how language functions in the discipline. Grounded in this report, we turned to teacher and administrator expertise during a weeklong Summer Institute to tailor the materials to the district's diverse learners.

First, the curriculum engages students in disciplinary practices by integrating inquiry-based instruction using the "5 E" model of inquiry to guide unit development: Engage, Explore, Explain, Elaborate, and Evaluate (Bybee, 1997). Inquiry-based instruction provides active, hands-on CS learning activities that stimulate authentic contexts for language use, making instruction more engaging for multilingual students (Estrella et al., 2018; Janzen, 2008; National Research Council [NRC], 2012; Rosebery et al., 2008). The curriculum was further aligned with the Common Core State Standards for English Language Arts (ELA), and the statewide Department of Education English Language Development (ELD) Standards to set clear guidelines and expectations for student learning.

Second, the curriculum was designed to stimulate rich classroom discourse through collaborative activities such as pair programming, small-group, and whole-class activities that facilitate the use of everyday and discipline-specific language across multiple contexts. Instructional materials were supplemented with professional development that guided the teachers' noticing of student peer-to-peer talk and suggested teacher-talk moves for facilitating productive discourse (Michaels & O'Connor, 2015).

Third, the curriculum integrated unplugged activities to build on students' existing resources. For example, when learning about loops, or programming concepts that cause a set of commands to repeat, the students might first do a dance, then map out how each move of the dance repeats, then map out how sequences of moves repeat. It is not until students have fully embodied the concept through physical activity that the term loop is introduced. In this way, students are able to leverage their everyday sense-making abilities to understand abstract concepts. To further build on students' cultural resources, we integrated children's stories depicting diverse pioneers in the field of computer science to provide role models that were relatable to students.

Fourth, the curriculum engages students in multiple modalities through the use of visualizations, simulations, gestures, pictures, and symbols to more effectively teach CS vocabulary and concepts (Lee et al., 2019). For example, before learning about parallelization, in which two programs are running simultaneously, students might play a "Simon Says" game in which they simultaneously act out certain gestures (i.e., walking, counting, tapping). After visualizing parallelization through computer simulations, students then learn the term, and finally practice it in Scratch, a media-rich programming environment, on their own or in groups.

Fifth, the curriculum provides linguistic scaffolding through the use of language frames that include the functional language of CS as well as that of social interaction. This scaffolding was presented to students on lesson placemats during reflection activities in which students were asked to describe their computational artifacts in pairs, and during whole-group presentations. The language frames were aligned with the ELA and ELD standards and we provided three levels according to the standards' proficiency guidelines: emerging, expanding, and bridging.

These strategies were embedded in the curriculum to promote multilingual student participation and inclusion in computer science. We aimed to leverage students' existing linguistic, social, cultural, and semiotic resources to engage them in CS disciplinary practices. Most notably, we took a "content first" approach toward CS learning by engaging students in CS content without bogging them down in unnecessary linguistic tasks that would tax their existing resources and divert attention away from learning (Lee et al., 2019). In this way, students learned as computer scientists would, who first develop their understanding of complex problems before assigning terms to efficiently describe perceived phenomena. Therefore, learning and understanding are foregrounded while language is used in service of engaging students in authentic disciplinary practices (Lee et al., 2019).

4.2 Scratch

Scratch is a media-rich programming environment designed for novice programmers that enables students to create, and then share, content online (Resnick et al., 2009) (see Figure 7.2). Scratch as a programming environment provides a rich context for actively cultivating students' computational thinking and facilitating opportunities for conversation about computational thinking. Scratch also provides a rich context for learning due to its design affordances, which provide a low floor with high ceiling to differentiate instruction for diverse learners (Resnick et al., 2009). Low floors provide entry points for emerging programmers while high ceilings extend learning

Figure 7.2. Screenshot of the Scratch Programming Environment

through more rarefied and complex opportunities (Resnick & Silverman, 2005; Wolz et al., 2009).

Additionally, the block-based nature of Scratch's programming environment provides scaffolding opportunities for the learning of computer programming without having to master strict syntax, while presenting advanced computational constructs for proficient coders (Resnick et al., 2009). Wide walls refer to the possibility of multiple pathways which coders of diverse ability levels can take to learning, represented by the varied presentation of media choices afforded by the Scratch programming environment (i.e., games, stories, animations, sprites,[1] backdrops, etc.) (Resnick et al., 2009).

4.3 Study Context

This study takes place within the context of a research practice partnership between the University of California Irvine, Santa Ana Unified School District, and the Orange County Department of Education. Researchers and practitioners put the partnership into action by developing, implementing, and testing a computational thinking curriculum designed to meet the needs of the district's culturally and linguistically diverse students. The district has

[1] In Scratch, a sprite is a character that can be programmed to execute a wide variety of actions. There are many different kinds of sprites in the Scratch library (i.e., people, animals, sports objects, food). Students can also upload pictures and videos from their computers and use a paint function to create their own sprites.

among the highest percentages of Latinx (96%), low-socioeconomic (91%), and multilingual students (63% in elementary grades) in the nation.

4.4 Participants

This case study is situated within a larger study in which we worked with the district's elementary coordinator to select seven teachers based on their extensive experience teaching computer science to elementary students. Within the broader study, the analysis for this chapter focuses on a dual-immersion school to more closely understand the relationship between bi/multilingualism and identity development in computer science learning. Within this school, we chose to focus on Angela's class because it is a dual-immersion classroom composed of students who predominantly speak Spanish as a first language, many of whom are designated as having mild to moderate disabilities. Angela describes herself as a Mild/Moderate Special Education Teacher who finds ways to provide instructional and socioemotional support to her students with special needs. She implemented the year-long curriculum as a visiting teacher during the technology hour of another elementary teacher's classroom. Angela is herself a Latina who is bilingual, speaking both English and Spanish. She provided bilingual instruction to her students during the piloting of the curriculum.

For the larger study, we interviewed four students from each of the seven classrooms (N=28) who demonstrated heterogeneous proficiencies in language and programming: two students with advanced proficiencies in either language or programming and two students with emerging proficiencies in either language or programming. We relied on teacher judgment to select students. For the purpose of this chapter, we chose two students from Angela's classroom to be interviewed based on their differences in language proficiency and programming experience. Amelia was selected as an advanced language learner as evidenced by her recent designation as Reclassified Fluent English Proficient (RFEP) and described as a novice programmer by her teacher. In contrast, Diego was classified as an emerging language learner as evidenced by his English Learner (EL) status and described as a highly proficient programmer by his teacher. We selected students with heterogeneous backgrounds to better understand the relationships between language and coding skills as they relate to identity development.

4.5 Intervention

The participating teachers piloted the year-long, five-unit computational thinking curriculum in their classrooms once a week for a lesson duration of 50 minutes.

4.6 Data Sources

4.6.1 Student Interviews

Two students were selected with input from the teachers for individual semi-structured interviews of about 15–20 minutes (see Appendix). For the student identity interview, questions explored their perceptions of computer science and interest in the profession. The constructs were grounded in research on the roles of family support (Gilmartin & Aschbacher, 2006), school experiences (Osborne et al., 2003), and self-perceptions (Eccles & Wigfield, 2000). Student responses were audio recorded, and video recordings of their projects (no faces) were captured.

4.6.2 End-of-Unit Scratch Projects

We collected and assessed students' final Scratch projects using a rubric that assesses overall proficiency in programming, user experience, and the use of coding and computational thinking constructs.

4.6.3 Teacher Interviews

Teachers were interviewed at the end of the school year about the instructional practices and activities they used to teach the computational thinking curriculum to multilingual students. They were asked to discuss their approach to teaching as well as any modifications they had made to the curriculum based on the needs of their students.

4.7 Data Analysis

We took a narrative approach to investigating the lived experiences of multilingual students as they express their agency to either invest or disengage themselves from computer science education. Narrative-based inquiry in L2 research has been particularly beneficial for examining the identity trajectories of multilingual students, especially those from marginalized groups based on factors such as language, class, ethnicity, gender, and age (e.g.,

Kinginger, 2004; Menard-Warwick, 2005; Pavlenko, 2001; Hall et al., 2004). This approach has represented a significant paradigm shift in the social sciences noted as the "discursive" or "narrative turn" (Lincoln & Denzin, 2003; Phillips & Hardy, 2002). Taking a constructionist approach to narrative accounts allows multilingual students to leverage their linguistic and cultural capital to enact their identities (Higgins & Stoker, 2011). All student and teacher names were replaced with pseudonyms.

5 Findings

5.1 Amelia

We turn to our data sources to examine how multilingual students invested in computer science identities while participating in a year-long computational thinking curriculum designed to meet their linguistic and sociocultural needs. To address this question, we turn to an interview transcript featuring a young girl named Amelia, author of About Me (see Figure 7.3) as she discusses her coding projects with the interviewer. Amelia was selected by her teacher for her advanced language proficiency and emerging programming skills

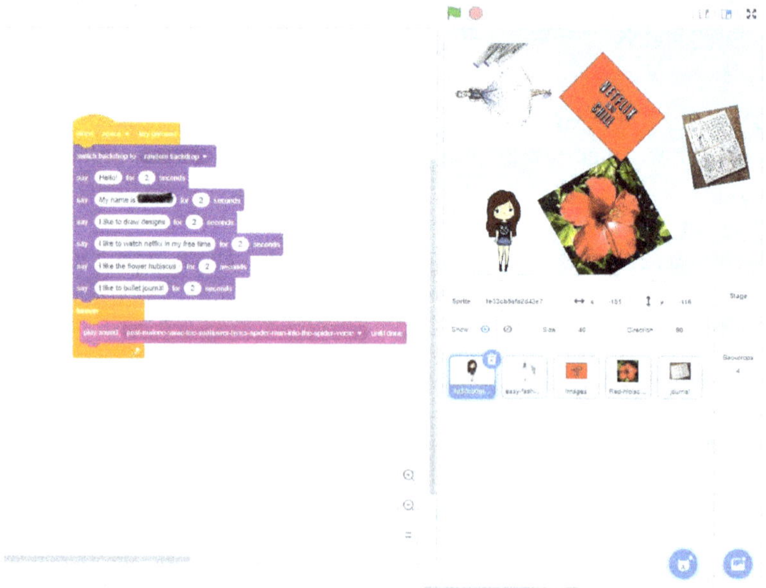

Figure 7.3. Screenshot of Amelia's About Me Project

and was described as a problem solver in math and science. The excerpts below help to describe how multilingual students such as Amelia engage in the process of programming and showcase the ways in which they choose to invest in the process.

Amelia's affinity for computer science was rooted in her ability to personalize her projects and be creative in her work.

> I like doing computer science because you get to create something on your own and you can personalize it and try ... to be creative with doing it like that.

For example, in describing her project, she mentions being able to choose from different sprites, or characters in the Scratch platform, and different blocks of code.

> We can choose different types of sprites to do it. We did different types of code. So, for example, I did "If hit the ground and you would lose the game and then you restart and then, um, the wallpaper would change when you made a score."

This excerpt exemplifies the perceived affordances and benefits that Amelia might acquire by participating in computer science, particularly through the Scratch platform. Amelia expresses her affinity for the choices embedded in Scratch, which allows her to leverage her existing knowledge to practice abstract concepts. These findings corroborate previous work from Howell et al. (2016) in which students' identification was increased through the personalization of designed artifacts. To illustrate, Amelia was able to take advantage of the multiple pathways embedded in Scratch to go above and beyond expectations, as evidenced by her sophisticated understanding of the computer science concepts involved in her games. She explained how she used conditional logic and variables to create rules and keep score in her game. Although she doesn't name the concepts using discipline-specific terms (i.e., conditionals, variables, operators), she correctly describes them using her everyday sense-making abilities. To this end, she is able to leverage her knowledge of how games work to articulate the rules that her program will follow. As Amelia was recently reclassified as Fluent English Proficient, she may have acquired communicative competence that enabled her to express abstract ideas but is still working on developing the discipline-specific terminology to deliver a more precise account of her programming processes.

Amelia feels that she can express herself in computer science by adding her personal touch to her projects and by helping people understand her perspective. For example, she describes her About Me, which was an interactive collage in which students shared characteristics about themselves with their classmates.

> I express myself through computer science, I like ... putting my own touch on it and helping people see what my perspective and stuff is ... Like in my About Me [Scratch project], you express yourself and you kind of explain what you like and maybe you can make a Scratch for people to explore and see what you created.

Through expressing herself in her About Me project, Amelia was able to use computer science to share her perspective with her classmates and the broader Scratch community while at the same time exploring the work of her fellow Scratchers.

Through her expression, Amelia selects cultural elements, such as music, art, and fashion to share about herself. In this example (see Figure 7.3), Amelia engages in the labor-intensive process of uploading images from the internetinstead of easily selecting sprites from the Scratch library to add personal touches to her projects. The ability to add culturally relevant images and sprites can be seen as an extension of concepts revealed by Eglash et al. (2013). Complex mathematical concepts are often embedded in art and music, and other cultural artifacts. The freedom and validation of cultural representation afforded this student a platform to increase her investment. Just as Eglash et al. (2013) saw certain crafts as proxies for formal math learning and expression, we see the Scratch platform as a proxy for cultural expression and articulation of language. Amelia shares some of her preferences with her classmates, such as fashion design, drawing, hibiscus flowers, and bullet journals, and even takes the time to upload a recording of a song by American rapper Post Malone, revealing her attention to detail and preference for realism. These cultural artifacts exhibit choiceful behavior that Amelia adopts as she activates her ideal L2 self as it relates to her bicultural identity (Arnett, 2002). Taken together, the excerpts above reveal how Amelia leverages her cultural capital to connect with the curriculum as she begins to envision herself as an active participant in the formal classroom setting (Darvin & Norton, 2017; Dörnyei, 2009).

Through her work in Scratch, Amelia also animated her projects using special effects that she learned from her peers and the broader Scratch community (see Figure 7.2). Using special effects pushes students to think in a more abstract way about how others will perceive their models, with the goal of enhancing the user's experience (Resnick et al., 2009). In the following excerpt, Amelia discusses how she explores Scratch at home and learns about programming by looking at other projects to see how others have created them.

> Sometimes in my house I explore in Scratch. I have access to a computer, so sometimes I go to Scratch and explore ... other projects. I look at other projects and use them and see how they created it.

In this example (see Figure 7.4), Amelia employed the change color special effect she learned from her peers to create dazzling images, and then extended this practice by incorporating rotation effects in an attempt to remix work she modeled after that of her peers. Amelia demonstrated her skills by sharing her work with her classmates, which represented a typical mechanism for passing computer science knowledge to other members in Angela's classroom. In this example, we see how multimodal elements of new technologies mediate language learning by leveraging students' social semiotic systems (Satar, 2015). Through interaction with her peers, Amelia symbolically negotiates meaning with them through non-verbal elements such as pictures, animations, example code, sound, color, and motion (Gumperz, 1982, 2005). By reusing and remixing existing projects into her own, Amelia positioned herself as an active member of the computing classroom, thereby developing a more durable sense of identity as a person who does computer science (Darvin & Norton, 2017).

Throughout her participation in the curriculum, Amelia expressed her agency by choosing to participate in what she perceived would provide affordances for her budding identity and engaged in discipline-specific practices in concert with their own perceptions and preferences. Taken together, the excerpts above suggest that the exploratory and collaborative nature of computer science, in addition to the freedom to choose how to express oneself, help to solidify multilingual students' budding computer science identities.

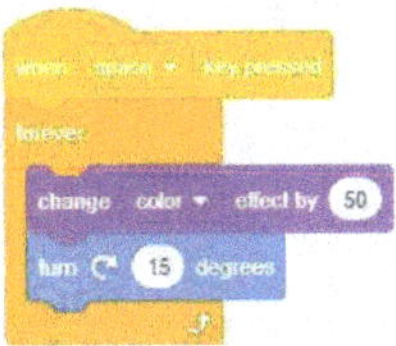

Figure 7.4. Screenshot of Amelia's Special Effects

5.2 Diego

We now turn to Diego, who is designated as an English learner and described by his teacher as having "high interest in coding" but his "behavior varies according to his focus level." The excerpt below describes Diego's lived experience with pair programming a holiday-themed Scratch project with his partner, Adrian. Pair programming is a paired computer science activity in which one student acts as the driver, who controls the computer and drags the code blocks to the scripts area, and the other student acts as the navigator, providing directions and corrective feedback to the driver. During pair programming activities, Angela would have students switch roles as driver and navigator every 15 minutes.

> Diego: Well, this is a project that Miss Valencia said we had to do for the Christmas thing. It was kind of annoying doing it because it kinda stressed me out doing it ... because me and my partner Adrian couldn't work good on the pair programming … Cause she wanted it [the reindeer Sprite] to move slower but I wanted it to move fast.
> Interviewer: Okay. So did you try what she wanted to do?
> Diego: Yeah, we tried it but it didn't work because it would end up like this.
> Interviewer: I see. Does she agree that it didn't work?
> Diego: Yeah, she agreed.
> Interviewer: Okay. And then you both changed it back?
> Diego: Yeah. And then we both agreed that we should make it 15 degrees and we should add some words to it. And that's why it goes fast and we added "follow mouse." So now it follows a mouse.

Although Diego seemed to have strong intrinsic motivation to program the joint project in specific ways, he still described the pair programming activity as stressful. He is frequently met with disagreement by his partner Adrian, encountering style disagreements with his classmates, which leads him to feel disinvested from the project. For example, the excerpt below discusses a compromise that he made with his partner that left him feeling that their program was "funky" and "weird looking."

> This was ... Adrian's designed Scratch cat. And look, I feel like it's kind of funky. It's kind of funky because of the look that it has. It

> looks literally funny. I am not going to lie. It looks very funny and it looks kind of weird though.

The negotiation of meaning through agreement and disagreement is a key skill that upper elementary students need to practice for successful collaboration. Research indicates that stimulating rich discourse through collaborative activities such as pair programming has positive outcomes on multilingual student learning in STEM (NASEM, 2018). However, successful collaboration occurs only when each member's feedback and expertise are recognized by the rest of the group. When patterns of social control in classrooms reveal themselves as necessitating conformity to be a respected member, socialization can lead to dramatic narratives that undermine strong students' contributions (Hand, 2010). Diego's compromising his ideals to conform to his partner's preferences leaves him feeling disempowered and disengaged from the project. It is plausible that presenting Diego with the linguistic functions for expressing agreement and disagreement could have facilitated the negotiating of pair programming moves with his partner. Due to the difficulty Diego experienced with pair programming, he expresses his lack of interest in formal computer science instruction, even despite his strong intrinsic motivation to create new projects and his high levels of competence noted by his teacher. To illustrate, in the excerpt below, Diego discusses his affinity for playing games in Scratch and compares them to classroom lessons, which he finds to be uninteresting.

> I think [games] would be a good way to entertain ourselves ... because sometimes I really get bored with some of the lessons and I like to explore sometimes.

While Diego is "bored" with the computer science lessons, he displays interest in programming games in Scratch on his own. In the excerpt below, he discusses a game he likes playing called Geometry Dash, describing how he could modify and improve the project.

> Um, and maybe I could make my own Geometry Dash game and try to replicate it so it'd be better than this game. I liked the slow-motion block ... Look, when you jumped it goes on slow motion! Maybe at the end of my own game I could use it too. I liked how it goes fast and then when you press the space bar, it's "slow motion" and how it gives you more time to like jump down.

This example echoes Amelia's responses by highlighting these students' affinity for popular culture, in Diego's case his interest in video games. We see an increase in investment when students can personalize and incorporate components of their culture. In these instances, the students' cultures are validated through their inclusion in a school project, where lessons rarely incorporate student agency and cultural components such as art and music. For example, throughout the interview, Diego mentioned how he incorporates elements of several popular video games such as Fortnite into his own games. In instances such as these, Diego is able to leverage his cultural capital by applying his own cultural references to computer science knowledge, skills, and attitudes. Unfortunately, Diego did not perceive his cultural referents to be valued in the classroom.

In the example above, he was motivated to create his own game based on an existing game, and incorporated elements of the existing game, such as the slow-motion effect, which gave characters more time to jump. However, when the interviewer probed further into whether he had made any games on his own, Diego said "I tried making my own game in school, but I ended up deleting it," suggesting he makes his own games at home but deletes them when he is in a formal learning environment. Together, the excerpts above reveal that despite his keen interest in practicing computer science, Diego's social capital is not viewed as legitimate by his teacher and peers, which leads to his disinterest in coding within the context of the classroom.

Angela, the classroom teacher, noted that due to her diverse range of students, she had to pay special attention while assigning students to pairs. In the excerpt below, she describes why she paid particular attention to students like Diego.

> Like anybody who has accepting behavior … accepting help from [students] versus someone like, you know, Diego, who is really bright and loves it and has no problem with trial and error and going back and forth. But because his personality is a little more domineering, he wasn't always my first choice to say go help [another student]. I had to specifically put somebody that I knew was friends with him, and say, "Hey, go help that friend." And then it would work out, you know, so personalities and people were really important. Um, who to pair him with. Um, what does an ideal connection look like for you?

In this example, we see how Angela chooses not to position Diego as an expert due to his "domineering" personality. Instead of fostering his enthusiasm during pair programming by providing extra opportunities to develop his budding interest in computer science, she co-constructs the narrative that Diego is a liability who might cause behavioral issues during pair programming.

6 Discussion

At the heart of computer science education lies the ability to develop instructional curricula and technologies that foster creativity, innovation, and inclusion for learners from traditionally marginalized communities, such as multilingual students. This provides them with the capacity to be competitive in a knowledge economy, promoting active and engaged learning. With the realization that multilingual students are developing their varied repertoires in informal learning environments came the desire to leverage their linguistic and cultural capital to empower them to become active creators of new technologies. This chapter sought to uncover the ways in which multilingual students invest in computer science, and how their investment is related to linguistic and sociocultural factors. The field of computer science presents valuable opportunities for educators and researchers who wish to develop multilingual students' budding identities, to make instructional materials relevant to their existing cultural and linguistic resources (Eglash et al., 2013; James DiSalvo et al., 2011), and to foster communication through multiple modalities (Fernandes et al., 2017). In addition, this chapter aims to showcase how computer science curricula can complement many of the aims of traditional elementary education.

For example, Amelia's experiences reveal that even when multilingual students are working in digital platforms such as Scratch, they still encounter the same demands as other content area classes, such as math, science, and English courses. By working in Scratch, multilingual students build upon key computer science and language concepts, such as communicating computer science terminology, algorithmic thinking, conditional logic, and design principles. However, despite the advanced understanding and proceduralized knowledge displayed by Amelia, our analysis reveals that multilingual students do not necessarily need an extensive background in language before they can communicate their understanding (Lee, 2005). This finding corroborates the growing body of work on multilingual students in computing, such as efforts to use translanguaging to engage multilingual students' full linguistic repertoires and foster participation in computational literacies (Vogel et al., 2020). Findings such as these present critical entry points for multilingual students in computing by providing access to complex computational concepts and practices without unnecessarily taxing linguistic resources (Lee, 2005).

Ultimately, Amelia was able to develop her budding identity in computer science because her linguistic and cultural capital was recognized as a legitimate form of classroom participation. Research on engaging multilingual students in STEM suggests that leveraging students' semiotic and cultural resources promotes content learning (NASEM, 2018). The multimodal elements of the curricular intervention enabled Amelia to draw upon her semiotic resources through the use of images, special effects, and video to express herself. Connected to her semiotic resources are the cultural references Amelia used in her projects – Amelia mixed CS design components with elements of Latina popular culture, including fashion design, drawing, hibiscus flowers, bullet journals, and music videos. These instances suggest that Amelia leveraged her cultural capital to engage in programming, thereby bridging her cultural assets with CS activities conducted in formal learning environments such as the classroom. This process solidified her perception of herself as a valuable member of the computer science classroom community while leveraging aspects of her cultural identity to shape how CS is enacted in formal settings.

Unfortunately, this was not the case for Diego. While Diego leveraged his cultural capital to remix a complex mathematical computing game, he did not upload it to the classroom project studio but instead deleted it. Both Diego and Amelia shared an affinity for embedding cultural references into their programs, but Diego did not view his particular referents to be pertinent to classroom dynamics. A plausible explanation for this observed phenomenon could be the quality of interactions that Diego experienced with his peers. While Amelia viewed her peers as assets, recreating special effects used by many of her classmates, Diego viewed his classmates as an obstacle to creating programs according to his own specifications. Research corroborates the critical role peer-to-peer interaction plays in successfully engaging multilingual students in STEM (Denner et al., 2014). Conversely, multilingual students are less likely to develop discipline-specific motivation if they do not have direct, high-quality contact with other L2 speakers (Dörnyei, 2009). In Diego's case, the teacher co-constructed an oppositional narrative between Diego and his peers, which was reified by Diego's lived experience with pair programming. While co-construction is generally recognized as the basis for characterizing dramatic narratives that arise through interaction (Hand, 2010), the sociocultural nature of these narratives is often overlooked when focusing on individual student characteristics (Hand, 2010), such as Diego's "domineering" nature. Ultimately, Diego's issues resulted from the narrative that was co-constructed around his participation that delegitimized the recognition of his cultural and linguistic capital by his peers and his teacher (Darvin & Norton, 2017; Hand, 2010). Future work should pay special attention to approaches to teaching computer science that leverage the assets of students with diverse language and computing proficiencies.

As mentioned above, the "content first" approach to our curriculum design allowed Amelia and Diego to access complex computational concepts without being bogged down in unnecessary linguistic tasks. In Amelia's case, she was able to use her everyday sensemaking abilities to describe advanced computing concepts such as conditionals and loops. However, during pair programming, Diego had difficulty negotiating design choices with his partner. While the curriculum was designed to stimulate rich discourse, future research should examine how student expertise is recognized and positioned during group work by peers and by the teacher. Despite the many affordances of Diego's classroom, certain classroom practices (e.g., aspects of pair work, teacher-designated "experts") may have had unintended consequences and caused some learners, such as Diego, to disinvest. Furthermore, while the curriculum these students participated in included linguistic scaffolds for the functions of social interaction, such as help seeking and asking for clarification, future work should examine the role that teaching the functions of agreement and disagreement plays in providing positive pair-programming opportunities for multilingual students.

In order for multilingual students to develop strong computer science identities, curricula must be responsive to their culturally and linguistically diverse backgrounds. This can be achieved by connecting schooling to their existing resources in a manner that allows them to become valued members of the classroom community. Curricula such as these might pave the way for higher engagement not only in computer science but in school as well. In this way, the field of computer science can form the bedrock for providing equitable participation which values the views and perspectives of marginalized youth. However, as we have seen in this chapter, curriculum designers need to attend to the factors that impede participation and refrain from including activities that perpetuate dominant narratives about who does computer science. Particularly in collaborative activities, students must be given the necessary scaffolds and supports that will enable them to be recognized as valued members by their teachers and their peers. Given the underrepresentation and inequities that exist in the field of computer science today, this chapter sheds light on the factors that contribute to fostering multilingual students' budding identities while identifying barriers to participation.

Studies such as this one underscore how giving multilingual students access to computer science promotes meaningful participation for all students.

References

Arnett, J. J. (2002). The psychology of globalization. *American Psychologist, 57*(10), 774–783.

Bourdieu, P. (1991). *Language and symbolic power*. Harvard University Press.

Bransford, J. D., Brown, A. L., & Cocking, R. R. (2000). *How people learn* (Vol. 11). Washington, DC: National Academy Press.

Brinton, D., Snow, M. A., & Wesche, M. B. (2003). *Content-based second language instruction*. University of Michigan Press ELT.

Bureau of Labor Statistics. (2015). Occupational outlook handbook, 2014–2015: Computer and information technology. Retrieved from https://www.bls.gov/ooh/computer-and-informationtechnology/home.htm

Bybee, R. W. (1997). *Achieving scientific literacy: From purposes to practices*. Heinemann.

Canagarajah, A. S. (2013). *Translingual practice: Global Englishes and cosmopolitan relations*. Routledge.

Cook, V. J. (1991). The poverty-of-the-stimulus argument and multicompetence. *Interlanguage Studies Bulletin (Utrecht)*, *7*(2), 103–117.

Cook, V. J. (2003). *Effects of the L2 on the L1*. Multilingual Matters.

Csizér, K., & Dörnyei, Z. (2005). The internal structure of language learning motivation: Results of structural equation modelling. *Modern Language Journal*, *89*(1), 19–36.

D'Amato, J. (1996). Resistance and compliance in minority classrooms. In E. Jacob & C. Jordan (Eds.), *Minority education: Anthropological perspectives* (pp. 181–208). Ablex.

Darvin, R., & Norton, B. (2017). Language, identity, and investment in the twenty-first century. *Language Policy and Political Issues in Education, Encyclopedia of Language and Education,* Springer International Publishing.

Denner, J., Werner, L., Campe, S., & Ortiz, E. (2014). Pair programming: Under what conditions is it advantageous for middle school students?. *Journal of Research on Technology in Education*, *46*(3), 277–296.

Dörnyei, Z. (2009). The L2 motivational self system. *Motivation, language identity and the L2 self, 36*(3), 9–11.

Eccles, J. S., & Wigfield, A. (2000). Schooling's influences on motivation and achievement. *Securing the future: Investing in children from birth to college*, 153–181. Russell Sage Foundation.

Eglash, R., Gilbert, J. E., & Foster, E. (2013). Toward culturally responsive computing education. *Communications of the ACM*, *56*(7), 33–36.

Estrella, G., Au, J., Jaeggi, S. M., & Collins, P. (2018). Is inquiry science instruction effective for English language learners? A meta-analytic review. *AERA Open*, *4*(2), 1–23.

Fernandes, A., Kahn, L. H., and Civil, M. (2017). A closer look at bilingual students' use of multimodality in the context of an area comparison problem from a large-scale assessment. *Educational Studies in Mathematics*, *95*(3), 263–282.

Fordham, S., & Ogbu, J. U. (1986). Black students' school success: Coping with the "burden of 'acting White.'" *Urban Review*, *18*(3), 176–206. https://doi.org/10.1007/bf01112192

Fryer, R. G. (2006). Acting White. *Education Next*, *6*(1), 52–59.

Gardner, R. C., & Lambert, W. E. (1959). Motivational variables in second-language acquisition. *Canadian Journal of Psychology/Revue canadienne de psychologie*, *13*(4), 266.

Gilmartin, S. K., Li, E., & Aschbacher, P. (2006). The relationship between interest in physical science/engineering, science class experiences, and family contexts: Variations by gender and race/ethnicity among secondary students. *Journal of Women and Minorities in Science and Engineering*, *12*(2–3), 179–207. https://doi.org/10.1615/jwomenminorscieneng.v12.i2-3.50

Gumperz, J. J. (1982). *Discourse strategies*. Cambridge University Press. http://dx.doi.org/10.1017/CBO9780511611834

Gumperz, J. J. (2005). Interactional sociolinguistics: A personal perspective. In D. Schiffrin, D. Tannen, & H. E. Hamilton (Eds.), *The handbook of discourse analysis*, pp. 215–228. Blackwell.

Hall, J. K., Vitanova, G., & Marchenkova, L. A. (2004). Authoring the self in a non-native language: A dialogic approach to agency and subjectivity. In Dialogue With Bakhtin on Second and Foreign Language Learning (pp. 150–170). Routledge.

Hand, V. M. (2010). The co-construction of opposition in a low-track mathematics classroom. *American Educational Research Journal*, *47*(1), 97–132. https://doi.org/10.3102/0002831209344216

Higgins, C., & Stoker, K. (2011). Language learning as a site for belonging: A narrative analysis of Korean adoptee-returnees. *International Journal of Bilingual Education and Bilingualism*, *14*(4), 399–412.

Howell, J., Tofel-Grehl, C., Fields, D. A., & Ducamp, G. J. (2016). E-textiles to teach electricity: An experiential, aesthetic, handcrafted approach to science. *Teacher pioneers: visions from the edge of the map.* pp. 232–245. ETC Press.

Jacob, S., Nguyen, H., Garcia, L., Richardson, D., & Warschauer, M. (2020, March). Teaching computational thinking to multilingual students through inquiry-based learning. *2020 Research on Equity and Sustained Participation in Engineering, Computing, and Technology (RESPECT)* (Vol. 1, pp. 1–8). IEEE.

Jacob, S., Garcia, L., & Warschauer, M. (2020). Leveraging multilingual identities in computer science education. *Technology and the Psychology of Second Language Learners and Users*, pp. 309–331. Palgrave Macmillan.

Jacob, S., Nguyen, H., Tofel-Grehl, C., Richardson, D., & Warschauer, M. (2018). Teaching computational thinking to English learners. *NYS TESOL Journal*, *5*(2), 1–12.

James DiSalvo, B., Yardi, S., Guzdial, M., McKlin, T., Meadows, C., Perry, K., & Bruckman, A. (2011, May). African American men constructing computing identity. *Proceedings of the SIGCHI Conference on Human Factors in Computing Systems* (pp. 2967–2970).

Janzen, J. (2008). Teaching English language learners in the content areas. *Review of Educational Research*, *78*(4), 1010–1038.

Kafai, Y., Searle, K., Martinez, C., & Brayboy, B. (2014, March). Ethnocomputing with electronic textiles: Culturally responsive open design to broaden participation in computing in American Indian youth and communities. In *Proceedings of the 45th ACM technical symposium on Computer Science Education* (pp. 241–246).

Kinginger, C. (2004). Alice doesn't live here anymore: Foreign language learning and identity reconstruction. *Negotiation of Identities in Multilingual Contexts*, *21*(2), 219–242.

Leander, K. M. (2002). Locating Latanya: The situated production of identity artifacts in classroom interaction. *Research in the Teaching of English*, *37*(2), 198–250.

Lee, O. (2005). Science education with English language learners: Synthesis and research agenda. *Review of Educational Research*, *75*(4), 491–530.

Lee, O., Llosa, L., Grapin, S., Haas, A., & Goggins, M. (2019). Science and language integration with English learners: A conceptual framework guiding instructional materials development. *Science Education*, *103*(2), 317–337.

Lincoln, Y. S., & Denzin, N. K. (Eds.). (2003). *Turning points in qualitative research: Tying knots in a handkerchief* (Vol. 2). Rowman Altamira.

McFarland, D. (2001). Student resistance: How the formal and informal organization of classrooms facilitate everyday forms of student defiance. *American Journal of Sociology*, 107(3), 612–678.

McFarland, D. (2004). Resistance as a social drama: A study of change-oriented encounters. *American Journal of Sociology*, *109*(6), 1249–1318.

McLeod, J. (1987). *Ain't no makin' it: Leveled aspirations in a low-income neighborhood*. Westview.

Menard-Warwick, J. (2005). Both a fiction and an existential fact: Theorizing identity in second language acquisition and literacy studies. *Linguistics and Education*, *16*(3), 253–274.

Michaels, S., & O'Connor, C. (2015). Conceptualizing talk moves as tools: Professional development approaches for academically productive discussion. *Socializing intelligence through talk and dialogue*, 347–362.

Moje, E. B., Ciechanowski, K. M., Kramer, K., Ellis, L., Carrillo, R., & Collazo, T. (2004). Working toward third space in content area literacy: An examination of everyday funds of knowledge and discourse. *Reading Research Quarterly*, *39*(1), 38–70.

National Academies of Sciences, Engineering, and Medicine (NASEM). (2018). *English learners in STEM subjects: Transforming classrooms, schools, and lives*. The National Academies Press. https://doi.org/10.17226/25182; https://www.nap.edu/catalog/25182/english-learners-in-stem-subjects-transforming-classrooms-schools-and-lives

National Research Council. (2012). *A framework for K–12 science education: Practices, crosscutting concepts, and core ideas*. National Academies Press.

Norton, B. (2013). *Identity and language learning: Extending the conversation*. Multilingual Matters.

Osborne, J., Collins, S., Ratcliffe, M., Millar, R., & Duschl, R. (2003). What "ideas-about-science" should be taught in school science? A Delphi study of the expert community. *Journal of Research in Science Teaching*, *40*(7), 692–720.

Pavlenko, A. (2001). "In the world of the tradition, I was unimagined": Negotiation of identities in cross-cultural autobiographies. *International Journal of Bilingualism*, *5*(3), 317–344.

Peppler, K. A., & Warschauer, M. (2011). Uncovering literacies, disrupting stereotypes: Examining the (dis)abilities of a child learning to computer program and read. *International Journal of Learning and Media*, *3*(3), 15–41.

Phillips, N., & Hardy, C. (2002). *Discourse analysis: Investigating processes of social construction* (Vol. 50). Sage Publications.

Pinkard, N., Erete, S., Martin, C. K., & McKinney de Royston, M. (2017). Digital youth divas: Exploring narrative-driven curriculum to spark middle school girls' interest in computational activities. *Journal of the Learning Sciences*, *26*(3), 477–516.

Resnick, M., Maloney, J., Monroy-Hernández, A., Rusk, N., Eastmond, E., Brennan, K., Millner, A., Rosenbaum, E., Silver, J., Silverman, B., & Kafai, Y. (2009). Scratch: programming for all. *Communications of the ACM*, *52*(11), 60–67.

Resnick, M., & Silverman, B. (2005, June). Some reflections on designing construction kits for kids. In *Proceedings of the 2005 Conference on Interaction Design and Children* (pp. 117–122). ACM.

Ricento, T. (2005). Considerations of identity in L2 learning. *Handbook of research in second language teaching and learning*, *1*, 895–910. Routledge.

Rosebery, A. S., Warren, B., & Conant, F. R. (2008). Appropriating scientific discourse: Findings from language minority classrooms. *The Journal of the Learning Sciences*, *2*(1), 61–94.

Satar, H. M. (2015). Sustaining multimodal language learner interactions online. *Calico Journal*, *32*(3), 480–507.

Schleppegrell, M. J., Achugar, M., & Oteíza, T. (2004). The grammar of history: Enhancing content-based instruction through a functional focus on language. *TESOL Quarterly*, *38*(1), 67–93.

Shaw, M., & Kafai, Y. (2020). Charting the identity turn in K-12 computer science education: Developing more inclusive learning pathways for identities.

Proceedings of the International Conference on the Learning Sciences (ICLS'20).

Smith, M. (2016, January 30). Computer science for all. [Web log comment]. Retrieved from https://obamawhitehouse.archives.gov/blog/2016/01/30/computer-science-all

Stinson, D. W. (2006). African American male adolescents, schooling (and mathematics): Deficiency, rejection, and achievement. *Review of Research in Education, 76*(4), 447–506.

Tissenbaum, M., Sheldon, J., & Abelson, H. (2019). From computational thinking to computational action. *Communications of the ACM, 62*(3), 34–36.

Vogel, S., Hoadley, C., Castillo, A. R., & Ascenzi-Moreno, L. (2020). Languages, literacies and literate programming: Can we use the latest theories on how bilingual people learn to help us teach computational literacies? *Computer Science Education, 30*(4), 420–443.

Weedon, C. (1997). *Feminist practice and poststructuralist theory* (2nd ed.). Blackwell.

Willis, P. (1977). *Learning to labor*. Columbia University.

Wing, J. M. (2006). Computational thinking. *Communications of the ACM, 49*(3), 33–35.

Wolz, U., Leitner, H. H., Malan, D. J., & Maloney, J. (2009). Starting with Scratch in Computer science 1. In Proceedings of the 40th ACM technical symposium on CS education, p. 23. ACM.

About the authors

Sharin Jacob is a PhD in Education candidate at the University of California, Irvine. Her research interests bring together theory from the learning sciences, computer science education, and applied linguistics to examine the linguistic and sociocultural factors that help multilingual students succeed in mastering computational thinking. She has five years' experience teaching English as a Second Language, where she taught all levels of proficiency, including sheltered math and science to newcomers. She was recently awarded the UCI Public Impact Distinguished Fellowship for her commitment to bringing actionable change for multilingual students in computing.

Jonathan Montoya is a Ph.D. student at the University of California Irvine. His research explores STEM and CTE pathways. Jonathan leverages his decades long experience as a practitioner in secondary and post secondary STEM and CTE classrooms to inform and ground his work. His most recent paper "Opportunity Gap and Women in the Energy Infrastructure Workforce" explores secondary and post-secondary STEM pathways for young women.

Mark Warschauer is a Professor of Education at the University of California, Irvine where he directs the Digital Learning Lab. His research focuses on uses of digital media to promote language and literacy development among culturally and linguistically diverse learners. He is Principal Investigator of a National Science Foundation-funded project developing a computational thinking curriculum for multilingual students. Dr. Warschauer is author and editor of a wide range of books, including, *Learning in the Cloud: How (and Why) to Transform Schools with Digital Medi*a. He is founding editor of *Language Learning & Technology* journal and inaugural editor of *AERA Open.*

Appendix

Student Computer Science Identity Interview

1. What is a computer scientist? What do computer scientists do?
2. How do you feel about doing computer science? Tell me more about that.
3. How do you practice computer science outside of school, if at all? (For example, do you write programs or build something using codes?)
4. What would you like your job to be when you grow up?
5. How do you express yourself through computer science, if at all? (How do you express yourself in your Scratch projects?)
6. How do you feel about your ability to learn computer science?
7. How do you feel when you make a mistake in your program?
   a Do you feel like you have the ability to fix your mistakes?
   b Give one example of a time when you made a mistake. How did you fix it?
8. How can computer scientists make a difference in this world, if at all?
9. Does anyone in your family do computer science? If so, who are they? And what do they do?
10. Do you know anyone outside of your family who does computer science? If so, who are they? And what do they do?
11. Do you talk with people about computer science outside of school? If so, with whom? And what do you talk about?
12. What does your family think about computer science? What does your family say when you tell them about your work in computer science?
13. What do your friends think about computer science? Do your friends enjoy doing computer science?
14. What do your friends say when you tell them about your work in computer science?

8 On *Becoming* Language Education Professionals: Reframing Doctoral Students' Perceptions of Language Teacher Identity Negotiations

Patrick Mannion and John I. Liontas

1 Introduction

Language teacher identity (LTI) has been the focus of much recent research in the field of second/foreign language (hereafter *L2*) teacher education (Barkhuizen, 2017; Yazan & Lindahl, 2020b). Said emphasis is based on widely held perceptions that LTI has a significant influence on language teacher education (Kayi-Aydar, 2019) and interest in how LTI relates to "[w]hat constitutes a 'good teacher' and 'good teaching'" (De Costa & Norton, 2017, p. 3). Research on LTI suggests teachers' beliefs about their identities have a relationship to their classroom practices (Kanno & Stuart, 2011; Kayi-Aydar, 2019), or, as De Costa and Norton (2017, p. 8) succinctly stated, "Language teaching is identity work." As such, the development of knowledge about teacher identity is of central importance to improving the quality of L2 teaching (Goh, 2015). This current interest in LTI and its relation to teacher education and teaching practices is equally reflected in the numerous publications on these subjects (Liontas, 2020a, 2020b; Yazan & Lindahl, 2020b).

While much research has focused on pre- and in-service LTI, relatively less research appears to exist on the identity perceptions of Second Language Acquisition (SLA) doctoral students, particularly in relation to educational technology (ET). In our study, we address this gap. Specifically, we discuss the findings of an exploratory and descriptive qualitative case study in which multilingual SLA doctoral students, enrolled in a summer course on the use of ET in L2 education, employed asynchronous online discussion forums and collaborative digital stories to negotiate and express beliefs and practices about their private and public identities. Utilizing multimodal digital texts, participants engaged in dialogic discourse as a community of doctoral students to address issues related to the use of ET in L2 education, including their developing beliefs about ideal ET-related practices. This research has particular relevance in the field of L2 teacher education because participants' perceptions and evolving beliefs are likely to have a direct influence on their future work as teacher educators and researchers alike. In what follows, we begin with a literature review involving LTI and digital storytelling. We then present the method of the research design and discoveries we were able to make. Finally, we discuss implications for both research and practice, as well as some concluding thoughts on how best to reframe multilingual doctoral students' perceptions of language teacher identity negotiations in communities of practice.

2 Literature Review

2.1 Research on Language Teacher Identity

As already noted, LTI occupies a prominent role in research on language teacher education and practices, and literature on LTI has appeared numerous times in a variety of academic publications. Interest in LTI resulted, at least in part, from an understanding in the field of L2 teacher education that "in order to understand language teaching and learning we need to understand teachers; and in order to understand teachers, we need to have a clearer sense of who they are" (Varghese et al., 2005, p. 22). The broad interest in LTI has also generated a diverse body of literature in terms of research contexts, types of participants, identity-related subject matter, inquiry methods, and theoretical frameworks. One result of this increasing interest has been calls to apply knowledge about LTI in teacher education practices (Liontas, 2020a, 2020b; Yazan & Lindahl, 2020b).

2.1.1 Contexts and Participants

To date, LTI research has taken place in a variety of contexts, including second (e.g., Farrell, 2011; Park, 2015) and foreign language (e.g., Mason & Chik, 2020) education. Studies have also involved participants from differing backgrounds, among them in-service K-12 teachers (Ding & Pawan, 2020), university instructors (Mason & Chik, 2020), writing instructors (Racelis & Matsuda, 2015), undergraduate (Ponzio, 2020) and graduate students (Vitanova, 2016), non-native speakers of the target language (Reis, 2015), and native and non-native speakers (e.g., Liontas, 2020b). Unsurprisingly, the body of literature on LTI is broad and extensive (Yazan & Lindahl, 2020b).

2.1.2 Foci and Theoretical Frameworks

Researchers have approached LTI from different theoretical perspectives (Barkhuizen, 2017; Cheung et al., 2015; De Costa & Norton, 2017). While organizing these into discrete categories may prove challenging, addressing their similarities is nonetheless a worthwhile pursuit. To begin with, the "social turn" in SLA research (Block, 2003; Firth & Wagner, 1997) coincided with or contributed to a growth of research focusing on the social or discursive nature of LTI development (De Costa & Norton, 2017; Varghese et al., 2005). These theories focus on various contexts and aspects of identity formation in that they embrace social interaction and socialization, and, more importantly, perhaps, the role the sociopolitical and sociocultural contexts play in LTI formation and identity work as relational process (Varghese et al., 2005). The "dialogic nature" of LTI – that is, how language teachers develop their identities through dialogic discourse with peers – is explored more closely in the work of Hallman (2015) and Liontas (2020b). This includes research undergirded by a Community of Practice framework (Wenger, 1998), which we discuss below. In other studies, authors have shifted the focus more to the characteristics or cognition of individual teachers. For example, research on LTI and teacher identity in general has indicated teacher knowledge or competence have an influence on teacher identity, which Beijaard et al. (2000) addressed in research on *professional* identity and the ways in which language teachers have engaged in identity work through their pedagogical practices (Kanno & Stuart, 2011; Racelis & Matsuda, 2015). However, as Trent (2015) and Xu (2017) point out, identity work involves collective and individual levels which influence each other. Still other researchers have adopted poststructural theoretical frameworks in teacher and LTI research to explore the identity constructs of non-native and native English speakers (Aneja, 2016) and the relationship between age and gender in TESOL instructors' identity perceptions (Mason & Chik, 2020).

2.1.3 Issues and Subjects

LTI research has also involved a number of issues and subjects related to teacher identity (Cheung et al., 2015; Yazan & Lindahl, 2020a). Chief among them are issues related to the dichotomy of native speakers and non-native speakers (Martinez, 2017); teacher knowledge (Kanno & Stuart, 2011; Yazan & Lindahl, 2020b); teacher affect or emotions (De Costa & Norton, 2017); language teachers performing multiple roles or concurrent identities (Farrell, 2011; Racelis & Matsuda, 2015); L2 teachers as researchers (Liontas, 2020b; Yazan & Lindahl, 2020b); social inequities related to in- or pre-service teachers' race (Gachago et al., 2014) or social class (van Galen, 2017); marginalization and privilege (Park, 2015); and monolingualism, multilingualism, and translanguaging (Ponzio, 2020). (For a detailed overview of theoretical frameworks and subjects in LTI research, see Barkhuizen, 2017, or LTI-related entries in Liontas, 2020a.)

2.1.4 Teacher Identity and Digital Storytelling

Teacher educators and researchers in different disciplines, including L2 education, have employed digital storytelling for a variety of identity-related purposes in multiple disciplines in teacher education. Although different definitions of digital storytelling exist today, we offer here the following brief synthesis of definitions from different sources, including those who focus on the use of digital storytelling for educational purposes: digital stories are typically brief videos consisting of still or moving images, the creators' voices for narration, and, optionally, background music (Lambert, 2013; Robin, 2016). In several digital storytelling studies, both pre- and in-service teachers have explored various social, gender, ethnic, racial, cultural, and linguistic issues in relation to their identities or the identities of their current or future students. Subjects of focus have included race and gender (Vitanova, 2016), and issues related to social and racial inequality or injustice (Gachago et al., 2014; van Galen, 2017). Other digital storytelling studies have focused on the pre- or in-service teachers' development of a Community of Practice (CoP) (Chigona, 2013), teacher attrition and resilience (Ng & Nicholas, 2015), and explorations and expressions of cultural or intercultural experiences (Dell Jones, 2018).

2.2 Community of Practice

According to Wenger-Trayner and Wenger-Trayner (2015, p. 1), "*Communities of practice are groups of people who share a concern or a passion for something they do and learn how to do it better as they interact regularly*" [italicized in original]. Three features that define a CoP are domain, community, and practices. First, the domain is an interest the community members share. Second, the community is a group of people who share interests and information, engage in the same practices, learn together, and support each other. Third, practice refers to members' development of "a shared repertoire of resources: experiences, stories, tools, ways of addressing recurring problems" (p. 2). Members of a CoP develop and express identities by forming and maintaining a community whose members share interests, exchange knowledge, and engage in similar practices. We chose CoP as a theoretical framework for this study because the participants represented a group (i.e., community) of doctoral students and nascent researchers and teacher educators who shared an interest (i.e., domain) in the use of ET in L2 education (i.e., practice), which was the primary subject of the course and related to their doctoral majors (SLA and ET).

So contextualized, we note that several authors have already employed a CoP framework in studies related to teacher education, teacher identity, or both (Breen, 2015; Chigona, 2013; Patton & Parker, 2017). Indeed, while some authors have focused on the construction and engagement within virtual or online CoP (Cumming-Potvin & Sanford, 2015; Moodley, 2019), others employed CoP as a theoretical framework in research on language teacher education and identity research (Clarke, 2008). Representative examples include how English-as-foreign-language teachers from Mexico on a teacher exchange program in the US engaged in online identity work (Ban, 2006), how the culture of an online CoP composed of ESL/EFL teachers influenced the members' engagement within their community and the impact their participation in the community had upon their professional knowledge (Kulavuz-Onal, 2013), how language teachers employed Twitter to create and engage within a virtual CoP that included both classmates in a teaching methods course and teachers in other locations in the US and Canada (Lord & Lomicka, 2014), and, finally, how researchers (Meihami & Rashidi, 2020) employed the CoP framework and a TESOL teacher identity model (Pennington, 2015) to explore EFL teachers' cultural identities.

Along similar lines of empirical research, we suggest the CoP framework would be particularly useful for the purposes of our study as we believed participants' perceptions of their membership in their community would no doubt play a central role in how they viewed themselves as doctoral students in general and nascent teacher educators and researchers in particular.

2.2.1 Competence and Artifacts

Other CoP concepts related to *practice* employed in this study are the notions of *competence* and *artifacts* (Mercieca, 2017; Wenger, 1998; Wenger-Trayner & Wenger-Trayner, 2015). Through participation, members develop *competence* with the practices of their community. They may also create *artifacts* reflecting that competence. Mercieca (2017, p. 13) described these notions thus:

> As participants further immerse themselves in a CoP, they build a level of competence through participating in shared decision-making and engaging creatively with problems as they arise (Wenger, 1998).

> The construction of artifacts, such as resources for others to use, further testifies to this competence.

We agree with Mercieca (2017) and note that, as we will show next, both pre- and in-service teachers develop dynamic identities through participation in the practices of a community. Furthermore, recognition of participants' competence with those practices bolsters the members' sense of identity and agency assertion. This is particularly true when participants engage in the collaborative construction of artifacts that attest to their evolving competence.

3 Method

3.1 Context

This study took place in a six-week summer doctoral seminar on the use of ET in L2 education. The seminar was a core course in a doctoral program focusing on Second Language Acquisition and Educational Technology in the College of Education at a large research university located in a suburban area in the southeast of the US. The course was hybrid and coupled weekly face-to-face classes with asynchronous online discussions. The assignments of the course were a collaborative digital storytelling project, asynchronous online discussions, a review of a software application or website, and an annotated bibliography of research on ET use in L2 education.

3.2 Participants

The participants were 16 doctoral students, one doctoral candidate, and one course instructor (hereafter *instructor*, the second author of this paper) in the doctoral program named above. The doctoral students were in their first, second, or third year in their program, and the doctoral candidate was in his fifth. The candidate participated in the course as an un-enrolled observer, attended all classes, and also engaged in the collaborative digital storytelling project the instructor named *digital stories with a twist* (or DS+). (A detailed account of DS+ is provided in Liontas, 2020b.) The 17 participants were from 10 different countries in East Asia, South Asia, the Middle East, North America, and South America. They were all multilingual and identified their native languages as Arabic, Chinese, English, Indonesian, Malaysian, Spanish, Tuareg, and Turkish. They had varying levels of interest in, knowledge of, and experience employing CALL-MALL technologies for personal and academic purposes. To protect their privacy, they are identified herein with numbers instead of names (P1, P2, P3, ... P17). We also note here that this group of participants represented a "sample of convenience" for the authors. The first author was in the same doctoral program as some of the participants, although in a different cohort, and therefore had some personal knowledge of some of them. The second author was the director of the doctoral program. The doctoral students were not offered any remuneration for participating in the study, and their participation did not affect course scores. Students enrolled in the course and the candidate all agreed to participate and signed informed-consent forms. Data collection commenced after the course had ended so as to avoid perceived violations of ethical conduct.

3.3 Data Collection

To triangulate the data and obtain deeper insight into participants' experiences and beliefs (Yin, 2014), two sets of data were collected: asynchronous online discussion forum posts and digital stories the participants collaboratively created. The university's institutional review board gave the authors permission to collect these data and conduct the proposed research. Both the entirety of data collection and the majority of data analysis occurred prior to the onset of the COVID-19 pandemic (World Health Organization, 2021).

3.3.1 Asynchronous Online Discussion Forums

The participants took part in six weekly asynchronous online discussions (henceforth *discussion*) in the course's Learning Management System. For each week's discussion, the instructor provided thoughtful prompts related to ET, L2 pedagogy, and/or the course's reading materials and learning objectives. He directed participants to first write posts in which they reflected critically on knowledge they had acquired from the course prior to responding to their classmates' posts. Collecting copies of these discussions provided a great many insights into participants' course experiences and their beliefs about ET, L2 education, multimodal digital texts, and their evolving identities.

3.3.2 Digital Stories

In another course assignment, groups of four or five students created digital stories, DS+, that promoted the use of ET in L2 education. The instructor asked participants to consider the audiences of their digital stories to be L2 teachers who were engaged in professional development. The digital stories were to be in a narrative format and a maximum of ten minutes in length. Participants were allowed to self-select group members and focus on any type of ET they desired. They created DS+ on four topics: (1) Gaming and Immersive Technologies, (2) Learning Management Systems (LMS), (3) Google Apps (Docs, Slides, Forms), and (4) Augmented Reality (AR).

3.4 Transcribing Digital Stories

For the DS+ transcription process, the first author followed recommendations by Meredith (2016) – multimodal transcripts should be characterized by "accessibility, usability, readability and reflecting the aims of the research" (p. 674) – and Bezemer and Mavers (2011) – multimodal transcribers need to keep in mind the purposes of the video creators, the transcriber's research purposes, the focus of the transcriptions, and what the transcriber chose to make salient in the transcriptions. To facilitate the DS+ transcription process, he created a tabular transcription template (Bezemer & Mavers, 2011) in a word-processing document. During transcription, he watched the digital stories and paused the story whenever the scenery on the screen changed in a manner that he believed was significant. He then took screen shots of the video and placed them in the transcription document. He also typed any text that appeared on the screen and wrote rich descriptions of the visual and audio elements. Below the screen shots, he transcribed any narration or dialogue that occurred during the scene word for word.

3.5 Thematic and Multimodality Analysis

To search for themes in the data, the first author employed thematic analysis (Guest et al., 2012). He first uploaded the DS+ transcripts and discussion forum posts into a qualitative data analysis software program, MaxQDA (VERBI Software, 2019), which enabled him to apply codes across all datasets. Next, he read through the data (transcripts, discussion posts) several times to familiarize himself with the contents. Thereafter, he read carefully through the data again and developed codes for meaningful chunks of the data. During this process, he also made notes and highlighted sections of text that seemed relevant to the purposes of this study. Following this, he looked for similarities, differences, and relationships among the codes in order to organize them into code groups. To ease this process, he employed a code-mapping tool in the qualitative data analysis software to create visual representations of the codes. Figure 8.1 shows an example of a preliminary

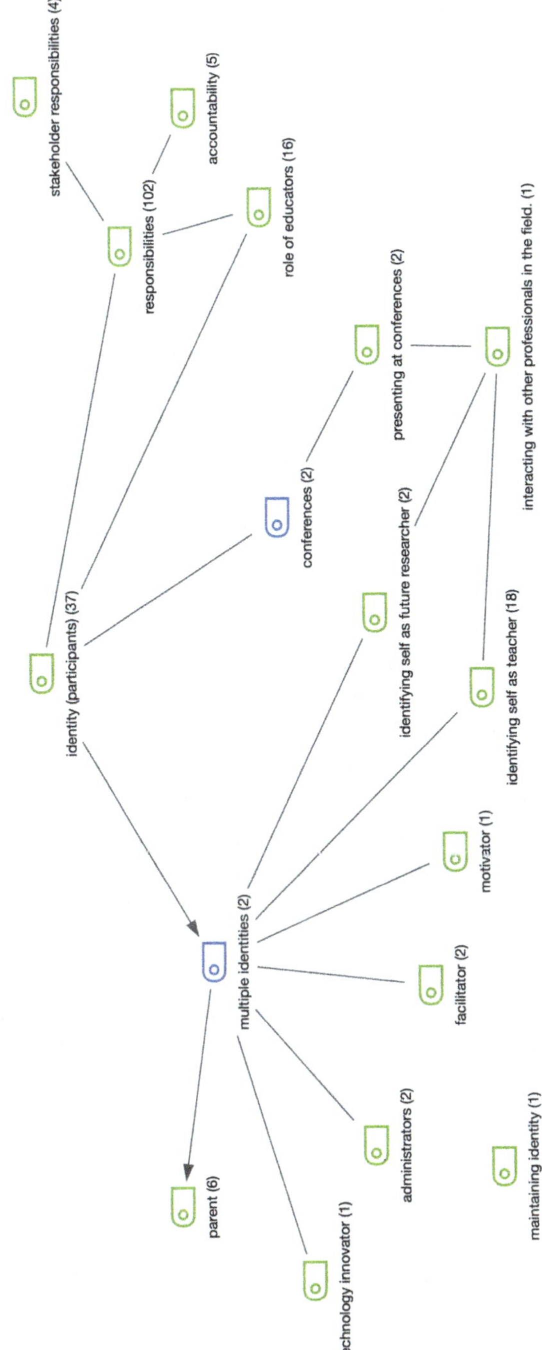

Figure 8.1. Example of Preliminary Code Map for Identity Coding

code map. He also printed the code maps and revised the code groupings manually with a pen. The coding process was also iterative, with him frequently checking and revising the codes and code groups as needed. In the final stages of thematic analysis, he developed themes from the groups of codes he had previously organized and consulted the second author about the codes and themes. Together they discussed ways in which these codes could be further refined while identifying the codified themes in a more practical and efficient manner.

To further explore how participants employed multiple semiotic systems (images, written language, spoken language) in their DS+ projects, the first author employed multimodal concepts from Unsworth's (2006) work on image–text relations. The three primary types of image–text ideational meaning relationships Unsworth described were (1) *concurrence* (Gill, 2002), (2) *connection*, and (3) *complementarity* (see Table 8.1). In the following paragraph, we offer brief descriptions of the primary types of image–text relations that we identified in the data (for a detailed description, see Unsworth, 2006).

Concurrence refers to the expression of similar ideational meanings by both images and texts and may involve a degree of *redundancy*, but there may also be differing or similar levels of generality between the image and language (Martinec & Salway, 2005). One of the modalities may also serve as an *instance* of the other. *Connection* can involve *projection* or *conjunctive relations*. With *projection*, one of the modes serves as the locution or thoughts of the other (Martinec & Salway, 2005). In *conjunctive relations* (Gill, 2002; Martinec & Salway, 2005), one of the modalities expresses "causal, temporal or spatial relations" (Unsworth, 2006, p. 65) for the other. Finally, *complementarity* refers to how images and language can either *augment* or *diverge* from each other's ideational meaning while making contributions to the overall meaning of the text. These concepts were employed during the thematic analysis coding process in an effort to analyze how participants had employed language and images together in their DS+ projects to express ideational meaning (Halliday & Matthiessen, 2014).

Table 8.1. Ideational Meaning Expressed in Image–Text Relations (Unsworth, 2006)

Connection	Concurrence	Complementarity
Projection	Redundance	Augmentation
Conjunction	Exposition	Divergence
	Instantiation	
	Homospatiality	

4 Discoveries

Through thematic analysis of the discussion forum posts, and thematic (Guest et al., 2012) and multimodal analysis (Unsworth, 2006) of the DS+ projects, two identity-related themes were identified in the data. One related to participants' explicit and implicit declarations and descriptions of their own multiple *digital* identities. The other involved participants' statements of beliefs regarding the ideal ET-related practices (e.g., roles, duties, obligations) of L2 teachers, which they considered themselves to be. We address both themes in detail in the following sections.

4.1 Digital Expressions of Teacher Identity

In the two datasets, participants focused much of their attention on their own digital identities and those of L2 teachers in general. In the discussion forums, they identified themselves, in both explicit and implicit terms, as performing multiple digital identities. They also described their perceptions of a community of doctoral students, of which they considered themselves members. In other discussion forum posts, they described their experiences in the course and doctoral program as a step in *a journey of becoming*. In the DS+ projects, they employed multiple modalities concurrently to express and delineate beliefs about their identities and the identities of other L2 education professionals.

4.1.1 Expressing Identities in Discussion Forums

In the discussion forums, participants primarily identified themselves as teachers, members of a doctoral program, and nascent researchers, although some mentioned performing other identities. Seven participants (P2, P3, P4, P5, P7, P10, P16) identified themselves "as educators" in discussion posts, and six of them (P3, P4, P5, P7, P8, P9) employed the inclusive plural pronoun *we* in discussions of the practices or duties of L2 teachers. P13 and P14 also explicitly identified themselves as researchers, with the latter declaring that "[i]t is our duty as SL/FL researchers to fill in the gaps that are in our field." Worth noting here is that declarations such as these about their language teacher-related identities appeared frequently in the discussion forums.

4.1.2 Members of a Community and a Family

In the discussion forums, the majority of participants (12 out of 17 to be precise) referred to themselves as members of their doctoral program.

Specifically, P4, P10, P12, P13, and P14 described their community as a *family*, and P13 and P14 employed the same phrase about it being "an honor to be a member of the [doctoral program] family." Several participants also described the nature of their community-family, including P13, who viewed the members as helpful and reliable: "You can count on the [doctoral program] family for guidance and support as you progress through the program." P4 and P10 expressed similar appreciation, with the former stating, "I was anxious and nervous because of the challenges ... pursuing a Ph.D. However, I found people who helped me and made me feel part of a 'team'; part of the [doctoral program] family. I really appreciated that." P7 and P15 expressed gratitude to their program mates for their positive experiences on the course. Statements such as these, in which participants identified themselves as members of a community (*family*) of doctoral students and/or showed appreciation to other members, appeared many a time throughout the discussion forums.

4.1.3 Education as a Journey

In addition to the term *family*, another identity-related metaphor six participants (P2, P3, P8, P9, P13, P15) employed was that of education representing *a journey of becoming*. The term *journey* referred to both the course and their doctoral education as a whole. P3 and P15, for example, described their course experiences as a *first* or *single step* in the journeys of their careers. Conversely, P15, who noted the course instructor frequently employed a Lao Tzu quote about journeys (Laozi, 3rd century B.C.E./2002) in class, expressed her view of education as a *journey* in her final discussion forum post:

> I would like to conclude with the quote that I was always being asked to read in class, "A journey of a thousand miles begins with a single step," as after a year's busy but fulfilling doctoral study, I noticed it is indeed the truth.

P3 also employed journey-like imagery to describe how the instructor had encouraged her and her classmates to examine the trajectory of ET use in L2 education to deepen their understanding of their profession: "We were asked to really understand where we came from and asked to foresee where we might be in the future that made it possible for me to truly understand and appreciate technology use in the classroom." As these quotes illustrate, some participants viewed their course and doctoral program experiences as stages (i.e., steps) in a process (i.e., *journey*) of *becoming* academics.

4.1.4 Multimodal Expressions of Identities

The participants employed the affordances of the multiple semiotic systems in their DS+ projects (e.g., images, background music, written and spoken language) to express and describe their identities. In particular, they identified themselves as L2 teachers who employ ET and promote its use among other L2 educators. For example, Group 2 employed ideational *concurrence* (Gill, 2002; Unsworth, 2006) in multiple scenes in their digital project by expressing similar meanings with both language and images. Two statements by Group 2's first narrator (P13), "I am a 21st-century teacher" and "We are the 21st-century teachers," occurred while images of people who seemed to be teachers appeared in the scene. Concurrent with the first statement, a teacher from a cartoon series appeared on the screen with the label "The 21C Teacher." During the latter statement, an image of people dressed in business attire, perhaps meant to represent teachers, appeared on the screen. In both instances, the narration and the images concurrently stated or suggested P13 was a teacher. Group 1's narrator similarly identified herself as a teacher by asking her audience (teachers engaged in professional development), "So how do *we* [emphasis added] overcome this problem?" during a discussion of the importance of employing authentic language in L2 education. Group 3 members, who did not explicitly identify themselves as teachers in their digital project, nevertheless employed multimodal methods to express their perceived identities. Their DS+ consisted of a series of dramatizations of classroom interaction in which one member played the role of a teacher and the other group members played the roles of students.

The four groups used other types of image–text relations in their DS+ projects. Group 1 employed *complementarity* (Unsworth, 2006) to express information about their digital identities. In a scene at the beginning of their digital story, on-screen text stated the total number of years of experience group members had with teaching languages and employing ET while images of each group member were visible on the screen. The two modalities augmented each other's ideational meaning in that the images provided information about the total number of group members and their physical characteristics (e.g., gender, general age), while the written text provided details about their professional experience. Group 4 also employed *complementarity* in a scene in which their narrator identified herself as being among L2 educators who teach a variety of languages: "The potential opportunities for AR use in the language classroom are as diverse as the languages *we* [emphasis added] are excited to teach." Concurrent with this narration, a world map containing multiple national flags appeared on the screen, which seemed to suggest L2 instructors, including Group 4 members (*we*), teach a wide variety of languages.

Another type of image–text relation Group 4 employed in their DS+ project was *projection*, a type of ideational *connection* in which either the image or the language represents the speech or thoughts of the other modality (Martinec & Salway, 2005; Unsworth, 2006). As P10 narrated Group 4's digital story, a cartoon character representing the narrator, who identified herself as a teacher, appeared in the scenes to advocate the use of AR in L2 education by describing the positive impact AR and ET in general can have on L2 learning processes and outcomes. The language in the narration (i.e., *locution*) and the image worked together to identify the narrator as a teacher.

4.1.5 Digital Expressions of Multiple Concurrent Identities

In addition to identifying themselves as teachers, researchers, and members of a community of doctoral students, participants claimed several other types of concurrent identities in both the digital stories and discussion forums. For example, P13 identified herself "as a teacher, parent, and 21st-century technology innovator" in Group 2's DS+ project. Expressions of various concurrent digital identities also appeared in the first week of the discussion posts, where some participants explicitly listed multiple identities and/or posted pictures which suggested other identities. For example, some participants' pictures included spouses and children. The current and past identities they explicitly or implicitly claimed in the two datasets (i.e., digital stories and discussion forums) included that of student, doctoral program member, teacher, researcher, technology innovator, mother, wife, speech-language pathologist, web designer, and secretary.

4.2 The Ideal Practices of L2 Education Professionals

As stated above, a second theme in the discussion forums and digital stories related to participants' beliefs about the ideal practices of L2 education professionals, a group of which they saw themselves as members. Their ideal L2 teacher role involved a student-centered approach to education. Relatively more specific ideal L2 teacher practices, which they viewed as duties or obligations of L2 teachers, included learning about and focusing on students, developing teacher competence (e.g., field- and ET-related knowledge), employing critical thought about reasons for ET use, and implementing ET to help students succeed in learning target language and culture.

4.2.1 Student-centered Teaching Roles

Several participants believed educational approaches should shift from a teacher-centered to a student-centered paradigm that involves focusing on learners and employing ET. In the discussion forums participants argued teacher roles should evolve from those of authoritative figures who impart knowledge to something more akin to a coach or guide who assists students in their learning. P9, for example, expressed a belief that "[e]ducators have a new role with technology in the classroom as guides, facilitators, motivators, and collaborators." P13 stated changes in L2 education should involve "going from 'teacher-centered instruction' to 'student-centered learning'." Comments such as these, about the need for L2 teacher roles to practice student-centered education and employ ET, appeared numerous times in the discussion forums.

The participants also addressed the topic of student-centered education in the DS+ projects. Group 2, for example, included five different images of classrooms of students employing computers, which seemed to suggest ET can promote student-centered education in which teachers facilitate learning rather than serve as sources of knowledge. In one of these scenes, Group 2 employed side-by-side images of classrooms from different eras. In the black-and-white photograph on the left, which was suggestive of teacher-centered education, a teacher appeared to be asking a student a question while pointing at a chalkboard. In the color image on the right, which appeared more student-oriented, a teacher looked over the shoulders of students who were focused on computer screens. Group 1 advocated a student-centered approach to L2 education involving games and play with the following quote by Crawford (2011): "Games are thus the most efficient and time-honored vehicle for education. We don't see mother lions lecturing cubs at chalkboards" (Chapter 2, para. 5). As these examples illustrate, participants expressed beliefs that ideal roles of L2 teachers involve creating student-centered classrooms and employing ET in a purposeful manner.

4.2.2 Duties of L2 Education Professionals

In both the digital stories and discussion threads, participants also expressed beliefs about relatively more specific duties or obligations of L2 education professionals (e.g., teachers, researchers). These duties included focusing on and learning about students, adhering to standards and becoming a competent teacher, learning about their discipline (e.g., SLA, CALL, MALL, ET), acquiring and keeping current with ET knowledge, applying critical thought about reasons for employing ET, and employing ET effectively for the benefit of L2 students.

The participants believed that L2 education professionals have a duty to learn about their students and to make them the focus of their attention. P13's post exemplified these concerns: "We, the next generation of researchers, need to advocate more for the FL learners." They recommended that L2 teachers learn more about their students because with that knowledge, they are better able to serve their students' needs and interests. On this topic, P9 stated, "*Without knowing your students, it is difficult to positively affect changes in their learning behaviors. Moreover, their personality provides crucial insights into how they* [*see*] *themselves and their abilities*" [italicized in original].

The emphasis on learning about students also appeared in the DS+ projects. Group 1's digital story included brief interviews in which P6 asked three language learners their opinions about different aspects of language learning. Group 2 pointed out that discussion forums in LMS can improve communication between teachers and students. The concern for students extended to recognition of individual students' differences and learning needs. P13, for example, expressed a belief in the discussion forums that successfully "igniting students' imagination" and improving their motivation comes from "being an attentive teacher responsive to the students' individual learning needs and learning styles." Participants also believed knowledge of students would help teachers decide what ET to employ and how to employ it. In another discussion post, P2 advised L2 teachers to "explore their needs, wants, skills, preferences, and styles before teaching them anything." She went on to say, "By doing so, we can utilize the appropriate technology that motivates our students to learn better and make progress." Comments such as these concerning the need to learn about and focus on students featured prominently in the data.

For participants, an important aspect of learning about and focusing on students was recognizing students' cultures and identities, along with helping students learn the target culture. On these topics, P9 expressed the following beliefs:

> [P]roviding a curriculum that highlights identity and culture within the language learning can benefit students immensely as it helps students cultivate their identity within the L2. Teachers and educators play a crucial role in providing this type of environment and I feel that this is part of their role as FL and SL educators. Teaching an L2

> is not only about language, it is about the culture, and developing their cultural literacy is an integral part of language learning.

P15 agreed with P9, stating, "[e]ven though incorporating every student's culture into the class is challenging, especially in a culturally diversified classroom, it is important for teachers to always bear that point in mind." P10 suggested learning about students' cultures and backgrounds with ET and then incorporating that knowledge into lessons. The need to learn about students and apply that knowledge in their teaching practices appeared in participants' statements with high frequency in the discussion forums.

In the discussion forums, participants frequently noted the need for L2 teachers to develop competence as teachers, meet professional standards, and be accountable for their teaching. For example, P4 stated, "As educators, we have the responsibility of finding effective ways to teach and create a positive environment where learning is the ultimate aim." In a discussion of educational games, P10 advocated flexible adaptation to the times: "We must adapt to the current academic and social environment of our time and refrain from continuing outdated educational practices."

Many participants expressed similar beliefs about the importance of *becoming* effective teachers and what effective teaching entails. They also believed professional standards, particularly those advanced by TESOL (TESOL International Association, 2020) and WIDA (2020), offer much-needed guidance for *becoming* effective L2 teachers. P4, for example, stated, "In my opinion, the professional standards guide the educators through the route to reach professional and educational goals." P7 shared her beliefs about professional standards serving "as guidelines in designing their curricula, syllabi, and lesson plans." P12 similarly advocated the use of TESOL and WIDA principles to help teachers develop "encouraging and effective language lessons and language classrooms." P4 noted that the "professional development workshops" organizations such as TESOL and WIDA offer can help teachers improve the quality of their teaching. As these examples attest, many participants believed L2 teachers should try to meet professional standards in order to *become* more effective teachers.

The participants also believed teachers have a duty to acquire and employ knowledge about SLA theories in order to improve the quality of L2 teaching. P8, for example, stated, "SLA professionals should always take SLA theories and models into consideration during the cross-disciplinary process of CALL design." P2 similarly believed that in order "[t]o design effective multimedia lessons, teachers should consider integrating these SLA hypotheses into their CALL instructional materials." As these examples demonstrate, several participants believed knowledge of SLA theories was necessary for L2 teachers to employ CALL-MALL effectively.

Learning about ET and keeping abreast of ET-related developments was important for improving the effectiveness of L2 education. As P16 put it, "We need to find ways to keep up with the latest technologies available to utilize in our classrooms today." P10 expressed similar beliefs: "If we do not stay up-to-date and offer our students a foundation in tech-based learning and literacy, they will be greatly disadvantaged when they leave our classrooms for their next step." Some participants advocated ET-related professional development for teachers and suggested that schools provide support for such training. P2, for example, stated, "there is a need for training sessions and workshops where teachers can learn about the latest technological tools to use in their classrooms."

The majority of participants stressed the need for L2 teachers to apply critical thought before implementing ET because they believed teachers should have sound reasons for its use. P5 cautioned against purposeless use of ET: "As warned by [the course instructor], implementations of technology in language classrooms *should always be done with a purpose and for a purpose*" [italicized in original]. P10 issued a similar caution regarding the utility of games in L2 education: "This must be done in a calculated and purposeful way. We are not entertainers, we are educators, and any component we incorporate into our curricula needs to serve a purpose." These statements are examples of views the majority of participants expressed regarding the need for sound reasons when employing ET in L2 education.

The participants also believed teachers have a duty to implement and employ ET in a determined manner to improve the processes and outcomes of teaching and learning. Regarding the importance of ET use, P2 stated, "I think in our field, technology plays a crucial role in teaching and learning, especially for the new generations," an opinion echoed in the words of P16: "Nowadays, it is almost impossible to teach without technology in the classroom." Regarding the consequences of teachers employing or not employing ET, P13 stated, "I believe it is important to remember technology won't replace teachers, but teachers who use technology will probably replace teachers who do not." On the subject of the potential positive impact ET can have on learning processes and outcomes, P5 explained, "The development of digital technology has transformed collaborative learning for the better, provided unprecedented access to learning resources, and improved learning experience as a whole." P7 also expressed multiple reasons for L2 teachers to employ ET, including that it could improve "digital literacy skills" and "provide authentic materials, accommodate different learning styles, serve the curricula, provide engaging FL/SL experience, increase collaboration in the language instruction and learning, etc." As these quotes attest, employing ET to improve the learning processes and outcomes in L2 education for the benefit of all students is an important consideration indeed.

5 Discussion

Both in the digital stories and in the discussion forums, the study's participants engaged in explorations, negotiations, and expressions of their professional identities and those of L2 teachers in general. Through the affordances of digital media, participants frequently identified themselves as members of a community of doctoral students who share common interests in SLA and ET, and as members of a larger community of L2 education professionals, teachers, and researchers in particular. Several of them viewed their experiences in the course and in their doctoral program as part of a process or journey of "becoming" and "being" language education professionals. They also expressed strong beliefs about the ideal ET-related roles and practices of L2 teachers. They believed teachers should practice a student-centered approach to linguacultural education, one that involves learning about students, developing teacher competence (e.g., learning about ET and SLA theory), employing critical thought about reasons for employing ET, and applying such knowledge to improve the processes and outcomes of L2 education.

In the following sections we apply specific elements of the CoP theoretical framework to discuss these findings and their implications for L2 teacher education practice and research.

5.1 Identity through Membership in Communities of Practice

5.1.1 Identifying the Domain

To construct and maintain their community, participants identified and defined a *domain* – a shared interest in employing ET and SLA theory to improve the quality of L2 education – through discourse in the discussion forums and multimodal expressions of beliefs in their digital stories (Wenger-Trayner & Wenger-Trayner, 2015). In these multisemiotic digital texts, they expressed beliefs that L2 teachers should make decisions regarding ET implementation after applying critical thought about its potential impact on the processes and outcomes of a student-centered approach to education. Their frequent references to professional standards, such as TESOL

(TESOL International Association, 2020) and WIDA (2020), both of which address the use of CALL-MALL technology in English language education, also served as clear indications of their shared interests in SLA and ET.

5.1.2 Self-identification as Members of a Community

Sharing an interest (i.e., *domain*) in ET use in L2 education, participants employed the digital and multimodal affordances of digital stories and discussion forums to create and maintain a CoP, or *family* in their parlance, in which they shared knowledge and negotiated and developed identities. Their community may also, to a degree, be characterized as a Virtual CoP (Mercieca, 2017) because much of their interaction in their hybrid course occurred in their asynchronous online discussion forums. They thus performed digital and multimodal identity work, employing the multiple semiotic systems offered by digital storytelling and discussion forums (spoken language, written language, and visual images), by identifying themselves as members of their local community (*family*) of doctoral students, but also as members of a global community of L2 teachers and nascent researchers. The perceptions of themselves as performing multiple public/personal identities, digital identities included, are consistent with the discoveries of other authors, including Racelis and Matsuda (2015), who found that L2 writing instructors perceived themselves as performing multiple concurrent identities, and Farrell (2011), whose participants believed they engaged in multiple identity roles.

Moreover, the self-identification discourse in which participants engaged within their community of peers is consistent with research findings that show people develop identities in relation to others through social interaction (Morton & Gray, 2018; Trent, 2015). As Thorne et al. (2015, p. 217) point out, "identity work is a relational process, involving the 'social positioning of self and other' (Bucholtz & Hall, 2005, p. 586) that is contingently enacted as a function of the recognition, confirmation, or rejection of other people (Butler, 1990)." In the present study, participants defined their developing identities (doctoral student, language teacher, nascent researcher, future teacher educator) by collectively creating, and locating themselves within, a community of doctoral students who shared an interest in employing ET to improve the quality of the processes and products of L2 education for the benefit of all students.

5.2 Language Teacher Practice, Competence, and Artifacts

The combination of digital storytelling and discussion forums as prime course activities enabled participants to engage in critical thought, reflection, and expression regarding the ideal *practices* and *competences* (Mercieca, 2017; Wenger-Trayner & Wenger-Trayner, 2015) of L2 teachers, particularly in relation to educational technology. They believed L2 teachers should engage in a student-centered approach to education that involves purposeful and effective use of ET. L2 teachers should learn about their students, engage in critical thought about ET use, and employ ET to improve the processes and outcomes of learning. They directed these exhortations at themselves as well. Discussions of the duties of L2 teachers reflected the ways they envisioned their future teaching practices. Their strong interest in teacher ET-related competence and knowledge is consistent with research by multiple authors who have found that teacher knowledge plays an important role in teachers' identity work (Beijaard et al., 2000; Liontas, 2020b; Racelis & Matsuda, 2015; Rogers, 2011).

While participants' DS+ projects enabled them to engage in identity work, the completed products also served as *artifacts* or testimonials to their evolving competence (Mercieca, 2017; Wenger, 1998) with SLA knowledge and ET use. By telling participants the imagined audiences of their digital projects were K-12 teachers engaged in professional development, the instructor positioned them as experts in the field of ET use in L2 education. Comments in the discussion forums indicated that many of them took great pride in their completed projects.

The participants' dual focus on identifying themselves as L2 education professionals and identifying the ideal practices and competences of L2 teachers is consistent with the findings of Racelis and Matsuda (2015), whose research on L2 writing teacher identity included a focus on "teachers' self-identification (e.g., 'I am a language teacher') and their discussion of classroom practices (e.g., 'I provide corrective feedback to facilitate language development')" (p. 205). In the present study, both the digital stories and discussion forums afforded opportunities for participants to employ the digital and multimodal affordances of digital storytelling and discussion forums to engage in identity work that involved self-identification and a description of the ideal practices and competence of L2 education professionals (Trent, 2015; Varghese et al., 2005).

6 Implications for Research, Practice, and Final Thoughts

Exploring ET- and identity-related beliefs of multilingual SLA doctoral students has value because as they begin their careers in academia, these beliefs are likely to have a discernible influence on future curricular developments and research in the field of L2 teacher education. The identity-related beliefs of participants, and other teachers or teacher educators in the field of SLA, may indeed influence their pedagogical practices (Leibowitz, 2017). Therefore, it is important to provide opportunities and dialogic space for doctoral students, along with pre- or in-service L2 teachers, to explore, reflect on, and express beliefs and practices about (perceived or imagined) language-teacher and teacher-educator identities, digital identities notwithstanding.

Course exercises such as collaborative digital stories and asynchronous online discussions may be a particularly effective combination because digital storytelling offers multiple modes with which to engage in dialogic discourse about identity, with both collaborators and audiences, and because asynchronous online discussions enable education majors opportunities to reflect critically on experiences (Johnson et al., 2017; Plešec Gasparič & Pečar, 2016) with course activities such as *digital stories with a twist* (Liontas, 2020b). These types of activities also afford opportunities for both pre- and in-service teachers, seasoned professionals and researchers included, to engage in meaningful discourse about what teachers should know (*competence*) and what they should do (*practice*) to meet student needs and interests in today's digital worlds of (mis/dis)information. Doing so also serves as a means for participants to rethink, redefine, recast, and, importantly, reframe L2 teacher competence in general and digital practice and expertise in particular. The participants are thus creating and redrawing the boundaries of what it means to be a language education professional in the 21st century – a future that is yet to be reimagined digitally.

Armed with such insights, there is indeed compelling value in employing and conducting research on coursework such as digital storytelling and asynchronous online discussion forums, both constructs of which provide ample opportunities for doctoral students, along with pre- or in-service L2 teachers, to explore, reflect on, and express beliefs about their perceived and apperceived (digital) identities. Said simply, these types of classroom practices and related research have value because the ways in which language teachers perceive themselves, and are perceived by others, influence and alter their reality of pedagogical CALL-MALL practices. In fact, agency change and subjectivity are but two facets deserving further investigation in the years ahead. More than 15 years ago, Varghese et al. (2005) described LTI as a multifaceted construct involving social and discursive aspects, along with cognition of individual teachers. They recommend employing multiple theoretical constructs to understand how language teachers engage in identity work. The findings of our study also suggest that combinations of course projects involving multiple modalities (digital storytelling) and different group dynamics (individual vs. collaborative work) may provide particularly effective means for L2 education professionals to engage in exploration, discussion, negotiation, and expressions of their identities and their beliefs about topics such as teacher practice and teacher knowledge concerning ET.

And while the future is promising indeed, it bears repeating that the course in which this study was conducted was only six weeks long and thus we were limited in the amount of data we were able to collect and analyze. The short duration of the course also limited our ability to explore how participants' beliefs about their personal and collective identities may have changed over time (Kanno & Stuart, 2011). Another limitation worth noting here is the nature of the relationship between the course participants and the first author – they were, after all, a sample of convenience. His personal knowledge of some of them may well have influenced interpretation of data and insights gleaned from the discussions he has had with the course instructor since then.

In closing, while there is much extant research on LTI, the study discussed in this chapter makes a direct contribution to research in the field of SLA by focusing on multilingual doctoral students whose dynamic LTI beliefs may indeed have an influence on their future research and teacher education practices. As researchers and teacher educators, their evolving beliefs and CALL-MALL practices may also influence the LTI of future L2 teachers employing ET-related constructs. Espousing a similar research framework, future research studies should be able to affirm the findings here reported. And while we wait for additional evidence to come in, one notion remains as true as ever: *becoming* language education professionals by reframing multilingual doctoral students' perceptions of language teacher identity negotiations is but *a single step in a journey of a thousand LTI miles*. The journey beckons, yet few heed the call.

References

Aneja, G. A. (2016). (Non)native speakered: Rethinking (non)nativeness and teacher identity in TESOL teacher education. *TESOL Quarterly*, *50*(3), 572–596. https://doi.org/10.1002/tesq.315

Ban, R. (2006). *Community of practice as community of learners: How foreign language teachers understand professional and language identities* [Doctoral dissertation, University of South Florida]. University of South Florida Scholar Commons. https://scholarcommons.usf.edu/cgi/viewcontent.cgi?article=3449&context=etd

Barkhuizen, G. (2017). Language teacher identity research: An introduction. In *Reflections on language teacher identity research* (pp. 1–11). Routledge.

Beijaard, D., Verloop, N., & Vermunt, J. D. (2000). Teachers' perceptions of professional identity: An exploratory study from a personal knowledge perspective. *Teacher and Teacher Education, 16*, 749–764. https://doi.org/10.1016/S0742-051X(00)00023-8

Bezemer, J., & Mavers, D. (2011). Multimodal transcription as academic practice: A social semiotic perspective. *International Journal of Social Research Methodology, 14*, 191–206. https://doi.org/10.1080/13645579.2011.563616

Block, D. (2003). *The social turn in second language acquisition.* Edinburgh University Press.

Breen, P. (2015). Letting go and letting the angels grow: Using Etienne Wenger's Community of Practice Theory to facilitate teacher education. *International Journal of Web-Based Learning and Teaching Technologies, 10*(1), 14–26. https://doi.org/10.4018/ijwltt.2015010102

Bucholtz, M., & Hall, K. (2005). Identity and interaction: A sociocultural linguistic approach. *Discourse Studies, 7*(4–5), 585−614. https://doi.org/10.1177/1461445605054407

Butler, J. (1990). *Gender trouble: Feminism and the subversion of identity.* Routledge.

Cheung, Y. L., Ben Said, S., & Park, K. (Eds.). (2015). *Advances and current trends in language teacher identity research.* Routledge.

Chigona, A. (2013). Using multimedia technology to build a community of practice: Pre-service teachers' and digital storytelling in South Africa. *International Journal of Education & Development Using Information & Communication Technology, 9*(3), 17–27.

Clarke, M. (2008). *Language teacher identities: Co-constructing discourse and community.* Multilingual Matters.

Crawford, C. (2011). *The art of computer game design.* Amazon.com. ASIN: B0052QA5WU

Cumming-Potvin, W., & Sanford, K. (2015). Countering a 'Back-to-Basics' approach to teacher education: Multiliteracies and on-line discussions in a community of practice. *Language and Literacy, 17*(1), 21–41. https://doi.org/10.20360/G29W20

De Costa, P., & Norton, B. (2017). Introduction: Identity, transdisciplinarity, and the good language teacher. *The Modern Language Journal, 101*(Supplement 2017), 3–14. https://doi.org/doi:10.1111/modl.12368

Dell Jones, J. (2018). *Intersecting stories: Cultural reflexivity, digital storytelling, and personal narratives in language teacher education* [Doctoral dissertation, University of South Florida]. University of South

Florida Scholar Commons. https://scholarcommons.usf.edu/cgi/viewcontent.cgi?article=8341&context=etd

Ding, A.-C. E., & Pawan, F. (2020). Multimodal identity construction of technology-using language teachers via stance taking in an online learning space. In B. Yazan & K. Lindahl (Eds.), *Language teacher identity in TESOL: Teacher education and practice as identity work* (pp. 83–100). Routledge.

Farrell, T. S. (2011). Exploring the professional role identities of experienced ESL teachers through reflective practice. *System*, *39*(1), 54–62. https://doi.org/doi:10.1016/j.system.2011.01.012

Firth, A., & Wagner, J. (1997). On discourse, communication, and (some) fundamental concepts in SLA research. *The Modern Language Journal*, *81*(3), 285–300. https://doi.org/10.2307/329302

Gachago, D., Condy, J., Ivala, E., & Chigona, A. (2014). “All stories bring hope because stories bring awareness”: Students’ perceptions of digital storytelling for social justice education. *South African Journal of Education*, *34*(4), 1–12. https://doi.org/10.15700/201412052108

Gill, T. (2002). Visual and verbal playmates: An exploration of visual and verbal modalities in children’s picture books. Unpublished B.A. (Honours), University of Sydney, Australia.

Goh, C. C. M. (2015). Foreword. In Y. L. Cheung, S. Ben Said, & K. Park (Eds.), *Advances and current trends in language teacher identity research* (pp. xii–xiv). Routledge.

Guest, G., MacQueen, K. M., & Namey, E. E. (2012). *Applied thematic analysis.* SAGE Publications. http://dx.doi.org/10.4135/9781483384436

Halliday, M. A., & Matthiessen, M. I. (2014). *Halliday's introduction to functional grammar* (4th ed.). Routledge.

Hallman, H. L. (2015). Teacher identity as dialogic response: A Bakhtinian perspective. In Y. L. Cheung, S. Ben Said, & K. Park (Eds.), *Advances and current trends in language teacher identity research* (pp. 3–15). Routledge.

Johnson, C., Hill, L., Lock, J., Altowairiki, N., Ostrowski, C., da Rosa dos Santos, L., & Liu, Y. (2017). Using design-based research to develop meaningful online discussions in undergraduate field experience courses. *International Review of Research in Open and Distributed Learning*, *18*(6), 36–53. http://dx.doi.org/10.19173/irrodl.v18i6.2901

Kanno, Y., & Stuart, C. (2011). The development of L2 teacher identity: Longitudinal case studies. *Modern Language Journal*, *95*, 236–252. https://doi.org/10.1111/j.1540-4781.2011.01178.x

Kayi-Aydar, H. (2019). Language teacher identity. *Language Teaching*, *52*, 281–295. https://doi.org/10.1017/S0261444819000223

Kulavuz-Onal, D. (2013). *English language teachers' learning to teach with technology through participation in an online community of practice: A netnography of Webheads in action* [Doctoral dissertation, University of South Florida]. University of South Florida Scholar Commons. http://scholarcommons.usf.edu/etd/4713

Lambert, J. (2013). *Digital storytelling: Capturing lives, creating community* (4th ed.). Routledge.

Laozi. (2002). *Tao te ching* [D. Hinton, Trans]. Perseus Books Group. (Original work published 3rd century B.C.E.)

Leibowitz, B. (2017). Language teacher identity in troubled times. In G. Barkhuizen (Ed.), *Reflections on language teacher identity research* (pp. 74–79). Routledge.

Liontas, J. I. (Ed.). (2020a). *The TESOL encyclopedia of English language teaching*. John Wiley & Sons, Inc.

Liontas, J. I. (2020b). Understanding language teacher identity: Digital discursive spaces in English teacher education and development. In B. Yazan & K. Lindahl (Eds.), *Language teacher identity in TESOL: Teacher education and practice as identity work* (pp. 65–82). Routledge.

Lord, G., & Lomicka, L. (2014). Twitter as a tool to promote community among language teachers. *Journal of Technology and Teacher Education, 22*(2), 187–212.

Martinec, R., & Salway, A. (2005). A system for image–text relations in new (and old) media. *Visual Communication*, *4*(3), 337–371. https://doi.org/10.1177/1470357205055928

Martinez, A. J. D. D. (Ed.). (2017). *Native and non-native teachers in English language classrooms: Professional challenges and teacher education*. De Gruyter Mouton.

Mason, S. L., & Chik, A. (2020). Age, gender and language teacher identity: Narratives from higher education. *Sexuality & Culture*, *24*, 1028–1045. https://doi.org/10.1007/s12119-020-09749-x

Meihami, H., & Rashidi, N. (2020). Cultural identity development in second language teacher education: Toward a negotiated model. *The Qualitative Report*, *25*(8), 3101–3127.

Mercieca, B. (2017). What is a community of practice? In J. McDonald & A. Cater-Steel (Eds.), *Communities of practice: Facilitating social learning in higher education* (pp. 3–26). Springer.

Meredith, J. (2016). Transcribing screen-capture data: The process of developing a transcription system for multi-modal text-based data. *International Journal of Social Research Methodology*, *19*(6), 663–676. https://doi.org/10.1080/13645579.2015.1082291

Moodley, M. (2019). WhatsApp: Creating a virtual teacher community for supporting and monitoring after a professional development programme. *South African Journal of Education*, *39*(2), 1–10. https://doi.org/10.15700/saje.v39n2a1323

Morton, J., & Gray, T. (2018). *Social interaction and English language teacher identity*. Edinburgh University Press.

Ng, W., & Nicholas, H. (2015). iResilience of science pre-service teachers through digital storytelling. *Australasian Journal of Educational Technology*, *31*(6), 736–751. https://doi.org/10.14742/ajet.1699

Park, G. (2015). Situating the discourses of privilege and marginalization in the lives of two East Asian women teachers of English. *Race, Ethnicity, and Education*, *18*(1), 108–133. https://doi.org/10.1080/13613324.2012.759924

Patton, K., & Parker, M. (2017). Teacher education communities of practice: More than a culture of collaboration. *Teaching and Teacher Education*, *67*, 351–360. http://dx.doi.org/10.1016/j.tate.2017.06.013

Pennington, M. C. (2015). Teacher identity in TESOL: A frames perspective. In Y. L. Cheung, S. Ben Said, & K. Park (Eds.), *Advances and current trends in language teacher identity research* (pp. 38–52). Routledge.

Plešec Gasparič, R., & Pečar, M. (2016). Analysis of an asynchronous online discussion as a supportive model for peer collaboration and reflection in teacher education. *Journal of Information Technology Education: Research*, *15*, 369–393. https://doi.org/10.28945/3538

Ponzio, C. M. (2020). (Re)Imagining a translingual self: Shifting one monolingual teacher candidate's language lens. *Linguistics and Education*, *60*, 1–11. https://doi.org/10.1016/j.linged.2020.100866

Racelis, J. V., & Matsuda, P. K. (2015). Exploring the multiple identities of L2 writing teachers. In Y. L. Cheung, S. Ben Said, & K. Park (Eds.), *Advances and current trends in language teacher identity research* (pp. 203–216). Routledge.

Reis, D. S. (2015). Making sense of emotions in NNESTs' professional identities and agency. In Y. L. Cheung, S. Ben Said, & K. Park, (Eds.), *Advances and current trends in language teacher identity research* (pp. 31–43). Routledge.

Robin, B. R. (2016). The power of digital storytelling to support teaching and learning. *Digital Education Review*, *30*, 17–29. https://doi.org/10.1344/der.2016.30.17-29_

Rogers, G. (2011). Learning-to-learn and learning-to-teach: The impact of disciplinary subject study on student-teachers' professional identity. *Journal of Curriculum Studies*, *43*(2), 249–268. https://doi.org/10.1080/00220272.2010.521262

TESOL International Association. (2020). *The 6 principles for exemplary teaching of English learners*. TESOL International Association. https://www.tesol.org/the-6-principles/about

Thorne, S. L., Sauro, S., & Smith, B. (2015). Technologies, identities, and expressive activity. *Annual Review of Applied Linguistics*, *35*, 215–233. https://doi.org/doi:10.1017/S0267190514000257

Trent, J. (2015). Towards a multifaceted, multidimensional framework for understanding teacher identity. In Y. L. Cheung, S. B. Said, & K. Park (Eds.), *Advances and current trends in language teacher identity research* (pp. 44–58). Routledge.

Unsworth, L. (2006). Towards a metalanguage for multiliteracies education: Describing the meaning-making resources of language-image interaction. *English Teaching: Practice and Critique*, *5*(1), 55–76.

van Galen, J. A. (2017). Agency, shame, and identity: Digital stories of teaching. *Teaching and Teacher Education*, *61*, 84–93. https://doi.org/10.1016/j.tate.2016.09.009

Varghese, M., Morgan, B., Johnston, B., & Johnson, K. A. (2005). Theorizing language teacher identity: Three perspectives and beyond. *Journal of Language, Identity & Education*, *4*, 21–44. https://doi.org/10.1207/s15327701jlie0401_2

VERBI Software. (2019). *MAXQDA 2020* [Computer software]. VERBI Software. https://www.maxqda.com/

Vitanova, G. (2016). Exploring second-language teachers' identities through multimodal narratives: Gender and race discourses. *Critical Inquiry in Language Studies*, *13*(4), 261–288. https://doi.org/10.1080/15427587.2016.1165074

Wenger, E. (1998). *Communities of practice: Learning, meaning, and identity*. Cambridge University Press.

Wenger-Trayner, E., & Wenger-Trayner, B. (2015). *Communities of practice: A brief introduction*. Wenger-Trayner. http://wenger-trayner.com/introduction-to-communities-of-practice/

WIDA. (2020). *Teaching with standards*. WIDA. https://wida.wisc.edu/teach/standards

World Health Organization. (2021). *Archived: WHO timeline – COVID-19*. World Health Organization. https://www.who.int/news/item/27-04-2020-who-timeline---covid-19

Xu, Y. (2017). Becoming a researcher: A journey of inquiry. In G. Barkhuizen (Ed.), *Reflections on language teacher identity research* (pp. 120–125). Routledge.

Yazan, B., & Lindahl, K. (Eds.). (2020a). *Language teacher identity in TESOL: Teacher education and practice as identity work*. Routledge.

Yazan, B., & Lindahl, K. (2020b). Language teacher learning and practice as identity work: An overview of the field and this volume. In B. Yazan & K. Lindahl (Eds.), *Language teacher identity in TESOL: Teacher education and practice as identity work* (pp. 1–10). Routledge.

Yin, R. K. (2014). *Case study research: Design and methods* (5th ed.). SAGE Publications, Inc.

About the Authors

Patrick Mannion has two decades of experience teaching English as a foreign language in K-12 schools and language institutes in Japan. He also holds a doctoral degree in Second Language Acquisition and Instructional Technology from the University of South Florida. His research interests are primarily pedagogy-focused, and include genre approaches to literacy informed by Systemic Functional Linguistics, multimodality, digital storytelling, idiomatic language education, and dialogic scaffolding. He is also interested in language teacher education and Japanese language education.

Dr. John I. Liontas is the 2014–2021 Director of the Technology in Education and Second Language Acquisition (TESLA) doctoral program at the University of South Florida where he teaches graduate courses in ESOL, SLA, idiomatics, and emerging digital technologies. He is an active member in (inter)national learned societies, distinguished thought leader, multiple award-winning author, researcher, and practitioner, and also the Editor-in-Chief of award-winning *The TESOL Encyclopedia of English Language Teaching* (Wiley, 2018), the first print and online encyclopedia for the TESOL International Association since its founding in 1966. He writes and presents worldwide on issues of idiomatics, emerging digital technologies, and game approaches.

9 Construction and Performance of Online Foreign Language Teacher Identity: A Case Study of Korean as a Foreign Language Teachers

Seojin Park

1 Introduction

This chapter addresses how critical reflexivity and the pedagogical practices of foreign language (FL) teachers work simultaneously to shape their language teacher identity in online classrooms. The chapter presents a qualitative case study that explores the complex identity construction and management processes that Korean as a foreign language (KFL) teachers use in their online classrooms. The study had a unique temporal setting: it focused on the performance of KFL teacher identity in the context of emergency remote online teaching during a pandemic. The outbreak of COVID-19 changed many things in people's daily lives, including modes of teaching and teaching practices. Many traditional in-person classes have become online classes, including FL courses. Due to this sudden change, there also have been many uncertainties and unfamiliar situations in classrooms.

This study aims to unveil some of the uncertainties in online learning and teaching by exploring how the KFL teachers' professional identities were constructed and managed in online classrooms. Teacher identity in a language classroom is a crucial element that can affect various teaching practices and student learning processes (Varghese et al., 2005). Therefore, it was crucial to understand teacher identities to understand teaching and learning processes in online classes. To this end, the study was guided by this research question: How do KFL teachers manage and construct their professional teacher identities in their online classes? The study shed new light on the field of teacher education for less commonly taught languages (LCTLs) and the close relationship between teachers' reflexive identity, positioning, and practices in digitally mediated language teaching contexts. Moreover, it indicates the importance of integrating online interaction training into teacher education programs.

2 Literature Review

2.1 FL Teacher Identity in LCTLs Classrooms

A teacher's identity in the language classroom has been heavily emphasized as a crucial component in determining how language teaching is carried out (Duff & Uchida, 1997; Morgan, 2004). While previous literature has suggested different definitions of language teacher identities based on various theoretical ideas, the following characteristics are often shared. Language teacher identities are "cognitive, social, emotional, ideological, and historical" (Barkhuizen, 2017, p. 4). They are (re)constructed through constant negotiation processes of struggles, challenges, and acceptances in social interactions (Barkhuizen, 2017; Beijaard et al., 2004; Gao, 2012; Pennington & Richards, 2016; Varghese et al., 2005). They are multiple, dynamic, and relational (Kayi-Aydar, 2015; Miller, 2009; Pennington, 2015; Phan, 2008; Racelis & Matsuda, 2014), and both personal and professional (Barkhuizen, 2017; Beijaard et al., 2000; Simon-Maeda, 2004).

Professional identity and disciplinary identity are two of the practice-centered frames of language teacher identity (Pennington, 2015). First, professional identity highlights the identity of a teacher as a subject matter, a pedagogical, and a didactical expert (Beijaard et al., 2000). This professional identity develops over time through being and acting as a language teacher in specific educational and work settings, and disciplinary knowledge and identity can be critically intertwined with a language teacher's professional identity. Disciplinary knowledge, which is the pedagogical content knowledge that provides a basis for language teaching (Pennington & Richards, 2016), plays an important role in shaping teacher identity (Connelly & Clandinin, 1999). Disciplinary identity relates to and is constructed in the teacher's academic knowledge, qualifications, activities, units of affiliation, and work on research (Pennington, 2015).

To understand the multifaceted and multidimensional aspect of teacher identity, previous studies have explored how teacher identity can be developed with other types of identities, such as ethnic, racial, cultural, gendered, and sexual identities (Cooper & Bryan, 2020; Kayi-Aydar, 2019). Some studies have focused on the development of multilingual teacher identity

(Canagarajah, 2017; Higgins & Ponte, 2017), highlighting how the values and beliefs of multilingual teachers are manifested in language classrooms and to learners. However, many of these studies have focused on multilingualism as a setting or characteristic of a language teacher. In other words, they examined how teacher identity develops and performs in multilingual classrooms, instead of exploring the intersection of language teacher identity and multilingual identity and how they influence each other. Multilingual identity, in this study, describes the identity one develops and reflects when they "identify as multilingual precisely because of an awareness of the linguistic repertoire one has" (Fisher et al., 2018, p. 449).

Previous studies have painted a complex picture of language teacher identity in their discussions of how it is performed. First, it is performed through teacher–student interactions and relations in a classroom (José, 2013; Pennington & Richards, 2016; Richards, 2006; Wolff & De Costa, 2017). In a classroom, where the teacher and students interact constantly with one another, the perceptions and actions of one party can affect the other. Students' senses and perceptions of the teacher are reflected in their actions and interactions and can influence the teacher's professional identity development.

Second, language teacher identity is performed through practices and evolves through various conflicts and negotiations of meanings (Gao, 2012; Pennington & Richards, 2016). Teacher identity is "neither fixed nor something imposed by others" (Sachs, 2005, p. 15); it is developed through different teaching practices and experiences. Conflicts and negotiations can result from several causes, including teacher–student relationships and the cultural and linguistic values of the target language (Gao, 2012). Previous studies on FL teacher identity have also shown that identity is "relational as well as experiential, reificative as well as participative, and individual as well as social" (Tsui, 2007, p. 678), and the teacher's identity strongly influences their students' perceptions of the FL and learning. However, two gaps in the body of research on teacher identity are particularly noticeable: the scarcity of explorations of teacher identity in LCTLs classrooms, and a lack of inquiry into FL teacher identity in digitally mediated classrooms. The present study helps fill this gap by focusing on the identity of LCTLs teachers, specifically KFL teachers.

While several LCTLs, such as Arabic, Chinese, and Korean, have seen dramatic growth in the United States over the last two decades (De Felice et al., 2019), there have been a limited number of studies investigating the identity of LCTLs teachers. In this section, I present two such studies. First, focusing on two Arabic instructors who were both pursuing master's degrees in the United States, De Felice et al. (2019) investigated the teachers' identities, experiences, and challenges in teaching. Through virtual semi-structured interviews, the researchers revealed the different positionalities of the two teachers based on their national, cultural, and religious identities and how they sometimes had to negotiate and reconcile those identities to develop their professional teacher identities.

Kim and Smith (2020) examined the identity negotiation processes of five graduate instructors who were teaching KFL at an American university. The researchers indicated how the teachers negotiated their emotions in both their perceptions of themselves as teachers and their interactions with students regarding different cultural norms. The teachers perceived that building a non-authoritative teacher identity into the process could improve classroom interactions with students.

While these two studies do suggest the complex intersectionality in terms of LCTLs teachers' professional identity development, they could not uncover how they performed their identities in their classrooms and how that affected their teaching practices. Moreover, the scarcity of research on LCTLs teachers' identities makes it difficult to understand the complex picture of their identity construction and performance in the classroom. Therefore, the present study aims to explore how KFL teachers' professional identities are constructed and performed in the process of interacting with their students, especially in online language classrooms.

2.2 Online Second Language Teacher Identity

Under the influence of globalization and increased mobility, digitally mediated second language (L2) learning has witnessed dramatic growth. Moreover, as the COVID-19 pandemic abruptly required language teachers and learners to move to various online platforms, there has been increased attention to online language learning and teaching. Paesani (2020) claims that "teacher professional development plays a key role in helping us navigate online language instruction during the pandemic and beyond" (p. 292). However, only a limited number of studies have investigated the identity of L2 teachers in online classrooms in order to understand their teaching practices. Most previous studies focus on teacher education programs and explore how pre-service language teachers develop their professional identities by engaging in various online activities (Arnold & Ducate, 2006; Doering & Beach, 2002; Kitade, 2014; Muller-Hartmann, 2006; Satar & Akcan, 2018; Uzum et al., 2020).

Those previous studies indicate that online activities and teaching could serve as sites of not only media literacy learning but also professional identity development for teachers (Kitade, 2014). In online collaboration with their students, online language teachers can perform several complex roles, including technology expert, joint learner, and learning mentor (Muller-Hartmann, 2006). Therefore, online FL teachers not only must maintain the various skills that in-person teaching requires but also need to develop different skills for the online context. They must acquire technical knowledge and management of the online classroom and deal with learner anxiety that can be caused by the online environment (Lewis, 2006). To help online FL teachers achieve and develop different skills, teacher education programs have been emphasizing the importance of increasing students' motivation in an online environment. Moreover, previous literature on online teacher development has noted the importance of the teachers' engagement in technologies and connecting them to their pedagogical and content knowledge (Adnan, 2018). In addition, online FL teachers need to reflect critically on their previous experiences of online learning and improve their teaching skills and knowledge by participating in different training programs (Adnan, 2018; Paesani, 2020).

While some studies have focused on the identity development of pre-service language teachers through their engagement in online activities, one study explored how identities of online in-service teachers are performed and reflected in their language teaching practices. Del Rosal et al. (2017) focused on a 10-week telecollaboration project at an American university and how 11 English teachers' identities influenced their online teaching practices and interactions with students. An analysis of the teachers' reflective journals and observation of online interactions revealed that in the online language teaching context, the teachers felt a strong need to build positive relationships with their culturally and linguistically diverse students to foster their participation and engagement in online interactions. To do so, the teachers acknowledged the importance of cultural awareness and sensitivity, which also influenced their identities as teachers. Moreover, the teachers positioned themselves as collaborators, learners, and friends in their online classrooms.

Despite increased online FL learning and the discussion of the various skills that online FL teachers need to acquire, few studies have investigated how online FL teachers perceived themselves in online classrooms and demonstrated their skills in various teaching practices. To understand how L2 teachers position themselves in a digitally mediated teaching environment, the present qualitative case study aims to investigate the negotiation and management of teacher identities. Moreover, the study focuses on how their professional teacher identities are reflected in their online teaching practices.

2.3 "Identity-in-Practice" and "Identity-in-Discourse"

To explore the identities of online KFL teachers, this study draws from the post-structuralist conceptualization of identity. Identity is constantly changing in various discourses; it is always contextual and situated. Identity is "constructed in our interaction with other people through language" (Andrew, 2016, p. 338) not only in our everyday social interactions with other people but also in the broader discourses surrounding us. Moreover, identity is not a simple listing of an individual's specific physical and social characteristics and group classifications. It is rather "a reflection of the context or activity in which the individual is situated" (Pennington & Richards, 2016, p. 6). For example, the identity of a teacher is built on the identities of the classroom, students, colleagues, and perhaps that of parents or even a partner. Identity negotiation takes place in every human relationship and daily practice, even in language classrooms. Since language teachers bring their identities with them into their classrooms, it is important to understand the identity of language teachers.

More specifically, this study draws on Varghese et al.'s (2005) notions of "identity-in-discourse" and "identity-in-practice" to analyze online KFL teacher identity. The concept of identity-in-discourse perfectly reflects the poststructuralist notions of identity and discourse. According to Varghese et al. (2005), in identity-in-discourse, "agency is discursively constituted, mainly through language, focusing primarily on critical reflexivity" (p. 39). Identity, therefore, is shaped through language and self-reflection, such as how people describe themselves and their identities during interviews.

Moreover, the perception of self is constructed within larger discourses surrounding the individuals in society. Identity-in-practice is intertwined with identity-in-discourse and is revealed through the performance and enactment of identity. Individuals not only shape and construct their identities in discourse but also actively perform them in their everyday life. More specifically, FL teachers' identity-in-practice can be related to their teacher agency, which is seen as "action-oriented and focusing on concrete practices and tasks in relation to a group and mentor(s)" (Varghese et al., 2005, p. 39). The enactment of an FL teacher's identity can also be revealed in their interactions with the students and colleagues and in planning and designing the class. In the present study, identity-in-practice is examined through how

KFL teachers' identities were constructed and reflected in their everyday teaching practices.

Adopting the notions of identity-in-discourse and identity-in-practice, Kanno and Stuart (2011) painted a concrete picture of novice language teachers' professional teacher identities through a combination of their narrated and enacted identities. The researchers found that L2 teachers' identity formation was central to teacher development and classroom practices and further highlighted the importance of teacher identity development in teacher education programs. Varghese et al. (2005) also argue for the incorporation of shared teaching practices and critical reflexivity into teacher education. In order to critically examine the identity construction and management of KFL teachers through their narrated and enacted identities, therefore, this study focuses on how identity-in-discourse and identity-in-practice interplayed in shaping KFL teacher identities in their online language classrooms.

3 Methodology

3.1 Sites and Participants

This study adopts a case study design (Yin, 2014) in order to understand how KFL teachers position themselves in a digitally mediated teaching environment. The case study approach was chosen to examine how KFL teachers shape and reflect their online teacher identities, which has not been discussed enough in the field of applied linguistics, in relation to given contexts, histories, and different factors that affect their teaching processes. The case study design enabled the researcher to document the processes and experiences of the participants' language use, identity construction and management, and their teaching practices in-depth (Yin, 2014).

The research sites were the online platforms that were utilized in teaching KFL at one university and one college in the southwestern United States. The classes of two KFL instructors were both small, with 10–20 students, and used Desire2Learn and Zoom as primary learning systems. After the COVID-19 outbreak in 2020, almost all the classes offered by schools were moved to an online teaching modality. This study took place when many instructors had to change their courses from face-to-face meetings to the online setting and were still getting used to online teaching. This study focused on how KFL instructors constructed and performed their teacher identities in these unfamiliar online teaching environments. To analyze their identities in the classroom, I chose online class meetings on Zoom as my research site.

Zoom is a widely used online video-conferencing tool that allows users to meet online, with or without video or audio.

Two female KFL instructors participated in this study; their names were changed to pseudonyms to keep their anonymity. The two instructors were chosen as participants in this case study since they showed shared but also distinctive online teaching experiences under the context of COVID-19. Min was a Korean instructor in her 40s at the time of the study. She had been living in the United States for 15 years. Min obtained her master's degree in Teaching English to Speakers of Other Languages (TESOL) in England. She was trained to be an ESL teacher and later began to teach Korean as an FL. Min had been teaching Korean language at various American institutions for 10 years.

The other participant, Yuna, also Korean, was in her 30s at the time of the study. She had been teaching KFL for about 10 years at the time of the study. She received her Ph.D. in Second Language Acquisition and Teaching in the United States. She taught KFL at several institutions there. Through many discussions regarding KFL classes and teaching practices, the researcher developed a good understanding of their teaching philosophies, styles, and characteristics. The researcher recognized Min and Yuna as enthusiastic KFL teachers who were interested in developing and implementing different teaching methods and activities. Min was a caring and warm-hearted teacher who was not afraid to try new technologies and activities in class. Yuna was a creative teacher who was not bound to textbook grammar and content and tried to incorporate various authentic materials in her teaching. The researcher's understanding of the two instructors had influenced the analysis and interpretations of their interactions with students and teaching practices, which was constantly reflected upon throughout the present study.

3.2 Data Collection

The data in this study consist of video recordings of six classes for each instructor, observation field notes of their class teaching practices, and semi-structured individual interviews with the two instructors. Before collecting the data, the participants were asked to sign a consent form that had been approved by the Human Subject Research Office. The researcher collected data from March to November 2020. Once classes changed to the online setting, both instructors recorded all their classes. With their permission, a total of 12 of those class recordings were examined. Each class lasted between 50 and 90 minutes; both instructors were teaching beginner-level students in classes of 15–25. While watching the class recordings, the researcher took field notes about any interesting incidents of teacher–student interactions and teaching practices. Lastly, during the courses, two semi-structured interviews were conducted with each instructor for about an hour in each case to understand their professional teacher identities. Due to COVID-19, those interviews were conducted in online Zoom meetings. The interview questions were translated to Korean by the researcher and the initial translation was backtranslated to ensure the reliability and validity of the translation. The interviews were conducted in Korean, which was the first language of both instructors. The questions were used to prompt the participants to talk about their past teaching experiences, teaching philosophies, and perceptions of online teaching and their interactions with students (see Appendix A for the interview questions). The background information and relevant life histories of the participants were also investigated to obtain an in-depth understanding of the participants' experiences as KFL teachers.

Stimulated recalls (Calderhead, 1981) were used during the interviews. This involved asking each participant to watch and describe three clips of 3–5 minutes each chosen by the researcher from among the class recordings. The researcher chose the clips because they offered insights on the KFL teachers' unique online teacher identity construction and management and how they were reflected in their teaching practices. They were also chosen to elicit the participants' perceptions of the interactions and their understandings of teaching practices. The researcher asked the participants to talk about what happened in the video and to share their thoughts on what they had seen. After watching each video, the participants explained what happened in the video, giving background information and why they acted in certain ways. Stimulated recall was used not only as a tool to understand the teacher's perceptions of these interactions but also to member-check the researcher's interpretations of the data. The entirety of both interview sessions was video-recorded with the participants' permission and transcribed by the researcher.

3.3 Data Analysis

Data analysis was conducted at two different levels: *within-case* and *cross-case* (Merriam, 1998). First, all data from the interview sessions and class recordings were transcribed. The data from each participant were first analyzed separately, extracting recurring themes in the following manner. The interview transcripts, which reflected the participants' identity-in-discourse, were read repeatedly, with initial impressions on and insights into online teacher identities noted on separate sheets of paper. The researcher especially focused on how the participants described themselves and their roles as KFL teachers in an online setting. The different topics were then highlighted and color-coded to generate initial categories.

The class recordings and field notes were analyzed carefully, with emerging categories of identity management and performance on separate sheets of paper, which allowed the coding categories to arise organically from the data. In this process, the researcher focused on how the teachers' identity-in-discourse was reflected in their teaching practices (identity-in-practice), including their interactions with students. Categories in interview transcripts and field notes in the two datasets were compared to each other multiple times to see how identity-in-discourse and identity-in-practice were either aligned or disjoined.

After the within-case analysis, the two instructors' coding categories were compared (i.e., cross-case analysis). In particular, the researcher gained insights by comparing and contrasting the online language teaching experiences of the two teachers. This enabled the researcher to identify shared and distinctive experiences of their online language teaching. Through this iterative procedure, some categories were modified or rejected, while new ones were developed. This process continued until the researcher obtained a rich and

Table 9.1. Analytical Coding Chart of the Participants

Similarities		Discourse and practice as a participation facilitator Discourse and practice as a mother Discourse and practice as a technology user Discourse and practice as a non-expert in the use of technology Practice: Initiation – response – feedback interactional patterns
Differences	Min	Discourse: Challenges to facilitate the students' participation and frustration Practice: Asking for participation/challenges to facilitate the students/making jokes about non-participation
	Yuna	Discourse: Disciplinary identity Practice: Explaining the rationale for class activities
		Discourse: Building a community in an online class Practice: The use of Zoom breakout room function/ collaborative learning
		Practice: Encouraging students to use different modes of communication

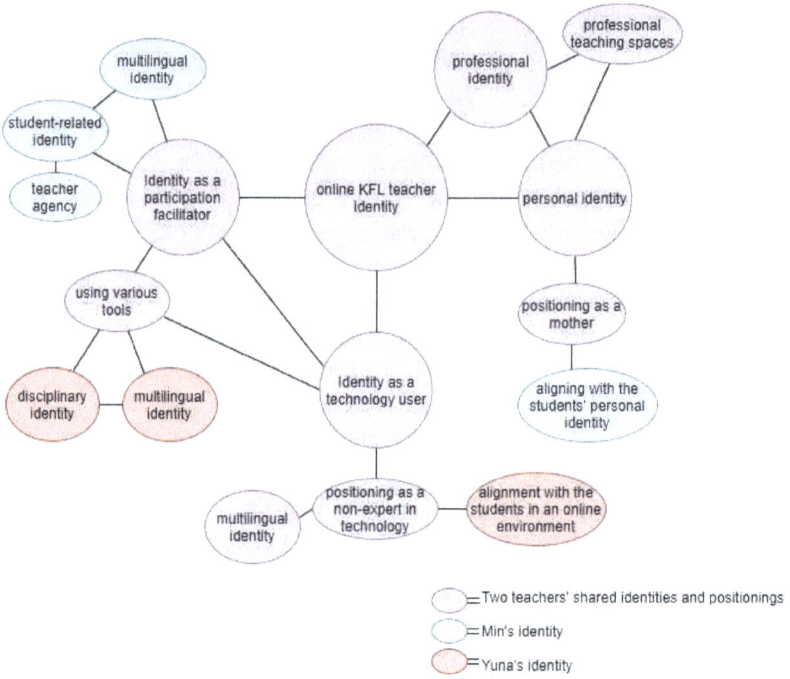

Figure 9.1. Categories of Min's and Yuna's KFL Teacher Identities

full picture of the data. Table 9.1 provides a comparative analytical coding chart for the within-case and cross-case analyses of the two participants. In the table, "discourse" represents how identity shapes and is shaped through language use and self-reflection of the teachers, while "practice" relates to their identity enactment in their teaching practices.

For internal reliability, peer examination was used. The transcripts and categories were read by an expert in the area of identity and L2 learning and teaching; based on that feedback, the researcher modified the categories. Then, three final themes that reflected the participants' online teacher identity construction and management were identified: identity as a participation facilitator; identity as a technology user; and personal and professional identity. Finally, the researcher chose the most representative excerpts from the data to illustrate each theme. Figure 9.1 visualizes the themes and categories of Min's and Yuna's online KFL teacher identities and the relationship between them.

4 Findings

4.1 Identity as a Participation Facilitator

Through their identity-in-discourses and practices, Min and Yuna revealed their identities as participation facilitators in their online classes. Min claimed, "In an online language class, I try to make them participate intentionally, to let them know I am paying attention to them, and they need to do something in class too" (Interview, April 19, 2020). To improve the students' participation and engagement, the teachers used different tools in their online classes. For example, during the online class observations, Yuna actively used the Zoom chat function to increase participation by students who could not turn on their cameras or microphones. Moreover, she often used a Zoom breakout room function to facilitate students' collaborative learning. Yuna showed her disciplinary knowledge in terms of the use of the breakout room function in her online teaching.

> **Excerpt 1.** (Interview, November 23, 2020)
>
> Yuna: I often do community-building with my students, such as students doing workbooks together in breakout rooms. I think it's better when two or three students explain things to each other using metalanguage. I think it can be included in my teaching philosophy.

Yuna's disciplinary knowledge led to a clear rationale for the use of breakout rooms in class. This disciplinary knowledge, which is the pedagogical content knowledge that provides a basis for language teaching (Pennington & Richards, 2016), is shown by the different terms she uses in the excerpt, such as community-building and metalanguage. It is also reflected by her knowledge of technological literacy. Her disciplinary identity shaped and reflected by her disciplinary knowledge often intertwined with her multilingual identity as an English speaker. Those sub-identities were actively performed in her teaching practices to explain and justify her teaching practices. For instance, before splitting a class-wide Zoom meeting into different breakout rooms and directing her students to those rooms for small group work, Yuna clearly explained the purpose of doing so by telling her students to help one another complete the task. She told them what to do in the breakout rooms and asked students multiple times whether they understood her instructions in English rather than Korean. Therefore, Yuna's online language teacher identity as a participation facilitator could be strengthened by the alignment of her disciplinary identity and multilingual identity, which helped her not only to justify her teaching practices but also to effectively explain them to the students.

However, Yuna's and Min's identities as participation facilitators were sometimes challenged when their students did not actively participate in online classes.

> **Excerpt 2.** (Class observation, October 7, 2020)
>
> (Students were not answering Min's questions and were being quiet)
> Min: It's a little weird. What happened to you guys, is it getting hard? Or did you just have lunch and get sleepy? (laugh) Shall we jump eight times to wake up?
> Ja [*Well*], what are you doing now, eo-tteoh-ge mal-hae-yo? [*how can we say that?*]

By making jokes about jumping eight times to wake up and trying to lighten the mood and class atmosphere, Min reflected her identity-in-practice as a participation facilitator. After watching the interaction in Excerpt 2 during the stimulated recall, Min explained that she code-switched in English to facilitate interaction with her students and to ask whether there were other reasons why her students could not answer her questions. Therefore, Min tried to overcome the students' low engagement and participation by exercising her multilingual identity as an English speaker.

> **Excerpt 3.** (Interview, November 23, 2020)
>
> Min: *I am particularly careful when I randomly call on my students to participate in class. I am directly feeling the burdens of the students these days. So, in terms of asking my students to participate, I feel intimidated as a teacher. There is this ambivalent mind in me, it's good to make my students less pressured (if I don't ask them to participate), but at the same time, how is it then different from a normal lecture?*

Min's teacher identity was often challenged because of her student-related identity (Pennington & Richards, 2016), which is the identity built into the relationship and interactions between teacher and students. Min's teacher identity as a participant facilitator was challenged in her online classes, as she felt the same difficulties and burdens that students felt for various reasons, including the COVID-19 pandemic and the sudden change to online language learning. Min was not able to make her class more student-centered and participatory because she paid heed to the emotional burden and stress among her students. This indicates that when the teacher's beliefs about online language teaching are challenged by her perceptions toward the students, it can weaken her agency as a teacher by not being able to make a class operate in the way she wants.

4.2 Identity as a Technology User

Integrated with their identities as participation facilitators, the two teachers actively performed their identities as technology and online tool users in their classes. During the class observations, they used a variety of technologies, such as the annotation and breakout room functions on Zoom, Google Docs, Google Forms, and Jamboard. However, one of the most interesting features that created different dynamics in online classes was the fact that not everyone was familiar with all the technologies, including the teachers. The teachers' technical issues sometimes positioned them as non-experts in technology, which reassured students who might have felt uncomfortable as non-experts themselves in their new online learning environment.

Excerpt 4. (Class observation, March 19, 2020)

Min: Where are the (0.5) breakout rooms ga eobs-eo-yo. Wae? [*There are no breakout rooms. Why?*] I-sang-ha-da. [*That's weird.*] I should have breakout rooms. Breakout rooms ga an-bo-i-ji-yo? [*You don't see breakout rooms, do you?*]
Students : (Silence)
...
Min: Somehow, I cannot see the breakout room on my computer. Ah, it is my
computer because my computer is not a good one. So I can see the breakout room on my office computer but not on my own computer (laughs).

Excerpt 5. (Class observation, October 28, 2020)

(Some students came back from breakout sessions)
Yuna: (Yuna talking but on mute)
Student: Seon-saeng-nim [*teacher*], you are muted.
Yuna: (laughs) O, go-ma-wo-yo. [*Oh, thank you.*] Oh, I didn't know! I was telling everything.
Student: (laughs)

> Yuna: This is a new life I have to get used to (laugh). Okay, let me bring back everyone.

While the two teachers' mistakes might seem comical or even trivial, they were significant in that they changed the interaction and power dynamics between them and their students. The majority of teacher–student interactions in Min's and Yuna's observed classes followed the teacher's initiation–student's response–teacher's feedback (IRF) structure, which is a teacher–student interaction structure found in many language classrooms (José, 2013). Following the IRF interaction pattern, the teachers had the authority to initiate conversations and the power to assess the correctness of an utterance and give feedback to the students. However, in Excerpts 4 and 5, the interaction structures have shifted because of the teachers' technical issues. In Excerpt 5, for example, one student points out that Yuna is on mute, positioning Yuna as a non-expert. By saying "I didn't know!" and correcting the problem by unmuting herself, Yuna accepts the identity imposed by her student. Therefore, the interactional deviation and the acceptance of an imposed identity challenged Yuna's traditional role of a teacher, in which she acted as an expert and information giver in the classroom. While watching the interaction shown in Excerpt 5 during the stimulated recall, Yuna mentioned that her students pointed out her "mistakes," which reflected her acknowledgment of her challenged identity as an expert in class. However, positioning herself as a non-expert in technology may also have given her a new identity that could be aligned with her students at the same time. By saying it was a new life she had to get used to in Excerpt 5, Yuna aligned her identity with the students to convey the message that not only students but also teachers were adapting to a new and unfamiliar environment and the transition could not always be easy and smooth.

Excerpts 4 and 5 also reveal the code-switching practices of the two teachers, shedding light on their multilingual teacher identities. While they could speak in English to facilitate interaction with their students and fix the technical problems, they were actively code-switching to Korean, especially when it was certain that their students could understand their Korean sentences (Breakout rooms ga an-bo-i-ji-yo? [*You don't see breakout rooms, do you?*], go-ma-wo-yo, [*thank you.*] Oh, I didn't know!). By exercising their multilingual identities, they were practicing their identities as language teachers who could help students practice their Korean listening and interaction skills. Hence, while the teachers' language teacher identity was sometimes challenged by the positioning of non-experts in technology, they were also actively exercising their language teacher identity by performing their multilingual identities as Korean speakers.

4.3 Personal and Professional Identity

One of the most distinctive characteristics of online language learning and teaching is that teachers and students can be in different places; indeed, they can be anywhere as long as they have reliable internet access. Zoom is a unique teaching and learning platform because when participants turn on their cameras and microphones, they are sharing information about their own surroundings. Because of this feature, the personal identities of Zoom participants, including teachers and students, can sometimes be exposed. The two teachers were quite open about this issue.

> **Excerpt 6.** (Interview, November 23, 2020)
>
> Yuna: There are various situations, such as a baby running around or younger siblings doing their homework in the background. Sometimes students talk with other people without muting their audio. ... Sometimes my baby comes in during the class, says "Hi" to my students, and goes out. Some of my students are holding their babies while taking class as well. Sometimes my baby cries, and I have to mute myself and make my students do something while I take care of the baby.

Excerpt 6 indicates how the personal identities of Yuna and her students could affect their teaching and learning experiences in class. Yuna's positioning as a mother, for example, affected her online teacher identities by blurring the situational boundaries of her personal and professional identities in online teaching practices.

While this blurred boundary could be seen as a challenge, Min could successfully overcome it through actively utilizing her personal identity instead of pushing it away from her professional teaching spaces.

> **Excerpt 7.** (Class observation, October 28, 2020)
>
> Min: Let me see. (student's name), bo-tong mol-e eo-tteoh-ge ga-yo? [*How do you usually go to a mall?*]
> Student: Ah, I didn't understand.
> Min: Ah, mall, shopping mall e bo-tong eo-tteoh-ge ga-yo? [*How do you usually go to a shopping mall?*]

> S: Oh ... bo-tong [*usually*] ... (a baby coughing and babbling loudly in the background)
> Min: Jeo-neun syo-ping mol-e [*I to a shopping mall*] (0.5) by what?
> S: Uh (the baby screaming loudly in the background) ja-jeon-geo? [*bicycle?*]
> Min: Ja-jeon-geo-lo ga-yo. [*I go there by bicycle.*] Thank you (laughs). It's okay. I totally understand because I have a son.

In Excerpt 7, by saying thank you, Min was appreciating students' participation regardless of the loud background noises that they might not have wanted to share with the entire class. Moreover, Min was positioning herself as a mother by telling students that she has a son, and that was why she understood their situations. This reflexive positioning as a mother enabled Min to align herself with her student who had to expose her personal identity as a sister with younger siblings, and let her students know she understood the distraction. In online teaching, therefore, where professional and personal identities co-exist, the teachers' positionings as mothers brought not only different perspectives on teaching but also a more understanding atmosphere of the learning environments in which some students were working.

5 Discussion

This chapter has reported on the study that explores how KFL teachers constructed and performed their professional teacher identities through both discourse and practices in their online classes. The two teachers' critical self-reflexivity and practices revealed that their online teacher identities 1) were performed to overcome the novel and unique challenges that online FL teaching entails, 2) are a complex of various situated positionings and sub-identities that were harmonized but also conflicted with each other, 3) critically influence their agency as online teachers and the construction of the students' learning environments, and 4) were co-constructed in a variety of interactions and relationships in online classrooms.

The findings revealed the common challenges that teachers face when teaching online classes, such as managing students' low motivation and engagement, using unfamiliar technological tools, and the exposure of personal identities in a professional teaching and learning environment. In online classes where students can decide whether to turn on their cameras and microphones, it is more difficult for teachers to manage class engagement (Choi & Chung, 2021; Sun, 2011; Atmojo & Nugroho, 2020). Min's identity-in-discourse reflected such challenges. However, Min and Yuna showed how online language teachers could overcome this challenge by performing their identity-in-practice as participation facilitators with different sub-identities, such as disciplinary and multilingual identities. Moreover, the two teachers' positioning as non-experts in technology and mothers intertwined with their professional identities as language teachers, which enabled them to overcome the challenges of using unfamiliar online tools and being flexible and understanding regarding the impact of their students' personal identities in class.

Teacher identity often consists of multiple sub-identities that are not always in a harmonious relationship (Miller, 2009; Pennington, 2015; Phan, 2008; Racelis & Matsuda, 2014). The findings in the present study revealed the two teachers' various sub-identities, and that they were often closely intertwined with the different skills that online language teachers need. The complex interplay of the teachers' identities and positionings further shaped the agency of the teachers and the students' learning environment in the online classroom (Hiver & Whitehead, 2018; Kanno & Stuart, 2011; Varghese et al., 2005; Yazan & Lindahl, 2020). This study revealed how Min's teacher agency was shaped and reflected by her teacher identity-in-discourse and identity-in-practice in the online classes. Moreover, when the sub-identities were well-integrated and harmonized, the teachers created secure and stable professional teacher identities, which may have also positively influenced the students' online language learning experiences. For instance, the alignment of disciplinary, multilingual, and teacher identity in Yuna's online teaching worked as a way to strengthen her professional online teacher identity.

However, teacher identity formation was also a struggle, as "teachers had to make sense of varying and sometimes competing perspectives, expectations, and roles that they had to confront and adapt to" (Beijaard et al., 2004, p. 115). The online KFL classrooms examined in this study were also a site of struggle due to the teachers' competing perspectives and expectations in relation to their students. In their classes, the two teachers followed their traditional roles as language and participation facilitators who conveyed disciplinary knowledge. However, Min's teacher identity-in-discourse was often challenged due to the students' increased stress and the burdens of online learning, which weakened her agency as a teacher. The teachers' identity as non-experts in technology also diverged from the expected role of a teacher who is an expert. This contradiction revealed how different expectations and roles of the teacher could create different power dynamics in an online FL classroom.

Lastly, the present study could contribute to the understanding of online KFL teacher identities by showing how the teacher's perceptions of students or the identity imposed on the teacher by students influenced the construction of teacher identity-in-discourse and identity-in-practice in an online environment. Previous studies on L2 teacher identity have shown that language teacher identity is performed and enacted through teacher–student interactions and relationships in the classroom (José, 2013; Pennington & Richards, 2016; Richards, 2006; Wolff & De Costa, 2017). According to Pennington and Richards (2016), teacher identity is constructed in a classroom, where "teacher and student are in a mutually interactive relationship in which the thinking and the actions of one reflect the thinking and the actions of the other" (p. 16). Min's and Yuna's interactions with their students and how they reacted to the identities imposed by those students co-constructed their online FL teacher identities. In addition, the teachers constructed and performed new identities by suggesting identities that were aligned with their students' experiences.

6 Conclusion and Implications

This chapter presented an empirical study that reveals how critical reflexivity and teaching practices of online KFL teachers simultaneously work to construct and perform their language teacher identities in digitally mediated environments. The class observation data collected for this study were obtained for a limited time period that was not lengthy enough to examine the long-term development of online FL teacher identity. A longitudinal study on the future of how language teachers continue to construct and maintain their identities in online classes will help strengthen the current understanding of online KFL teacher identity. Despite this limitation, this study is significant in that it provides insights into the online identities of LCTLs teachers, which has not been studied before. It was especially insightful because it discussed how KFL teachers used different sub-identities to overcome the common challenges that online language teachers face in their classes, such as the students' low level of engagement and participation and their lack of familiarity with using new technology. This links to the unique setting of the current study, which is the pandemic-instigated emergency transition to remote online teaching. The two teachers showed how they constructed their identity-in-discourse under the context and how they performed their identity-in-practice to overcome the challenges of this time. The performance of their unique teacher and multilingual identities helped them analyze and manage the difficulties in online teaching. Moreover, this study also revealed the complex interplay between teachers' identities-in-discourse and identities-in-practice. Those concepts enabled a comprehensive understanding of how language teacher identity was portrayed and enacted in online KFL classes. Teacher identity and agency were discursively constructed through language and actions in an online classroom (Varghese et al., 2005). In many cases, Min's and Yuna's identities-in-discourse were well aligned with their identities-in-practice and online teaching practices.

Although the present study focused on the KFL teachers' identity construction and performance, the findings bring up significant issues for the field of FL teacher education. Based on these findings, this chapter reflects the need to integrate teachers' meta-awareness and self-reflection and their teaching practices into the field of FL teacher education. FL teacher education programs need to recognize the close relationship between the teacher's reflexive identity, positionings, and teaching practices in digitally mediated language teaching contexts. Based on the findings of the study, I argue that there needs to be more discussion on how online FL teachers can overcome unique challenges they might face in online teaching by performing their various sub-identities and positionings in interactions with their students and teaching practices. It can be advantageous to create space for the online FL teachers to narrate, discuss, and analyze the complex relationship between their identities, positionings in classrooms, and teaching practices, including various challenges they face in teaching. Moreover, the study raises the importance of integrating online interaction training in language teacher education programs since teacher identity is actively constructed and performed through interactions with other members in classroom communities. By encouraging language teachers to critically reflect on their identities, cognitions, and interactions in their classes, we can encourage educators to be critical and proactive, even in online teaching contexts.

References

Adnan, M. (2018). Professional development in the transition to online teaching: The voice of entrant online instructors. *ReCALL, 31*, 88–11. https://doi.org/10.1017/S0958344017000106

Andrew, P. (2016). Constructing age identity: The case of Mexican EFL learners. In S. Preece (Ed.), *The Routledge handbook of language and identity* (pp. 337–350). Routledge.

Arnold, N., & Ducate, L. (2006). Future foreign language teachers' social and cognitive collaboration in an online environment. *Language Learning & Technology, 10*(1), 42–66. http://dx.doi.org/10125/44046

Atmojo, A. E. P., & Nugroho, A. (2020). EFL classes must go online! Teaching activities and challenges during COVID-19 pandemic in Indonesia. *Register Journal, 13*(1), 49–76. https://doi.org/10.18326/rgt.v13i1.49-76

Barkhuizen, G. (2017). Language teacher identity research: An introduction. In *Reflections on language teacher identity research* (pp. 1–11). Routledge.

Beijaard, D., Meijer, P. C., & Verloop, N. (2004). Reconsidering research on teachers' professional identity. *Teaching and Teacher Education, 20*(2), 107–128. https://doi.org/10.1016/j.tate.2003.07.001

Beijaard, D., Verloop, N., & Vermunt, J. D. (2000). Teachers' perceptions of professional identity: An exploratory study from a personal knowledge perspective. *Teacher and Teacher Education*, *16*, 749–764. https://doi.org/10.1016/S0742-051X(00)00023-8

Calderhead, J. (1981). Stimulated recall: A method for research on teaching. *British Journal of Educational Psychology*, *51*(2), 211–217. https://doi.org/10.1111/j.2044-8279.1981.tb02474.x

Canagarajah, S. (2017). Multilingual identity in teaching multilingual writing. In G. Barkhuizen (Ed.), *Reflections on language teacher identity research* (pp. 67–73). Routledge.

Choi, L., & Chung, S. (2021). Navigating online language teaching in uncertain times: Challenges and strategies of EFL educators in creating a sustainable technology-mediated language learning environment. *Sustainability*, *13*, 1–14. https://doi.org/10.3390/su13147664

Connelly, F. M., & Clandinin, D. J. (1999). *Shaping a professional identity: Stories of educational practice*. Teachers College Press.

Cooper, A., & Bryan, K. (2020). Reading, writing, and race: Sharing the narratives of Black TESOL professionals. In B. Yazan & K. Lindahl (Eds.), *Language teacher identity in TESOL: Teacher education and practice as identity work* (pp. 125–142). Routledge.

De Felice, D., Lanier, A., & Winke, P. (2019). Serving the less-commonly-trained teacher: Perspectives from Arabic instructors. *The Qualitative Report*, *24*(9), 2309–2327. https://nsuworks.nova.edu/tqr/vol24/iss9/15

Del Rosal, K., Conry, J., & Wu, S. (2017). Exploring the fluid online identities of language teachers and adolescent language learners. *Computer Assisted Language Learning*, *30*(5), 390–408. https://doi.org/10.1080/09588221.2017.1307855

Doering, A., & Beach, R. (2002). Preservice English teachers acquiring literacy practices through technology tools. *Language Learning & Technology*, *6*(3), 127–146.

Duff, P. A., & Uchida, Y. (1997). The negotiation of teachers' sociocultural identities and practices in postsecondary EFL classrooms. *TESOL Quarterly*, *31*(3), 451–486. https://doi.org/10.2307/3587834

Fisher, L., Evans, M., Forbes, K., Gayton, A., & Liu, Y. (2018). Participative multilingual identity construction in the languages classroom: A multi-theoretical conceptualisation. *International Journal of Multilingualism*, *17*(4), 448–466. https://doi.org/10.1080/14790718.2018.1524896

Gao, F. (2012). Teacher identity, teaching vision, and Chinese language education for South Asian students in Hong Kong. *Teachers and Teaching*, *18*(1), 89–99. https://doi.org/10.1080/13540602.2011.622558

Higgins, C., & Ponte, E. (2017). Legitimating multilingual teacher identities in the mainstream classroom. *The Modern Language Journal*, *101*(S1), 15–28. https://doi.org/10.1111/modl.12372

Hiver, P., & Whitehead, G. E. K. (2018). Sites of struggle: Classroom practice and the complex dynamic entanglement of language teacher agency and identity. *System*, *79*, 70–80. https://doi.org/10.1016/j.system.2018.04.015

José, F. (2013). "What makes a teacher": Identity and classroom talk. *Cuadernos De Lingüística Hispánica*, *22*, 127–146.

Kanno, Y., & Stuart, C. (2011). Learning to become a second language teacher: Identities-in-practice. *Modern Language Journal*, *95*(2), 236–252. https://doi.org/10.1111/j.1540-4781.2011.01178.x

Kayi-Aydar, H. (2015). Teacher agency, positioning, and English language learners: Voices of preservice classroom teachers. *Teaching and Teacher Education*, *45*, 94–103.

Kayi-Aydar, H. (2019). Language teacher identity. *Language Teaching*, *52*, 281–295. https://doi.org/10.1017/S0261444819000223

Kim, H. K. (2008). Beyond motivation: ESL/EFL teachers' perceptions of the role of computers. *CALICO Journal*, *25*(2), 241.

Kim, J., & Smith, H.-Y. (2020). Negotiation of emotions in emerging language teacher identity of graduate instructors. *System*, *95*, 1–10. https://doi.org/10.1016/j.system.2020.102365

Kitade, K. (2014). Second language teachers' identity development through online collaboration with L2 learners. *CALICO Journal*, *31*(1), 57–77. https://doi.org/10.11139/cj.31.1.57-77

Lewis, T. (2006). When teaching is learning: A personal account of learning to teach online. *CALICO Journal*, *23*(3), 581–600. https://doi.org/10.1558/cj.v23i3.581-600

Merriam, S. B. (1998). *Qualitative research and case study applications in education* (2nd ed.). Jossey-Bass.

Miller, J. (2009). Teacher identity. In A. Burns & J. C. Richards (Eds.), *The Cambridge guide to second language teacher education* (pp. 172–181). Cambridge University Press.

Morgan, B. (2004). Teacher identity as pedagogy: Towards a field-internal conceptualisation in bilingual and second language education. *International Journal of Bilingual Education and Bilingualism*, *7*(2–3), 172–188. https://doi.org/10.1080/13670050408667807

Muller-Hartmann, A. (2006). Learning how to teach intercultural communicative competence via telecollaboration: A model for language teacher education.

In J. A. Belz & S. L. Thorne (Eds.), *Internet-mediated intercultural foreign education* (pp. 63–84). Thomson Heinle.

Paesani, K. (2020). Teacher professional development and online instruction: Cultivating coherence and sustainability. *Foreign Language Annals*, *53*(2), 292–297. https://doi.org/10.1111/flan.12468

Pennington, M. C. (2015). Teacher identity in TESOL: A frames perspective. In Y. L. Cheung, S. Ben Said, & K. Park (Eds.), *Advances and current trends in language teacher identity research* (pp. 38–52). Routledge.

Pennington, M. C., & Richards, J. C. (2016). Teacher identity in language teaching: Integrating personal, contextual, and professional factors. *RELC Journal*, *47*(1), 5–23. https://doi.org/10.1177/0033688216631219

Phan, L. H. (2008). *Teaching English as an international language: Identity, resistance and negotiation.* Multilingual Matters.

Racelis, J. V., & Matsuda, P. (2014). Exploring the multiple identities of L2 writing teachers. In Y. L. Cheung, S. B. Said, & K. Park (Eds.), *Advances and current trends in language teacher identity research* (pp. 203–216). Taylor and Francis Inc.

Richards, K. (2006). Being the teacher: Identity and classroom conversation. *Applied Linguistics*, *27*(1), 51–77. https://doi.org/10.1093/applin/ami041

Sachs, J. (2005). Teacher education and the development of professional identity: Learning to be a teacher. In P. Denicolo & M. Kompf (Eds.), *Connecting policy and practice: Challenges for teaching and learning in schools and universities* (pp. 5–21). Routledge.

Satar, H. M., & Akcan, S. (2018). Pre-service EFL teachers' online participation, interaction, and social presence. *Language Learning & Technology*, *22*(1), 157–183. https//dx.doi.org/10125/44586

Simon-Maeda, A. (2004). The complex construction of professional identities: Female EFL educators in Japan speak out. *TESOL Quarterly*, *38*(3), 405–436. https://doi.org/10.2307/3588347

Sun, S. Y. H. (2011). Online language teaching: The pedagogical challenges. *Knowledge Management & E-Learning: An International Journal*, *3*(3), 428–447. https://doi.org/10.34105/j.kmel.2011.03.030

Tsui, A. (2007). Complexities of identity formation: A narrative inquiry of an EFL teacher. *TESOL Quarterly*, *41*, 657–680. https://doi.org/10.1002/j.1545-7249.2007.tb00098.x

Uzum, B., Akayoglu, S., & Yazan, B. (2020). Using telecollaboration to promote intercultural competence in teacher training classrooms in Turkey and the USA. *ReCALL*, *32*(2), 162–177. https://doi.org/10.1017/S0958344019000235

Varghese, M., Morgan, B., Johnston, B., & Johnson, K. (2005). Theorizing language teacher identity: Three perspectives and beyond. *Journal of Language, Identity, and Education*, *4*(1), 21–44. https://doi.org/10.1207/s15327701jlie0401_2

Wolff, D., & De Costa, P. (2017). Expanding the language teacher identity landscape: An investigation of the emotions and strategies of a NNEST.

Modern Language Journal, *101*(S1), 76–90. https://doi.org/10.1111/modl.12370

Yazan, B., & Lindahl, K. (2020). Language teacher learning and practice as identity work. e B. Yazan & K. Lindahl (Eds.), *Language teacher identity in TESOL: Teacher education and practice as identity work* (pp. 1–10). Routledge.

Yin, R. K. (2014). *Case study research: design and methods*. SAGE.

About the Author

Seojin Park (M.A., Sookmyung Women's University) is a Ph.D. student in Second Language Acquisition and Teaching at the University of Arizona. Her research interests are identity (re)construction and second language learning/teaching of socially and culturally minoritized groups of learners/teachers.

Appendix A: Interview Questions

[Demographic information]

- Demographic questions, including gender, age, race, ethnicity, and educational and teaching backgrounds.

[Teaching philosophy]

- How did you decide to become a Korean language teacher?
- What is your teaching philosophy? / What are your beliefs about teaching in general? / What are your beliefs about teaching the Korean language?

[Professional teacher identity]

- When you reflect on your professional identity as a teacher, how would you describe it?
- Do you see yourself as a professional Korean language teacher?
- Please describe the experiences that have shaped your professional identity as a teacher. What do you recall as the most memorable moment that made you realize that you are a professional Korean language teacher?
- Do you think your roles and relationships with the students change when you interact with them outside of class? If so, what are your roles/relationships in class teaching, and what are they in out-of-class interactions?
- Do you think of yourself as a different person when you teach in the classroom and when you don't teach outside of class?

[Teacher–student relationship]

- How do you think your students perceive you in the classroom?
- Do you feel any challenges when you interact with your students in class?

[Online language teaching]

- How has your online teaching been? What are the benefits and challenges of online language teaching? What did you learn from your online teaching experiences?
- What aspects of teaching do you focus on the most when you teach online?
- How has your teaching changed from in-person to online teaching?
- How have your relationship and interaction with your students changed in online teaching?

Appendix B: Transcription Conventions

?	Raised intonation
.	Full stop marks falling intonation
(laugh)	Laughing
::	Long prolongation of immediately prior sound
(0.5)	Elapsed time in tenths of seconds
(silent)	Silent and no response
italic	English translation of the original text

10 Engagement in the Expression of Learners' Identity Within Virtual Exchange Asynchronous Discussions

Ana Sevilla-Pavón and Anna Nicolaou

1 Introduction

This study examines the expression of linguistic and cultural identity construction processes experienced by 78 Cypriot and Spanish learners of English as an Additional Language (EAL) within a virtual exchange project. The importance of interpersonal communication and accurate argumentation strategies in learners' online discussion forum entries, which are the main foci of this study, has been highlighted by authors such as Coffin and Hewings (2004) and Coffin and O'Halloran (2005). Previous studies focused on characterizing the learners' use of engagement and interpersonal communication resources in English academic writing (Vega Garrido, 2018) as well as determining whether argumentations were successful (Wu, 2006; Wu & Allison, 2005) in the realization of stance and stance support (Chandrasegaran & Kong, 2006) and in the creation of robust arguments with a variety of expanding and contracting strategies (Ryshina-Pankova, 2014). As for learners' cultural reflections, which are also analysed in this study, they have been one of the main components of research on virtual exchange (Basharina, 2007; Belz, 2003; Belz & Thorne, 2006; Elola & Oskoz, 2008; Helm, 2013, 2016, 2018; Liaw, 2006; Lomicka, 2006; O'Dowd, 2007, 2016; Sevilla-Pavón & Nicolaou, 2020; Ware & O'Dowd, 2008) for the last few decades. Numerous studies focusing on intercultural communicative competence (Byram, 1997, 2000) in foreign language (FL) teaching have shown that virtual exchange participants generally display curiosity and interest in other cultures, overcoming difficulties resulting from differences in cultural engagement styles (Belz, 2003; Ware & O'Dowd, 2008) when discussing topics aimed at fostering cultural exchanges and discovery (Elola & Oskoz, 2008). Building on the prior research on how L2 learners co-create knowledge and build arguments collaboratively in asynchronous written discussions (Oskoz & Gimeno-Sanz, 2019; Oskoz, Gimeno-Sanz & Sevilla-Pavón, 2018), this study analyses FL learners' use of contracting and expanding strategies when building arguments about experiences with and views of their own and their additional or target language(s) and culture(s) in EAL settings.

The main focus of the study is interpersonal communication strategies used for the projection and negotiation of cultural identities, understood as subsets of someone's overall global identity, which in turn are viewed not as fixed and static but rather as multiple and fluid (Helm, 2018), as well as situated. Cultural identity has to do with an individual's identification with and sense of belonging to a specific group with shared systems of symbols, meanings, and behavioural norms (Collier & Thomas, 1988). Nowadays, our current digital age and the context of liquid modernity (Bauman, 2005, 2007), globalization, massive migratory movements across the globe, constant mobility and changes in relationships and identities within our highly complex societies, together with an increase in technological "normalization" (Bax, 2003; Chambers & Bax, 2006), have all influenced the current notions of cultural identity (Hall, 1992; Jensen, 2003; Kim, 2009). Thus, cultural contrasts have been reduced and new multicultural, transnational individuals (Jensen, 2003, 2011) with millennium, hybrid multilingual/multicultural identities (Higgins, 2015) have emerged. These transnational individuals no longer perceive reality as inertial, traditions no longer influence their learning processes, and they no longer see the possibilities for their future as pre-determined or finite (Helm, 2018). Their fluid identities align with what Appadurai (1996) identified as "transcultural flows" in the domains of ethnoscapes (involving flow of people), mediascapes (flow of information), technoscapes (flow of technology), financescapes (flows of finance), and ideoscapes (flow of ideology or ideas).

In order to gain insight into the expression of the linguistic and cultural identity construction processes of such transcultural and transnational individuals, the empirical study conducted adopted the discourse-semantic subsystem of Appraisal Theory (Martin & White, 2005; White, 2000) known as Engagement. It was considered appropriate as a framework to capture argumentation strategies used in online forum discussions (Coffin & Hewings, 2004), as it involves "all those locutions which provide the means for the authorial voice to position itself with respect to, and hence to engage with, the other voices and alternative positions construed as being in play in the current communicative context" (Martin & White, 2005, p. 94). In other words, Engagement refers to how writers position themselves in relation to other voices (Hyland & Jiang, 2016) and has been considered "probably the most theory-grounded study of the functions and forms of evaluative meaning in English" (Hunston, 2011, p. 2) as well as "the most systematic analyzing tool that offers a typology of evaluative resources available in English" (Hyland, 2005, p. 174). The role of Engagement is thus crucial in the expression of authors' viewpoints and dialogistic positioning to engage their readers with their arguments, and can be performed through linguistic features such as reporting verbs, modal auxiliaries, or intensifiers. Therefore, Appraisal Theory and its Engagement subsystem (Martin & White, 2005) was deemed a suitable framework to explore the identity that writers/speakers assume and project when they produce text (that is, the "group affiliation" aspect of identity), as well as the identity these text producers assign to the other voices that participate in the text (in other words, the "value structure of writers") (O'Donnell, 2013).

This chapter delineates the context of online discussion forums in learning and presents a discussion of the Engagement strategies of contracting and expanding. This is followed by the analysis and discussion of virtual exchange participants' process of identity construction. The data for this analysis come from the corpus generated from two different datasets. The first dataset resulted from participants' online forum posts and narratives that reported positive and negative experiences using their L2(s) in different contexts, as part of a "language memories" task which will be described in more detail in the Methodology section. As for the second dataset, it originated from a "DNA Journey" discussion in which students shared their reflections on their identity and their willingness to explore various cultural or ethnic affiliations from their genealogical tree, as will be explained in the Methodology section. Given the increasing attention that virtual exchange has attracted over the past few years, this study attempts to shed light on the extent to which the topic being discussed can influence L2 learners' interpersonal communication discourse strategies, as well as on the specific Engagement (Contractive and Expansive) strategies used. This study thus poses the following questions:

1. How do Cypriot and Spanish L2 learners express their linguistic and cultural identity construction processes within a virtual exchange project in terms of the inclusion of other voices in the discourse (monoglossia or heteroglossia)?
2. How do L2 learners from Cyprus and Spain express their cultural and linguistic identity construction processes through the use of Engagement discourse strategies (Contraction and Expansion) when

referring to culture one (C1), culture two (C2), and topic (T) in virtual exchange forum discussions?

3. How do L2 learners from Cyprus and Spain express their cultural and linguistic identity construction processes by means of Engagement discourse strategies, depending on the topic (language memories or DNA Journey), when referring to C1, C2, and T in virtual exchange forum discussions?

2 Theoretical Framework

2.1 Online Discussion Forums in Virtual Exchange

Online threaded discussion forums[1] have been utilized as an internet-based communication tool for a few decades (Cameron & Anderson, 2006) and their popularity as teaching tools has increased steadily (Salter & Conneely, 2015). The affordances of threaded discussion forums in computer-mediated instruction have been documented in numerous studies (Arnold & Ducate, 2006; Meyer, 2004; Mooney et al., 2014). According to Mooney et al. (2014), asynchronous online threaded discussions "are widely recognized as a tool to enhance learning in the virtual classroom since they can serve as a mechanism for reinforcing material and promoting a deeper understanding of course content." Sull (2009) noted that threaded discussions where students post weekly in response to topics related to the course subject and engage in conversations with their peers and the instructor are considered "the beating heart of online courses" (p. 65). Rizopoulos and McCarthy (2009) stated that online dialogic communities "have become a ubiquitous tool that transforms student learning and course delivery" (p. 373), while Cole et al. (2020) emphasized that threaded discussion is considered to be a key tool in enabling e-learners to develop skills such as critical thinking, reflection, and engaged learning.

Various studies have examined the success of online discussion forums towards achieving satisfactory engagement, interaction, and participation of students in the forum's activities. Salter and Conneely (2015), for example, compared structured and unstructured discussion forums and concluded that

[1] Online threaded discussion forums are understood as online postings on a specific topic, usually initiated by the instructor, where students are asked to post their answers and can read the messages posted by other participants as well as respond to them. Each group of messages on a specific topic with the initial message and responses is considered a "thread."

structured forums were generally perceived by students to be more engaging. A study by Mokoena (2013) found that discussion forums are more effective in increasing students' interaction if instructors establish social presence and provide participants with support. However, Andresen (2009) emphasized that the instructor's level of intervention in asynchronous discussion forums should only revolve around motivating discussions and keeping students on track as "an instructor that contributes significantly to a discussion tends to decrease the length of discussions (this does not necessarily decrease the quality of the discussion, however) as well as their frequency" (p. 251). Nevertheless, the instructors' lack of intervention in forum discussions does not mean overlooking the provision of guidance regarding how students can make culturally-appropriate contributions to those discussions. In fact, as pointed out by Hanna and de Nooy (2003), successful participation in forum discussions where participants from different cultural and linguistic backgrounds interact depends on awareness of cultural and generic conventions and netiquette rules, as well as on the ability to work within and/or with them. These authors argue that it is the role of instructors to help raise students' awareness about such issues so that their participation in electronic discussions can move beyond simple linguistic training and it becomes actual engagement with other cultural practices. They also remind us that despite the ideal of a borderless, neutral internet society, there are cultural differences which influence communication styles and may incite cultural clashes (Hanna & de Nooy, 2009).

In language learning, online discussion forums can be beneficial as they provide EAL learners with an opportunity to join in discussions that "they may not have felt comfortable contributing to in class during face-to-face interactions" (Rizopoulos & McCarthy, 2009, p. 377). Lee (2009) noted that threaded discussions can result in establishing a shared virtual space where students have equal opportunities to express their opinions, offer support and feedback to each other, work collaboratively and create knowledge, and sustain communication beyond the classroom walls. Integrating online threaded discussions in language instruction can be an enjoyable, motivating, and meaningful experience provided they are designed with caution (Nicolaou, 2020). A study by Lee (2009) suggests three elements that are needed to optimize the effectiveness of discussion boards in language instruction: "1) use of carefully designed tasks that prompt critical thinking, 2) scaffolding strategies for keeping account of group discussions, and 3) inclusion of online etiquette to avoid confusion and minimise personal conflicts" (p. 212).

As for virtual exchange, it is "a well-known pedagogical approach in foreign language education which involves engaging classes in online intercultural collaboration projects with international partners as an integrated part of their educational programmes" (O'Dowd, 2020, p. 1). In the context of virtual exchange, online discussion forums have served as venues for asynchronous interaction, provision of personal opinions, reflections, and reactions to local and international peers' contributions in many telecollaborative projects (Basharina et al., 2008; Chun, 2011; Liaw & Bunn-Le Master, 2010; Loizidou & Savlovska, 2020; Loizidou & Mangenot, 2016; Nicolaou & Sevilla-Pavón, 2016; Sevilla-Pavón & Nicolaou, 2020; Turula, 2017; Ware & Kramsch, 2005). Previous research on learners' intercultural online written interactions has shown that despite possible problems that may lead to communication breakdowns resulting from participants' dissimilar cultural engagement styles (Belz, 2003; Ware & O'Dowd, 2008), expressions of curiosity are common, as well as willingness to engage in discussions that foster intercultural discovery (Elola & Oskoz, 2008). Online discussion forums offer useful locations for engagement in conversations which promote intercultural exploration and discovery, as they provide participants with an opportunity and time for reflection, reaction, search of additional information to support and counteract different points of view, co-creation of knowledge and building of arguments collaboratively when discussing their C1 and C2 (Oskoz et al., 2018), as well as their L1(s) and L2(s). This can be achieved even in cases where "missed communication" (Ware, 2005) may occur. In fact, as Ware and Kramsch note, "discussion of such moments of miscommunication can be valuable learning opportunities for both students and teachers" (2005, p. 190). Therefore, as O'Donnell (2013) explains, the participants' identity development is viewed from a social semiotic perspective, as the language used to project identities is assumed to be a meaning-making system within which the meanings that language producers make are not constrained by a particular sense of reality.

This means that an author can project any identity in a discussion forum, whether it conforms or not with their own sense of identity, and that identities can be negotiated. However, the language user does not need to accept an author's projected identity and may be more willing to accept a projection which is closer to their perception of social reality. An author could choose to project an identity different from their own perception for multiple reasons: renegotiating one's public identity so as to be perceived in the way they would like to be perceived, adopting the character of another as a joke, or to deceive others (O' Donnell, 2013).

2.2 Engagement: Expanding and Contracting Strategies

The Systemic Functional Linguistics (SFL) language model proposed by Halliday focuses on the variations of language in use depending on context and the inner workings reflected in its surface structure (Eggins, 2004). Based on this model, White (1998, 2001, 2015) and Martin (2000a, 2000b) developed their interpersonal communication framework, the Appraisal Framework (AF). In this framework, Engagement refers to "those resources by which a text references, invokes and negotiates with the various alternative social positions put at risk by a text's meanings" (White, 1998, p. 13). Engagement can thus be considered a subsystem of Appraisal, the resources of which are used for introducing additional voices into a discourse through a set of different strategies. In other words, engagement has to do with speakers allowing space for negotiation of meaning into their talk, and this in turn determines the degree to which a text is relatively monoglossic or heteroglossic. The other subsystems of Appraisal, which are beyond the scope of this chapter, are Attitude and Graduation.

As noted earlier, the AF assumes a social semiotic perspective, according to which the language used to project identities is considered a meaning-making system. Thus, the meanings that language producers make are not constrained by a particular sense of reality. This means language producers can manipulate the linguistic resources available to them in order to project the reality they desire. When applied to the analysis of identity, an author can project any identity, regardless of whether it is aligned or not with their own sense of identity (O'Donnell, 2013). Martin (2014) argues that Appraisal as a system is needed to connect feelings with lexical-grammatical choice, thus providing a way to describe evaluation as it relates to the negotiation of identity.

The appropriateness of the AF in the exploration of identity and the social construction of the self has been tested in previous studies. McKinley (2018) found out that the AF could be used linguistically to operationalize an analysis to explore the "possibilities for selfhood" (Clark & Ivanic, 1997) and provide insights into teachers' and students' use of metalanguage for the social construction of selves and the projection of those identities in writing. His main finding was that identity construction in academic settings was mainly influenced by instructors' expectations and, to a lesser extent, by personal beliefs (McKinley, 2017).

Another example of the AF being used when examining identity in academic settings is provided by Alonso Belmonte (2012), who explored the empirical insights that the AF could provide to explore student teachers'

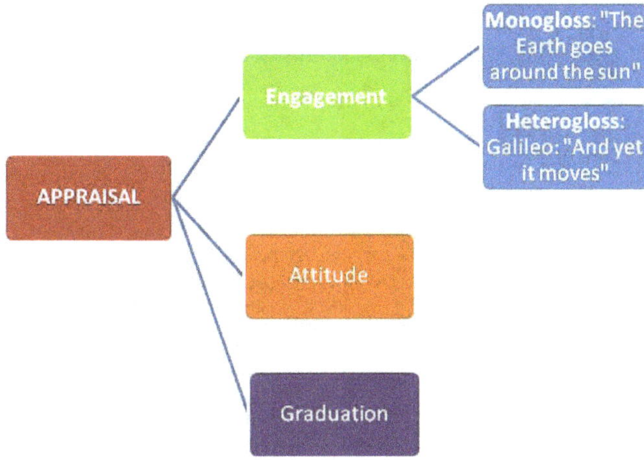

Figure 10.1. Appraisal Framework. Adapted from White, 2001

emerging professional identities. Meanwhile, O'Donnell (2013) applied the AF to shed light on the identity assumed by writers/speakers when writing, and on the identity assigned to the other voices that participate in the text produced by those writers/speakers.

Within the AF, as shown in Figure 10.1, monoglossia occurs when a text is monoglossic, that is, when the communicative context is construed as a single voice. In other words, utterances which do not make reference to other voices and viewpoints can be said to be monoglossic. Examples of this include: "The Earth is the only planet that has liquid water on its surface"; "The Earth goes round the sun." Meanwhile, heteroglossia offers space for the inclusion of the audience. Therefore, heteroglossic utterances are found when the communicative context is construed as more than one voice and/or when a text offers space for the inclusion of the audience, such as in this example taken from Martin and White (2005): "It is believed an asteroid or comet might have caused the extinction of dinosaurs" (Figure 10.2).

When applied to learning contexts, such as the one examined in this chapter, the AF can provide learners with multiple benefits. For instance, it can help them gain a better understanding of discourse, fostering critical reading while effectively stimulating and cultivating learners' abilities to think and reflect. Furthermore, the concept of Engagement in the AF can be applied to reading teaching focusing on critical assessment and identification of the author's value judgment, writing positioning, and creative purpose. A deeper understanding and critical analysis of discourse in general and of

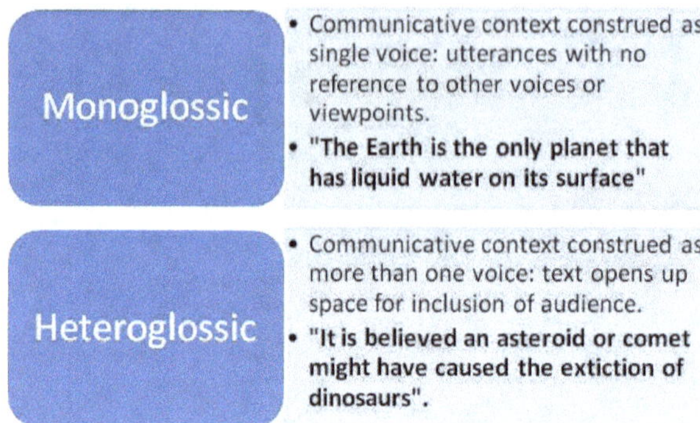

Figure 10.2. Monoglossia and Heteroglossia. Adapted from Martin & White, 2005

value judgment in particular can help learners become more effective in both projecting their identities and critically examining the identities portrayed by their interlocutors. As mentioned earlier, the first aspect of identity has to do with identified social values. These can be explored within the AF through the evaluative style: an author's preference for specific evaluative resources and the identification of the characteristics that the author values and dis-values (O'Donnell, 2013). The second aspect of identity is connected to the author's group affiliation: an analysis within the AF can give close insights to the identity of the author in terms of the people, organizations or ideas the author values and thus affiliates with (O'Donnell, 2013).

3 Methodology

3.1 Settings and Participants

Seventy-eight (N=78) university students from two different higher education institutions took part in the virtual exchange project. The 45 (n=45) first-year students from the Cyprus University of Technology (CUT, Limassol, Cyprus) were Cypriot nationals who were enrolled in the Business Management program. Meanwhile, the 33 (n=33) participants from the University of Valencia (UV, Valencia, Spain) were students from the International Business degree offered by that university.

The participants from both institutions were between 18 and 25 years of age and their English proficiency level was between B1 and B2 according to the CEFR (Council of Europe, 2001, 2018). It is worth noting that all participants considered themselves multilingual and listed in the pre-project needs analysis survey the languages they spoke (apart from English) as follows: Greek, Spanish, Catalan, French, Danish, Swedish, German, Russian, Chinese, Romanian, Italian, Dutch, Bulgarian, Portuguese, Armenian, and Azerbaijani. The learners were divided into multinational groups of 4–5 students, each group having at least two students from either institution who interacted with each other throughout the semester (from September to December). Students interacted online both synchronously and asynchronously, sharing knowledge and experiences connected to their own language(s) and culture(s) while developing new knowledge about different languages and cultures.

3.2 Data Collection

The data analysed in this study, using both quantitative and qualitative procedures, were gathered from the two main forum discussions within the virtual exchange project. In other words, the data were made up of the narratives and reflections exchanged by participants over the course of one semester on the Google+ forum. To obtain informed consent, the participants were asked to give both instructors their permission to use their anonymized data for educational and research purposes. All participants agreed to take part in the study and thus signed the permission forms. A separate Community was created by the instructors in Google+ which served as an asynchronous online milieu for the exchange.

The study focuses on the asynchronous component of participants' intercultural discussions in the form of narratives reporting both positive and negative experiences using participants' additional or target language(s) (L2s),[2] in different contexts, as well as a discussion about hypothetically tracing their ethnic origins through a DNA test and the implications of doing so. A total of 235 utterances were selected for in-depth analysis within a corpus of nearly 25,000 words. The 235 utterances were selected based on whether they belonged to one of the two main discussions carried out in the exchange project: the "Language memories" and the "DNA Journey" discussions. These were connected to the tasks which provided participants with the most opportunities to reflect on their cultural and linguistic identities as well as to project those identities in their narratives and reflections. Both the "Language memories" narratives and the "DNA Journey" reflections, which

[2] Despite acknowledging the different implications and contextual meaning nuances of the terms "second language," "third language," and "foreign language," in this chapter only the terms "additional language" and "target language" (L2) will be used to refer to any of the former terms, unless stated otherwise.

are explained below, were framed within the third stage of the project, "Information exchange: exploring and sharing knowledge." In these two tasks, each participant was equally involved in the discussion and contributed an average of three utterances. As for the utterances resulting from other discussions, they are beyond the scope of this study and thus have not been addressed in this chapter.

The first part of the project's third stage focused on exchanging "Language memories" narratives. The topic was inspired by the celebration of the European Day of Languages, which coincided with the time period when the specific activity took place during the exchange.

A total of 116 utterances were exchanged within the "Language memories" task in the form of narratives which described each student's personal recollections and anecdotes connected to either positive or negative experiences related to the use of their L2(s) which, in most cases, was English but also included Spanish, French, and German, among others. These narratives were prompted by the following statement, formulated by the participants' instructors from both institutions in the form of an introductory forum post which started a new thread:

> The European Day of Languages is celebrated every year on 26 September. It's a day to encourage language learning for young and old. Let's mark this day by sharing our language memories. Write a brief personal story of a good or bad memory regarding the use of language, INDIVIDUALLY, and share it as a Comment to this post. Use linking words, verbs in the past and at least 10 sentences in a paragraph."

Another 119 utterances corresponded to the second part of the third stage, the "DNA Journey" discussion, in which students reflected on questions connected to their identity and their willingness to explore various cultural or ethnic affiliations that were present in their genealogical tree. This task was part of the "Global awareness – Discussing social issues: Comparison and contrast" component of the project and it was included in the task sequence of this virtual exchange project with the goal to spark discussion and reflection on the importance of breaking boundaries, being tolerant and respectful to others, and embracing diversity (Nicolaou, 2020). The initial thread on this topic included a prompt which was based on a video the students were asked to watch prior to sharing their reflections:[3]

[3] The DNA Journey video is available at: https://www.youtube.com/watch?v=tyaE-QEmt5ls, last accessed August 11, 2021.

> The DNA Journey: Our DNA reveals so much about where we come from. Most of us are far more diverse and have much more in common with people from other countries than we would ever have thought. We have started The DNA Journey because we want people to understand that there are more things uniting us than dividing us. a) Are you interested in finding out where you come from based on your DNA? b) Would you dare question who you really are? c) How connected do you feel to the rest of the world? d) Is there a country that you feel you are most connected with? e) Is there a country that you feel you absolutely have no connection with? f) What if you are genetically related to a certain group of people you normally associate with bad feelings? g) Would you like to travel to all the countries you are genetically related to? Write your reflections on the Google+ Community and respond to each other.

The "DNA Journey," a video campaign launched by Momondo in 2016, intended to create a more open and tolerant world by showing participants how we, as people, have more things uniting us than dividing us. Their videos were viewed more than 28 million times on Facebook and more than 5 million times on YouTube, as well as being shared more than 600,000 times globally and commented on by thousands of people from all over the world.

3.3 Data Analysis and Procedure

Learners' postings were subjected to quantitative and qualitative content analysis using a modified version of the Appraisal model (Martin & White, 2005; Oskoz et al., 2018). To examine the Engagement strategies used by participants, each narrative was divided into utterances, understood as pieces of speech beginning and ending with a clear pause (Kaplan, 2007), as students' informal forum comments resembled spoken discourse. Within each utterance, lexical items, understood as a single word, a part of a word, or a chain of words that form the basic elements of a language lexicon, were identified. In addition, those utterances were categorized as referring to the C1, the C2, general statements referred to the topic (T) but without addressing any specific culture, and dynamics (D) for instances such as salutations and ice-breaking exchanges (Sevilla-Pavón & Nicolaou, 2019). It should be noted that C1 referred to the students' own culture(s) (Spanish and any other additional cultures in the case of students from Spain, Cypriot and any other additional cultures in the case of students from Cyprus, and so on) while C2 referred to their target culture(s), which in turn were connected to the L2 being learned. The D utterances were not analysed in this study.

Secondly, the utterances were categorized into monoglossic or heteroglossic. Within heteroglossic utterances, the analysis focused on whether the statements could be considered as including the voices of others, either through an expansion strategy considering the perspectives of others as legitimate or supporting one's own, or through a contraction strategy as an active challenge of the views of others (Oskoz et al., 2018). In some cases, an utterance could fall into more than one category, that is, it could follow more than one strategy. In other words, heteroglossic utterances were further subdivided into the following main subcategories, which are illustrated by different examples:

- Heteroglossic/Expand/Entertain: "I think it is important to know yourself so you really can understand and accept others" (Astrid, Swedish UV student, "DNA Journey" discussion).
- Heteroglossic/Attribute (acknowledge readings or others): "As Gilbert Highet said: New pieces bud out, spread into leaves, and become big branches, proliferating" (Petra, Austrian UV student, "DNA Journey" discussion).
- Heteroglossic/Contract/Disclaim/Deny: "I think it would be nice to travel to the countries which are part of my DNA except for a specific country whose behavior I don't like" (Karisa, Cypriot CUT student, "DNA Journey" discussion).
- Heteroglossic/Contract/Disclaim/counter readings or others: "I have met a lot of people from different countries during my summer job but my favorite one is Israel. They are very friendly and tell me about their habits, teach me Hebrew, and appreciate the work of others. I cannot say 100%. But I believe that if I were genetically related to a group of people I associated with bad feelings, I would accept that" (Maria, Cypriot student, "DNA Journey" discussion).

In the initial stages of the data analysis process, inter-rater reliability was sought first by discussing the framework and then coding 25% of the data (from the two subsets), comparing results, and ensuring there were not any inconsistencies. Cohen's kappa coefficient (κ) was used to measure inter-rater reliability (and also intra-rater reliability) regarding the analysis of the utterances. The analysis determined that there was very strong agreement between the two raters, $\kappa = 1.000$, $p < .0005$, and Cohen d sizes for the significant differences regarding means between the two groups of learners or between the two discussions were small. Subsequently, after agreeing upon the categories, one of the researchers coded both datasets.

The discussions were always initiated in class under the guidance of the instructors. Students from both groups were provided with relevant videos, articles, and reference materials that they could use as an anchor point. Furthermore, they could refer to those materials at any given point in their discussion. In addition, students were encouraged to provide information from websites, journals, videos or books that they deemed relevant to the discussion. All group members were required to provide personal opinions and share personal experiences, and they had to post a minimum number of comments. Furthermore, when replying to other students' contributions, participants were required to try to comment first in those conversations with fewer comments. This was done with a view to making everyone feel included in the learners' community, and also as a way to keep the conversations alive by incorporating ideas from their project partners' comments into their own comments.

4 Results and Discussion

The research questions that guided the study were connected to Cypriot and Spanish L2 learners' expressions of their linguistic and cultural identity construction processes within a virtual exchange project in connection to 1) the use of the different discourse resources in terms of the inclusion of other voices in the discourse (monoglossia or heteroglossia); 2) the use of Engagement discourse strategies (Contraction and Expansion) when referring to culture one (C1), culture two (C2), and topic (T); and 3) the use of Engagement discourse strategies, depending on the topic (language memories or DNA Journey), when referring to C1, C2, and T.

The first subset of data analysed came from the forum posts the participants from CUT and UV exchanged about their individual "Language memories," which resulted in 116 utterances, as explained above. Since the language memory shared by each participant was connected to the use of a language other than their mother tongue(s), the utterances referred to the students' target culture(s) (C2) in almost all cases, except for two utterances which referred to their own culture(s) (C1). The number of monoglossic utterances within the "Language memories" discussion was 83, while the remaining 22 were heteroglossic. This big difference could be explained by the fact that the language memories students recalled had to do with experiences which were highly personal and showed their conclusions or implications for their future. Similar results were reported by Vega Garrido (2018), who found in her analysis of rhetorical stages that results differed depending on the prompt. In this study, participants' monoglossic statements were mostly in the present tense as well as the present continuous. As for the most frequently used lexical-grammatical resources within the Entertain subcategory, these included the modal verbs "will" and "can." In the case of the Contract/Deny subcategory, the strategies used included the negative modals "don't," "will not," and "can't." Finally, the Contract/Counter strategies were limited almost in their entirety to the conjunction "but" with a few comment adjuncts.

An example of a monoglossic statement connected to a highly personal view is provided by Darío (note that all students' names were replaced by pseudonyms), a student from UV: "Whenever I meet someone from another country, I love asking questions about their way of being, their behaviour, to know other cultures and traditions." In this case, as in many other similar cases in this discussion, the utterance is monoglossic in nature, but that does not necessarily mean that the underlying ideology is monoglossic, as the student presents a pluralistic, open-minded attitude toward other ways of being, behaviors, cultures, and traditions. In other words, many of the monoglossic statements found in the "Language memories" discussion could not be considered as "bare assertions" (Bakhtin, 1986, 2010) but they could be interpreted instead as an effort to "create ideological spaces that move away from monoglossic language ideologies toward heteroglossic language ideologies and implementational spaces that provide concrete tools for enacting this vision" (Flores & Schissel, 2014).

As for the 24 heteroglossic statements found in the "Language memories" discussion, 5 belonged to the subcategory of "Expand," including the following examples: "In my opinion, languages are the best way to get knowledge while you are establishing bonds with other people from anywhere around the world" (Darío, UV, Heteroglossic/Expand/Entertain) and "In my opinion, learning a language is difficult, but when you finally know enough and you are able to speak in other languages you experience a unique feeling of satisfaction" (Carolina, UV, Heteroglossic/Expand/Entertain). Meanwhile, 19 statements belonged to the subcategory of "Contract." Some examples are: "My first week there was one of the best experiences of my life, but as time went on, I had to face my first big challenge: the language" (Mara, UV, Heteroglossic/Contract/Disclaim/Counter) and "In fact, language is not a set of words created in order to communicate but to both identify with each other and feel that we all are part of something bigger" (Mara, UV, Heteroglossic/Contract/Disclaim/Counter).

Following Martin and White's AF, the examples above can be considered illustrative of contractive dialogue, since in each case the author proclaims and more specifically pronounces an initial utterance which is immediately followed by a disclaiming utterance aimed at countering the previous assumption. In the first example, Mara's initial statement that her first week in a foreign country was one of the best experiences in her life is countered by the subsequent reference to the challenges she had to face when trying to communicate in her L2.

As for the second example, the participant uses a similar disclaiming/countering strategy in order to highlight her view of language as a tool to not just communicate but identify with each other and "feel that we are part of something bigger," thus "insisting upon her point of view when it [...] is in contrast with a preceding proposal or assumption" (Aijmer, 2007, p. 335). Even though the two utterances belong to statements by the same author, and in spite of the fact that both of them fall into the same category within the AF, a contrast in Mara's portrayed cultural and linguistic identities can be observed.

The identity she projected earlier in the project may be interpreted as less open toward other languages, as she frames her experience with the foreign language in such a way that the emphasis is placed on the challenges she faced when trying to communicate in that language. This aspect of her identity coexists with another one projected later on in the project, an identity which appears to be more in alignment with a new multicultural, transnational perspective (Jensen, 2003, 2011), which is closer to a millennium, hybrid multilingual/multicultural identity (Higgins, 2015), since it emphasizes feelings of empathy, connection, and belonging among people from different linguistic and cultural backgrounds.

Regarding the second subset of data analysed, it came from the forum posts the participants from CUT and UV exchanged within the "DNA Journey" discussion, which resulted in 119 utterances, as explained earlier. Within those, 87 utterances were monoglossic, while the remaining 32 were heteroglossic. Ninety-five of those utterances were connected to the students' C2, while only 8 had to do with their C1, and the remaining 14 belonged to the categories of group dynamics or general statements not connected to any languages or cultures in particular (and thus were not included in the analysis). This again resonates with the results obtained by Vega Garrido's study (2018), with differences connected to the kind of prompt students were replying to. In this case, students had to give a highly personal opinion about whether they would be willing to undertake a "DNA Journey" to reveal their origins and whether this might affect their cultural identities or the way they view other languages and cultures.

Examples of monoglossic statements connected to this hypothetical DNA test revealing the students' ethnic background, which were chosen because of the fact that they were representative of how other students responded, include the following statement from Anna, a Swedish exchange student at UV: "A few years ago my grandmother did some research about our family back in the days and it was super interesting to get information about who we were back then. So yes, I am interested in finding out more about my family's past." Another example of a monoglossic statement came from Antigone, a student at CUT: "I generally love to travel and I would really like to travel especially to all the countries I am genetically related to, if I haven't been there already. I'm definitely interested in finding out from what other places I come from, based on my DNA."

Similar to the examples selected from the "Language memories" discussion, these monoglossic statements cannot be seen as "bare assertions" (Bakhtin, 1986, 2010) which "present the speaker as a solitary voice unengaged with any dialogic partners or alternatives" (White & Sano, 2006, p. 192) but rather as contributions which attempt to create heteroglossic ideological spaces (Flores & Schissel, 2014), as the speakers show their willingness to know more about their ethnic backgrounds and even to visit all the places in the world that are connected to their DNA.

Concerning the 32 heteroglossic statements found in the "DNA Journey" discussion, 18 of them belonged to the subcategory of "Expand," including the following example from an Austrian exchange student at UV from a Croatian background: "I don't know about you but in my opinion, languages are changing constantly – that's one of the reasons why languages are so interesting for me: Do you like languages? If yes or no, tell me why? I think it's funny how many meanings a word can have – so we always have to watch out what and how we say it. Especially the different pronunciation of the same word in different countries amazes me" (Krista, Austrian-Croatian student from UV, Heteroglossic/Expand/Entertain). Meanwhile, 15 "DNA Journey" utterances belonged to the subcategory of "Contract," an example of which can be found in the post by Andreas, a student from CUT: "I do not feel closer to one country in particular but I don't feel like I don't have any connections with other countries" (Heteroglossic/Contract/Disclaim/Deny). This and other examples of Disclaim/Deny formulations used by students illustrate "maximally contractive" propositions, as they simultaneously negate a position and by virtue of the negation acknowledge its implicit positive version. In this way, the propositions are dialogistic but at the same time they contract the dialogical space.

In line with the results of previous research (Vega Garrido, 2018), this study shows students participating in the online discussions around their linguistic and cultural identities within the virtual exchange project used a majority of monoglossic, Expand/Entertain and Contract/Deny resources in their posts. In addition, the results show that among heteroglossic strategies, participants prefer the use of Expanding (e.g., Entertain) and Contracting (e.g., Disclaim) strategies in the verbal expression of their linguistic and cultural identity construction processes, which also coincides with the findings of previous studies (Oskoz & Gimeno-Sanz, 2019; Oskoz et al., 2018). Furthermore, also in line with the findings of previous studies, the monoglossic-heteroglossic utterances ratio seems to have been influenced by the topic and the kinds of prompts provided to initiate the discussions (Vega Garrido, 2018), as discussed below.

On the one hand, the number of monoglossic utterances within the "Language memories" discussion was 83 (out of 116), while the number of heteroglossic utterances was 22. On the other hand, in the "DNA Journey" discussion, 87 monoglossic utterances (out of 119 utterances) were found, while the remaining 32 were heteroglossic. The apparent preference for monoglossic utterances students show when portraying and projecting their linguistic and cultural identities seems to have been motivated by the prompt and the main topics dealt with in the discussions (Vega Garrido, 2018), as mentioned earlier. In the first one, the language memories recalled by students were connected to highly personal experiences, feelings, and conclusions or even lessons learned for the future. Meanwhile, in the second discussion students expressed highly personal opinions about their hypothetical participation in a "DNA Journey" which would reveal their origins and might even encourage them to see their cultural identities (as well as other languages and cultures in general) in a new light.

In both cases, the analysis revealed that the predominance of "monoglossic" utterances did not mean that those utterances were "bare assertions" (Bakhtin, 1986; 2010). In other words, the imbalance between monoglossic and heteroglossic statements was not necessarily an indicator of monolithic, fixed, or rigid cultural and linguistic identities, as participants displayed pluralistic, open-minded attitudes toward other ways of being, behaviors, cultures, and traditions. In fact, many utterances portray conscious efforts to offer ideological spaces that lead to heteroglossic language ideologies (Flores & Schissel, 2014). Those efforts in creating such dialogical spaces portray cultural and linguistic identities which are not fixed and static but rather multiple, fluid (Helm, 2018), and situated. Furthermore, these identities seem to have been influenced by the current digital age and liquid modernity (Bauman, 2007), globalization, massive migratory movements across the globe, constant mobility, and changes in relationships and identities within our highly complex societies (Hall, 1992; Jensen, 2003; Kim, 2009), as well as an increase in technological "normalization" (Bax, 2003; Chambers & Bax, 2006). Thus, when referring to their linguistic and cultural identities, participants tended to minimize or play down differences and contrasts, choosing to focus instead on aspects which could be connected with new multicultural, translational individuals (Jensen, 2003, 2011) with millennium, hybrid multilingual/multicultural identities (Higgins, 2015).

5 Concluding Remarks

This study has shed light on the way 78 Cypriot and Spanish EAL learners expressed their identities by sharing knowledge and views about their own language(s) and culture(s) while developing new knowledge about different languages and cultures through virtual exchange asynchronous online forum discussions, which resulted in a corpus of nearly 25,000 words from which 235 utterances from the "Language memories" and "DNA Journey" discussions were selected and analysed.

The mixed-methods analysis was informed by the Engagement subsystem of the interpersonal communication framework known as Appraisal (Martin & White, 2005; Oskoz et al., 2018), which follows an SFL approach. SFL views participants' identity development from a social semiotic perspective, thus assuming that the language used to project identities is a meaning-making system within which the meanings that language producers make are not constrained by a particular sense of reality. This analysis helped characterize participants' use of the language resources denoting interpersonal engagement meanings and to describe the engagement patterns that emerged when discussing their cultural and linguistic identities.

In adopting the AF, the researchers followed previous studies which highlighted the appropriateness of the Appraisal model to capture argumentation strategies used in online forum discussions (Coffin & Hewings, 2004); to explore the identity that writers/speakers assume and project when they produce text and the identity these text producers assign to the other voices that participate in the text (O'Donnell, 2013); to delve into the identity negotiation and the social construction of the self (McKinley, 2018) while looking into the "possibilities for selfhood" (Clark & Ivanic, 1997) and the projection of identities in writing; to inquire into emerging professional identities (Alonso Belmonte, 2012); and to shed light on both the identity assumed by writers/speakers when writing and the identity assigned to the other voices that participate in the text produced by those writers/speakers (O'Donnell, 2013).

The limitations of the study lie in the areas of validity and reliability of the research approach. This study has the potential to improve by adopting the principle of triangulation in the analysis of the students' texts. For example, analysing different empirical data obtained from various sources, such as interviews and focus groups with students, would render this study more reliable and valid. In spite of these limitations, the project forum discussions analysed can be seen as an example of how genres build or enact social practice, and theorizing about this contributes to building a comprehensive theory of social action, revealing the usefulness of systemic functional analysis in addressing the social construction of reality (Christie & Martin, 1997; Iedema et al., 1994). Since educational settings provide contexts for apprenticeship into such genres, the application of Appraisal Theory can assist professionals in the field of critical analysis of texts in any form (written, oral or computer mediated), upgrading their skills at appreciation/evaluating language usage.

As for the analysis of learner discourse, it can provide useful information about how identities, opinions, and views are negotiated, as well as the evolution of the learner's value judgment and writing positioning. Appraisal Theory can therefore propose pedagogic ways to enhance transformative change. Thus, future research could focus on achieving this goal by bringing divisive topics and deliberatively addressing conflicting worldviews to favor the move beyond the exchange of information, which is deemed as a superficial approach to virtual exchange (O'Dowd, 2018). An additional advantage of using AF to investigate students' discourse may offer new ways of including an ongoing reflective component that requires learners to consider different worldviews.

This chapter examined the ways in which students of English as an Additional Language in two dispersed geographical contexts engaged in identity construction in a shared virtual space. By applying Appraisal Theory, the students' monoglossic and heteroglossic utterances were explored. The study concluded that even though the students' monoglossic discourse exceeded their heteroglossic engagement, virtual spaces seem to afford opportunities for translingual and transcultural practices in the cases where the topic of discussion incites heteroglossic positioning and global identity formation.

Acknowledgments

The authors would like to thank the Spanish Ministry of Science, Innovation and Universities for supporting this research through the project VELCOME: Virtual exchange for learning and competence development in EMI classrooms (Ref: RTI2018-094601-B-100), for the period 2018–2021.

References

Aijmer, K. (2007). Modal adverbs as discourse markers. In J. Rehbein, C. Hohenstein, & L. Pietsch (Eds.), *Connectivity in grammar and discourse* (pp. 329–344). John Benjamins.

Alonso Belmonte, I. (2012). "I feel as if I were a real teacher": An analysis of EFL student teachers' evaluative discourse through Appraisal Theory. *Revista Canaria de Estudios Ingleses*, 65, 13–28.

Andresen, M. A. (2009). Asynchronous discussion forums: Success factors, outcomes, assessments, and limitations. *Journal of Educational Technology & Society*, *12*(1), 249–257.

Appadurai, A. (1996). *Modernity at large: Cultural dimensions of globalization*. University of Minnesota Press.

Arnold, N., & Ducate, L. (2006). Future foreign language teachers' social and cognitive collaboration in an online environment. *Language Learning and Technology*, *10*(1), 42.

Bakhtin, M. M. (1986). *Speech genres and other late essays*. University of Texas Press.

Bakhtin, M. M. (2010). *The dialogic imagination: Four essays* (Vol. 1). University of Texas Press.

Basharina, O. K. (2007). An activity theory perspective on student-report contradictions in international telecollaboration. *Language Learning & Technology*, *11*(2), 82–103.

Basharina, O., Guardado, M., & Morgan, T. (2008). Negotiating differences: Instructors' reflections on challenges in international telecollaboration. *Canadian Modern Language Review*, *65*(2), 275–305.

Bauman, Z. (2005). *Liquid life*. Polity Press.

Bauman, Z. (2007). *Consuming life*. Polity Press.

Bax, S. (2003). CALL—Past, present, and future. *System*, *31*(1), 13–28.

Belz, J. A. (2003). Linguistic perspectives on the development of intercultural competence in telecollaboration. *Language Learning & Technology*, 7(2), 68–99.

Belz, J. A., & Thorne, S. L. (2006). Introduction: Internet-mediated intercultural foreign language education and the intercultural speaker. In J. A. Belz & S. L. Thorne (Eds.), *Internet-mediated intercultural foreign language education* (pp. iix–xxv). Annual Volume of the American Association of University Supervisors and Coordinators. Heinle & Heinle.

Byram, M. (1997). *Teaching and assessing intercultural communicative competence*. Multilingual Matters.

Byram, M. (2000). Assessing intercultural competence in language teaching. *Sprogforum*, *18*(6), 8–13.

Cameron, D., & Anderson, T. (2006). Comparing weblogs to threaded discussion tools. *International Journal of Instructional Technology & Distance Learning*, *2*(11), 1–16.

Chambers, A., & Bax, S. (2006). Making CALL work: Towards normalisation. *System*, *34*(4), 465–479.

Chandrasegaran, A., & Kong, K. M. (2006). Stance-taking and stance-support in students' online forum discussion. *Linguistics and Education*, *17*(4), 374–390. DOI: 10.1016/j.linged.2007.01.003

Christie, F., & Martin, J. R. (Eds.) (1997). *Genre and institutions: Social processes in the workplace and school* (pp. 161–195). Cassell.

Chun, D. M. (2011). Developing intercultural communicative competence through online exchanges. *CALICO Journal*, *28*(2), 392–419.

Clark, R., & Ivanic, R. (1997). *The politics of writing*. Routledge.

Coffin, C., & Hewings, A. (2004). IELTS as preparation for tertiary writing: Distinctive interpersonal and textual strategies. In L. Ravelli & R. Ellis (Eds.), *Academic writing in context: Social-functional perspectives on theory and practice* (pp. 153–171). Continuum.

Coffin, C., & O'Halloran, K. (2005). Finding the global groove: Theorising and analysing dynamic reader positioning using appraisal, corpus and a concordancer. *Critical Discourse Studies*, *2*(2), 143–163.

Cole, M. T., Swartz, L. B., & Shelley, D. J. (2020). Threaded discussion: The role it plays in e-learning. *International Journal of Information and Communication Technology Education (IJICTE)*, *16*(1), 16–29.

Collier, M. J., & Thomas, M. (1988). Identity in intercultural communication: An interpretive perspective. In Y. Kim & W. B. Gudykunst (Series Eds.), *International and intercultural communication annual: Vol. 12. Theories of intercultural communication* (pp. 99–120). Sage. https://doi.org/10.1080/17405900500283607

Council of Europe (2018). *Common European Framework of Reference for Languages: Learning, teaching, assessment. Companion volume with new descriptors.* Council of Europe Publishing.

Council of Europe. Council for Cultural Co-operation. Education Committee. Modern Languages Division. (2001). *Common European Framework of Reference for Languages: Learning, teaching, assessment*. Cambridge University Press.

Eggins, S. (2004). *An introduction to systemic functional linguistics*. Continuum.

Elola, I., & Oskoz, A. (2008). Blogging: Fostering intercultural competence development in foreign language and study abroad contexts. *Foreign Language Annals*, *41*(3), 454–477. DOI: 10.1111/j.1944-9720.2008.

Flores, N., & Schissel, J. (2014). Dynamic bilingualism as the norm: Envisioning a heteroglossic approach to standards-based reform. *TESOL Quarterly*, *48*(3), 454–479. https://doi.org/10.1002/tesq.182
Hall, S. (1992). Race, culture, and communications: Looking backward and forward at cultural studies. *Rethinking Marxism*, *5*(1), 10–18. DOI: 10.1080/08935699208657998
Hanna, B., & de Nooy, J. (2003). A funny thing happened on the way to the forum: Electronic discussion and foreign language learning. *Language Learning & Technology*, *7*(1), 71–85. http://dx.doi.org/10125/25188
Hanna, B., & de Nooy, J. (2009). *Learning language and culture via public internet discussion forums.* Palgrave Macmillan.
Helm, F. (2013). A dialogic model for telecollaboration. *Bellaterra Journal*, *6*(2), 28–48.
Helm, F. (2016). Facilitated dialogue in online intercultural exchange. In R. O'Dowd & T. Lewis (Eds.), *Online intercultural exchange: Policy, pedagogy, practice* (pp. 150–172). Routledge.
Helm, F. (2018). *Emerging identities in virtual exchange*. Researchpublishing.net.
Higgins, C. (2015). Intersecting scapes and new millennium identities in language learning. *Language Teaching*, *48*(3), 373–389. DOI: https://doi.org/10.1017/S0261444814000044
Hunston, S. (2011). *Corpus approaches to evaluation*. Routledge.
Hyland, K. (2005). *Metadiscourse: Exploring interaction in* writing. Continuum.
Hyland, K., & Jiang, F. (2016). "We must conclude that…": A diachronic study of academic engagement. *Journal of English for Academic Purposes*, *24*, 29–42.
Iedema, R., Feez, S., & White, P. R. R. (1994). *Media literacy. Disadvantaged schools program*. NSW Department of School Education.
Jensen, L. A. (2003). Coming of age in a multicultural world: Globalization and adolescent cultural identity formation. *Applied Developmental Science*, *7*(3), 189–196.
Jensen, L. A. (2011). Navigating local and global worlds: Opportunities and risks for adolescent cultural identity development. *Psychological Studies*, *56*(1), 62–70.
Kaplan, N. (2007). *La construcción discursiva del evento conflictivo en las noticias por televisión*. Universidad Central de Venezuela, Unpublished Ph.D. dissertation.
Kim, Y. Y. (2009). The identity factor in intercultural competence. *The Sage handbook of intercultural competence: 1* (pp. 53–65). Sage.
Lee, L. (2009). Scaffolding collaborative exchanges between expert and novice language teachers in threaded discussions. *Foreign Language Annals*, *42*(2), 212–228.
Liaw, M. (2006). E-learning and the development of intercultural competence. *Language Learning & Technology*, *10*(3), 49–64.
Liaw, M. L., & Bunn-Le Master, S. (2010). Understanding telecollaboration through an analysis of intercultural discourse. *Computer Assisted Language Learning*, *23*(1), 21–40. https://doi.org/10.1080/09588220903467301

Loizidou, D., & Mangenot, F. (2016). Interactional dimension of online asynchronous exchange in an asymmetric telecollaboration. In B. O'Rourke, M. Kurek, & S. Jager (Eds.), *New directions in telecollaborative research and practice: Selected papers from the Second Conference on Telecollaboration in Higher Education* (pp. 155–161). Research-publishing.net.

Loizidou, D., & Savlovska, D. (2020). Taking care of their positive online face? Reasons and strategy development. In M. Hauck & A. Muller-Hartmann (Eds.), *Virtual exchange and 21st century teacher education: Short papers from the 2019 EVALUATE Conference* (p. 71). Research-publishing.net.

Lomicka, L. (2006). Understanding the other: Intercultural exchange and CMC. In L. Ducate & L. Arnold (Eds.), *Calling on CALL: From theory and research to new directions in FL teaching* (pp. 63–86). Equinox.

Martin, J. R. (2000a). Beyond exchange: Appraisal systems in English. In S. Hunston & G. Thompson (Eds.), *Evaluation in text* (pp. 142–175). Oxford University Press.

Martin, J. R. (2000b). Design and practice: Enacting functional linguistics in Australia. *Annual Review of Applied Linguistics*, 20 (20th anniversary volume "Applied linguistics as an emerging discipline"), 116–126.

Martin, J. R. (2014). Evolving systemic functional linguistics: Beyond the clause. *Functional Linguistics*, 1–3. DOI: 10.1186/2196-419X-1-3.

Martin, J. R., & White, P. R. (2005). *The language of evaluation. Appraisal in English.* Palgrave. DOI:10.1057/9780230511910.

McKinley, J. (2017). Identity construction in learning English academic writing in a Japanese university. *Journal of Asia TEFL, 14*(2), 228–243. DOI: 10.18823/asiatefl.2017.14.2.2.228

McKinley, J. (2018). Integrating appraisal theory with possible selves in understanding university EFL writing. *System, 78*, 27–37. DOI: 10.1016/j.system.2018.07.002.

Meyer, K. A. (2004). Evaluating online discussions: Four different frames of analysis. *Journal of Asynchronous Learning Networks, 8*(2), 101–114.

Mokoena, S. (2013). Engagement with and participation in online discussion forums. *Turkish Online Journal of Educational Technology-TOJET, 12*(2), 97–105.

Mooney, M., Southard, S., & Burton, C. H. (2014). Shifting from obligatory discourse to rich dialogue: Promoting student interaction in asynchronous threaded discussion postings. *Online Journal of Distance Learning Administration, 17*(1), 1–12.

Nicolaou, A. (2020). *The affordances of virtual exchange for developing global competence and active citizenship in content-based language learning.* Unpublished doctoral thesis, Trinity College Dublin, University of Dublin.

Nicolaou, A., & Sevilla-Pavón, A. (2016). Exploring telecollaboration through the lens of university students: A Spanish–Cypriot telecollaborative exchange. In S. Jager, M. Kurek, & B. O'Rourke (Eds.), *New directions in telecollaborative research and practice: Selected papers from the Second Conference on*

Telecollaboration in Higher Education (pp. 113–119). Research-publishing.net. https://doi.org/10.14705/rpnet.2016.telecollab2016.497

O'Donnell, M. (2013). Exploring identity through Appraisal Theory: A corpus annotation methodology. *Linguistics and the Human Sciences*, *9*(1), 1–15.

O'Dowd, R. (2007). Evaluating the outcomes of online intercultural exchange. *ELT Journal*, *61*(2), 144–153. DOI: 10.1093/elt/ccm007

O'Dowd, R. (2016). Emerging trends and new directions in telecollaborative learning. *CALICO Journal*, *33*(3), 291–310. DOI: 10.1558/cj.v33i3.30747

O'Dowd, R. (2018). From telecollaboration to virtual exchange: State-of-the-art and the role of UNICollaboration in moving forward. *Journal of Virtual Exchange*, 1, 1–23. 10.14705/rpnet.2018.jve.1.

O'Dowd, R. (2020). A transnational model of virtual exchange for global citizenship education. *Language Teaching*, *53*(4), 477–490. DOI: 10.1017/S0261444819000077

Oskoz, A., & Gimeno-Sanz, A. (2019). Engagement and attitude in telecollaboration: Topic and cultural background effects. *Language Learning & Technology*, *23*(3), 136–160. http://hdl.handle.net/10125/44700

Oskoz, A., Gimeno-Sanz, A., & Sevilla-Pavón, A. (2018). Examining L2 learners' discourse strategies usage in telecollaborative written interactions. In B. Mousten, S. Vandepitte, E. Arnó, & B. Maylath (Eds.), *Cooperation on multilingual writing in global virtual learning environments* (pp. 200–220). IGI-Global.

Rizopoulos, L. A., & McCarthy, P. (2009). Using online threaded discussions: Best practices for the digital learner. *Journal of Educational Technology Systems*, *37*(4), 373–383.

Ryshina-Pankova, M. (2014). Exploring academic argumentation in course-related blogs through engagement. In G. Thompson & L. Alba (Eds.), *Evaluation in context* (pp. 281–302). John Benjamins.

Salter, N. P., & Conneely, M. R. (2015). Structured and unstructured discussion forums as tools for student engagement. *Computers in Human Behavior*, *46*, 18–25.

Sevilla-Pavón, A., & Nicolaou, A. (2019). *Business English 3.0: Hands-on online and virtual collaboration tasks.* Editorial Comares.

Sevilla-Pavón, A., & Nicolaou, A. (2020). Artefact co-construction in virtual exchange: "Youth entrepreneurship for society." *Computer Assisted Language Learning*, 1–26 DOI: 10.1080/09588221.2020.1825096

Sull, E. C. (2009). The (almost) complete guide to effectively managing threaded discussions. *Distance Learning*, *6*(4), 65.

Turula, A. (2017). Teaching presence in telecollaboration. Keeping an open mind. *System*, *64*, 21–33.

Vega Garrido, M. E. (2018). *Characterizing level IV students' use of Engagement resources in academic writing in English: An exploratory study from a systemic functional perspective*. Doctoral Thesis. RED Colombiana de información científica: Repositorio Uninorte. http://hdl.handle.net/10584/8125

Ware, P. (2005). "Missed" communication in online communication: Tensions in a German–American telecollaboration. *Language Learning & Technology*, *9*(2), 64–89.

Ware, P. D., & Kramsch, C. (2005). Toward an intercultural stance: Teaching German and English through telecollaboration. *The Modern Language Journal*, *89*(2), 190–205.

Ware, P. D., & O'Dowd, R. (2008). Peer feedback on language form in telecollaboration. *Language Learning & Technology*, *12*(1), 43–63.

White, P. R. R. (1998). *Telling media tales: The news story as rhetoric.* Unpublished doctoral thesis. University of Sidney.

White, P. R. R. (2000). Dialogue and intersubjectivity: Reinterpreting the semantics of modality and hedging. In M. Coulthard, J. Cotterill, & F. Rock (Eds.), *Working with with dialogue* (pp. 67–80). Neimeyer.

White, P. R. R. (2001). *Appraisal: An overview.* http://www.grammatics.com/appraisal/AppraisalGuide

White, P. R. R. (2015). Appraisal theory. In K. Tracy, T. Sandel, & C. Ilie (Eds.), *The International encyclopedia of language and social interaction*. DOI: 10.1002/9781118611463.wbielsi041

White, P. R. R., & Sano, M. (2006). Dialogistic positions and anticipated audiences – a framework for stylistic comparisons. In K. Aijmer & A. M. Simon-Vandenbergen (Eds.), *Pragmatic markers in contrast* (pp. 189–214). Elsevier.

Wu, S. M. (2006). Creating a contrastive rhetorical stance: Investigating the strategy of problematization in students' argumentation. *Relc Journal*, *37*(3), 329–353. DOI: 10.1177/0033688206071316

Wu, S. M., & Allison, D. (2005). Evaluative expressions in analytical arguments: Aspects of appraisal in assigned English language essays. *Journal of Applied Linguistics*, *2*(1), 105–127. DOI: https://doi.org/10.1558/japl.v2.i1.105

About the Authors

Ana Sevilla-Pavón is an Associate Professor in the Department of English and German Philology at Universitat de València, Spain and holds a Ph.D. in Applied Linguistics from Universitat Politècnica de València, Spain. She has participated in numerous research projects, including the iTECLA project, which she coordinated, and VELCOME. Her research interests include Computer-Assisted Language Learning and Assessment, Intercultural Education, 21st Century Learning, English for Specific Purposes, and Augmented Reality in Virtual Exchange.

Anna Nicolaou is an English Language Instructor at the Language Centre of the Cyprus University of Technology in Cyprus. She holds a Ph.D. from the School of Linguistics, Speech and Communication Sciences at Trinity College Dublin. She has participated in various research projects, such as VALIANT, DC4LT, DE-TEL, and EUt+. Her research interests include Intercultural Education, Virtual Exchange, Multilingualism, Computer-Assisted Language Learning, 21st Century Learning, and Extended Reality.

11 Cycles of Translanguaging and Group Identity Performances in Multi-Party Video-Mediated Telecollaboration: Triggers, Consequences, and Implications

Liudmila Klimanova

1 Introduction

Recent research on computer-mediated communication (CMC) has shown that systematic and intentional multilingual practices are a common phenomenon in today's global virtual communication (Ortega, 2017). This dynamic process in which multilingual speakers navigate complex social and cognitive demands through the strategic deployment of multiple languages is known as *translanguaging* (Blommaert, 2010; Otsuji & Pennycook, 2010; Wei, 2011). Translanguaging involves more than a mere alternation of linguistic codes at specific points of a communicative episode; it is an active process of meaning- and sense-making, where language users draw upon multiple linguistic, cognitive, semiotic, and non-linguistic resources to make meaning and make sense (García, 2009; Wei, 2011, 2018). A translanguaging speaker switches between "diverse languages that form their repertoire as an integrated system" (Canagarajah, 2011, p. 401).

Although translanguaging has received significant attention in language acquisition studies, current CALL literature is limited to studies of multilingual and multimodal written CMC, predominantly in naturalistic social-networking contexts (e.g., Kulavuz-Onal & Vásquez, 2018; Schreiber, 2015) and, to a lesser degree, in instructional settings (e.g., Adinolfi & Astruc, 2017; Satar, 2016, 2020). Furthermore, while the focus on translanguaging as an activity of engaging in the speaker's semiotic repertoire (Helm & Dabre, 2018) brings to the fore dynamic choices speakers make in an act of interaction, the external mechanisms triggering such choices in digitally mediated contexts remain under-researched because of a predominantly agentive approach to examining an individual multilingual speaker rather than observing multilingual speakers in relation to the socio-cultural context in which they operate (Kramsch, 2009). In this regard, scrutinizing translingual practices within a *digital micro-community of multilingual speakers* opens new possibilities for examining *translanguaging as a token of conversation* determined by the conversation structure and its participants.

This chapter addresses this gap by examining the practice of translanguaging in synchronous videoconferencing sessions involving up to five at a time multilingual speakers, hereafter MPVC (multi-party videoconferencing sessions), where participants engage in a content-oriented communicative task embedded in the framework of institutional virtual exchange. The focus of this analysis is when, how, and for how long participants of a multi-party video chat employ their multilingual repertoires and switch among mutually intelligible languages when collaborating in a group on a task-based assignment, but also how these uses of multilingual repertoires contribute to *the emerging virtual group dynamic*. The research questions posed for this exploration are as follows:

1. How does translanguaging happen in MPVCs, and what linguistic, social, and contextual factors may trigger the use of multiple languages in a multi-party video-mediated conversation among multilingual speakers?
2. In what ways do translanguaging practices signal emerging *multilingual group identity* performances in MPVC?

By scrutinizing the dynamics of MPVC conversations in the same group of participants over time, this chapter proposes the notion of multilingual *virtual group identity* to explain how translanguaging practices codify group-specific meanings, socially shape within group-specific identities as well as create norms that serve to organize interaction and maintain desirable social climates (Baym, 1998, p. 62). In this exploration, MPVC is conceptualized as a *fluid micro-community* – a virtual group consisting of the same individuals who engage in social interaction and establish social presence, or the capacity to project one's identity socially and affectively into a community of inquiry (Rourke et al., 1999), thus fostering participants' ability to "communicate purposefully in a trusting environment and develop inter-personal relationships by way of projecting their individual personalities" (Garrison, 2009, p. 352). In this communicative context, participants' multilingual repertoires enable them to negotiate shared meaning, project social presence, and shape an emerging virtual group identity and a sense of belonging (Walker, 2017).

This chapter draws on insights from the sociolinguistic theory of identity-in-interaction (Bucholtz & Hall, 2005) and computer-mediated conversation analysis (González-Lloret, 2011) to explore how plurilingual communication can be a product of an integrated communicative micro-ecology in the context of a multilingual "community of practice" and group identity performances. I first provide important definitions of key concepts and present selected transcripts of exchanges taking place among multilingual participants of an MPVC. I then examine the instances of translanguaging in the transcripts and describe possible triggers of multilingual use. Finally, I will extend these analyses by drawing from an ecological approach to language data to explain the dynamics of *group identity enactment* in a multilingual multi-party video chat.

2 Literature Review

2.1 Multi-Party Conversation (MPC)

Multi-party conversation is not a new phenomenon, and it has been the focus of conversation analysis for decades. In multi-party conversations, more than two communication partners are involved in the consecutive or simultaneous exchange of turns. Where dyadic conversations only include the roles of speaker and addressee, MPC also involves roles of side participants and overhearers. From this perspective, a multi-party conversation has a complex conversational system with often unpredictable turn-taking patterns (Matsuyama et al., 2015). Even a participant who is listening to a conversation between two other speakers without being directly addressed is included in the structure of a multi-party conversation since the presence of this third interlocutor shapes and directs the actions of the other two (Goffman, 1981).

To explain the inclusion of third and more participants in a conversation structure, Goffman (1981) proposed this notion of *ratification,* which explained whether a participant was officially included in the interaction or not. A *ratified participant* is one who, in a speech event, has the role of speaker, addressee, or intended audience. Such a social imbalance problem cannot be solved easily because participation roles do not always share common ground among the ratified participants.

One of the complex features of MPC is turn-taking (Goffman, 1981). In face-to-face dialogical communication with two speakers, the basic clue for specifying addressees is turning one's face toward the addressee. In contrast, in voice-only or text-based communication, the explicit declaration of the addressee's names is more common. In conversations with three and more participants, engagement and turn-taking cannot always be identified among the participants. Each participant is assigned a participant's role considered by the current speaker, where the speaker, the addressee, and the side participant are "*ratified participants*." The interaction occurs between two dominant speakers, while the third participant cannot properly take the floor to speak until they are promoted to a speaker or an addressee by one of the dominant speakers. These side participants "tend to get left behind, even though all participants are ratified" (Matsuyama et al., 2015, p. 2). For example, the third participant might not be able to "assume the floor to speak for a while and thus, from their viewpoint, is left out of the dominant conversation, even though floor exchanges may be well maintained among participants from the dominant speakers' viewpoints" (p. 2). Hence, *engagement density* (Matsuyama et al., 2015) – or the number of contributions made by interactants in a conversation – may vary between dominant participant and side participants. The dominant participants' engagement can be strong and the side participants' engagement with others can be relatively weak.

> Consequently, socially imbalanced multi-party-participant situations dictate the need for *an additional facilitator participant* to help the left-behind participants "*harmonize*" with the other participants. In this context, "harmonize" means maintaining equality of engagement density within the group. (p. 2)

2.2 Multi-Party Videoconferencing Conversation

The conversation structure in a video-mediated multi-party conversation, such as a multi-party Zoom video call, unfolds in a similar but not entirely identical way. Multi-party videoconferencing sessions have some of the same features as multi-party face-to-face conversations, but the medium may dictate necessary modifications to the conversation system. Speakers need to adapt to the medium in terms of interaction management. Studies show that video-mediated multi-party conversations operate on a varied set of rules, and usually exhibit more adaptable and changing conversation structures (in other words, the roles participants assume on entering such conversations are less stable and may change as communication unfolds) (Muñoz, 2016).

Every form of conversational exchange must be initiated. Procedures for initiation are different from face-to-face conversations as being online does not necessarily mean being engaged in a conversation (Mondada, 2008). Participants are expected to display availability, for example by activating individual video cameras, turning on a microphone, and using interaction management tools (e.g., Zoom reactions, such as hand raises, thumbs-up) to signal their availability and willingness to engage verbally or with the use of paralinguistic semiotic tools, or change a conversation role to that of the dominant speaker. Another feature of videoconferencing is overlapping speech or simultaneous *talk/double talk*. When double talk happens, all participants turn silent followed by an extended pause. Then, all participants start speaking again at the same time, pause, and double talk starts again (Yankelovich et al., 2006).

Delayed video/audio output and limited visual cues to signal turn-taking prediction and regulation are another unique feature of videoconferencing. Depending on the layout and device, participants might appear on the screen as small thumbnails, which hinder the recognition of non-verbal cues like nods, gazes, and head shakes. From the technical perspective, each participant in a videoconferencing session may have a potentially different perception of a social situation because of synchronization between video clients. Turn-taking cues and affirmation cues, such as facial expressions, gaze, backchannels, and body language, are hence quite limited in video-mediated communication. Therefore, multi-party video-based conversation lacks the physicality available in face-to-face interactions (Schmitt et al., 2014).

In terms of the spatio-temporal frame, videoconferencing sessions occur in the "third space without a physical context and can begin instantaneously and end abruptly" (Bezemer & Kress, 2016, as cited in Satar, 2020, p. 132), for example due to wi-fi interruptions or participants leaving the conversations due to external distractions or for personal reasons. Because spatial and temporal continuity is weak, "linguistic choices of participants are more prominent in establishing and maintaining social presence" (Satar, 2020, p. 132), but also in building a sense of groupness and intimacy and establishing self-positioning, and individual identity projections. This is particularly important in multi-party conversations among participants from distinct cultures because they may not share linguistic, social, and cultural contexts, and often need as a group to negotiate a conversation structure when their conversation begins to unfold in real-time. In this sense, exploring translanguaging practices among multilingual participants of video-mediated conversation is particularly intriguing.

On a broader social scale, a virtual multi-party videoconferencing group consisting of the same individuals that engage in multiple sessions of task-oriented videoconferencing can be described as a *micro-community*. While in language-focused studies of CMC a community can be viewed as a marginal notion, a social perspective on CMC operationalizes "community" as a central construct that underlies the linguistic and multimodal practices of its members (Androutsopoulos, 2006, 2007). In earlier studies, online or virtual communities were known as "social aggregations that emerge from the Net when enough people carry on […] public discussions long enough, with sufficient human feeling, to form webs of personal relations in cyberspace" (Rheingold, 1993, p. 5). Research shows that online communities do not follow the same patterns of communication and interaction as physical communities (Castells, 2000; Wellman et al., 2002). This consideration has prompted a considerable amount of research on the interactional dynamics of online interactions. More recently, an online/virtual community has been defined as a group of people who interact in a virtual environment, share the same affinity, have consistent language practices, and use specific vocabulary and forms of non-verbal communication (Baym, 2000, 2003; Herring, 2010). These features of a virtual *micro-community* are established through continuous communication among its members, who form a speech community sustained by dense interaction, a shared communicative history, and language practices (Hoflich, 1997, as cited in Androutsopoulos, 2006, p. 422). In the case of multilingual communities, these language practices can be monolingual, following an established formal or informal protocol of communication, or multilingual – where interactants can "translanguage" or draw from their mutually shared multilingual repertoires to construct complex and rich meanings (Wei, 2011).

2.3 Translanguaging in CMC

As stated earlier, translanguaging is a dynamic process in which speakers navigate complex social and cognitive demands through the strategic employment of multiple languages as an integrated communication system (García & Wei, 2014; Wei, 2018). As a social and linguistic phenomenon, translanguaging could be an all-encompassing term for diverse multilingual and multimodal practices, replacing terms such as code-switching, code-mixing, code-meshing, and code-crossing that restrict the understanding of multilingual practices as a mere exchange of linguistic codes (Canagarajah, 2013). It is an active process of meaning- and sense-making, where language users draw upon multiple resources to make meaning and make sense (Wei, 2018). Translanguaging relies on a heteroglossic language ideology, which views bilingual and multilingual communication as valuable and rich in meanings.

Translanguaging is also important for embracing positioning, which, according to Davies and Harré (1990), is "the discursive process whereby selves are located in conversations as observably and subjectively coherent participants in jointly produced storylines" (p. 48). Translanguaging explains meaning-making through a range of semiotic resources within a person's individual semiotic repertoire. Therefore, research on translanguaging investigates speakers' switches between "diverse languages that form their repertoire as an integrated system" (Canagarajah, 2011, p. 401). Systematic and intentional multilingual practices are a common phenomenon in today's global virtual communication (Ortega, 2017; Warschauer et al., 2007). What is still not clear is when and how translanguaging occurs among multilingual speakers in educational settings and what digitally mediated contexts and conversation structures are more conducive to the use of multiple semiotic codes in communication.

3 Participants and Data Collection

The MPVC data for this exploration come from a class-to-class virtual exchange between language classes in two public universities in the American Southwest and northern Kazakhstan – Russian (second language, or L2) learners (sixth semester of language instruction) and English (L2) learners (third year of instruction at the university level) respectively. At the core of this exchange were participants' experiences with living in geopolitical border towns, and a discussion of topics and issues associated with borderland living (see Klimanova and Hellmich (2021) for more details about the "Connecting the Borderlands" project). The exchange spanned eight weeks of in-class discussions and asynchronous activities. For the synchronous component of the exchange, the participants were grouped into three teams of 4–5 students based on their weekly availability during out-of-class hours, with 2–3 participants from each university in each group. The same groups met twice for one hour of videoconferencing via Zoom (a popular videoconferencing platform for conducting multi-party video calls) outside the class time. For each meeting, a list of conversation prompts was provided to facilitate conversation among participants. Zoom allows automated recording, which was activated by the researcher who was not on the Zoom call during the videoconferencing sessions. The recordings were transcribed using the Jefferson Transcription System, a conversation analysis code for identifying speech patterns and annotating conversations (Bolden, 2015; Lester &

O'Reilly, 2019). The corpus of MPVC data included six transcribed and coded Zoom sessions.

4 The Analytical Approach

All instances of translanguaging at the intra-sentential and inter-sentential levels were identified in the transcribed conversations and coded using the conversation analysis of computer-mediated communication (González-Lloret, 2011; Herring, 2004) (Table 11.1). Analysis of translanguaging episodes was conducted using two approaches. First, the turns where MPVC participants code-switched (used multiple languages) were coded as intra-sentential or inter-sentential, and each episode was scrutinized for possible triggers. In this analysis, a *translanguaging episode* was defined as a turn or a series of turns where participants draw on multiple languages to construct meaning. Each instance of translanguaging was coded and analyzed for possible triggers, duration, social purpose in the multi-party conversation, and its position in the interactional turn-taking sequence. Identified codes were then analyzed further and grouped, depending on a linguistic or interactional trigger that initiated a translanguaging sequence, into six distinct patterns. Second, the same excerpts were considered in the context of the entire MPVC conversation structure as evidence of a developing multilingual code adopted by MPVC participants in two group sessions and sustained over time.

Table 11.1. Summary of Translanguaging Episodes* per Group

Session #	Group 1 (n=5)	Group 2 (n=4)	Group 3 (n=5)
Session 1	87	27	39
Session 2	98	15	54
Languages used	English Russian French	English Russian Kazakh	Russian English Spanish
Predominant language of exchange	English (60% of turns)	English (89% of turns)	Russian (70% of turns)

* Each instance of switching from one language to another within a turn or between turns was counted as one translanguaging episode.

5 Translanguaging Practices in MPVC

To illustrate how the multilingual code of interaction was established over time throughout two videoconferencing sessions, this section includes examples from the transcripts of Zoom sessions attended by the same group of participants, including David, Amy, and Joshua – three American learners of Russian – and Aisulu and Sholpan– two English learners in Kazakhstan (all names are pseudonyms) (Figure 11.1). These participants shared two languages, English and Russian, among five of them, and Kazakh, Spanish, and French, which were shared by some participants but not by all members of the group. Amy had some knowledge of Spanish and Kazakh. Kazakh was also Aisulu's and Sholpan's native language, while Joshua and Amy were also French (L2) speakers, which was Aisulu's and Sholpan's L2 as well.

The participants entered the MPVC room one after another at varied time intervals. The delays allowed the participants who entered the MPVC room first to begin to engage with one another until the next participant would join the group as either a *harmonized speaker* or an *unharmonized speaker.* In the first role, this new participant would engage in the interaction with other participants immediately after the greeting turn; in the second role, the new participant would remain on the sidelines of the interaction as a *ratified listener*. The same pattern was repeated in the second session where the participants already knew each other and felt more confident in engaging upon entering the Zoom space. All five participants could see each other in their activated video cameras.

In Excerpt 1 (first MPVC session), David is the first participant to enter the Zoom room. After 13 minutes, his Kazakh partner, Aisulu, connects to the Zoom room. After an exchange of formulaic greetings in English, David uses the English word "gym" in Line 8, then repeats the word (which is an

Figure 11.1. Screenshot of the Zoom Session (Group 1, First Session).

Excerpt 1 (session 1)

1.	David:	0:00-13:07 ((David is awaiting other participants))
2.	David:	((Aisulu entered Zoom session)) Aisulu?
3.	Aisulu:	Yes.
4.	David:	Well, there's two of us.
5.	Aisulu:	yes, I think others are not ready yet.
6.	David:	(.) I believe you are correct. How are you this evening?
7.	Aisulu:	I'm good (.) and you?
8.	David:	I'm good this morning(.)I have already been to the gym.
9.	Aisulu:	Hmm (.)
10.	David:	Спортивный зал (.) So, I'm awake (.) ((Amy enters Zoom session)) Oh, I think Amy is here (.) good morning Amy *[Gym]*
11.	Aisulu:	I can't see her.
12.	Amy:	Доброе утро (.) Здравствуйте *[Good morning. Hello.]*
13.	David:	Доброе утро (.) Сейчас я понимаю, почему ты не использоваешь (.) твоя мобильник. I called you earlier and it goes straight to voicemail (.) you haven't set it up *[Good morning. Now I understand why you don't use your mobile]*
14.	Amy:	I'm glad you guys were able to get it on
15.	David:	I haven't seen Josh yet
16.	Amy:	[Ok]
17.	David:	he hasn't answered his phone (.) I called him at (.) you remember he said he'd probably be up at (.) two minutes before (.) I called, and it eventually went to voicemail
18.	Amy:	Okay
19.	David:	[If we] just have the three of us (.)excuse me just a second (4.5) I just had to get something (.) S::o is the correct pronunciation 'shu::lpan'↑
20.	Aisulu:	sholpan, yes, it's right
21.	David:	[isn't gonna] be here or (<)
22.	Aisulu:	oh (1) I wrote her (1) but she hasn't registered yet
23.	David:	a::hh okay
24.	Aisulu:	{laugh}

adjective-noun phrase in Russian) in Line 10, maintaining the rest of the conversation in English.

In the same excerpt, Amy, who is the third participant to join the session, enters the Zoom room when David uses the Russian phrase. As the transcript shows, Amy's entrance into the room is delayed as the other two participants can see her joining the session before her audio is activated. Upon joining, Amy immediately picks up on David's use of Russian in Line 10 and greets David and Aisulu in Russian. David responds in Russian in Line 13 but bounces back to English in the same turn. In this episode, the exchange of turns between David and Amy is constructed in two languages, constituting a continuous multilingual exchange without participants repeating any

Excerpt 2 (session 1)

26. Amy: should we start introducing ourselves first?
27. David: su:re (1) Меня зовут Дейвид но я использоваю Дейв (.)
Я старый человек (.) вчера был мой день рождения (.)
мне пятьдесят шесть лет (.) я пенсионер я изучаю
русский язык потому что я могу (.) Я хочу я::
((Josh enters Zoom session))
[My name is David, but I often use Dave. I am an old person. Yesterday was my birthday. I am 56 years old. I am a retiree. I'm studying Russian because I can. I want. I..]
28. Amy: [Hi] ((addressing Josh))
29. David: Я был в армии (.) и когда я был в армии, я был
разведчиком (.) yeah (.) I worked intelligence
((Laughter))
[I was in the Army, I worked as an intelligence officer]
30. David: моя семья (1.0) я один(.)мой отец умер от рака в
тысяча девятьсот восемдесять году и мать умерла от
от инфаркта в двухтысяч третьем году (.) У меня нет
братьев или (.) сестёр (.)that's pretty much the
basics for me.
[My family. I'm alone. My father dies from cancer in 1980 and my mother dies from a heart attack in 2003. I don't have brothers or sisters.]
31. Amy: ладно(.)Josh(.)we are introducing ourselves real
quick before we get started
[Okay, 'you are done']
32. Josh: can you hear me? Yes? No?
33. David: oh (.)now I see him.
34. Amy: we can hear you
35. David [Good morning, Josh]
36. Josh: здравствуйте (.) I woke up just 4 minutes ago
37. David: I called but you didn't answer But I called six
minutes ago
[Hello]
38. Josh: Ah(.)
39. David: [you are] still asleep
40. Josh: [Меня] зовут Джош я из X. Моя специальности
информатику(.)да::
[My name is Josh. I'm from X. My major is informatics. Yeah..]
41. Amy: это все?
((Josh, Aisulu, and David are laughing))
42. Josh: It takes a little bit for my brain to get going(.)да
(.)это всё.
[Yes, that's it.]
43. Amy: Круто (1.5)
[This is cool.]

of the words in two languages. Rather, each language adds a new meaning to the exchange.

As the conversation continues to unfold, two languages, English and Russian, work together to produce various personal meanings. In Except 2, two instances of translanguaging are interspersed in the group conversation. This excerpt begins with Amy suggesting that the group start with self-introductions. David immediately volunteers to go first in Line 27. After confirming his intent in English, he continues with his self-introduction in Russian. He then concludes his introduction with the English "That's about it," which frames his personal account and creates a dynamic bilingual narrative – where *English* regulates turn-taking by signaling the beginning and end of his turn and Russian serves to express personal meaning. In the same set of turns, David explains in Russian that he is in the army and works as an intelligence officer, then enhances this meaning with the phrase "Yeah, I worked intelligence" in English before switching back to Russian for the rest of his self-instruction. In this instance, the use of English adds an important clarification that contextualizes the Russian expression for "intelligence officer" in the context of English military talk. In Line 31, Amy takes the role of facilitator by "ratifying" Josh, who joined the session earlier in the exchange but was not invited to participate in the conversation at that point. Amy's use of translanguaging is instrumental in raising Josh to the position of *ratified speaker*. The first word in Line 31 is in Russian, which signals to David that his turn to speak has concluded and Amy intends to engage the new speaker, whom she addresses in the following sentence with the phrase "Josh, we are introducing ourselves…." It can be observed that Josh is stalling rather than entering the conversation in full mode. He wants to ascertain that the other members are able to see and hear him, and he asks in English whether they can hear him. He then proceeds with the greeting in Russian, which signals his Russian speaker identity, but bounces back to English to explain that he almost missed the meeting time due to the very early hour and hence was late to join the videoconference session. In Line 40, Josh finally introduces himself to the group in Russian, followed by Amy's "That's it?" as a signal that Josh's turn has concluded.

Excerpt 3 from the second session of the group shows a different trigger for translanguaging. In this segment, the last participant, Sholpan, joins the session. She then remains in the role of a bystander while the group continues to discuss the class assignment in English. In Line 72, Amy attempts to engage Sholpan in the conversation and addresses her in Russian – by doing so she ratifies her as a speaker in this conversation. Sholpan then takes the turn to introduce herself to the group in English, but quickly runs out of words. To accommodate her language level, David takes the turn in Line 77 and encourages Sholpan to continue her introduction in Russian, her first language. This switch to Russian was likely to be motivated by David's attempt to accommodate a less proficient English speaker. Their interaction continues in Russian, with which Sholpan is comfortable, until it hits a communication breakdown in Line 81, where David asks Sholpan to say a few words about her family but makes a pronunciation error, making his turn unintelligible for Sholpan. In Line 82, Sholpan signals the problem and David

Excerpt 3 (session 1)

(Timestamp: 22:40) Sholpan enters the Zoom room.
********** Conversation continues in English only ***********
(Timestamp: 25:19) Amy addresses Sholpan

72: **Amy:** Здравствуйте Шолпан (.)
[Hello Sholpan]
73: **David:** прив::ет Шолпан
[Hi Sholpan]
74: **Aisulu:** привет Шолпан
[Hi Sholpan]
75: **Sholpan:** приве::т hello my name is sholpan(.)nice to meet you.
[Hi]
76: **Amy:** nice to meet you too (.) thank you for coming.
77: **David:** пожалуйста (.) скажите нам о себе
[Please tell us about yourself]
78: **Sholpan:** кто я?
[Who, me?]
79: **David:** [по-английски] или по-русски
80: **Sholpan:** меня зовут Шолпан(.) мне 19 лет (.)я учусь в университете (.) в X (1.0) не знаю что сказать еще ((laugh)) (2.0) Что хотите знать? Что ещё сказать?
[My name is Sholpan. I'm 19. I go to school in X. I don't know what else to say. What do you want to know? What else can I say?]
81: **David:** Ah (.) о семе↑ ((pronunciation error))
[About familia]
82: **Sholpan:** Hm↑ (3.0)
83: **David:** мать (.) брат и так далее
[Mother, brother and so on]
84: **Aisulu:** About your family (1.0) Sholpan
85: **Sholpan:** oh (.) моя семья живёт в X (.) у меня (.) у меня большая семья(.)они живут в X (.) я учусь здесь. (.)Мы редко видимся (4.0)
[My family lives in X. I have. I have a big family. They live in X. I go to school here. We do not see each other much.]
86: **Amy:** очень познакомились (3.0) у вас есть вопрос для нам
[Nice to meet you. Do you have a question for us?]
87: **Sholpan:** (2.0) А сколько вы уже учите русский язык? Какой у вас курс? второй курс?
[How long have you been studying Russian? What year?]
88: **Amy:** это моя(.)на четвертом курсе (.)
[I'm senior.]
89: **Sholpan:** [↓↓ на четвертом] ((appearing disappointed))
[or four years]
90: **Amy:** но я (.) I took a lot of accelerated courses (.) so I've only been studying for one year (.) About (.) только один год (2.0)
[But I… only one year]
91: **Sholpan:** good ↓↓

attempts a repair by reformulating what he said to Sholpan in the previous turn. This communication is repaired by another participant, Aisulu, in Line 83 where she rephrases what David said in English for Sholpan, and Sholpan continues with her turn. What's interesting about this episode is that the communication breakdown is negotiated by the speaker and the addressee, in this case, David and Sholpan, but is repaired by another participant who

Excerpt 4 (session 2)

(Timestamp: 34:40)

```
267: Amy:       У меня есть вопрос(.) Мы узнали в классе как Казахстан
                переводит кириллицу на латиницу (.) Что вы думаете об
                этот вопрос?
                [I have a question. We learned in class that Kazakhstan
                is switching from Cyrillic to the Latin alphabet. What
                do you think about this issue?]
268: Josh:      очень вопрос (.) Очень вопрос
                [very 'good' question. Very 'good' question]
269: David:     ДА
                [yes]
270: Aisulu:    (5:00) Шолпан (.) ответишь?
                [Sholpan, will you answer?]
271: Sholpan:   не = я подумаю (.)сейчас подожди
                [No, I will think about it. Wait a minute]
272: Aisulu:    хорошо (.) я начну (.)а ты потом может еще
                скажешь=Вообще-то у нас в университете проводилось
                много уроков (.) пар (.)дебатов на эту тему (2.5) стоит
                ли переводить казахский язык на латиницу или не стоит
                (.) Я(.) была в числе тех кто сказал не стоит (.) …
                [okay, I will begin, and you can say something later.
                In general, in our university, we had many classes and
                debates on the topic of whether the Kazakh language
                should have a Latinized alphabet or not. I was among
                those who said that it's not worth it…]
                *************
274: Aisulu:    но как бы то ни было (.) уже = Вы видели наш принятый
                алфавит.
                [In any case, did you see our accepted alphabet?]
277: Sholpan:   как французский=там есть буквы с accent aigu что-то
                там (1.0)
                [just like French - there is a letter with a sharp
                accent something like that]
278: Aisulu:    have you seen our alphabet (h)
                ((Aisulu and Sholpan are laughing))
279: Amy:       д::а
                [yees]
289: David:     ДА
                [YES]
279: Amy:       =it looks hard to distinguish the different letters (.)
                a (1.5) с диакритиком [with diacritic] ((Amy
                demonstrates the direction of the diacritic symbol with
                a gesture by raising and lowering her hand in the video
                frame of the camera)) (1.0) do you guys remember the
                word for diacritical hm
```

steps up from her position of *listener* to remedy the problem and then returns to her listener role right after the repair. In Line 91 Sholpan finally aligns with the communication code of the group by switching to English and signalizing she is now comfortable mixing English and Russian as the rest of the group did in this videoconferencing session.

In the last example, the group discusses a language reform in Kazakhstan where the government introduced a change of the Kazakh language alphabet, leading to its Latinization. In Line 277 Sholpan attempts to describe the new look of the Kazakh alphabet by drawing simultaneously from multiple semiotic resources – Russian, English, and French (the latter is another language the group understands). In Line 278, Aisulu repeats Sholpan's question in English – "Have you seen our alphabet?" – and David and Amy explain in Russian that indeed they have seen the new alphabet. To confirm her understanding of Sholpan's description of a new diacritic, Amy draws the diacritic in the air while the rest of the group watch her hand move in her video frame. In this excerpt, the participants collaboratively draw from three languages to create a visual description of the new Kazakh alphabet.

This excerpt reveals a complex relationship between language play and non-verbal communication accomplished through Amy's engagement with the videoconferencing tool (a "tool-related critical incident," (Fuchs, 2019)) and reliance on the video in making her translingual sequence accessible for the entire group. Such dynamic engagement with the Zoom platform can also be observed in the turns where participants first ascertain that the group is able to hear them and see their video stream before they begin to engage in a group conversation. For example, in Lines 2–3 (Excerpt 1), David resorts to rising intonation to check that Aisulu can hear him. In Lines 32–34 (Excerpt 2), Josh engages in a similar sequence on entering session when he asks if the group can hear him. Almost formulaic in the form and illocutionary function, these sequences are uniquely prevalent in audio- and video-mediated talks, allowing participants to signal to the audience their availability, social presence, and willingness to be promoted to the speaker status (Munoz, 2016). Since these sequences typically announce the arrival of a new participant, the language in which participants initiate their engagement with the individual or group in MPVC may play a role in establishing a translingual code of communication. Interestingly, in David's and Josh's turns, English serves as a lingua franca and a "service language" for negotiating the terms of engagement in a multi-party video chat.

6 Analysis of Triggers and Consequences in MPVC Translanguaging

Research on multilingual use and code-switching draws from various linguistic theories to explain the mechanism of code-switching. Among theoretical linguists, the consensus is that code-switching can be explained by speakers' level of language proficiency, interactional context, group affiliation, and typological distance between languages (de Bot et al., 2009). At the same time, it has been argued that it is impossible to predict with certainty when code switches may occur (Sankoff, 1998).

From the perspective of conversation analysis, translanguaging originates in the conversational structure and turn-taking mechanisms and is interactionally motivated (e.g., Bucholtz & Hall, 2005; Wei, 1998) and should be analyzed by scrutinizing conversation turns and turn-taking mechanisms leading up to a code switch. In this regard, the analysis of translanguaging episodes in the previous section shows a number of recurring patterns in the way translanguaging was triggered, initiated, and completed by the participants. These patterns may be the outcome of the speaker's idiosyncratic choice to draw from their multilingual repertoires but may also be socially motivated by the dynamics of the conversation itself as well as be prompted by the technological affordances of the medium where the interaction is unfolding (Wei, 2018).

The excerpts illustrate how translanguaging occurs with more than two participants involved in a translanguaging episode where code switches are collaboratively constructed and sustained, affecting individual words, intra-sentential segments, and the entire turns. These switches are triggered by a variety of social and interactional stimuli and can be described through the consistent use of translanguaging patterns that form a dynamic multilingual code mutually agreed upon by all participants of an MPVC session. From the perspective of social interaction and meaning making, these patterns can be broadly attributed to the following categories:

- *Pattern 1*: rendering one word or phrase in two languages. In this pattern, the MPVC participant repeats the same word or phrase/utterance in two languages in the adjacent turns, often supplying the exact L2 equivalent immediately after saying the word or phrase in the L1, or vice versa (for example, Excerpt 1, lines 7–9).
- *Pattern 2*: aligning with the speaker's choice of language, usually in response to a question or comment. In this pattern, the addressee switches to the language used by another speaker in the turn preceding the speaker's turn. For example, if the preceding turn was in one language, the same language was used in response (for example, Excerpt 1, lines 12–13). This pattern, however, was not consistent across all the translanguaging episodes, and participants frequently exchanged turns in different languages, particularly in the second session where the multilingual code was already mutually accepted and mutually maintained.
- *Pattern 3*: using one word or phrase to provide a richer and/or more accurate description of a concept or phenomenon. In this pattern, the idea expressed by a word or phrase in one language is rendered

again using a word or phrase in another language within the same turn. The second "rendition" typically added a necessary clarification to the idea or signaled the speaker's intention to enhance the cultural meaning of the phrase said in one language by using a similar word or phrase in another language, which made the initial meaning of the utterance richer (for example, Excerpt 1, lines 12–13).

- *Pattern 4*: inter-sentential code switch. In this pattern, the dominant speaker began the turn in one language and switched to L1 within the same turn, either at the intra-sentential or inter-sentential level, and returned to L2 or L1 toward the end of the turn. This pattern was observed in Lines 90 (Amy) and Line 92 (David) and was common in the other MPVC sessions. Participants constructed bilingual (and on a few occasions trilingual) turns where the ideas expressed by multiple languages formed a coherent narrative structure understood only by an addressee who was also proficient in the same set of languages.
- *Pattern 5*: translanguaging as a mechanism of meaning negotiation. In this pattern, participants use L1 and L2 to repair a communication breakdown in order to accommodate one of the speakers in the multi-party conversation. For example, in Excerpt 3 (Line 84), Aisulu switches to Sholpan's L2 to mediate a conversation breakdown between Sholpan and David.
- *Pattern 6*: switching to the speaker's L1 for accommodation purposes. In the last pattern, the dominant speaker would switch to the addressee's L1 to accommodate a less proficient or reticent speaker and encourage them to join the conversation. In a multi-party conversation, this accommodation was typically provided by the dominant speaker, but also by the side participant, as we see in Line 81 where David attempts (unsuccessfully) to accommodate Aisulu's low proficiency in English by suggesting a new topic for her self-introduction and encouraging her in Russian to remain in the dominant speaker role in the following turn.

It can be generalized that these patterns of translanguaging are highly dependent on the dynamic role play in a multi-party session where one participant could be promoted from being an unharmonized side participant to a harmonized side participant and ratified speaker, while the other participant could be demoted to the role of ratified listener. This can be observed in Excerpt 2 where Josh is gradually introduced to the bilingual code of the group between Line 27 and Line 40, and in Excerpt 1 where David is demoted by Amy to Line 3 via a translanguaging sequence.

7 The Conversation Analysis of Multilingual Video-Mediated Conversation

Analysis of dynamic code switches in two consecutive videoconferencing sessions points to the systemic nature of translanguaging patterns, which appear to be chaotic and unpredictable early in the videoconferencing chat and gradually develop into a mutually acceptable and sustained communication code as the group continues to interact via MPVC. Conversation analysis, with its focus on observable interactional features of code switches and the organization of turn taking, contributes to unpacking hidden mechanisms of translanguaging with a more nuanced understanding of linguistic and interactional contexts that underlie the conversational structure of a videoconferencing multi-party group chat.

When the monolingual code is not prescribed by a class assignment, participants of a multi-party conversation attempt to establish and naturalize their own locally construed translingual code in turn-by-turn contributions to the ongoing exchange. Appearing unplanned at the beginning of the exchange (for example, David's engagement in language play where he switches from English to Russian and then back to English to ensure that he is understood in Excerpt 1), this emergent code gradually begins to establish normative expectations where language mixing emerges as a *normative practice* rather than evidence of communicative deficiency. Through translanguaging practices, the participants strive to position themselves as multilingual speakers, as we see in Sholpan's turn in Line 277, where she finds herself navigating across the language boundaries of English, Russian, and French to convey through words a complex visual depiction of the Latinized Kazakh alphabet. We can also see how the conversation transgresses the pure linguistic cannon to adapt non-verbal sign language in Line 279, when Amy balances between two languages, Russian and English, in a single turn, but also resorts to hand gestures to show the direction of the diacritic symbol in the visual frame of her Zoom camera.

As an epistemological approach rather than a mere analytical tool, conversation analysis unveils a complex structure of video-mediated conversation, mechanisms of translingual interaction, and turn-taking in a multi-party videoconferencing session. By scrutinizing the sequence of turns and participants' speaker and listener roles, we can observe how participants construct a shared, digitally mediated social medium while bound by the constraints of temporal and spatial reality (for example, Sholpan and Aisulu finding themselves in the future space for Amy, David, and Joshua due to a significant fourteen-hour time difference between their distant geographical locations). But they are also situated in the virtual third space where participants share a common social setting, claim individual and group affiliations through emergent and shared translanguaging practices, and abide by a locally construed multilingual code.

With more than two interactants participating and the complex nature of turn-taking in videoconferencing discussed above, the structure of multi-party virtual conversation frequently shows asymmetry in engagement density for participants, where Amy and David, dominant, harmonized speakers, regulate turn-taking and grant the right to speak for Josh, Sholpan, and Aisulu. The latter balance between being harmonized bystanders and listeners and ratified side participants and speakers in the complex architecture of the multi-party conversation – in other words, engaging in what Wooffitt (2005) coins "the wider interpersonal or social functions served by a passage of talk" (p. 80). These emergent power structures in the multi-party conversation cannot be interpreted within the paradigms of conversation analysis alone (Kramsch & Whiteside, 2008) but they are detectable from the close reading of talk-in-interaction transcripts, pointing to the emergence of larger social and ideological forces at play in this micro-community. They signal the collaborative construction of groupness through language-in-interaction and the emergence of *a micro-group identity*, that is dynamic, fluid, and co-constructed.

8 Virtual Group Identity-in-Interaction

Group identity, while widely researched outside SLA and CALL fields, has not received sufficient attention in relation to virtual minimal groups. Previous research demonstrated that group affiliation and the formation and maintenance of minimal groups affect subsequent behavior of group affiliates in how they treat other members of their group compared with an "out-of-group" individual (Edwards, 2009). In this sense, group identity, as a person's sense of belonging to a group, emerges upon the formation of groupness and entails social influence within the group. This influence may be based on some social category or on interpersonal interaction among group members, making individuals interdependent on one another. In psychology, groupness is a function of the basis and outcome of interpersonal exchanges between people (Thibaut & Kelley, 1959). Forging common bonds among group members occurs through the norms of interaction (Edwards, 2009). In this light, if the poststructuralist notion of individual identity signals "how a person understands his or her relationship to the world, how that relationship is structured across time and space, and how the person comprehends possibilities for the future" (Norton, 2000, p. 5; Norton, 2013), then group identity is how a person understands and projects their relationship and belonging to a group through language use and self-positioning.

Bucholtz and Hall (2005) stated that identity is the product of linguistic and other semiotic practices, and hence it is primarily a social and cultural phenomenon. Considering individual identity as an object of analysis, they propose that identities are linguistically indexed and relationally constructed through self and other, and are an outcome of interactional negotiation. In a similar vein, language use influences the formation of group identity, to the same extent as group identity influences language use (Sachdev & Bourhis,1990; Trofimovich et al., 2013). In the examples of various translanguaging practices described in the previous section, translanguaging episodes are not only oriented toward meaning-making but also signify interpersonal dependence among MPVC participants rooted in *emergent groupness* and group identity performances in the shared third space and communicative activity. David and Amy's regulation of turn-taking by engaging in translanguaging can be interpreted as an attempt to sustain groupness by ratifying "bystanders" and engaging unharmonized but *legitimately peripheral* participants (Wenger, 1998) in a multi-party conversation. We can also observe group identity enactment in Patterns 5 and 6 where side participants engage in code switches in order to repair a communication breakdown and maintain continuous interaction during a videoconferencing session. Groupness as a binding feature of a multi-party conversation may be stronger as a community-building mechanism in a digitally mediated videoconferencing session where participants cannot "walk away" from the conversation when they feel that they are no longer engaged in it or their physical proximity to dominant speakers is no longer felicitous. On the contrary, all participants of an MPVC are required to maintain a minimal degree of social presence and remain in the same virtual space even when their role is that of bystander or unharmonized listener (e.g., a participant whose video camera is off and the microphone is muted technically remains a participant in an MPVC, however with minimal direct engagement with the other participants).

9 From Micro-community to Micro-ecology

One way to explain the rich interactional dynamics of MPVC sessions is through the ecological analysis of multi-party videoconferencing as a product of an integrated *communicative micro-ecology* in a multilingual "community of practice" (Wenger, 1998). From the ecological perspective, translanguaging practices can be viewed as the enactment, reenactment, and stylization of past language practices, and the rehearsal of potential multilingual identities (Kramsch & Whiteside, 2008). As the data demonstrated, the translingual code in the multi-party videoconferencing group was shaped over time and also collaboratively by the socially motivated actions of each individual participant. Engaging in tranlanguaging practices, the MPVC participants normalized the multilingual code of communication, which allowed them to express complex meanings and engage in social bonding in a technological medium where social cues are subdued and the emotional states of interlocutors are not easily interpretable (for example, in Lines 39–41, where the translanguaging episode initiated by Josh concludes with group laughter). Their translingual code of interaction would not be considered a norm outside the virtual space of their MPVC sessions; it is construed and sustained strictly locally by the members of their MPVC micro-community. The languages used by the group (English, Russian, French in the examples above, but also Kazakh and Spanish in other MPVC groups in this study) index various ethnic, cultural, and even professional identities (for example, for Sholpan and Aisulu who are trained to become language translators in their university), and evidence the emergence of *a collective multilingual group identity* as individual participants begin to draw from their own and their partners' multilingual repertoires to construct mutually accessible meanings.

Kramsch and Whiteside (2008) propose to examine such rich multilingual exchanges as dynamic complex systems "to see the various languages used by the participants as part of a more diversified linguistic landscape with various hierarchies of social respectability among codes and added layers of foregrounding the code itself rather than just the message" (p. 662). Even though the choice of language was not dictated by the project task and the instructor was not present to police language use, David and Josh opted to "reenact" their language learner identity in Excerpt 2 where they performed the role of language students who were asked to introduce themselves in the L2. It is not surprising that their introductions came off as "artificial" and "performed," which made the other participants of the group laugh. Both use English to frame these "Russian performances of L2 learner identity" within a larger mostly English-dominated conversation structure as an act of mobilization of an entire repertoire of identity features and languages converted into complex and subtle moment-to-moment speaking positions (Blommaert, 2005). In other words, the translanguaging practice identified in the previous analysis signals symbolic action.

Performing social action in multilingual contexts activates more than a simple ability to communicate in an effective and appropriate way. Kramsch and Whiteside (2008) propose the notion of *symbolic competence* to explain the fluid capacity of multilingual speakers to play with linguistic codes and their various spatial and temporal resonances – "not only to approximate and appropriate for oneself someone else's language but to shape the very context in which the language is learned and used" (p. 664). In online social spaces, language choice is motivated by the situated ecologies of individual participants, which are shaped by their various backgrounds but also by the perceived expressiveness of various languages to create personal meanings (Barton & Lee, 2013) and by how different languages position their speakers in different symbolic spaces (Kramsch & Whiteside, 2008). Even brief switches to the languages that one may even not speak fluently are construed as online multilingual literacy practice. In Kulavuz-Onal and Vásquez's study (2018), for example, Arabic, Spanish, and English were used by Facebook group members for different purposes and functions, including relationship building and establishing solidarity, even though English was the only language shared among them. The authors argued that community, affordances of the internet, and socialization shape multilingual use in a digitally mediated community, even in an online space where English may appear to be the dominant lingua franca. In another study, the use of the native language in one-on-one videoconferencing serves a compensatory function of projecting oneself socially and emotionally in a digital environment where interpersonal bonding is delayed due to a lack of physical proximity (Satar, 2020), and where embodied resources, such as gesture and gaze, serve as mechanisms to sustain effective, interactive, and cohesive dimensions of social presence. Similarly, in the transcripts above, resorting to Russian or French or Kazakh or Spanish appears entirely unnecessary since all participants seem comfortable with English being the "service" language of multi-party exchange. Yet, language switches are preeminent and performative in all three groups and across videoconferencing sessions (see Table 11.1), establishing within the social space of a Zoom session the alternative categories of legitimacy and normativity in the cycles of a translingual play. Multilingual game play increases "the contact surfaces among symbolic systems and the potential for creating multiple meanings and identities" (Kramsch & Whiteside, 2008, p. 667), while the technological features of multi-party videoconferencing platforms complexify group interactions, requiring participants to negotiate turn-taking in ways that lead to the building of a micro-community and multilingual group identity performances.

10 Conclusion and Implications for CALL Research

Multi-party video-based conversations involving participants from diverse cultures and language backgrounds offer rich opportunities for the conceptualization of fleeting and sustainable translanguaging practices as *multilingual group identity performances*. Videoconferencing platforms (such as Zoom, Adobe Connect, Skype, Microsoft Teams) create a third space (Soja, 1996) where tangible temporal and spatial dimensions are replaced by the intangible categories of "virtual rooms" that can be "entered," "occupied," and "vacated," and communication spaces within the visual-audio-textual interfaces of the medium where all participants are expected to interact with one another, unlike social-media chats where participants can remain silent and passive (e.g., Rosenbaun et al., 2016).

In videoconferencing spaces, locally construed communication mechanisms are forged from multiple semiotic resources into a complex conversational structure with unpredictable turn-taking sequences and intricate joint interactional work (Muñoz, 2016). Participants' cultural and linguistic capitals merge into idiosyncratic multilingual codes whose cultures-of-use are strictly contained within a particular virtual "room" situated metaphorically in between participants' physical bodies, technological materialities, and the intangible spatiality of shared virtual social space and its other human occupants. As the data discussed in this chapter demonstrate, translanguaging practices in linguistically unstructured (i.e., not imposed externally) multi-party video chats are socially motivated, and this motivation to sustain uninterrupted and rich interaction among multiple participants is conducive to the emergence of strong social bonds and virtual micro-group identities. The translanguaging patterns identified in these MPVC interactions vary in length and duration in ways that are unpredictable and are occasionally interspersed by mode switches (Sindoni, 2014) – from purely verbal communication to gestures, gazes, backchannels, visual language, and pragmatic cues (see also the data discussed in Muñoz, 2016). Hence, the conversational structures of the MPVC sessions discussed in this chapter are unique and non-generalizable. The rich meanings collaboratively created by the multilingual speakers cannot be replicated in monolingual instructional settings of foreign language classrooms (also see Hafner et al., 2015). Further research on multi-party video conversations can shed light on the impact of such critical experiences on the development of multilingual and symbolic competences (Kramsch & Whiteside, 2008; Kramsch, 2021), assertive subject positionings, and individual and group identity performances, and will help operationalize the concept of *digital group identity* in the context of an MPVC micro-ecology.

Transcription Notation

Brief interval between utterances	(.)
Pause (in seconds)	(2:00)
Emphasis	[wor::d]
Overlapping talk	[okay]
Analyst comment/description	(( ))
English translation	*[cursive]*
Loud breath	(h)
Marked shift in pitch	(↓down) (↑up)

References

Adinolfi, L., & Astruc, L. (2017). An exploratory study of translanguaging practices in an online beginner-level foreign language classroom. *CercleS, 7*(1), 185–204.

Androutsopoulos, J. (2006). Introduction: Sociolinguistics and computer-mediated communication. *Journal of Sociolinguistics*, *10*(4), 419–438.

Androutsopoulos, J. (2007). Language choice and code switching in German-based diasporic web forums. In B. Denet & S. C. Herring, *The multilingual Internet: Language, culture, and communication online.* https://doi.org/10.1093/acprof:oso/9780195304794.003.0015

Barton, D., & Lee, C. (2013). Language online. Routledge. https://doi.org/10.4324/9780203552308

Baym, N. K. (1998). The emergence of on-line community. In S. Jones (Ed.) *CyberSociety 2.0. Revisiting computer-mediated communication and community* (pp. 35–68). Sage.

Baym, N. K. (2000). *Tune in, log on: Soaps, fandom, and online community*. Sage.

Baym, N. K. (2003). Communication in online communities. In K. Christiansen and D. Levinson (Eds.), *Encyclopedia of community* (Volume 3, pp. 1015–1017). Sage.

Bezemer, J., & Kress, G. (2016). *Multimodality, learning, and communication: A social semiotic frame.* Routledge.

Blommaert, J. (2005). *Discourse.* Cambridge University Press.

Blommaert, J. (2010). The Sociolinguistics of globalization. In *The sociolinguistics of globalization* (pp. xvi–xvi). Cambridge University Press. https://doi.org/10.1017/CBO9780511845307

Bolden, G. B. (2015). Transcribing as research: "Manual" transcription and conversation analysis, research on language and social interaction. *Research on Language and Social Interaction, 48*(3), 276–280. https://doi.org/10.1080/08351813.2015.1058603

Bucholtz, M., & Hall, K. (2005). Identity and interaction: A sociocultural linguistic approach. *Discourse Studies*, *7*(4–5), 585–614.

Canagarajah, S. (2011). Codemeshing in academic writing: Identifying teachable strategies of translanguaging. *The Modern Language Journal*, *95*(3), 401–417. https://doi.org/10.1111/j.1540-4781.2011.01207.x

Canagarajah, A. S. (2013). *Translingual practice: Global Englishes and cosmopolitan relations*. Routledge.

Castells, M. (2000).*The rise of the network society* (2nd ed.). Blackwell.

Davies, B., & Harré, R. (1990). Positioning: The discursive production of selves. *Journal for the Theory of Social Behaviour, 20*(1), 43–63. https://doi.org/10.1111/j.1468-5914.1990.tb00174.x

de Bot, K., Broersma, M., & Isurin, L. (2009). Sources of triggering in code-switching. In L. Isurin, D. Winford, & K. De Bot (Eds.), *Multidisciplinary approaches to code-switching* (pp. 85–102). John Benjamins Publishing.

Edwards, J. (2009). *Language and identity*. Cambridge University Press. https://doi.org/10.1017/CBO9780511809842

Fuchs, C. (2019). Critical incidents and cultures-of-use in a Hong Kong–Germany telecollaboration. *Language Learning & Technology*, *23*(3), 74–97. http://hdl.handle.net/10125/44697

García, O. (2009). *Bilingual education in the 21st century: A global perspective*. Wiley-Blackwell.

García, O., & Wei, L. (2014). *Translanguaging: Language, bilingualism and education*. Palgrave Macmillan.

Garrison, D. R. (2009). Communities of inquiry in online learning. In P. L. Rogers (Ed.), *Encyclopedia of distance learning* (2nd ed., pp. 352–355). IGI Global.

Goffman, E. (1981). *Forms of talk*. University of Pennsylvania Press.

González-Lloret, M. (2011). Conversation analysis of computer-mediated communication. *CALICO Journal*, *28*(2), 308–325. http://citeseerx.ist.psu.edu/viewdoc/download?doi=10.1.1.456.8944&rep=rep1&type=pdf

Hafner, C. A., Li, D. C. S., & Miller, L. (2015). Language choice among peers in project-based learning: A Hong Kong case study of English language learners' plurilingual practices in out-of-class computer-mediated communication. *Canadian Modern Language Review*, *71*(4), 441–470.

Helm, F., & Dabre, T. (2018). Engineering a "contact zone" through translanguaging. *Language and Intercultural Communication*, *18*(1), 144–156.

Herring, S. C. (2004). Computer-mediated discourse analysis: An approach to researching online behavior. In S. A. Barab, R. Kling, & J. H. Gray (Eds.), *Designing for virtual communities in the service of learning* (pp. 338–376). Cambridge University Press.

Herring, S. C. (2010). Computer-mediated conversation: Introduction and overview. *Language@Internet*, *7*(2). http://www.languageatinternet.org/articles/2010/2801

Hoflich, J. R. (1997). Electronic communities as social worlds: Toward a sociosemiotic analysis of computer mediated interpersonal communication. In W. Noth (Ed.), *Semiotics of the media* (pp. 507–518). de Gruyter.

Klimanova, L., & Hellmich, E. A. (2021). Crossing transcultural liminalities with critical virtual exchange: A study of shifting border discourses. *Critical Inquiry in Language Studies*, *18*(3), 273–304. https://doi.org/10.1080/15427587.2020.1867552

Kramsch, C. (2009). *The multilingual subject: What foreign language learners say about their experience and why it matters.* Oxford University Press. https://doi.org/10.1111/j.1473-4192.2006.00109.x

Kramsch, C. (2021). *Language as symbolic power*. Cambridge University Press.

Kramsch, C., & Whiteside, A. (2008). Language ecology in multilingual settings. Towards a theory of symbolic competence. *Applied Linguistics*, *29*(4), 645–671. https://doi.org/10.1093/applin/amn022

Kulavuz-Onal, D., & Vásquez, C. (2018). "Thanks, shokran, gracias": Translingual practices in a Facebook group. *Language Learning & Technology*, *22*(1), 240–255.

Lester, J. N., & O'Reilly, M. (2019). *Applied conversation analysis: Social interaction in institutional settings*. Sage. https://doi.org/10.4135/9781071802663

Matsuyama, Y., Akiba I., Fujie, S., & Kobayashi, T. (2015). Four-participant group conversation: A facilitation robot controlling engagement density as the fourth participant. *Computer Speech & Language*, *33*(1), 1–24.

Mondada, L. (2008). Using video for a sequential and multimodal analysis of social interaction: Videotaping institutional telephone calls. *Qualitative Social Research*, *9*(3).

Muñoz, A. S. (2016). Attending multi-party videoconference meetings: The initial problem. *Language@Internet*, *13*(3). https://www.languageatinternet.org/articles/2016/munoz

Norton, B. (2000). *Identity and language learning: Gender, ethnicity, and educational change*. Pearson Education Limited.

Norton, B. (2013). *Identity and language learning: Extending the conversation.* Multilingual Matters.

Ortega, L. (2017). New CALL-SLA research interfaces for the 21st century: Towards equitable multilingualism. *CALICO Journal*, *34*(3), 285–316.

Otsuji, E., & Pennycook, A. (2010). Metrolingualism: Fixity, fluidity, and language in flux. *International Journal of Multilingualism*, *7*(3), 240–254, DOI: 10.1080/14790710903414331

Rheingold, H. (1993). *The virtual community: Homesteading on the electronic frontier*. Addison-Wesley.

Rosenbaun, L., Rafaeli, S., & Kurzon, D. (2016). Participation frameworks in multiparty video chats cross-modal exchanges in public Google Hangouts. *Journal of Pragmatics*, *94*, 29–46.

Rourke, L., Anderson, T., Garrison, D. R., & Archer, W. (1999). Assessing social presence in asynchronous text-based computer conferencing. *The Journal of Distance Education*, *14*(2), 50–71. http://www.ijede.ca/index.php/jde/article/view/153/341

Sachdev, I., & Bourhis, R. Y (1990). Language and social identification, In D. Abrams & M. A. Hogg (Eds.), *Social identity theory: Constructive and critical advances*. Harvester Wheatsheaf.

Sankoff, D. (1998). A formal production-based explanation of the facts of code-switching. *Bilingualism, Language and Cognition, 1*, 39–50.

Satar, M. (2016). Meaning making in online language learner interactions via desktop videoconferencing. *ReCALL, 28*(3), 305–325.

Satar, M. (2020). L1 for social presence in videoconferencing: A social semiotic account. *Language Learning & Technology, 24*(1), 129–153.

Schmitt, M., Gunkel, S., Cesar, P., & Bulterman, D. (2014). Asymmetric delay in video-mediated group discussions. *2014 Sixth International Workshop on Quality of Multimedia Experience (QoMEX)* (pp. 19–24). https://doi.org/10.1109/qomex.2014.6982280

Schreiber, B. R. (2015). "I am what I am": Multilingual identity and digital translanguaging. *Language, Learning & Technology, 19*, 69–87.

Sindoni, M. G. (2014). Through the looking glass: A social semiotic and linguistic perspective on the study of video chats. *Text & Talk, 34*(3), 325–347.

Soja, E. W. (1996). *Thirdspace: Journeys to Los Angeles and other real and imagined places.* Blackwell.

Thibaut, J. W., and Kelley, H. H. (1959). *The social psychology of groups*. John Wiley & Sons.

Trofimovich, P., Turuševa, L., & Gatbonton, E. (2013). Group membership and identity issues in second language learning. *Language Teaching, 46*(4), 563–567. doi:10.1017/S026144481300030X

Walker, U. (2017). Discursive construction of social presence and identity positions in an international bilingual collaboration. *Distance Education, 38*(2), 193–215.

Warschauer, M., El Said, G. R., & Zohry, A. (2007). Language choice online. In B. Denet & S. C. Herring, *The multilingual Internet: Language, culture, and communication online*. DOI:10.1093/acprof:oso/9780195304794.003.0013

Wei, L. (1998). The "why" and "how" questions in the analysis of conversational code switching. In P. Auer (Ed.), *Code-switching in conversation: Language, interaction and identity* (pp. 156–176). Routledge.

Wei, L. (2011). Multilinguality, multimodality, and multicompetence: Code- and mode-switching by minority ethnic children in complementary schools. *The Modern Language Journal, 95*(3), 370–384.

Wei, L. (2018). Translanguaging as a practical theory of language. *Applied Linguistics, 39*(1), 9–30. https://doi.org/10.1093/applin/amx039

Wellman, B., Boase, J., & Chen, W. (2002). The networked nature of community: Online and offline. *IT & Society Journal, 1*(1), 151–165. http://www.ITandSociety.org

Wenger, E. (1998). *Communities of practice: Learning, meaning, and identity.* Cambridge University Press.

Wooffitt, R. (2005). *Conversation analysis and discourse analysis. A comparative and critical introduction*. Sage.

Yankelovich, N., Kaplan, J., Provino, J., Wessler, M., & DiMicco, J. (2006). Improving audio conferencing. *Computer Supported Cooperative Work: Proceedings of the 2006 20th Anniversary Conference on Computer Supported Cooperative Work*, 333–342. https://doi.org/10.1145/1180875.1180926

About the Author

Liudmila Klimanova, Ph.D., is an Assistant Professor of Russian and Second Language Acquisition in the College of Humanities, University of Arizona, USA. Her research focuses on topics related to (critical) virtual exchange, task-based language learning, and identity deployment in digital spaces.

12 Cultural Identity and Intercultural Learning: Individual Learners' Experiences in Telecollaboration

Anastasia Izmaylova

1 Introduction

Collaborative web technologies and social networking sites have become virtually ubiquitous in the last two decades. With the number of social media users steadily growing worldwide, these sites and applications become complex multilingual and multicultural digital spaces, where intercultural communication takes place on a regular basis (Noels et al., 2012). Successful and effective interaction in these contexts requires a certain level of intercultural competence (IC), loosely defined as an awareness, understanding, and respect for various cultural beliefs, values, and norms. Reflecting the need to foster students' IC development and prepare them for the multicultural communication in digital spaces, scholars suggest that telecollaboration projects may be the most suitable and authentic activity (Godwin-Jones, 2013; Helm & Guth, 2010; Jin, 2015). Telecollaboration is generally defined as an online exchange between students in remote locations, and in the case of language learners, such exchanges are typically intercultural.

In addition to promoting the development of IC, telecollaboration, especially one that is conducted on social networking sites, lends itself to be a simulation of real-life multilingual and multicultural interactions online, where users construct their virtual identities that may or may not align with their off-line identities. These virtual identities are fluid (De Costa & Norton, 2016) and constantly changing based on the context, experiences, and interlocutors. Numerous studies explore how multilingual individuals construct and enact their virtual identities in such exchanges, with some studies looking at language learners in instructed settings (Helm, 2018; Klimanova & Dembovskaya, 2013; Kohn & Hoffstaedter, 2017) and others examining such identity construction "in the wilds" (Thorne, 2010, p. 144), i.e., in the non-instructional digital contexts such as blogs, online communities, and social media (Lam, 2000; Schreiber, 2015; Sharma, 2012). As part of a larger project on IC development in telecollaboration, this multiple case study examines three language learners' experiences in an intercultural exchange on a social networking site and how their cultural identities shaped their positioning, learning, and IC development in the exchange.

2 Literature Review

2.1 Intercultural Competence

Broadly speaking, IC is a set of skills necessary for effective intercultural communication. While IC is often discussed in various fields, it is not easily defined (Martin, 2015; Schulz, 2007) and numerous terms, such as intercultural sensitivity, intercultural awareness, global competence, and others, are used to refer to this concept (Fantini, 2009), with some researchers suggesting that they all refer to different types of skills (Chen & Starosta, 1996) and others using them interchangeably. However, there is a general agreement on the nature of IC. It is understood as a continuum (Bennett, 1993; Hammer, 2008; Paige et al., 2003) and a complex, multifaceted set of knowledge, skills, and abilities (Bennett, 1993; Byram, 1997; Fantini, 2009; Paige et al., 2003).

In the field of foreign language education, there are several influential models and theories of IC. One of them is Bennett's Developmental Model of Intercultural Sensitivity (1993). This model conceptualizes intercultural sensitivity as a continuum of six stages in viewing cultural differences, ranging from the least to the most accepting of other cultures. The first three stages – denial, defense, and minimization – represent an ethnocentric orientation, where an individual puts their own culture at the center of their worldview. The following three stages – acceptance, adaptation, and integration – represent an ethnorelative orientation, where an individual understands their culture as one of many equally valid ones and is able to view it from the perspectives of people from other cultures.

Another important model is Byram's (1997) Intercultural Communicative Competence (ICC) model, where he proposed a concept of an intercultural speaker, an individual who has some or all components of IC to a certain extent. The five components essential to becoming an intercultural speaker (see Figure 12.1) are attitudes of curiosity and openness to other cultures; knowledge about products and practices of one's own and the target cultures; ability to interpret and relate documents or events from one's own and

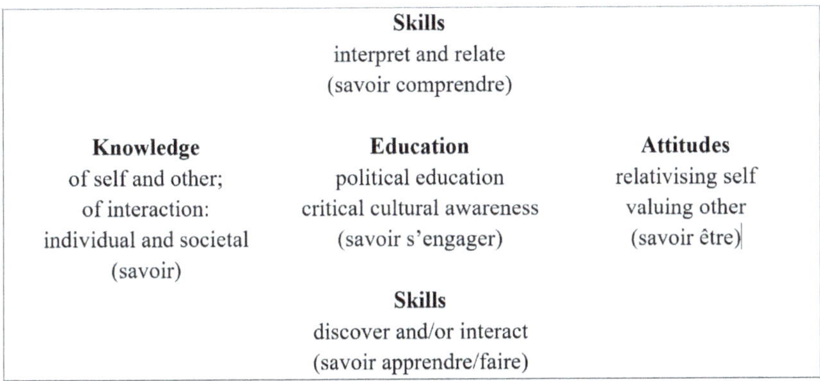

Figure 12.1. Byram's (1997) ICC Components (p. 34)

other cultures; ability to acquire knowledge about a culture and its practices through communication; and critical cultural awareness, or an ability to critically evaluate cultural products, practices, and perspectives.

Finally, theories proposed by Kramsch (1993, 2006) have been prominent in discussions of culture learning and IC. In these theories, Kramsch views culture as a product of perceptions, where real events are combined with imagined characteristics. For that reason, she proposed that in order to have "a more complete and less partial understanding" of one's own and other cultures, it is important to develop a "third place," a perspective that allows one to "take both an insider's and an outsider's view on [home and target cultures]" (Kramsch, 1993, p. 210). More recently, Kramsch (2006) proposed that the third place is a symbolic process of cultural understanding and meaning making where culture is constructed by personal stories and consists of many versions. This means that an interculturally competent individual needs to be able to accept multiple and sometimes conflicting discourses of one culture.

In this study, I relied on these three approaches to interpret the data and analyze participants' cultural orientations, as well as their IC development.

2.2 Telecollaboration and IC Development

Telecollaboration has been implemented in foreign language education for the last three decades (O'Dowd, 2018). While there is a recent movement to unite various approaches to online interactions under the term "virtual exchange," this study uses the term "telecollaboration" as it is more traditionally used in the field of foreign language education and reflects the practice of instructors integrating online class-to-class interactions into their language courses (O'Dowd, 2018). Telecollaborative exchanges have shown potential in promoting the development of learners' IC (Lamy & Goodfellow, 2010; O'Dowd, 2007), improving learners' language skills (Belz & Kinginger, 2002; Liaw & English, 2013), and increasing their motivation (Lee, 2007; Vinagre, 2007). However, the data on IC development through telecollaboration is not conclusive. Some studies show that telecollaboration provides a rich environment where forming personal connections with peers from target cultures, negotiating for meaning, and finding out cultural information from authentic sources leads to a greater understanding of cultural aspects and differences (O'Dowd, 2013; Wilden, 2007), as well as eradication of biases and stereotypes (Chase & Alexander, 2007; O'Dowd, 2013; Vinagre, 2007). Yet studies also report potential problems that may hinder culture learning. For instance, mismatched language proficiency and unequal participation have led students to viewing the target culture more negatively (Belz, 2002, 2003). Additionally, institutional exchanges do not necessarily lead to community-building and personal relationships that increase intercultural understanding (Fuchs & Snyder, 2013; Liaw & English, 2013) and can even result in stereotype reinforcement (Flowers et al., 2019; Guth et al., 2012; Kirschner, 2015).

In light of these contradictory research findings, there is a need for more studies exploring different aspects of telecollaboration and IC development. Möllering and Levy (2012) suggested that such research should focus on individual learners' experiences and called for semester-long qualitative studies. In addition, many earlier telecollaboration projects used email, discussion boards, and text chats (Guth & Thomas, 2010), and the more recent studies that utilized collaborative web technologies relied primarily on blogs, wikis, and videoconferencing, while the use of social networking sites has been limited (Avgousti, 2018; Jin, 2015). At the same time, social networking sites appeal to students and contribute to their enjoyment and participation in the exchanges (Jin, 2015; Lee & Markey, 2014), making them a promising platform that may help learners develop the ability to communicate in a variety of contexts and environments.

2.3 Cultural Identity and IC

In the past two decades there has been a surge of interest in research on identity and language learning (De Costa & Norton, 2016). Scholars in the field of second language acquisition view identity as a dynamic, post-structuralist concept (Norton, 2000), where the "post-modern subject" does not have a fixed identity but rather "assumes different identities at different times," which can be contradictory among themselves (Hall, 1992, p. 277). Cultural identity can be understood as a subcategory of an individual's overall global identity. Collier and Thomas (1988) defined cultural identity as "identification with and perceived acceptance into a group that has shared systems of symbols and meanings as well as norms/rules for conduct" (p. 113). Globalization, international migration, and the spread of internet technologies have affected the idea of cultural identity (Hall, 1992; Jensen, 2003; Kim, 2009). Some scholars suggested that in today's interconnected world, cultural contrasts have started to diminish, leading to the creation of multicultural, transnational identities. Some proposed that adolescents and young adults are especially predisposed to develop such multicultural identities as they grow up among a variety of cultural practices and beliefs (Jensen, 2003). Higgins (2015) referred to this as "millennium identities," or individuals who are culturally hybrid due to increased multilingualism and multiculturalism in the society (p. 373). However, the blurring of the lines between cultures may lead to polarization and an *us* versus *them* mentality (Kim, 2009), where individuals try to emphasize the uniqueness of their cultural values and characteristics (Wang, 2007), making their identity and belonging to a group even more pronounced.

Collaborative web technologies offer a space where users can construct and negotiate their virtual identities (Helm, 2018) positioning themselves as transnational individuals, emphasizing their unique cultural background, or shifting between the two. An individual's positioning in regard to their cultural identity may then influence the nature of their engagement in intercultural communication and the level of IC they possess. Kim (2009) proposed that cultural identity is "a core underlying dimension of IC" (p. 59). He discussed notions of identity inclusivity and identity security as the main predictors of one's ability to engage in collaborative and effective intercultural communication. Identity inclusivity refers to one's inclusive orientation toward members of other groups and a more personalized, less stereotypical way to perceive others. Identity security, in turn, is the degree of one's confidence in one's own identity. Kim suggested that the more inclusive and secure identities lead to greater intercultural engagement, while the less inclusive and secure identity will lead to avoidance of such engagement and a more prejudiced view of others. Zarate (2003) also linked one's identity with IC and posited that in order to become an intercultural mediator, one needs to renounce their "immediate identity-related solidarities" and "distance themselves from all the affiliations which are generally involved in communication," thereby achieving a true third position (p. 96). In other words, one must suspend their cultural beliefs in order to be truly unbiased in their cultural mediation. Parmenter (2003) also suggested that when a national or cultural identity is deeply embedded in an individual, it may be very difficult for them to, in Byram's (1997) terms, relativize themselves as it could mean "complete restructuring … of identity" and values associated with it (p. 131).

The issue of cultural identity is rarely examined in relation to telecollaboration. In one study, Helm et al. (2012) found that telecollaboration helped students explore their cultural identities. At the same time, they changed their positioning in the exchange according to the discussion topics and people present in their groups. This study seeks to further explore how learners with different cultural identities experience telecollaboration and the extent of their learning overall and IC development in particular. The following research questions guided the study:

1. How do individual learners experience telecollaboration in terms of their attitudes, participation, and learning?
2. How does a learner's cultural identity affect their IC development through telecollaboration?

3 Methodology

3.1 Telecollaboration Project Description

The telecollaboration took place during the spring semester of 2016 and lasted eight weeks. On one side of the exchange was an entire section (19 students) of the fourth-semester Spanish course at a large Midwestern university. On the other side was an entire class of students enrolled in the third semester of English as a foreign language course at a higher education institution in Bogotá, Colombia. The exact number of students in the Colombian class was not disclosed.

Each week students posted pictures, videos, or text on the Facebook Group Wall responding to that week's prompt. The prompts were broad cultural topics with guiding questions for students to consider (Appendix A). In addition to the original post, students were required to comment on at least two posts made by their intercultural exchange partners. The goal of the project was for both Colombian and American students to practice their target languages and learn about their target cultures. For that reason, all students made their original posts in their native languages, while their comments were in their target languages. In this manner, all posts and conversations about Colombian culture were in Spanish, while all posts and conversations about the U.S. culture were in English. The exchange was constructed as a many-to-many interaction in a private Facebook Group, where all students' posts were visible to all of the other students in the group (see Appendix B for a sample screenshot). Facebook was chosen as the exchange platform due to it being able to accommodate students' preferences for both synchronous and asynchronous communication, although by nature it was an asynchronous exchange.

Along with the discussions on Facebook, the U.S. students engaged in brief class discussions and analyses of the new information they learned from their Colombian peers. At the end of the project the U.S. students wrote portfolios about their experiences. These portfolios were a collection of various instances where students felt that they learned something new about their own or the target culture, as well as about culture in general. Students described several interactions where they learned something and provided a brief reflection on those learning moments.

3.2 Data Collection and Analysis

This study is a part of a larger research project on telecollaboration and IC development. This section describes the data collection and initial analysis for the larger project, then expands on the parts that pertain to this study in particular.

The project focused on the telecollaboration experiences of the U.S. students. For the larger study, out of 19 students enrolled in the class, 15 agreed to volunteer as study participants. They allowed the researcher access to their Facebook interactions, class discussion participation, and end of project portfolios for data analysis. In addition, they completed two surveys (background and telecollaboration expectations) and one interview prior to the telecollaboration. After the exchange participants completed a survey and one interview about their experiences. Surveys were mostly used as preparation for the one-on-one interviews (see Appendix C for interview protocols). This study used data from portfolios, surveys, and interviews to perform interpretive qualitative analysis. This "basic qualitative study" method aims to "*understand* how people make sense of their lives and their experiences" (Merriam, 2009, pp. 22–23, italics in the original). In line with qualitative research tradition, data analysis was concurrent with data collection, and all data sources were used in conjunction, supporting each other. The researcher read through the data sources multiple times looking for recurring themes, identifying potential categories and codes, and writing analytical memos and notes. Following this initial analysis, coding process for the larger project began.

After collecting and analyzing the pre-telecollaboration data, the researcher identified three focal participants for the more detailed study of individual students' experiences. Multiple case study was chosen as a way to get an insight into different experiences that students have in the same telecollaboration. The first focal participant, James, was identified as a case study because of his unique approach to the telecollaboration project and the nature of his experience, which was different from that of the other participants. The two other focal participants, Paul and Maddie, were chosen because of their different positioning in relation to their cultural identities. The selection of focal participants in this study was a combination of maximum variation with convenience sampling. The researcher chose the participants who exhibited different levels of IC based on their pre-project interviews, different types of involvement in the telecollaboration, and different self-proclaimed cultural identities. At the same time, the researcher sought out case studies that had provided sufficient data in their interviews that would allow for a rich, "thick" description inherent to descriptive case studies (Merriam, 2009, p. 43).

Each case study was treated and analyzed separately. The researcher began the analysis by reading interview transcripts, portfolios, and surveys repeatedly, making notes and analytical memos about significant parts. These sources were treated as new data, and codes and categories from the larger study were not used. Using different data sources allowed for triangulation of the data and a fuller picture of each participant's experiences. In this analysis, descriptive, or topic, coding was used to identify general themes. The researcher was particularly looking for evidence of IC development using the three models described earlier, as well as for themes in terms of participants' learning and participation in the exchange. In the next stage of analysis, subcoding was applied to split the information into more specific categories. Then, the categories in participants' pre- and post-project data were compared to analyze students' development. Finally, the major themes among the three participants were compared to establish similarities and differences in their telecollaboration experiences and outcomes.

4 Results and Discussion

4.1 Case Study #1: James

4.1.1 Background

The first case study was James, a 19-year-old sophomore. Born in the U.S. in a family with Mexican and Native American heritage, James self-identified as a Mexican American, which, to him, meant being different from the dominant White U.S. culture. Some of the differences he mentioned were in his ways of relating to his parents, his typical pastimes, and "cultural tastes." In addition to his cultural heritage, James's background was different in that he grew up in a large West Coast city in a multicultural, lower-socioeconomic neighborhood, while most of his classmates were of white Midwestern, mostly middle-class, origin.

Due to his experiences, James was naturally engaged in intercultural communication on a daily basis. Interestingly, despite being aware of his cultural background, James constructed himself as a more generalized U.S. American when discussing his intercultural communication experiences prior to the telecollaboration. In fact, he only thought of the interactions he had with foreigners as representative of intercultural communication. James discussed his experience working with a group of Chinese workers in a warehouse and, while describing it as negative, he was very careful to emphasize that it was his particular experience with that particular group and he did not make generalizations about the whole Chinese culture. Refraining from stereotypes and generalization shows that James already had a certain degree of IC prior to the telecollaboration (Byram, 1997). As for James's identity, it went from a strong identification with being Mexican American in the beginning of the pre-project interview to a more general American identity once he discussed his understanding of intercultural communication. As discussed later, James also employed this American identity in the exchange with Colombian students.

4.1.2 Attitude Toward and Participation in the Telecollaboration

Prior to the start of telecollaboration, James was interested in the project and expected to learn about daily life in another country, which he thought would allow him to become a more "well-rounded person" (James, pre-project interview). He also mentioned it would be "cool" to directly interact with someone from a different culture. Once again, James positioned himself as a monocultural individual who could benefit from learning about another culture, disregarding his own multiple cultural identities and cultural knowledge and experiences he already had.

After telecollaboration, James said that he enjoyed the experience and was excited to share the important parts of his culture since he was proud of his Mexican American background. However, in his actual posts he only mentioned his Hispanic ancestry in the introduction and then never referred to it again. When asked about it in the interview, James explained that he wanted to highlight how the U.S. culture is different from others and to introduce it the right way, enacting his U.S. American identity, even though in the pre-project interview he self-identified as Mexican American and explained how that was different from the Caucasian American. James seemed eager to take on the role of the culture mediator and allow Colombian students to see his culture the way he does:

> I take that personally, I really want that person to see it the way I do, so if I really like my own culture, if I really enjoy it, I want to give it the best evaluation, the best display, the best way, so that they can enjoy it the way I do.

It appears that James took on a role of a cultural representative and highlighted the parts of the culture he liked and enjoyed. In this quote James showed his understanding of what it is like to try to put yourself in another's shoes, demonstrating his developing third-place perspective (Kramsch, 1993). James also said that participating in the project made him even more eager to learn about other cultures and what he called "international culture." This demonstrates his openness and curiosity, which, according to models of IC (Bennett, 1993; Byram, 1997), is one of its essential components. Although it seems that James already had some of these skills and mindsets before the project, the telecollaboration allowed him to practice and expand them. It could be that his multiple-culture background had prepared him for such an activity and naturally provided him with a certain level of IC.

Despite his interest in the telecollaboration, James did not go beyond the required number of posts and comments. He said that the level of his Spanish language skills prevented him from interacting with Colombian students' posts more as it was sometimes difficult to communicate exactly what he wanted. While he was a heritage speaker, he grew up speaking English at home and had formal Spanish instruction in high school and college. James referred to his preference for meaningful and deep discussion as opposed to small talk, and he did not feel comfortable with his ability to engage in such conversations. James may have been more worried about his language because it misaligned with his identity as a Mexican American, even though he did not portray that part of his identity in the exchange. He also mentioned that he wanted to improve his Spanish skills as he wanted to "be able to interact with people from [his] background, [his] own culture," demonstrating that in his mind language was a part of an identity. Language is often theorized as a tool for negotiating of identities (Noels et al., 2012), which may have been the reason it was important to James to be able to express himself well in Spanish.

4.1.3 Learning Experience in the Telecollaboration

One learning experience for James was his engagement in an analysis of the U.S. culture, where he seemed to position himself as a monocultural U.S. American and did not bring his multiple cultural identities into the discussion. When discussing differences in cultural practices, James always tried to find reasons for those differences and came up with hypotheses to explain them, which demonstrates his developing critical cultural awareness (Byram, 1997). The project also made him think about culture outside of class time. He mentioned that several times after class he further thought about class discussions and felt that his classmates and he could benefit from a deeper analysis of cultural differences in order to understand their own culture. It appears that James's multiple cultural identities primed him for being more analytical in his reflection on culture as he had to negotiate cultural identities his whole life and, thus, had accumulated some experience doing so. James claimed that he had never thought about American culture as much prior to the telecollaboration. He even admitted that he had always assumed that certain preferences and customs pertinent to the U.S. culture were universal, which was a common theme for most of the U.S. telecollaboration participants. This is consistent with Bennett's (1993) minimization stage of the ethnocentric worldview. It appears that the exchange prompted James to develop his IC and become more culturally aware. He also developed a critical view of his culture, citing individualism, excess consumerism, and the culture of entitlement as some of the negative characteristics of the U.S. culture. He admitted that he did not particularly like them and said that he wanted to be more conscious about it. This demonstrates an increased self-awareness and willingness to question his existing beliefs, which shows James's further development of IC as described in the attitudes part of Byram's (1997) model.

While James did not participate in the Facebook discussions beyond the requirement, he claimed to have assumed the role of a distant observer in the group conversations. James said that although it did not contribute to a richer discussion, it allowed him "to view the project from a different perspective" and to see a "bigger picture," which he thought was helpful to him and resulted in the most important type of learning:

> I found this project pretty interesting because the difference . . . between me and everybody else in the class is that I have a little bit of both, where I do have some Latin American or Hispanic culture, but it's very Americanized. So some things I do more Hispanic, and some things I do more American. So I thought that was really interesting, that showed me that I really do have both. . . . [I tried to] predict what people from my culture are going to say . . . I guess it's kind of an affirmation of do I understand my own culture, or the culture of the country that I'm in.

In this excerpt, James explained that he was interested in seeing which culture he would identify with in the exchange. Every week he tried to predict what most students' posts would be about and see whether his predictions were right. Whenever the posts fell in line with his predictions, it served as an affirmation of his understanding and belonging to one or the other culture. While some topics, such as sports, helped him realize that he was "definitely Americanized," others, like superstitions, showed that he did not know about some aspects of the U.S. culture but was familiar with the Colombian ones. Based on these observations, James concluded that he had "a little bit of both [cultures]," but was not "completely knowledgeable on either side." He thought it was an unexpected but positive experience to think about and analyze his own identity and sense of belonging to both Hispanic and U.S. cultures. In fact, James claimed it to be one of the major take-aways from the project for him. James's exploration of his identity is an example of the potential of telecollaboration to be a personal learning experience, as well as a place to analyze and construct one's identity. Telecollaboration gave James a space to legitimize his U.S. American identity as he positioned himself as a monocultural U.S. student in the visible part of the exchange. At the same time, it was a space for him to privately explore his multiple identities and verify his belonging to the Hispanic culture. James's shifts in positioning demonstrate the multiplicity of identity and its dependence on the context (Noels et al., 2012), with certain identities becoming more salient in certain situations (Clément & Noels, 1992) and being negotiated through contrasting the self with others (Collier & Thomas, 1988).

4.2 Case Study #2: Paul

4.2.1 Background

Paul was a 21-year-old student who took the class to fulfill a requirement but was interested in Spanish language and culture. Paul grew up in the suburbs of a large Midwestern city in what he referred to as a "typical white, suburban, middle-class family." By mentioning the race and the socioeconomic status of his family as indicators of cultural background, Paul demonstrated his awareness of the existence of multiple layers within U.S. culture, which shows a thoughtful grasp of the concept of culture from the beginning. While Paul was aware of his monocultural background, he did not identify with it and positioned himself as a more transnational, globally-oriented individual (Risager, 2007):

> I don't really like to call myself an American even though I know I am. I'm like a very poster child image of it, but I don't really like to identify with any national, nationalistic idea … I'm definitely not proud to be an American.

When asked what culture he did identify with, Paul mentioned belonging to the "weird kids" group that shared similar beliefs and interests, "sort of underground culture." In addition, Paul claimed that he did not like the idea of completely adapting to one culture, which aligns with Adler's (1982) idea of a multicultural identity, or an identity defined by not "owning or being owned by a single culture" (p. 391). Paul had never been abroad at the time and did not have much experience in intercultural communication. Before the exchange, Paul was already critical of the U.S. culture and seemed to romanticize other cultures, especially Hispanic ones. He was open to other cultures, valued different perspectives, and was willing to integrate other cultures' practices while questioning his own. This shows an ethnorelative worldview (Bennett, 1993) and a great degree of IC prior to the telecollaboration. However, Paul also exhibited ethnocentric characteristics in his overgeneralizations about cultures and persistent criticism of the U.S. culture along with praise for foreign cultures. For instance, speaking of his experience working alongside Mexican and U.S. workers at a construction site, he compared the two groups by describing his Mexican coworkers as open and friendly, while the U.S. workers were "group-oriented, shut-off, and angry." He clearly put the two cultures in stark contrast, without making distinctions among individuals in each group. It appears that he idealized the Mexican group to a certain extent and desired to associate and identify himself with that community. This positioning continued throughout the telecollaboration and affected Paul's learning in the project.

4.2.2 Attitude Toward and Participation in the Telecollaboration

Paul enjoyed the telecollaboration experience, but said he would have been more interested if the conversation topics had been more profound and had included a political or critical component. He said that he often used Facebook to talk about things in U.S. politics and culture that he disliked, which was why he thought it would have been interesting to share that with his Colombian peers, while learning about things they wanted to change in their culture. It appeared that Paul wanted to reinforce his identity as someone resisting or not conforming to the mainstream culture, but the prompts and other students' responses did not allow him a space to do it. In fact, in his posts Paul never demonstrated his transnational identity and, similar to James, portrayed a general U.S. American identity (Figure 12.2).

My favorite holiday is thanksgiving. There us nothing better than tons of food, and getting drunk with your family that you haven't seen in ages. The tradition has always been the same. My dad fries one turkey, and we oven bake another filled with stuffing. Thanksgiving has always been my favorite holiday because ita not about getting a bunch of stuff. Its the mist primal of our holidays: eat and drink with family.

Figure 12.2. Paul's Post on Favorite Holidays

In this example, Paul explains why his favorite holiday is Thanksgiving. While he does mention that he likes it because it is "not about getting a bunch of stuff," this reference to consumerism embedded in most holidays is not explained at all. Paul made one post per week most of the time and reported reading other people's posts, but did not comment very much. His main reason for not commenting more was related to Colombian students' low activity on the interactional part of the project. Paul complained that he rarely got responses to his questions, which was frustrating to him given his genuine interest. However, Paul was always very active in weekly class discussions and deemed them one of the most interesting parts of the course.

4.2.3 Learning Experience in the Telecollaboration

One of the big themes in Paul's learning in the exchange was his persistent romanticizing of the target culture, while criticizing the U.S. culture. As discussed above, even prior to the exchange Paul tended to idealize Hispanic cultures in general:

> I feel like every Spanish-speaking country is surrounded by a beautiful coast … there's just something so romantic about like some other place … it'd be beautiful to just exist in that.

In this conversation, when the researcher pointed out that the U.S. also has places with beautiful and varied landscapes, Paul admitted that he did not view them as favorably. This contrasting continued in Paul's analysis of the two cultures in the project. For example, one of the most surprising things that Paul learned about Colombian culture was the custom of greeting each other with a kiss on the cheek. He suggested that Colombians are closer to each other socially, while Americans want to have "the biggest bubble" for themselves, which he thought represented an "entitled" culture. Such overgeneralization seems to be a far-reaching conclusion about a whole culture based on one custom. It shows that Paul may have already had a conclusion that he had predetermined to be true, and he used this new knowledge as an example to support that conclusion. His counter-culture identity seemed to affect everything he was learning and to steer his understanding of cultural differences into continued criticism of the U.S. culture and romanticization of the target culture.

Another example of Paul contrasting the two cultures was his discussion of differences in celebrating Halloween. He was surprised that his Colombian peers go trick-or-treating with their families while the U.S. students "just go out to bars and party." He suggested that it was the reflection of "social relationships" in the two cultures and demonstrated the closeness of family in the Colombian culture. At the same time, Paul painted an unfavorable picture of the U.S. students, and concluded that his observation made him sad about his culture, which again is a rather strong statement to make based on one holiday celebration. He also did not take into consideration that college students often do not live close to their families and thus cannot go trick-or-treating with them, further demonstrating that in his analysis he jumped to conclusions that aligned with his predetermined view of his own culture.

While he exhibited overgeneralizations and idealized the target culture, Paul nevertheless enhanced his existing IC skills and developed some new ones as a result of the telecollaboration. Prior to the exchange, some of Paul's opinions indicated an ethnocentric worldview (Bennett, 1993), such as considering some U.S. cultural norms and values to be universal. The continuing cultural comparisons in the telecollaboration made Paul realize that other cultures have different practices and values. In line with his pre-existing attitudes of openness to other cultures, he expressed interest in incorporating some of the new practices into his own culture. In particular, he said that learning about other cultures is important because he can "incorporate the cool things that [he] like[s] into [his] culture" and if it does not work, he would "still have an image of a better way to do things."

Another important learning point for Paul happened when he analyzed his classmates' responses to the prompts. He thought that they painted a stereotypical picture of the U.S. and only considered their own Midwestern experiences, while disregarding how certain views and practices may be different in other regions or among other populations in the country. He added that he "took everything the Colombians said for the truth," which was why he thought that they would also believe everything the U.S. students said was a universal truth for the U.S. culture. Paul lamented that it was not representative of the culture as a whole, but he did not attempt to clarify these points for his Colombian peers during the exchange. In this instance Paul was putting himself in the Colombian students' shoes and predicting what they might think when they read their American peers' posts. This demonstrates Paul's movement toward the third place (Kramsch, 1993), or a cultural mediator position where he could see it both from an insider and an outsider perspective. He also demonstrated a complex view of the culture and was able to distinguish the cultural differences within his own culture, which are important components of IC (Byram, 1997).

4.3 Case Study #3: Maddie

4.3.1 Background

Maddie was an 18-year-old freshman minoring in Spanish. Maddie grew up in a large Midwestern city and described her cultural background as Irish:

> My family is super Irish. Like my mom is like 90% Irish, so I guess we are really Irish Catholic people . . . I went to Catholic school my whole life until high school, and my mom is like that, and so are my grandparents, aunts, and uncles. We are all just really Irish people.

While she claimed a strong affiliation with Irish culture and Catholicism, she struggled explaining what it meant to her and only mentioned a few stereotypes, such as being "really loud," as well as celebrating St. Patrick's Day and liking beef stew. Interestingly, later in the interview Maddie said she did not express her Irish identity and culture very much because she did not speak Gaelic, which suggests that she may equate culture with language. These examples show that Maddie's discussion of culture and cultural identity consisted of the most visible cultural products and practices, while the idea of cultural perspectives was largely absent. This, in turn, suggests that Maddie did not have a high level of IC since understanding all aspects of the concept of culture is a prerequisite to IC development (Drewelow, 2012). It also appeared that Maddie did not understand, or at least was not able to articulate, what her cultural identity meant to her.

Prior to the exchange, Maddie had a lot of exposure to different cultures through extensive traveling. She claimed to enjoy learning about how other people lived and said that the intercultural communication on her trips was easy. However, when she gave examples of intercultural communication and cultural learning, Maddie did not demonstrate significant intercultural awareness and focused on observable cultural differences or even disregarded other cultures. Similar to Root and Ngampornchai's (2012) findings, Maddie's example shows that simple exposure to or even immersion into other cultures does not guarantee IC development. Despite her proclaimed interest in other cultures, Maddie held a rather ethnocentric worldview. She considered the U.S. cultural practices and perspectives largely universal and did not attempt to put herself in the shoes of someone from another culture. Maddie's ethnocentric views and a strong monocultural affiliation align with an in-group orientation (Kim, 2009). While she seemed to genuinely enjoy learning about new cultures as a tourist, this interest was not the same as Byram's (1997) attitudes of openness and curiosity, who emphasized the difference between a tourist's desire to collect exotic experiences and one's willingness to question their own beliefs in the process of learning about other perspectives.

4.3.2 Attitude Toward and Participation in the Telecollaboration

Maddie enjoyed the telecollaboration and thought it was a good way to learn about another culture. She fulfilled the exchange requirements every week, but lamented that she did not get many responses. However, unlike Paul, the main reason she was frustrated about not getting a response was that she had nothing to say in the class discussion afterwards. This shows that her interest in Colombian peers' responses was motivated by the desire to have something to share with her classmates, rather than by genuine curiosity about the target culture.

Similar to the other case studies, Maddie did not mention or portray her cultural identity in the telecollaboration posts. While in the interview she emphasized her Irish heritage, in her telecollaboration posts she took on the mainstream U.S. American identity. She also did not refer to her stated cultural identity in the analysis of cultural differences.

4.3.3 Learning Experience in the Telecollaboration

Maddie reported learning a lot about Colombian culture and her portfolio and post-project interview also showed that she experienced a development in some areas of IC. In particular, she seemed to have moved along the intercultural sensitivity continuum (Bennett, 1993) toward a more ethnorelative worldview and demonstrated a development of a third-place perspective (Kramsch, 1993), where she could mediate between the two cultures.

Similar to Paul, one of the most shocking things for Maddie was the difference in greetings as she found it "weird" to greet people with a kiss on the cheek. She said that the class discussion was helpful in understanding and accepting it as a thing that people do, but she would not understand or accept it if an American did that. She did, however, attempt to understand the connection of the customary greetings to cultural perspectives. She suggested that "Americans keep their own personal space," which is why their greetings are more reserved than those in Colombia. This shows that Maddie moved from the stage where cultural differences are viewed negatively toward a more open view, where one can appreciate these differences and understand that the same practice may have different meanings. Maddie was trying to understand a practice and accept it as valid in another culture, but she was far from adapting to it or integrating it into her own culture.

Another example of Maddie attempting to explain cultural differences was her discussion of the typical living arrangements. She suggested that Americans prefer to move out of their parents' houses as early as possible because they enjoy being by themselves and do not want to interact with other people, which she thought "says a lot about [Americans]," although she could not explain it further. While her conclusions were somewhat overgeneralized, Maddie looked for reasons behind different practices, demonstrated an understanding that these differences are culturally determined, and was more aware and accepting of such differences.

In her post-telecollaboration interview, Maddie also showed a developing third perspective where she could take on an insider's and an outsider's view on both home and target culture. For instance, she was surprised to learn about the various traditions Colombians have on New Year's Eve and mentioned that she had always thought that it was celebrated the same everywhere. She then added that in the U.S. there is a tradition of watching the Times Square ball drop and as she was saying it, she realized that it may seem like an odd tradition to other cultures. In this instance Maddie thought about a typical cultural practice of her own culture and looked at it from the outsider perspective of Colombian students, which made her realize that the tradition that seems normal to Americans may be strange to Colombians.

Finally, Maddie demonstrated taking on an outsider's perspective when discussing some of her classmates' posts. She mentioned several examples where she thought the posts were not appropriate as they included jokes that could have been misinterpreted. She also identified a missed opportunity for an interesting conversation, where an American student mentioned an Amish community in their post but did not answer questions about it from Colombian students. In these examples, Maddie was trying to predict how her Colombian peers would react to the posts about U.S. culture and thought that more explanation was needed. This shows not only her developing third-place stance (Kramsch, 1993) but also the potential to be a mediator between cultures, where she would recognize culturally-determined information and predict potential conflict (Byram, 1997). Although she was far from renouncing her cultural beliefs and affiliations to fully become an intercultural mediator (Zarate, 2003), it appears that Maddie's telecollaboration experience led her to begin developing a more multilingual and multicultural identity.

Figure 12.3 provides a summary of learning themes for the three participants, representative quotes from them, and connections to the three models of intercultural competence used in the data analysis.

Participant	Learning theme	Representative quote	Intercultural competence model
James	U.S. culture analysis • Reasons for cultural differences • Critical view of home culture	"During some of the discussions we were talking about [how] in America … we are a little bit selfish, bigger is better country … I think that provided some insights as some things that we can change about ourselves as Americans"	• Critical cultural awareness (Byram, 1997) • Willingness to question own culture (Byram, 1997)
	Identity analysis • Legitimization of the U.S. identity	"[I wondered if I could] predict what people from my culture are gonna say, so that I have an understanding of my culture … I guess it's kind of an affirmation of do I understand my own culture, or the culture of the country that I'm in." "I didn't think I was gonna learn this in particular, you know, all these things about myself"	
Paul	Romanticizing target culture while criticizing home culture	"I feel like [Colombians] are just much more closer socially and here we just want the biggest bubble that we can" "I think it says more about our culture being kind of like entitled."	Skills of interpreting and relating (Byram, 1997) Critical cultural awareness (Byram, 1997)
	• Incorporating target culture practices • Taking on an outsider's role	"[Learning about other cultures is important because] then I can incorporate the cool things that I like into my culture!" "As I took everything the Colombians said for the truth, they probably took everything we said for truth, and [what some U.S. students posted] is not representative of the culture."	Willingness to suspend (Byram, 1997) Adaptation & integration stages (Bennett, 1993) Third place position (Kramsch, 1993)
Maddie	• Movement toward ethnorelative worldview • Analysis of reasons for cultural differences • Taking an outsider's role: potential cultural mediator	"[The greetings are different in the U.S. because] Americans keep their own personal space and … I usually don't like being touched" "I was kinda weirded out at one person's post… I know you're joking right now, but like they're not gonna get that, so… like they're not gonna receive that as sarcasm"	Critical cultural awareness (Byram, 1997) Willingness to question own culture (Byram, 1997) Acceptance stage (Bennett, 1993) Third place (Kramsch, 1993)

Figure 12.3. Summary of Learning Points

5 Conclusion

This study examined how students' cultural identities and positioning in relation to other cultures impacted their experience and learning in telecollaboration. Similar to findings in Helm et al. (2012), telecollaboration allowed learners a space to explore their identities and their experience both shaped and was shaped by the participants' positioning. James, who identified as multicultural and demonstrated an inclusive identity (Kim, 2009), used the project to verify his belonging to both cultures. At the same time he reimagined his Mexican American identity and portrayed it as a more general U.S. American one, possibly legitimizing that identity for himself. Paul, who identified as a transnational, global individual, used the digital space of the exchange as a way to resist the mainstream white U.S. ideologies, although he did not show that resistance to his Colombian peers. Finally, Maddie, who exhibited a monocultural identity and an ethnocentric worldview (Bennett, 1993), continued having a strong "in-group" identification with her own culture (Kim, 2009) and viewed the target culture as "other." Interestingly, although all three participants expressed different cultural identities in their interviews, they all portrayed themselves as monocultural U.S. Americans in the exchange, negating the plurality of their identities. It may be that the contrastive nature of the project made them affiliate with the "majority" and not demonstrate their unique identities.

In addition, in line with previous research (Chun, 2011; Jin, 2015), the findings showed that all three subjects were able to develop their IC skills. The experience of performing cultural comparisons and analysis allowed them to move toward a more ethnorelative orientation (Bennett, 1993) and develop various components of IC, such as openness to other cultures, willingness to question their own culture, and some degree of critical cultural awareness (Byram, 1997). Finally, all three participants demonstrated a potential for cultural mediation and third-place positioning (Kramsch, 1993), although the degree of that potential depended on each participant's cultural identity.

While the findings of this study provide a valuable insight into the interplay of learners' identities and their experiences in telecollaboration, it is important to acknowledge its limitations. Given the nature of qualitative case studies, the conclusions are not directly transferable to other contexts. Participants' language proficiency, cultural identities, and IC levels may affect their experiences and learning. A different set-up (e.g., pair or small-group interactions) may also lead to different outcomes. Another limitation is that the study relied only on self-reported information. While we triangulated several data sources to minimize the threat to validity, adding a data source that is not self-reported (e.g., conversation or discourse analysis) would provide additional support to the findings. Future studies would benefit from exploring different contexts and set-ups of the exchanges. Using different tasks may also offer a more in-depth look at learners' IC development and cultural identity enactment in their interactions.

This study demonstrated that telecollaboration is an effective way to simulate real-life multilingual and multicultural communication in digital spaces, while fostering learners' IC development. Such exchanges also provide a space for learners to explore their cultural identities in relation to other cultures. At the same time, learners' positioning may guide their learning. For this reason, it is important to direct their attention to self-analysis and provide guidance on making meaning out of the new information they learn in order to foster learners' development as intercultural speakers and mediators, as well as provide space for their identity exploration.

References

Adler, P. (1982). Beyond cultural identity: Reflections on cultural and multicultural man. In L. Samovar & R. Porter (Eds.), *Intercultural communication: A reader* (3rd ed., pp. 389–408).Wadsworth.

Avgousti, M. I. (2018). Intercultural communicative competence and online exchanges: A systematic review. *Computer Assisted Language Learning, 31*(2), 1–37. https://doi.org/10.1080/09588221.2018.1455713

Belz, J. (2002). Social dimensions of telecollaborative foreign language study. *Language Learning & Technology, 6*(1), 60–81. https://doi.org/10125/25143

Belz, J. (2003). Linguistic perspectives on the development of IC in telecollaboration. *Language, Learning & Technology, 7*(2), 68–99. https://doi.org/10125/25201

Belz, J., & Kinginger, C. (2002). The cross-linguistic development of address form use in telecollaborative language learning: Two case studies. *The Canadian Modern Language Review, 59*(2), 189–214. https://doi.org/10.3138/cmlr.59.2.189

Bennett, M. J. (1993). Towards ethnorelativism: A developmental model of intercultural sensitivity. In R. M. Paige (Ed.), *Education for the intercultural experience* (pp. 21–71). Intercultural Press.

Byram, M. (1997). *Teaching and assessing intercultural communicative competence*. Multilingual Matters.

Chase, C., & Alexander, P. (2007). The Japan–Korea culture exchange project. In R. O'Dowd (Ed.), *Online intercultural exchange: An introduction for foreign language teachers* (pp. 259–263). Multilingual Matters. https://doi.org/10.21832/9781847690104-016

Chen, G. M., & Starosta, W. J. (1996). Intercultural communication competence: A synthesis. In B. Burleson (Ed.), *Communication yearbook 19* (pp. 353–383). Sage.

Chun, D. (2011). Developing intercultural communicative competence through online exchanges. *CALICO Journal*, *28*(2), 392–419. Retrieved from: https://www.jstor.org/stable/10.2307/calicojournal.28.2.392

Clément, R., & Noels, K. A. (1992). Towards a situated approach to ethnolinguistic identity: The effects of status on individuals and groups. *Journal of Language and Social Psychology*, *11*, 203–232.

Collier, M. J., & Thomas, M. (1988). Cultural identity: An interpretive perspective. In Y. Y. Kim & W. B. Gudykunst (Eds.), *Theories in intercultural communication* (pp. 99–120). Sage Publications.

De Costa, P., & Norton, B. (2016). Identity in language learning and teaching: Research agendas for the future. In S. Preece (Ed.), *The Routledge handbook of language and identity* (pp. 586–601). Routledge.

Drewelow, I. (2012). Learners' perceptions of culture in a first-semester foreign language course. *L2 Journal*, *4*, 283–302. https://doi.org/10.5070/L24213257

Fantini, A. (2009). Assessing IC: Issues and tools. In D. K. Deardorff (Ed.), *The SAGE handbook of IC* (pp. 456–476). Sage.

Flowers, S., Kelsen, B., & Cvitkovic, B. (2019). Learner autonomy versus guided reflection: How different methodologies affect intercultural development in online intercultural exchange. *ReCALL FirstView*, 1–17. https://doi.org/10.1017/S0958344019000016

Fuchs, C., & Snyder, B. (2013). It's not just the tool: Pedagogy for promoting collaboration and community in social networking in CMC. In M.-N. Lamy & K. Zourou (Eds.), *Social networking for language education* (pp. 117–134). Palgrave Macmillan. https://doi.org/10.1057/9781137023384_7

Godwin-Jones, R. (2013). Integrating IC into language learning through technology. *Language Learning & Technology*, *17*(2), 1–11. https://doi.org/10125/44318

Guth, S., Helm, F., & O'Dowd, R. (2012). University language classes collaborating online: Report on the integration of telecollaborative networks in European universities. https://www.unicollaboration.org/wp-content/uploads/2016/06/1.1-Telecollaboration_report_Executive_summary-Oct2012_0.pdf

Guth, S., & Thomas, M. (2010). Telecollaboration with Web 2.0 tools. In S. Guth & F. Helm (Eds.), *Telecollaboration in education, volume 1: Telecollaboration 2.0: Languages, literacies and intercultural learning in the 21st century* (pp. 39–68). Peter Lang AG.

Hall, S. (1992). The question of cultural identity. In T. McGrew, S. Hall, & D. Held (Eds.), *Modernity and its futures: Understanding modern societies, Book IV* (pp. 274–327). Polity Press in association with The Open University.

Hammer, M. R. (2008). The intercultural development inventory (IDI): An approach for assessing and building IC. In M. A. Moodian (Ed.),

Contemporary leadership and IC: Understanding and utilizing cultural diversity to build successful organizations (pp. 203–217). Sage.

Helm, F. (2018). *Emerging identities in virtual exchange*. Research-publishing.net. https://files.eric.ed.gov/fulltext/ED585082.pdf

Helm, F., & Guth, S. (2010). The multifarious goals of telecollaboration 2.0: Theoretical and practical implications. In S. Guth & F. Helm (Eds.), *Telecollaboration in education, volume 1: Telecollaboration 2.0: Languages, literacies and intercultural learning in the 21st century* (pp. 69–106). Peter Lang AG.

Helm, F., Guth, S., & Farrah, M. (2012). Promoting dialogue or hegemonic practice? Power issues in telecollaboration. *Language Learning & Technology 16*(2), 103–127. https://doi.org/10125/44289

Higgins, C. (2015). Intersecting scapes and new millennium identities in language learning. *Language Teaching, 48*(3): 373–389. https://doi.org/10.1017/S0261444814000044

Jensen, L. A. (2003). Coming of age in a multicultural world: Globalization and adolescent cultural identity formation. *Applied Developmental Science 7*(3), 189–196. https://doi.org/10.1207/S1532480XADS0703_10

Jin, S. (2015). Using Facebook to promote Korean EFL learners' IC. *Language Learning & Technology, 19*(3), 38–51. https://doi.org/10125/44429

Kim, Y. Y. (2009). The identity factor in IC. In D. K. Deardorff (Ed.), The SAGE handbook of intercultural competence (pp. 53–65). Sage.

Kirschner, L. L. (2015). Combining Skype with blogging: A chance to stop reinforcement of stereotypes in intercultural exchanges? *The EuroCALL Review, 23*(1): 24–30. https://doi.org/10.4995/eurocall.2015.4656

Klimanova, L., & Dembovskaya, S. (2013). L2 identity, discourse, and social networking in Russian. *Language Learning & Technology, 17*(1), 69–88. http://dx.doi.org/10125/24510

Kohn, K., & Hoffstaedter, P. (2017). Learner agency and non-native speaker identity in pedagogical lingua franca conversations: Insights from intercultural telecollaboration in foreign language education. *Computer Assisted Language Learning*, 1–17. http://dx.doi.org/10.1080/09588221.2017.1304966

Kramsch, C. (1993). *Context and culture in language teaching*. Oxford University Press.

Kramsch, C. (2006). From communicative competence to symbolic competence. *The Modern Language Journal, 90*(2), 249–252. https://www.jstor.org/stable/3876875

Lam, W. S. E. (2000). Second language literacy and the design of the self: A case study of a teenager writing on the internet. *TESOL Quarterly, 34*, 457–482. https://doi.org/10.2307/3587739

Lamy, M.-N., & Goodfellow, R. (2010). Telecollaboration and learning 2.0. In S. Guth & F. Helm (Eds.), *Telecollaboration in education, volume 1: Telecollaboration 2.0: Languages, literacies and intercultural learning in the 21st century* (pp. 107–138). Peter Lang AG.

Lee, L. (2007). One-to-one desktop videoconferencing for developing oral skills: Prospects in perspective In R. O'Dowd (Ed.), *Online intercultural exchange: An introduction for foreign language teachers* (pp. 281–291). Multilingual Matters. https://doi.org/10.21832/9781847690104-020

Lee, L., & Markey, A. (2014). A study of learners' perceptions of online intercultural exchange through Web 2.0 technologies. *ReCALL, 26*(3), 281–297. https://doi.org/10.1017/S0958344014000111

Liaw, M.-L., & English, K. (2013). Online and offsite: Student-driven development of the Taiwan–France telecollaborative project Beyond These Walls. In M.-N. Lamy & K. Zourou (Eds.), *Social networking for language education* (pp. 158–176). Palgrave Macmillan. https://doi.org/10.1057/9781137023384_9

Martin, J. N. (2015). Revisiting intercultural communication competence: Where to go from here. *International Journal of Intercultural Relations, 48*, 6–8. https://doi.org/10.1016/j.ijintrel.2015.03.008

Merriam, S. (2009). *Qualitative research: A guide to design and implementation.* Jossey-Bass.

Möllering, M., & Levy, M. (2012). Intercultural competence in computer-mediated-communication: An analysis of research methods. In M. Dooly & R. O'Dowd (Eds.), *Telecollaboration in education, volume 3: Researching online foreign language interaction and exchange: Theories, methods, and challenges* (pp. 233–264). Peter Lang AG. https://doi.org/10.3726/978-3-0351-0414-1

Noels, K. A., Yashima, T., & Zhang, R. (2012). Language, identity and intercultural communication. In J. Jackson (Ed.), *The Routledge handbook of language and intercultural communication* (pp. 52–66). Routledge.

Norton, B. (2000). *Identity and language learning: Gender, ethnicity, and educational change*. Longman.

O'Dowd, R. (2007). *Online intercultural exchange: An introduction for foreign language teachers*. Multilingual Matters. https://doi.org/10.21832/9781847690104

O'Dowd, R. (2013). Telecollaboration and CALL. In M. Thomas, H. Reinders, & M. Warschauer (Eds.), *Contemporary computer-assisted language learning* (pp. 210–236). Bloomsbury Academic.

O'Dowd, R. (2018). From telecollaboration to virtual exchange: State-of-the-art and the role of UNICollaboration in moving forward. *Journal of Virtual Exchange, 1*, pp. 1 – 24. https://doi.org/10.14705/rpnet.2018.jve.1

Paige, R. M., Jorstad, H. L., Siaya, L., Klein, F., & Colby, J. (2003). Culture learning in language education: A review of literature. In D. L. Lange & R. M. Paige (Eds.), *Culture as the core: Perspectives on culture in second language learning* (pp. 173–236). Information Age Publishing.

Parmenter, L. (2003). Describing and defining intercultural communicative competence – international perspectives. In M. Byram (Ed.), *Intercultural Competence* (pp. 119–147). Council of Europe.

Risager, K. (2007). *Language and culture pedagogy: From a national to a transnational paradigm.* Multilingual Matters. https://doi.org/10.21832/9781853599613

Root, E., & Ngampornchai, A. (2012). "I came back as a new human being": Student descriptions of IC acquired through education abroad experiences. *Journal of Studies in International Education, 17*(5), 513–532. https://doi.org/10.1177/1028315312468008

Schreiber, B. R. (2015). "I am what I am": Multilingual identity and digital translanguaging. *Language Learning & Technology, 19*(3), 69–87. https://doi.org/10125/44434

Schulz, R. A. (2007). The challenge of assessing cultural understanding in the context of foreign language instruction. *Foreign Language Annals, 40*(1), 9–26. https://doi.org/10.1111/j.1944-9720.2007.tb02851.x

Sharma, B. K. (2012). Beyond social networking: Performing global Englishes in Facebook by college youth in Nepal. *Journal of Sociolinguistics, 16*(4), 483–509. https://doi.org/10.1111/j.1467-9841.2012.00544.x

Thorne, S. L. (2010). The intercultural turn and language learning in the crucible of new media. In S. Guth & F. Helm (Eds.), *Telecollaboration 2.0: Language and intercultural learning in the 21st century* (pp. 139–165). Peter Lang.

Vinagre, M. (2007). Integrating tandem learning in higher education. In R. O'Dowd (Ed.), *Online intercultural exchange: An introduction for foreign language teachers* (pp. 240–249). Multilingual Matters. https://doi.org/10.21832/9781847690104-014

Wang, Y. (2007). Globalization enhances cultural identity. *Intercultural Communication Studies XVI, 1*, pp. 83–86.

Wilden, E. (2007). Voice chats in the intercultural classroom: The ABC's online project. In R. O'Dowd (Ed.), *Online intercultural exchange: An introduction for foreign language teachers* (pp. 269–275). Multilingual Matters. https://doi.org/10.21832/9781847690104-018

Zarate, G. (2003). Identities and plurilingualism: Preconditions for the recognition of intercultural competencies. In M. Byram (Ed.), *IC* (pp. 85–118). Council of Europe Publishing.

About the Author

Anastasia Izmaylova is the Director of the Center for Languages and Intercultural Communication at Grinnell College in Grinnell, Iowa. She works with faculty and students to promote and coordinate language and culture learning. In her research, Dr. Izmaylova focuses on intercultural competence and issues surrounding teaching and learning of culture. Her other research area is the use of web technologies in language instruction. In particular, she explores the use of social media as platforms for projects aimed at community-building and the development of interpersonal and intercultural communication skills.

Appendix A: Telecollaboration Prompts

Week #	Topic	Possible questions to consider
1	Short video introducing yourself (3–5 mins)	What do you study? Where are you from? What is your cultural background? What are your interests?
2	Good/bad luck	What are some common superstitions in your culture? Are there certain days or numbers that have a specific meaning? Are there any actions that bring good/bad luck? Do you have any good luck charms or totems? What are some taboo things in your culture?
3	Sport and its role in your life	What is your favorite sport to watch/play? Is it a big part of your life? How so? Was sport important to you when you were younger? Do you have any friends/family who are involved in sports? What are the sports that typical Americans do? What sports do typical Americans watch? Is it an important part of culture?
4	Typical family dinner	How often do you have it? Where? What is it like? How big is your family? What do you normally talk about? Is it the same every day? Do you think it is similar to family dinners in other American families?
5	Your free time	What do you do for fun? Where? With whom? Are your activities typical of most other college-aged people in your community?
6	Holidays that you celebrate	What are your favorite holidays? What is their origin? How do you celebrate them? Is it similar for everyone in your community?
7	Interpersonal communication etiquette	What are some major dos and don'ts in communicating with other people? How do you greet your friends/family/professors? How do you approach new people? How do you ask someone out? What are some things a foreigner should be aware of? Are there certain gestures or body language that have a significant meaning?
8	Transportation	What is your preferred type of everyday transportation? How do you get to places (school/movies/visit your family)? Is it similar for everyone in your community? At what age did you learn how to drive and got a driver's license? What do you think public transportation is? How often do you use it? For what purpose? What is it like?

Appendix B: Screenshot of the Facebook Group Wall

Appendix C: Interviews Protocols

Pre-telecollaboration semi-structured interview protocol

- How do you feel about this project? Why?
- Do you think you will learn anything from it? What?
- Do you think learning about other cultures is important in general? Why (not)?
- Do you think it is important for language learners to also learn about the culture or is it just about the language? Why?
- Do you have a lot of experience interacting with people from other countries or cultures? What were they like?
- In your opinion, what is culture?
- How would you describe your cultural background?
- What culture(s) did you grow up in?
- What culture(s) do you identify with?

Post-telecollaboration semi-structured interview protocol

- Have you changed your opinion about the project over the course of the semester? How?
- What did you learn in this project?
- What word would you use to describe your emotions when posting and reading your peers' posts on Facebook?
- In the questionnaire you said that you participated [in class/small groups/large groups] [more/less] as a result of participating in this project. Why is that?
- How did you feel about having to explain your culture to Colombian students?
- In your opinion, what is culture?
- Do you think learning about other cultures is important in general? Why (not)?
- Do you think it is important for language learners to also learn about culture? Why (not)?
- How did you feel when this happened [specific interactions]?
- If you were told that you would have to participate in a similar exchange again, what changes would you like to see in the project? Why?
- Tell me about one instance when you felt that you couldn't explain something well. Why did it happen? How did you resolve it?

- Tell me about one instance when you thought that one of the Colombian traditions was weird or you could not understand it.
- Would you like to learn more about Colombian culture? Why/Why not?
- Would you like to participate in a similar project with a different country?
- Do you think that everything Colombian students were posting about was representative of their culture?
- Do you think that everything American students were posting about was representative of your culture? Was there a time when you didn't agree with the explanation given by one of your classmates? Tell me about it. Did you intervene? How? If not, why not?
- Tell me about an instance where you had to describe something in your culture that you don't like very much.
- Tell me about an instance where you felt uncomfortable about a video, explanation, or comment posted by one of your classmates.
- How did you pick which posts to respond to?
- Why did you respond to this post [specific interactions]?
- How did you pick when to jump into conversations your classmates were having with Colombian students?
- Tell me about an instance where you were proud to share a certain aspect of your culture.
- What is your overall impression of the project?

13 The Effects of Multimodal Communication on the Development of New Types of Learner Imagination

Borbala Gaspar

1 Introduction

Drawing on different empirical and theoretical perspectives, in recent years researchers have highlighted the benefits of digital spaces for identity work, especially because digital contexts – and in particular multilingual contexts – can better capture the complexities of social interactions. In these contexts, learners may express themselves more freely (Lam, 2000; Schreiber, 2015; Yang & Yi, 2016), construct and (re)negotiate their identities (Klimanova & Dembovskaya, 2013; Thorne et al., 2009), resist (Iwasaki, 2011), perform relevant identities (Thorne et al., 2009), build meaningful relationships, and manage social bonds in local and global communities (Chen, 2013; Garcia-Pastor, 2020). Identity plays an important role in language learning, as it reflects how learners adjust their level of participation in different communities of shared practices.

As learners become more proficient in a foreign language, they expand on the available identities (Pavlenko & Norton, 2007), a process in which imagination has been found to play a key negotiating role (Yashima, 2013) as it strongly impacts identity construction (Kanno & Norton, 2003). Imagination is part of our everyday life and has been addressed by many scholars (Anderson, 2006; Kanno & Norton, 2003; Norton, 2000, 2001; Pavlenko & Norton, 2007). Several of these studies explore how the future is imagined by learners and how this imagined future can affect the language learner's engagement in language learning (Norton, 1997, 2000). When imagination is paired with other concepts related to engagement, it has been shown to help learners acquire not only new identities (Norton, 2000; Kanno, 2000,

2003) but in some cases temporary identities as well (Vandergriff & Fuchs, 2009; Warner, 2004).

Yet most of these studies on imagination limit their primary focus to the imagined and planned future of the language learner in relation to their career or the development of proficiency, overlooking other forms of imagination, such as co-constructed imagination. Imagination, as a tool (Szpunar & McDermott, 2009) and as a key element in identity negotiation (Yashima, 2013), remains unexplored in the virtual context, particularly in relation to foreign language learners.

This study is situated in the *digital wild* – the digital spaces where informal language learning takes place (Sauro & Zourou, 2019). It examines how four foreign language learners of Italian use their imagination, plan their future, engage in fantasy, and create mental images through their use of the language exchange app HelloTalk. Based on the analysis, the following questions guide this study:

1. How did the learners perceive themselves and others when engaging with the language exchange application?
2. What types of imagination did these learners use when engaging with HelloTalk?

The findings demonstrate how the learners, transcending space and time, acquired a new position as participants in the time/space of their (Italian) correspondents and, temporarily or instantaneously, imagined being and living in Italy as a local. While the imagination presented in this study overlaps in some respects with previously described concepts of imagination, it also provides some new insights. As the learners interacted with their language exchange partners using the app as a mediating tool of social semiotic activity (Ochs, 2002), they engaged, both synchronously and asynchronously, in co-constructed imagination. The central argument of this paper is that the collaborative imagination afforded by multisensory communication may better capture learners' desires, fantasies, relationships, and the *feltness* of their experience, particularly the affective aspect of their engagement in language learning. The study concludes with implications for future research and suggests the use of co-constructed imagination as an alternative to investment and imagination for the investigation of learners' engagement in digital contexts. The next section will orient this study in the field of second language teaching and learning and the prior research exploring the possible forms of imagination and identity construction.

2 Literature Review

2.1 Identity and Investment

This first section begins by situating this study within recent discussions of identity, investment and imagination in the digital context, in the field of second language teaching and learning. Imagination, then, relates to similar concepts that although do not directly address it, greatly inform our understanding of it.

Traditionally, the term *identity* was used to explain how a person connects and identifies with social groups, what emotions surface, and what connections are made between them (Tajfel, 1974, 1978). Norton (2000), incorporating critical sociology (e.g., Bourdieu, 1997, 1991) and poststructuralist, feminist theory (Weedon, 1997), focused on the positions and relationships a person has in the world, including power relations, which are subject to change. She connected identity development with the notion of investment as it refers to the degree of commitment of language learners to language learning (Peirce, 1995). Learners, therefore, can be motivated, but it does not mean that they will invest in language learning and in their imagined future.

Recent studies on English learners' investment have found that students are more invested in digital literacy activities because the digital technologies make more identities available, such as imagined futures and imagined identities (Early & Norton, 2014; Norton & Williams, 2012). These and similar studies inspired Darvin and Norton (2015) to reframe the model of investment to better reflect the constantly changing global environment. Their new model places investment in relation to identity, ideology, and capital, and extends the possible questions to pose when examining investment. Within their framework, learners invest in the present as well as the future; however, it does suggest that learners invest in a predetermined goal, which may not completely reflect the possible engagement types found in the digital context. Research on identity construction and investment in the digital space have demonstrated the complexities of identity negotiation and investment in digital spaces, in particular the role of collaboration and the possibilities for new social positions in digital spaces. Some of these studies, which I present below, are closely connected to the current study as they demonstrate the role of collaboration and the construction of alternative space that the digital context may afford.

Using the notions of identity and investment, Klimanova and Dembovskaya (2013) explored the types of connections that learners make within social groups and their role in identity negotiation and investment in an instructional setting. As learners of Russian spoke to Russian speakers through a series of telecollaborative tasks on *VKontakte*, a popular Russian social networking space, they invested in the learning and negotiated their identities – as heritage speakers, learners, or experts – as relational and embedded in the language and context. These learners constructed collaborative relations of power that allowed them to more fluidly move between native speaker and language user identities. This proved particularly beneficial for heritage learners who were in the process of making sense of and constructing their heritage identity. As this study demonstrated, the collaborative construction of power and identities is possible in a digital instructional setting.

Another example that demonstrates the potential for constructing alternative spaces and new identities in digital space, resulting in greater investment in the digital context, is the story of Almon, by Eva Lam (2000). Almon constructs an imaginative "I" in online discourse that allows him to acquire a new social identity. Almon distinguishes two different worlds: the realistic and the imaginational. He demonstrates how these can be interwoven and can affect each other. Almon becomes more engaged with learning English through the affordances of digital literacy, which differs from the academic setting. Almon's interactions with the other members of the community help him create an imagined space where he feels a sense of belonging. In this study, digital literacy served as a tool to trigger imagination and influenced Almon's investment in a future goal.

Identity can also be defined as a semiotic potential in a repertoire (Blommaert, 2005). This performative view of identity contributes to an understanding of how learners perform, and simultaneously shape their learning and organize and make sense of social contexts within a digital, multilingual space. Of particular relevance to digital settings, and consequently this study, is the concept of *multilingual subjectivities* (Kramsch, 2009). This concept offers a way to capture the experiences of learners, as it includes the emotions, desires, and fantasies that may emerge – especially in multilingual digital settings. As discussed above, imagination played an important role in Almon's identity construction, which increased his investment in learning English. Similarly, multilingual subjectivities describe multilingual learners who might playfully fantasize about other identities, creating virtual selves in both contexts – the internet and real life – without necessarily having in mind an imagined future, career goal or level of language proficiency. To better understand the possible development of, and distinction between, different forms of imagination, such as desire and fantasies, in the next section we will take a closer look at imagination.

2.2 Imagination

Imagination was first discussed in relation to identity in Anderson's *Imagined Communities* (2006), which describes how, when we communicate with communities, we feel their existence more concretely through our imagination. However, this is not the only way in which imagination contributes to community (Wenger, 1998). Wenger defined imagination as "expanding oneself by transcending our time and space and creating new images of the world and ourselves" (p. 176). Building on these concepts, Kanno and Norton (2012), in their concept of imagination and imagined identity, discuss learners' future relationships and affiliations, such as transnational communities and nationhood. There is still more that we can learn about the way in which learners use their imagination in the online multilingual context.

Multisensory communication in digital spaces offers possibilities for learners to use their imagination in different ways and invites us to consider exploring the concept beyond these previously examined perspectives. Positioning theory (van Langenhove & Harrè, 1999) is frequently used to examine how, through social interactions, learners emerge into and locate themselves, with rights and obligations, within a community. Similarly, as will be further discussed in the "Methodology" section, this study uses positioning theory to examine learners' perceptions as they engage in a co-constructed form of imagination.

The conceptualization of imagination in the field of psycholinguistics provides additional perspectives to consider when looking at possible forms of imagination, especially those that are triggered by multisensory communication. According to Kendall Walton's (1990) theory of make-believe, all images convey information and create a virtual presence for the viewer, inviting them to pretend to participate in the space. When we formulate a desire, we need to simulate in detail how to achieve it (Pham & Taylor, 1999; Taylor et al., 1998); positive images can help to achieve these desires. During a simulation, we can elicit perceptual activity that resembles what would have occurred, with the same feelings, as if the action happened in reality, because our brain processes imagined actions in the same way as actual ones (Decety & Grezes, 2006, p. 5). Informed by previous studies, this study takes a closer look at these developing desires and emotions in relation to imagination and the possible effect they have on language learners. To better understand the process forms of these desires and fantasies, the following section will first examine language play.

2.3 Language Play

To explore the affective and playful aspects of subjectivities, research on language play can provide insight into how, as learners engage in social practices in the digital space, they may initiate language play and, by doing so, display their subjectivities, emotions, and desires. In a multilingual context, learners can engage in language play in different ways, such as by playing with individual, relational, and social identities by changing or assuming new roles, taking new positions, and constructing new relationships (Ochs, 1996). For instance, Warner (2004) explored how German students engaged in language play using a synchronous network-based medium. One theory on social interaction that complements the abovementioned study is Cook's (2000), who outlined three main categories of play: 1) linguistic play (which refers to rhythm, sound, rhyming), 2) pragmatic play (performance of the speaker), and 3) semantic play (role play, alternative reality). While some of these elements were recognizable in the language play of German students, Warner (2004) further contributes to our understanding of learners' play in the digital context by providing examples of three types of play: a) play with form, b) play with content/concept, and c) play with frame. In particular, combining elements of Cook's concept of pragmatic play (2000) and Bakhtin's concept of parody (1984), Warner defines *play with the frame* as a way of performing with pieces of discourse that may also include certain behaviors but is not necessarily addressed to others. For example, Jany, as she engaged in a play with frame, sometimes by playing a character in a role play and other times taking on her student identity, provided evidence of play in her language choices that went beyond the *play with language form*.

Another playful use of language was discussed by Vandergriff and Fuchs (2009), who examined German students' foreign language play in both face-to-face and computer-mediated communication (CMC) and distinguished a type of temporary identity play between participants that occurred only in CMC. Similarly, the participants presented in this paper took on temporary identities and engaged in complex meaning making triggered by their imagination, through multisensory communication. The abovementioned studies on language play helped to develop the framework for this study for analyzing the formulation of imagination by taking a closer look at the possible multisensory forms of play with the frame that this study further explores. As in the case of Almon, who moved between spaces and created alternative ones, the spaces learners occupy as they engage in multisensory communication have an important role to play in shaping the possibilities for learners.

2.4 Transcending Time and Space Collaboratively

Although it does not explicitly address imagination, Malinowski's (2014) study explores the role of *synesthesia* and refers to how foreign language learners of French imagined being in the same space with their correspondents. Through drawings, learners collaboratively linked spatial and bodily meanings. These learners imagined and illustrated a symbolic space in their drawings where they interacted with their correspondent. Malinowski (2014) argues that multimodal environments allow foreign language learners to "draw themselves into" (p. 29) the space of the language community. This study shows us the fluidity of time and space that is possible to co-construct through multisensory communication that the digital spaces afford. The affective aspects and the effects of them on learners' participation during a co-constructed engagement in a digital context, however, remains unexplored.

2.5 Co-constructed Imagination

Multisensory communication in digital spaces is complex and can engage learners in different ways. Drawing on previous studies, this study provides a new way of looking at imagination in digital spaces. Imagination is considered to be dynamically changing, fluid, and co-constructed, and not a property of the learner. By describing imagination as co-constructed I am referring to the multimodal communication with the language exchange partners that learners may engage with online. It is dynamically changing and co-constructed because through conversations, learners create, share, and recreate an image (symbolic or actual), and in so doing, they interweave their physical and virtual presence and their connections to each other.

Thus, it serves as a tool that creates opportunities for learners to (self) position (van Langenhove & Harrè, 1999) in the here and now and to create imagined spaces or take on temporary subjectivities (Kramsch, 2009) – or simply to engage in a fantasized role play for their enjoyment.

When co-constructed imagination occurs, we can also detect the affective aspects that are associated with imagination. The affective aspects are important elements as they indicate the level of engagement and participation in learning, and thus can provide us a more comprehensive view of learners in the complex multisensory spaces. To examine the types of imagination and how imagination affects the learner and language learning, this study draws on the concepts of multilingual subjectivities (Kramsch, 2009), positioning theory (Langehove & Harrè, 1999), and language play with the frame (Warner, 2004). The following section offers a detailed overview of the methodology.

3 Methodology

3.1 Research Context and Design

The study was conducted in an institution in the southwest United States, located in a multicultural city were only few Italian speakers live. The study centers on three intermediate Italian courses that were taught by the author between 2016 and 2017, during which the data for this study were collected. Italian is only taught at the university. For many students who have not been to Italy, social connections to Italy and communication with Italian speakers are only imagined. Therefore, this study was developed with the desire to engage learners of Italian and provide opportunities for them to develop Italian social connections beyond the classroom environment.

The intermediate class met four times a week for 50 minutes. Classes were taught primarily in Italian. In order to provide practice opportunities in Italian outside of the class, all students were encouraged to use an interactive language exchange application, called HelloTalk, for at least 35 minutes

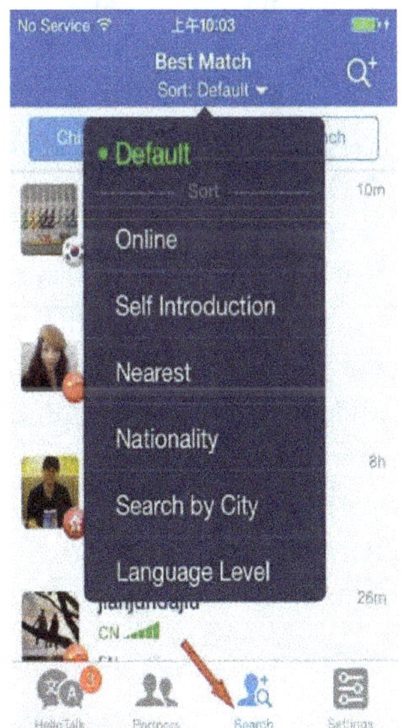

Figure 13.1. How Learners Find an Exchange Partner

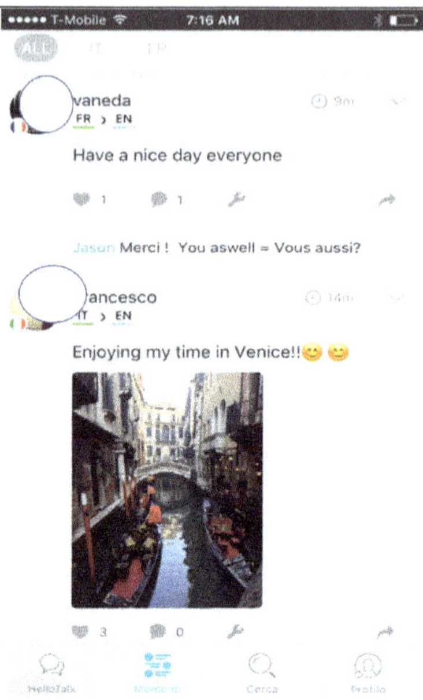

Figure 13.2. Moments: A Message Board to Communicate with the Learner Community

a week. HelloTalk is a free language exchange application, where learners can find and select Italian-speaking individuals learning English to engage in a language exchange, based on the self-introduction in their profile (Figure 13.1). App users can send messages to registered members (audio messages, images, videos) and can make phone calls or write on their Moments page – similar to a Facebook wall (Figure 13.2).

Because this is a language exchange application, once learners select who they want to chat with, they must establish the way they want to converse. In class we discussed options such as asking their partners to write in both languages or alternating the days when they practiced Italian and English.

It was noticeable that students commented enthusiastically on the pictures and videos they received, particularly the point-of-view shots. This triggered my interest to further investigate their multimodal engagement and playful interactions in the digital space.

3.2 Participant Selection

This study explores participants' lived experiences with Italian while using HelloTalk, rather than giving an in-depth analysis of their histories. The data reported here come from four selected participants who were enrolled in Intermediate Italian courses between 2016 and 2017. The participants were selected based on their emerging pattern of imagination, as well as the richness of the information that they provided. The majority of participants were American students (one participant was from Belgium). They all came from multicultural backgrounds. Overall, three female students (Carla, Laura, and Silvia) and one male student (Matteo) participated in the study. They were between 19 and 26 years old. Three of the selected participants (Carla, Silvia, and Matteo) were enrolled in two intermediate courses and used the app for a prolonged period of time.

3.3 Data Collection and Analysis

Data included classroom artifacts (screenshots of app conversations, reflection essays, photographs) and three fully transcribed semi-structured interviews. As a secondary data source, classroom observations of classroom discussions were also carried out.

Once a week, participants discussed their use of the language exchange app in a class activity called *Sharing Day*, during which learners shared one interesting image, word or story they had learned from their conversation partners. They included at least ten screenshots of their conversations and wrote short weekly reports in English (ten in total). Students openly wrote about their experiences in these weekly reports, which provided rich data sources, considering the fact that all knowledge is based on stories (Shank & Abelson, 1995). The data sources are summarized in Table 13.1.

Table 13.1. Data Types and Sources

Observations	Classroom discussions Discussions before/after class
Artifacts	Course work, including 4 compositions, 10 reflection reports, 1 portfolio (total of 400 pages of submitted assignments, 50 pages of coded data relating to the focus of inquiry) Follow-up questions on the students' reports and portfolio
Semi-structured interviews/recordings	Three semi-structured interview recordings, 25–30 minutes' duration each (total of 85 minutes of fully transcribed data)

3.4 Analytical Procedure

More than 400 pages of the students' weekly reports and final portfolios were reviewed, of which around 50 pages were selected and color-coded. These were judged to be representational of the participants' work. The screenshots were collected and marked, and connections were sought between the reports, the semi-structured interviews, and the screenshots of the conversations that students had submitted.

The data were coded using short keywords such as "imagined weekend in Italy" and "imagined future," although in some cases direct quotes were used, such as "I felt I was there." This pre-analysis helped to formulate some initial ideas. The codes were grouped into themes/nodes, and these were organized into larger categories. As discussed earlier, imagination can take on different forms (desire, fantasies, imagined presence, future or self), which do not necessarily lead to the development of new or temporary subjectivities. To better distinguish these differences and to better understand the use of multisensory communication, the notion of language play was used. Specifically, play with the frame (Warner, 2004) helped in pinpointing what learners played with and how they used multisensory communication to construct their imagination. Using Warner's definition, play with the frame refers to play with performance and the role of the speaker and is defined by pieces of discourse that might be derived from previous utterances and can be constructed in the form of behavior. To add to this definition, I considered not only previous utterances but multisensory conversations, including the exchange of images and other multimodal forms of communication that the learners utilized as they engaged in play with the frame. Finally, I used positioning theory (van Langenhove & Harrè, 1999) to analyze how participants positioned themselves and others in their narrative and conversations, demonstrating how they located themselves in social interactions.

I did not have access to all the conversations that participants had with their HelloTalk partners; the data included only the conversations that participants selected and wanted to share. Coincidentally, the screenshot examples of imagination that I had access to emerged only in conversations that occurred in English. While participants shared many screenshots in which they used mostly Italian, these did not contain examples of imagination and were therefore excluded. The collected data show prolonged use of the application (for at least two semesters), which in many cases resulted in developing friendships.

4 Findings

Two different types of co-constructed imagination could be identified in the data: 1) imagined projected self, and 2) imagined co-presence. As learners engaged in a multisensory conversation, they engaged in more complex forms of imagination, transcending the constraints of time and space and connecting with different epochs and spaces, turning them from static to more fluid ones. Through their multisensory communication, learners imagined how their partners lived their everyday lives. Thus, imagination served as a mediating element between physical and symbolic spaces, for example between the place one is sitting and the images in the HelloTalk exchange. Not all forms of imagination resulted in the construction of new or temporary subjectivities.

In some cases, learners reported on an imagined projected self that was either momentary or a projected future self. In other cases, they constructed their co-presence in a more playful way for their enjoyment. In both these types of imagination, emotions, desires, and fantasies are present and play an important role. In the following sections, examples are given of these two types of imagination, starting with the imagined projected self.

4.1 Imagined Projected Self

Imagined projected self refers to a type of imagination in which learners imagine being and moving within the space of their language exchange partner. This type of imagination is based on factual multisensory information exchanged by participants. The learners used multisensory communication to engage in a play with the frame by showcasing their familiarity with the Italian space. This allowed them to imagine entering into the space of their language exchange partners and regarding it as familiar. It resulted in their acquisition of temporary subjectivities such as *soon to be local*, *a young Italian*, and *local*. Participants made these plans for their future, but solely for their personal desires. The following sections present three examples of imagined projected self, each demonstrating a different aspect of the concept. The first example showcases Matteo's construction of temporary subjectivity as a soon to be local, reinforcing his multilingual subjectivity of a global citizen. The second example shows Laura's engagement in a role play of being a young Italian, and the third example shows Clara's multisensory play with the frame to project the self as a local.

4.1.1 Imagined Projected Self: Soon to Be Local

Matteo, who had never been to Italy, was a philosophy major, a veteran, a husband, and a father. He used the language exchange application very actively for two semesters. Using multisensory communication, he constructed an elaborate view of the space where his HelloTalk friend lived. His imagined view had an impact on his desires and helped him reinforce his subjectivities of being a global citizen and a multilingual.

> I was lucky enough to receive not only pictures of the famous Piazza, but how you get there. Which is by an old-style rail trolley. It's things like this that make me want to continue to travel the world because places like this have unfathomable stories to tell and are jaw dropping to witness in person, especially when you think about how long ago they were built and with so little resources for their time.

In the first sentence, Matteo positions himself as an insider, using the multimodal information he has gained from his HelloTalk friend. We can note the confidence in his explanation, demonstrated by the expression "how you get there," which shows his knowledge of and familiarity with the geographical space. When he describes the square, he engages in a translingual turn when he uses the word "piazza" in Italian, which indicates a shift toward the social identity of a multilingual speaker who is familiar not just with the space but with the language of the context as well, someone who easily moves between spaces.

Furthermore, Matteo explains how a "piazza" can trigger positive feelings in general. He uses the words "jaw dropping" and "unfathomable," which not only connect his emotional reaction to his past travel experiences but also show how he has built on those experiences in his imagination, thanks to the photos he has received from his partner. Both the expressed emotions and his display of knowledgeability about the space demonstrate the impact of his imagination. The multisensory communication allowed Matteo entrance into the community to desire and construct a subjectivity of a soon to be local. Although Matteo has never been to Italy, he did travel extensively during his military years. He has visited many Asian countries and started to learn Italian because of his passion for traveling. Engaging with Italian through multisensory communication reinforced his experiences so much that he started imagining himself in the space of his language exchange partner as a soon to be local.

> I will encourage my partner to keep sending me photos like this as she travels, which she does quite often. I also hope to be able to not only return the favor with some places from around here but one day show her some places she has been through my perspective.

The expression "I hope to be able to show her" not only shows his knowledgeability but also indicates his desire for the future to be in Italy, not just symbolically but also physically. Matteo expresses confidence that he will move around the same space in the near future, which shows that he has gained a cultural knowledge that has triggered his imagination and engagement.

At the beginning of the semester, Matteo's plan was to visit Italy with his wife and son; however, in a later reflection he wrote that it was "very thought engaging" and that while talking to his friend about his travel experiences, he realized that these were the times when he felt the happiest. He decided to make a "semi-permanent move to northern Italy," positioning himself as an active future participant in the Italian community. Below, the second example of imagined projected self demonstrates how Laura engaged in role play and took on a temporary subjectivity of a young Italian.

4.1.2 Imagined Projected Self: A Young Italian

Laura was a 19-year-old student who was planning to study abroad in Italy. In her report, Laura wrote that she often imagined and fantasized about being in Italy, and the images she received through HelloTalk made her want to go even more. Her engagement suggests that her interactions and construction of social relationships with her HelloTalk partner, similarly to Matteo, contributed to her projecting and constructing herself as a local, rather than as a tourist visiting the sights. Laura reflected on what she learned from the young Italians she communicated with, and how she positions their problems as her own problems, positioning herself as a future multilingual who can not only visit Italy as a study-abroad student but can also live as a young adult in Italy.

> She explained to me what it is like being a young adult in Italy. I thought this was important because it puts in perspective life in the United States compared to life in Italy at my age. It's something I'm about to have to deal with in a few short weeks and it makes you appreciative of the opportunities we have living in the United States. I never realized there was such a lack of jobs in Italy and if you want to find a job you have to move across the country to find one.

In this excerpt, Laura first takes an object position: "she explained to me" refers to her friend explaining and teaching her about the situation. But then, in the second sentence, she switches position: "something I'm about to have to deal with" is an expression that demonstrates her knowledgeability with regards to the social context and positions her as part of the community of Italians who are going through difficulties. It is also a play with the frame, as she switches from being a speaker-as-narrator to a speaker who imagines experiencing what the narrator reports on. The expressions "you want to find a job" and "you have to move" index "you" as someone living in Italy, but also position Laura as someone who is well informed about the situation. Because she mentions "I'm about to have to deal with [the situation]," the general "you" is also used to describe herself. If she were to say, "they have to find" and "they have to move," she would have excluded herself; instead, she opts to take an insider position.

Laura mentions that she is planning to study abroad the following semester. Typically, when students are planning to study abroad, they do not need to deal with finding a job. She imagines living the life of a young Italian, not that of a study-abroad student. She becomes a virtual participant in the Italian community and not only that, but her co-constructed imagined activities contribute to a change in her perception of studying abroad.

4.1.3 Imagined Projected Self: Moving in the Space as a Local

Carla, the third participant, used the HelloTalk application for about a year. During the study period, she communicated with the same HelloTalk friend for about six months. Carla was a graduate student on the course, working toward a PhD in astronomy. She was learning Italian for leisure, simply because she enjoyed it. She already spoke French, Flemish, Dutch, and English fluently. From her reports, it is clear that she spoke with her language exchange partner, Giovanni, every day and that they developed a special friendship. During the course, Carla mostly wrote about her friend Giovanni; she established a great connection with him, and they even decided to send each other gifts for Christmas. They exchanged many photos and audio messages on HelloTalk. Carla, like Matteo and Laura, became the speaker of the culture. She constructed an imagined getaway weekend in Giovanni's hometown. In her reflection essay, Carla talked about an imagined weekend that she would spend with Giovanni if she visited him and positioned herself as someone who could (hypothetically) function as a local in the Italian space of her friend.

> I have been imagining what a weekend would look like if I were to visit him. He has told me enough about his nights out with friends that I could imagine joining them when he goes back to Imperia during the weekend. If I were to go to Italy, we would probably start in Genoa, hopefully take the train (if it were to work again) or his car (and have to go through all the tolls) to go to Imperia. From there, we might stop at his grandparents' house, which seems like they would be awesome. His grandma would make me food, because she loves cooking for people. We would then go to his mom's house in the country. She lives about 20 minutes away from a city, so I think that it would be a very nice and pleasant drive.

Carla has constructed her imagined weekend based on the multisensory conversation that she had with her friend; this is clear from the information she has placed in parentheses, which contributes to the credibility of her imagined weekend by adding real-life details. For example, Carla playfully mentions about the train, "if it were to work again," because she knows from an image her language exchange friend sent her that the train was not operating because a truck got stuck on the tracks.

In her narrative, she enters into Giovanni's space, taking on the temporary identity of an expert and engaging in a play with the frame by using pieces of multisensory discourse to validate her temporary subjectivity as an expert of the local space.

The next section discusses the second type of imagination, imagined co-presence.

4.2 Imagined Co-Presence

Imagined co-presence refers to a type of imagination that happens instantly and co-constructively in the here and now, through synchronous conversations. It is not goal oriented, i.e., for the purposes of language learning, career or future plans, but is motivated by a playful, immediate enjoyment that may result in a felt experience and positive emotions in learners. During this form of imagination, the goal is not for learners to negotiate power or subjectivities but to play with the frame by taking advantage of the affordances of multisensory communication that allow learners to immerse themselves in each other's space instantaneously. Below, I present two examples: the first demonstrates the affective aspects learners experience as they enter the virtual space, while the second demonstrates the multisensory tools they playfully use to create their virtual presence.

4.2.1 Imagined Co-Presence: Affective Aspects of Entering a Virtual Space

Silvia, the fourth participant, was a major in early child education and a fan of Italian soccer. Through her multisensory conversations, she imagined being in Italy and taking part in the activities of her language exchange partner, which triggered an emotional reaction in her.

> These pictures really helped me picture what it is like to be there. Some of the pictures were so detailed it looked like and I feel like I was actually there in their exact shoes.

Silvia describes this embodiment with the use of two of her senses – "it looked like and I feel like I was actually there" indicates that what she has seen with her eyes, she can also physically feel with her body. She is able to feel emotions and temporarily take part in the space of her language exchange partner.

For both of her oral exams in two different courses Silvia chose to research and discuss Italian soccer. One of the photos she received from her language exchange partner was a point-of-view shot of him sitting in the stadium of the Juventus soccer team watching a game. When she received the photo, she immediately imagined being there with him. She perceived this photograph as different from other photos she had seen of the stadium because she considered it a "live image." This perception indicates that, just like Matteo who described the photos as "real life," Silvia also considered them to be dynamic rather than static, thereby emphasizing the make-believe power that these photos carry because of the social connections interwoven in them. This photo became a live image because it was a piece of a discourse Silvia synchronously constructed with her partner. The photo created the possibility for Silvia to not only enter into the space of her friend but also to synchronously feel the same emotions of experiencing a soccer game with her partner.

> He sent me a picture of the Juventus soccer stadium where he was sitting, and it felt like I was there in person experiencing the same thing he was experiencing. I immediately reacted and was in shock because it is my dream to watch Juventus play in person. This has been my dream since I was a little girl.

All the photos the participants sent to each other were taken with their cell phones, from the place where they were standing, sitting or walking. Point-of-view shots allow the viewer to enter into a narrative position and view the image from a subject position. And besides these point-of-view photos, other multisensory tools enriched them, so that they were perceived as "live" images. Through this image, Silvia was able to simultaneously be in the "here" position of her own space and a live "there" position of the Italian space; by doing so, she was able to virtually experience being at the game. Therefore, "I… was in shock" not only refers to her reaction upon seeing the picture of the Juventus stadium but also to the co-constructed experience of feeling as if she was at the game with her friend.

Silvia wrote about a couple of other cases when she felt as if she was there with her friend. In her reflection portfolio, she wrote about how these images and the accompanying experience triggered in her a desire to go to Italy and take part in the Italian lifestyle. The next example demonstrates how this co-presence may occur instantaneously in a conversation.

4.2.2 Imagined Co-Presence: Multisensory Tools to Create Virtual Presence

Matteo and his HelloTalk partner talked about a concert event synchronously. This direct discourse, pictured in Figure 13.3, shows a shared imagination taking shape instantly and a play with a frame that includes the use of non-verbal tools such as emojis that helped them imagine entering into the same space and acquiring new positions as participants in a common space.

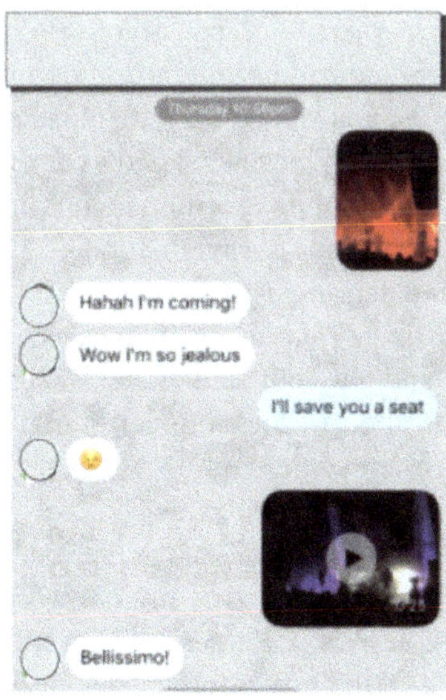

Figure 13.3. Matteo and his Exchange Partner Create a Virtual Common Space

When Matteo sent an image of the concert to his friend, she immediately responded, saying, "I'm coming!" In reply, Matteo entered into the imagined make-believe scene and answered, "I'll save you a seat," showing his friend that her virtual presence was welcomed and expected. His friend then sent an emoji of a winking face, acknowledging the participation in the make-believe game, in which they both imagined a physical presence that is replaced by a virtual one, in the space they created synchronously. As a follow-up, Matteo also sent a video of the concert, thinking of his friend and in this way contributing to a virtual space that included multiple channels, multiple synchronous semiotic elements of sound, image, and action. Through co-constructed imagination, Matteo and his friend acquired new positions as participants in their space(s). Their playful use of multisensory tools (videos, emojis) helped them enter into a play with the frame, during which they both positioned themselves as participants in the same time and space. Matteo and his language exchange partner did not engage in this type of imagined co-presence with a specific goal of language learning, career or future plans in mind but simply for their own enjoyment.

5 Conclusion

This chapter has explored how the informal multilingual digital space provides opportunities for learners to co-constructively imagine themselves as part of the Italian culture and language. I have presented two types of imagination: 1) imagined projected self, and 2) imagined co-presence. I propose that co-constructed imagination be considered as a new model for analyzing learners' engagement and use of imagination in multilingual digital contexts. In previous studies, the concepts of imagination and investment have often been connected to a predetermined goal related to language learning. However, the notion of investment reflects the learners' engagement in the present or an imagined future and may not fully cover the complexity afforded by multisensory communication in multilingual digital spaces. Although the discussed examples present some overlap with previously described concepts of imagination, there are recognizable complex forms and outcomes of imagination that differ from them. The main contribution of this paper is that the collaborative imagination afforded by multisensory communication may better capture learners' desires, fantasies, relationships, lived experiences, and the affective aspects of their (playful) engagement in language learning, which can lead to greater engagement and the development of (temporary) multilingual subjectivities.

Learners may invest in language learning with a goal related to language learning, such as negotiating the identity of an expert (Klimanova & Dembovskaya, 2013). Similarly, the participants presented here also (temporarily) position themselves as experts, or soon-to-be experts like locals; however, these positions are afforded to them through the multimodal exchange of multisensory co-constructed conversations, made possible by the digital space. Furthermore, not all cases presented here led to the development of new or temporary multilingual subjectivities. As demonstrated in the examples of co-constructed imagination, learners fantasize through a play with the frame using multisensory tools shared collaboratively. Co-constructed imagination can be considered an alternative to concepts of investment and imagination, as it shows how learners can (playfully) engage and participate in learning, can desire (temporary) subjectivities that do not necessarily relate to their future aspirations in connection with language learning but are potentially more fluid and relate to their emotional engagement, desires, and fantasies in the moment.

There are some noticeable connections between the types of imagination and language play with the frame (Warner, 2004; Vandergriff & Fuchs, 2009). In both examples, learners play with the frame by conducting a role play with different identities – although not necessarily for the purpose of negotiating power or an identity. The multisensory conversation in which participants exchanged pictures, emojis, videos, and messages evoked in them the feeling of presence and helped them (playfully) construct a co-presence, thereby allowing them the possibility of using this multimodal information to perform and take on different roles, such as experts – Italian locals – or momentary participants.

Malinowski (2014), using the concept of *synesthesia*, provided a great example of a form of imagination that describes how learners deconstruct time and space, without having a specific learning goal in mind. Similarly, in this study, all participants felt as if they were experiencing the same events as their language exchange partners, as demonstrated by their reported emotions and feelings. These learners experienced foreign language learning on an emotional as well as a linguistic level, and with the virtual presence of their bodies they were able to engage in meaning making (Kramsch, 2009) through co-constructed imagination. The examples presented here show us that co-constructed imagination can serve as an alternative to imagination and investment, as it better captures the affective aspects of learning and the process and complexity of how learners (playfully) maneuver in multilingual spaces. Because imagination creates an internalized view of our possible actions, it is a "staging ground for action" (Appadurai, 1996, p. 7); thus, it can influence learners' development of multilingual subjectivities.

6 Implications for Further Research

Throughout the study, students often remarked that the images they received had special meaning to them because they created a connection with their friend, or because their friend was in the image (behind the camera or in the picture itself). The social connections they formed appeared to be key to their imagination. What made the difference and engaged the learner more was the connection they made through the images and multimodal conversations with their friends. Future research and pedagogical approaches using virtual reality, augmented reality, and similar technologies can benefit from the study of co-constructed imagination, particularly in relation to learners' engagement and construction of multilingual subjectivities. For example, when such activities are designed, the inclusion of elements that allow for collaboration might contribute to co-constructed imagination. Because the learners in this study had access to the multilingual multicultural space, it helped them imagine alternative, momentary or future selves and participation in spaces where they could easily switch the language they used or utilize the possibilities of multisensory communication. Thus, participants' language-proficiency levels did not create barriers.

Looking at the level of investment in the HelloTalk application, although a detailed description of it goes beyond the remit of this paper, it is important to highlight that, based on the students' reports, the fact that the mobile app resembled a leisure activity was appealing to many. Like the participants in Malinowski (2014), learners were able to "draw themselves into" (p. 29) the time and space of their partners; therefore, pedagogies that make use of technology should consider creating opportunities for this type of engagement.

The limitation of the present study is that the examples from HelloTalk were those which students submitted and wanted me to see. Just because this study found evidence for the use of imagination only in conversations mostly carried out in English, it cannot be assumed that it did not happen in conversations that included more Italian (with other typical modes of digital communication). The multilingual and multisensory communication, however, certainly helped learners move more easily between spaces. My hope is that future studies will continue to explore the function and the power that co-constructed imagination has in multilingual and multisensory digital communication. Imagination in digital spaces, as described in this paper, can be a useful tool to explore the complexities of learners' online engagement and their ways of expressing their desires, needs, and fantasies and their construction of (temporary) multilingual subjectivities.

Acknowledgment

The author wishes to thank Dr. Chantelle Warner, the 2022 CALICO volume editor and anonymous reviewers for their valuable time and constructive feedback. Finally, I am grateful for the students who agreed to participate in this study, for their support and for sharing their work and time with me.

References

Anderson, B. (2006). Imagined communities: Reflections on the origin and spread of nationalism. Verso Books.

Appadurai, A. (1996). Modernity at large: Cultural dimensions of globalization (Vol. 1). University of Minnesota Press.

Bakhtin, M. (1984). Problems of Dostoevsky's poetics. Theory and History of Literature, Vol. 8. Transl. C Emerson (from Russian). University of Minneapolis Press.

Blommaert, J. (2005). Discourse: A critical introduction. Cambridge University Press.

Bourdieu, P. (1991). Language and symbolic power. Harvard University Press.

Bourdieu, P. (1997). Selections from the logic of practice. In A. D. Schrift (Ed.), The logic of the gift: Toward an ethic of generosity (pp. 190–230). Routledge.

Chen, H. I. (2013). Identity practices of multilingual writers in social networking spaces. Language Learning & Technology, 17(2), 143–170. doi: http://128.171.57.22/bitstream/10125/44328/17_02_chen.pdf

Cook, G. (2000). Language play, language learning. Oxford University Press.

Darvin, R., & Norton, B. (2015). Identity and a model of investment in applied linguistics. Annual Review of Applied Linguistics, 35, 36–56. doi: https://doi.org/10.1017/S0267190514000191

Decety, J., & Grèzes, J. (2006). The power of simulation: Imagining one's own and others' behavior. Brain research, 1079(1), 4–14. doi: https://doi.org/10.1016/j.brainres.2005.12.115

Early, M., & Norton, B. (2014). Revisiting English as medium of instruction in rural African classrooms. Journal of Multilingual and Multicultural Development, 35(7), 674–691.

García-Pastor, M. D. (2020). Researching identity and L2 pragmatics in digital stories: A relational account. Calico Journal, 37(1), 46–65. doi: https://doi.org/10.1558/cj.38777

Iwasaki, N. (2011). Learning L2 Japanese "politeness" and "impoliteness": Young American men's dilemmas during study abroad. Japanese Language and Literature, 67–106.

Kanno, Y. (2000). Bilingualism and identity: The stories of Japanese returnees. International Journal of Bilingual Education and Bilingualism, 3(1), 1–18. doi: 10.1080/13670050008667697

Kanno, Y. (2003). Negotiating bilingual and bicultural identities: Japanese returnees betwixt two worlds. Routledge.

Kanno, Y., & Norton, B. (2003). Imagined communities and educational possibilities: Introduction. Journal of Language, Identity, and Education, 2(4), 241–249.

Kanno, Y., & Norton, B. (2012). Imagined communities and educational possibilities: A special issue of the Journal of Language, Identity, and Education. Routledge.

Klimanova, L., & Dembovskaya, S. (2013). L2 identity, discourse, and social networking in Russian. doi: http://dx.doi.org/10125/24510

Kramsch, C. (2009). Cultural perspectives on language learning and teaching. Handbook of foreign language communication and learning (pp. 219–245). Mouton de Gruyter.

Lam, W. S. E. (2000). L2 literacy and the design of the self: A case study of a teenager writing on the Internet. TESOL Quarterly, 34(3), 457–482. DOI: https://doi.org/10.2307/3587739

Malinowski, D. (2014). Drawing bodies and spaces in telecollaboration: A view of research potential in synaesthesia and multimodality, from the outside. Pedagogies: An International Journal, 9(1), 63–85. doi: https://doi.org/10.1080/1554480X.2014.877559

Norton, B. (1997). Language, identity, and the ownership of English. TESOL Quarterly, 31(3), 409–429.

Norton, B. (2000). Identity and language learning: Gender, ethnicity and educational change. Editorial Dunken.

Norton, B. (2001). Non-participation, imagined communities and the language classroom. Learner Contributions to Language Learning: New Directions in Research, 6(2), 159–171.

Norton, B., & Williams, C. J. (2012). Digital identities, student investments and eGranary as a placed resource. Language and Education, 26(4), 315–329.

Ochs, E. (1996). Linguistic resources for socializing humanity. Cambridge University Press.

Ochs, E. (2002). Becoming a speaker of culture. In C. Kramsch (Ed.), Language acquisition and language socialization: Ecological perspectives (pp. 99–120). Continuum.

Pavlenko, A., & Norton, B. (2007). Imagined communities, identity, and English language learning. In International handbook of English language teaching (pp. 669–680). Springer US.

Peirce, B. N. (1995). Social identity, investment, and language learning. TESOL Quarterly, 29(1), 9–31.

Pham, L. B., & Taylor, S. E. (1999). From thought to action: Effects of process- versus outcome-based mental simulations on performance. Personality

and Social Psychology Bulletin, 25(2), 250–260. Doi: https://doi.org/10.1177/0146167299025002010
Sauro, S., & Zourou, K. (2019). What are the digital wilds? Language Learning and Technology, 23(1), 1–7. doi: https://doi.org/10125/44666
Schreiber, B. R. (2015). "I am what I am": Multilingual identity and digital translanguaging. Language Learning & Technology, 19(3), 69–87.
Shank, R., Abelson, R., & Abelson, R. (1995). Knowledge and meaning: The real story. Advances in Social Cognition, 5–81.
Szpunar, K. K., & McDermott, K. B. (2009). Episodic future thought: Remembering the past to imagine the future. Handbook of imagination and mental simulation, pp. 119–130.
Tajfel, H. (1974). Social identity and intergroup behaviour. Information (International Social Science Council), 13(2), 65–93. doi: https://doi.org/10.1177/053901847401300204
Tajfel, H. E. (1978). Differentiation between social groups: Studies in the social psychology of intergroup relations. Academic Press.
Taylor, S. E., Pham, L. B., Rivkin, I. D., & Armor, D. A. (1998). Harnessing the imagination: Mental simulation, self-regulation, and coping. American Psychologist, 53(4), 429. doi: https://doi.org/10.1037/0003-066X.53.4.429
Thorne, S. L., Black, R. W., & Sykes, J. M. (2009). Second language use, socialization, and learning in Internet interest communities and online gaming. The Modern Language Journal, 93(s1), 802–821. doi: https://doi.org/10.1111/j.1540-4781.2009.00974.x
van Langenhove, L., & Harré, R. (1999). Introducing positioning theory. Positioning theory: Moral contexts of international action (pp. 14–31). Blackwell Publishers Ltd.
Vandergriff, I., & Fuchs, C. (2009). Does CMC promote language play? Exploring humor in two modalities. Calico Journal, 27(1), 26–47.
Walton, K. L. (1990). Mimesis as make-believe: On the foundations of the representational arts. Harvard University Press.
Warner, C. N. (2004). It's just a game, right? Types of play in foreign language CMC. Language Learning & Technology, 8(2), 69–87.
Weedon, C. (Ed.). (1997). Post-war women's writing in German: Feminist critical approaches. Berghahn Books.
Wenger, E. (1998). Communities of practice: Learning, meaning, and identity. Cambridge University Press.
Yang, S. J., & Yi, Y. (2016). Negotiating multiple identities through eTandem learning experiences. Calico Journal, 34(1), 97–114.
Yashima, T. (2013). Individuality, imagination and community in a globalizing world: An Asian EFL perspective. The applied linguistic individual-sociocultural approaches to identity, agency and autonomy. Equinox eBooks Publishing, pp. 46–58. doi: 10.1558/equinox.20857

About the Author

Borbala Gaspar is a Lecturer of Italian at the University of Arizona. Her research focuses on how (underrepresented) language learners maneuver through social and symbolic power as they gain agency, use imagination, and engage in pedagogies such as project-based learning, task-based learning, and (multi)literacies.

14 Re-establishing Multilingual Identities through Telecollaborative Experience

Se Jeong Yang

1 Introduction

Telecollaboration is "generally understood to be Internet-based intercultural exchange between people of different cultural national backgrounds, set up in an institutional context with the aim of developing both language skills and intercultural communicative competence through structured tasks" (Guth & Helm, 2010, p. 14). Telecollaboration can take place between two or more groups of people with different first language (L1) or two individual people with different L1. In many situations, telecollaboration participants are second language (L2) learners who want to learn their partner's first language. At the same time, the participants teach their L1 to their partners. Given the nature of telecollaboration which includes interactions among target language learners and target language speakers, scholars have examined how telecollaboration affects participants' linguistic competence (Cheon, 2012; O'Dowd, 2005; Goertler et al., 2018; Llopis-García & Vinagre, 2014; Taskiran, 2019) and cultural competence (Hagley, 2016; Mullen & Bortoluzzi, 2019; Toscu & Erten, 2020).

Studies have found that the reciprocal relationship of the telecollaboration allows language learners to improve their L2 and cultural knowledge (Goertler et al., 2018). In addition, by teaching to and learning from their partners, participants play multiple roles. In this process of interaction, the participants can negotiate their identities. However, there have not been many studies that focused on the concept of identity in the telecollaborative context. Particularly, there is a lack of studies examining heritage language learners' identity construction in a telecollaborative context. In order to have a better understanding of heritage language learners' identity construction during telecollaboration, the current study aims to fill this gap and explore one Korean heritage language learner's (KHL) construction of her identities in relation to the community to which she aspires to belong. Heritage language in this paper refers to a language which has "a particular family relevance" and can be transmitted across generations, but may or may not be used at home (Fishman, 2001, p. 169). The current study investigates a heritage language learner's identity construction and negotiation as well as heritage language development. By examining identity work and L2 learning in the online community as social practices, this study explores the following two research questions: 1) How does a heritage language learner construct her identities in a telecollaborative learning context? 2) How are heritage language practices related to a heritage language learner's identity construction in an online context? In fact, second or foreign language learning has different approaches from the heritage language learning area. However, considering that the current study includes English language learners who are learning English as their foreign or second language and Korean language learners who are learning Korean as their heritage language as partners, I use the term second language (L2) in a general way and I group a Korean heritage language as well as English language learners into a second language learner category. This chapter first introduces two theoretical frameworks, communities of practice (CoP) and imagined communities, before offering a discussion of one case study.

2 Theoretical Frameworks

According to a sociocultural theory (SCT) (Vygotsky, 1978), language learning is constructed through social interaction. The SCT framework views the human's development as "mediated by others, whether they are immediately present as in the case of parents guiding children or teachers guiding students, or displaced in time and space, as when we read texts produced by others or participate in activities such as work, organized in specific ways by a culture" (Lantolf, 2007, p. 32). As Lantolf and Thorne (2006) point out, the SCT framework understands mediation as "the process through which humans deploy culturally constructed artifacts, concepts, and activities to regulate (i.e. gain voluntary control over and transform) the material world or their own and each other's social and mental activity" (p. 79). Culturally constructed artifacts can be physical tools (e.g. technology) or symbolic tools (e.g. literacy, language). Thus, according to the SCT perspective, a human's development is mediated by tools like language or technology which connect humans. Wenger's (1998) idea of communities of practice is in line with the SCT framework in that the social interaction is critical in human development.

CoP is defined as "groups of people who share a concern, a set of problems, or a passion for a topic, and who deepen their knowledge and expertise in this area by interacting on an ongoing basis" (Wenger et al., p. 4). From a CoP perspective, learning requires active participation in a particular community of practice which includes the concept of legitimate peripheral participation in which "newcomers" are socialized by "old-timers" to become legitimate members of community through learning how to complete tasks (Lave & Wenger, 1991). Wenger (1998) explains that participation in a community of practice includes "a more encompassing process of being active participants in the practices of social communities and *constructing identities* in relation to these communities" (p. 4). Through this process, novices become experts in the practices of a community. Thus, a CoP perspective suggests that learning which entails participation in a community of practice transforms "who we are and what we can do… it is a process of becoming – to become a certain person," which refers to one's identity construction (Wenger, 1998, p. 215). Thus, learning inevitably affects one's identity. This is connected to Gee's (2003) explanations on the relationship between identity and learning. According to Gee, active learning leads to the construction of identity formation and constructing one's identity is one of the important processes leading to successful learning.

According to post-structuralists, "identities are contingent, shifting and context-dependent, and that while identities or positions are often given by social structures or ascribed by others, they can also be negotiated by agents who wish to position themselves" (Norton & Toohey, 2011, p. 418). These flexible and fluid natures of identities are connected to the process of learning (Gee, 2003). Second, foreign, or heritage language learners particularly can construct their identities in relation to a target language community to which they wish to belong. Norton (2001) explains this idea using the term "imagined communities." Imagined communities refer to "groups of people, not immediately tangible and accessible, with whom we connect through the power of imagination" (Kanno & Norton, 2003, p. 241). Norton (2001) explains that "imagined communities are best understood in the context of a learner's unique investment in the target language and the conditions under which he or she speaks and practices it" (p. 165). Wenger (1998) suggested that imagination is one form of belonging to a particular community and a way in which individuals locate themselves (Kanno & Norton, 2003; Pavlenko & Norton, 2007). Drawing on the idea of imagined communities, Sung (2019) examined one L2 student's lived experiences of learning a second language. This L2 student put his effort to learn English selectively according to his association with his own imagined communities. Since this L2 student aspired to work in a multilingual, multicultural environment in an international company, he made an extra effort to establish a social circle with English speakers in his work space. The study showed how learners' varying degrees of L2 investments across contexts are closely related to identities that the learner constructed and their future career and communities which they wanted to access.

3 Identity Construction in Online Contexts

According to Turkle (1995), the identity construction can be more complex in an online context since it can provide an opportunity of "a fundamental reconsideration of human identity" (p. 321). Considering that L2 learning often occurs online, there have been some empirical studies that examined second, foreign, or heritage language learners' identity constructions online.

One of the seminal studies, Black's (2005, 2006, 2008) online fanfiction study, showed how L2 learners of English used not only English but also other semiotic resources to express their multilingual identities in one online fanfiction site. Fanfiction studies show that the online fanfiction sites provide a great way of developing literacy and identity practices, which are different from the traditional offline classroom learning (Black, 2008; Sauro, 2017).

More studies of online context with the topics of identity construction of L2 learners have come out recently. As Turkle (1995) argued, L2 learners seem to construct new online identities which are different from their offline identities, which is also tightly related to their increasing level of confidence since they interact with target language speakers online and do not have to worry about losing face. This newly constructed online identity as L2 learners helps develop their L2 skills (Cappellini, 2016; Dooly & Sadler, 2013; Jin, 2017; Luzón, 2018; Rezaei & Latifi, 2020). Although there have not been many telecollaborative studies exploring the topic of identity construction for heritage language learners specifically, the existing telecollaborative studies including heritage language learners have found distinct advantages of using telecollaborative contexts for heritage language learners including 1) cultural connection to their family (Yang & Yi, 2017), 2) community access (Deusen-Scholl, 2018), and 3) multilingual identity (Klimanova, 2020). As Reyes and Vallone (2007) point out, particularly for heritage language learners, the online environments of telecollaboration could offer a chance to "access their [heritage] language and culture [which] allows them to 'read the world' through a multicultural lens" (p. 8). The online interaction can allow them to rethink their identities and cultures, while learning their heritage languages and cultures.

In sum, previous studies showed that online contexts allow language learners to construct their new identities while interacting with other learners. Drawing from previous research, the current study examines heritage language learners' identity construction in a telecollaborative context. Grounded in the theoretical concepts of CoP and imagined communities that highlight the importance of social interaction in learning, the current study aims to explore how one heritage language learner's community participation could affect her identity construction and heritage language learning.

4 Methodology

4.1 Participants and the Context

The current study adopts a qualitative case study research paradigm (Yin, 2003). Data for this chapter were drawn from a larger study which was conducted over a period of nine months, with the focus on exploring the concepts of identity and second language learning with eight pairs of adult participants. The larger study (Yang & Yi, 2017) included two adult language groups: Korean-dominant English language learners (ELLs) whose first language is Korean, and English-dominant Korean heritage learners (KHLs) whose first language is English. The volunteers in the two groups ranged in age from 21 to 45 and had a variety of professional occupations. Ten were females and five were males.

ELLs are Koreans who grew up in Korea and came to the U.S. for various reasons; they were learning English at the time of the study. KHLs are Korean-Americans who were born and raised in an English-dominant society such as the U.S. and Canada. They were learning Korean as their heritage language at the time of the study. All the participants had varying degrees of proficiency in both Korean and English. Their second language proficiency was based on their self-evaluation and the researcher's observation. The researcher partnered a member of one language group with a member from the other language group based on their self-rated L2 proficiency and their interests as reported in a pre-project questionnaire and an initial individual face-to-face interview. ELLs and KHLs were connected using Google Blogger, Google Hangout, and email. This chapter presents a case study of one KHL, Kristine (pseudonym), and examines two topics – identity construction and

L2 learning – in the telecollaborative learning context. Kristine's story is representative of the KHLs' experience and clearly illustrates one heritage language learner's struggles with her identity construction and the development of heritage language skills. By focusing on one focal participant, a researcher can capture more nuanced and holistic views on an individual's identity construction online (Duff, 2008). Since a case study design emphasizes a thorough investigation of the context in which an individual's thoughts and lifestyle can be closely captured (Yin, 2003), a qualitative case study design was an ideal research method for the current study in order to capture the nature of identity construction of the participant in an online context.

4.2 Data Collection Procedures

In the larger study, in order to diversify the participant pool, the researcher recruited participants using various sources such as online social media, personal connection, and a snowball recruitment procedure. Once the participants were identified, they completed the pre-project questionnaire and the initial interview with the researcher as the first data collection process. Then, in the first week of collaboration, each pair exchanged an introductory email with their partner. In the following weeks, the participants were asked to complete weekly online tasks, such as participant blogs using Google Blogger, online chatting using Google Hangout, reflective journals via email, and community blog writing using Google Blogger. These four required tasks focused on the topic announced by the researcher every week. The weekly topics included L2 learning experience, food, movies, the Korean Wave – the increasing popularity of Korean pop culture around the world, memories from school, Korea's reunification, English fever in Korea, immigration, travel, and online friends. As the first weekly task, the participants were asked to write a blog post about the weekly topic in their L2 for the shared blog space (Figure 14.1) between the partners. This shared space was where each partner was asked to exchange their feedback on the other's posts in terms of content and language. Thus, KHLs wrote their blog posts in Korean as their L2 and ELLs wrote their blog posts in English as their L2, and they gave their feedback on their partner's writing. Then, each pair had one 30-minute text chat session every week in both their L1 and L2. After that, the participants were asked to join the group discussion in the community blog and choose either L1 or L2 for communication purposes. While the shared blog was for interaction between each pair, the community

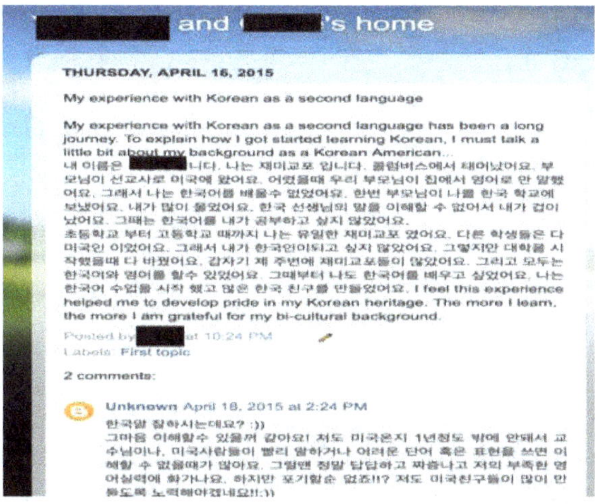

Figure 14.1. A Screenshot of a Shared Blog Between Partners

blog was for more diverse interactions among all the participants where each participant could share their ideas with other participants. Finally, as the last weekly task, they were asked to write a weekly reflective diary about their interactions with their partner or other participants, either in L1 or L2, with a minimum of 200 words, and send it to the researcher. Depending on their schedule, some pairs had daily interactions using the blog and chatting, while others had one- or two-day interactions to complete these four tasks. Bi-weekly, the researcher also interviewed each participant to check the status of weekly tasks and discuss any difficulties that they might have had during the projcct.

The current study draws on Kristine's data including her blog posts, interviews, and reflective diary. She completed all the tasks, which included ten blog entries in her shared blog, 25 posts of varying lengths in the community blog, and the chat sessions with her partner which usually lasted more than an hour, as well as seven interviews.

4.3 Data Analysis

Kristine's case study necessarily required data not only from interview scripts and her entries in the personal blog and the reflective journal but also from her chatting scripts with her partner, the feedback she was given from her partner, and her interactions with other members in the community blog. Central to the current study is identity construction in relation to L2 learning.

Table 14.1. Meta-codes and Properties of the Themes that Emerged

Meta-code	Property
Community	Imagination/imagined communities
L2 learning (i.e., Korean heritage language learning)	Investment
	L2 practice
Identity construction	Confidence/self-perception
	Koreanness/heritage Identity/multilingual self

This study used content analysis (Kondracki et al., 2002), which is for classification of written or oral materials (Cho & Lee, 2014).

The researcher began reading the data from beginning to end to obtain a general understanding (Tesch, 2013). Then the researcher reread the data to derive codes by highlighting text that appeared to signal identity construction and the focal participant's heritage language learning. Through this process, the researcher made notes of the impressions, thoughts, and initial analysis. As this process continued, some key words for codes emerged. These became the initial coding scheme. The researcher examined the data based on these codes. Finally, the researcher examined the final codes to group codes into meaningful clusters. After preliminary analysis, the researcher checked with the participant to share her analysis and get her insights for member checking to establish trustworthiness. Based on the identified codes (see Table 14.1), the findings were organized into three subsections: the focal participant's identity construction, her L2 practices, and her multilingual identity. The other meta code, community, was embedded and described in these subsections.

5 Findings

5.1 Reconceptualizing Koreanness

Kristine was born in the U.S. to Korean parents. At the time of the study, Kristine was in her 30s and worked as a nurse. While growing up, she did not communicate with her parents in Korean, although she mentioned that her parents regretted not raising their children with the language of their heritage. Her parents spoke in English to each other and to Kristine. They worked full time and did not have time to pay attention to their children's Korean language skills. Kristine reported that she was the only Korean in her middle and high schools, which sometimes led her to feel confused about her heritage identity. In this study, Kristine was partnered with Jin, a Korean ELL learner in his late 20s who was studying economics at a U.S. college. Jin was an intermediate English language learner and often made some grammatical mistakes in his English writing.

During the first week of the exchange, Kristine expressed excitement for the project as well as a high level of anxiety related to her inability to express ideas in Korean more professionally: "I was very nervous the first time because I did not want [my partner] to laugh at my Korean" (online interview, 4/25/15). At the beginning of the study, she was not confident about her writing proficiency in Korean and was worried that her exchange partner was looking down on her due to her poor Korean language skills. In the first week's journal, Kristine mentioned that she "was easily embarrassed by my language deficiencies" (reflective journal, 4/19/15). Although there was no one who attempted to evaluate her Korean language skills, her self-evaluative term for her Korean language proficiency as "deficien[t]" in her reflective journal signals her identity as a low-proficient Korean language learner. Her low self-competence in the Korean language seems to connect to her cultural identity. She seemed to struggle with her identities. In the community blog, she mentioned: "I am proud of my Korean heritage... but I do not feel like I am fully Korean" (5/30/15, group discussion). This phrase signifies her aspiration to identify herself as Korean but her pride does not result in a Korean identity. She felt intimacy with a Korean community, but her saying "I do not feel like I am fully Korean" implies her psychological distance from the Korean community, which shows her struggle in claiming her heritage identity. Her struggles with her identities seemed to be also caused by her perception of Koreanness. She attributed certain characteristics of Korean which she thought that she lacked to her insufficient status as Korean as she mentioned, "I guess I assumed certain personality traits were common to all Koreans. I did not carry these traits, which I assumed would make me Korean" (online interview, 6/19/15). Although Kristine did not explain exactly the traits to be Korean, her whole dataset implies that she connected language proficiency to her heritage identity as one of the important traits. Her experience in this online community seemed to provide her with insights into her identity as Korean. Another statement in her diary shows she appreciated this project for that reason.

> [This online learning experience] has connected me with my Korean heritage in a meaningful and fun way. This was something I always wanted, but I could not experience until now. What my parents could

> not do – teaching me Korean and showing me Korean things – I learned from this project (reflective journal, 6/19/15).

By saying "I always wanted," Kristine longed to join her imagined Korean community, in which she could celebrate her pride as Korean. Having the imagined community seemed to affect her language practices. She was one of the most enthusiastic learners in this study. For the weekly writing task, she mentioned to the researcher in a personal communication that she spent an enormous amount of time and effort in finding better ways to express her ideas in Korean sentences and consulted her Korean-speaking parents about syntactic rules. She showed her motivation and investment in improving her Korean language skills. She also mentioned that her purpose for joining this project was to learn the Korean language and culture, and she wanted to be close to a Korean-speaking community.

She had wanted to join Korean communities but she did not feel confident to claim as Korean, showing her identity struggle. However, this struggle with her identities began to abate as she interacted with different Korean participants in this online community. As one of the most active participants, she had many opportunities to interact with the participants in a community blog. Through this interaction, she learned new perspectives on some topics from other Korean speakers. For the sixth weekly topic, Kirogi family, she initiated her entry including her negative views toward Kirogi family. The term "Kirogi families" refers to families who live separately in different countries in order to provide a better learning environment for their children. The phenomenon of Kirogi families was partly derived from Koreans' aspiration to master English. As a native English speaker who was eager to learn the Korean language and culture, Kristine thought that it was "strange to [her] that people would want to come here as international students" (reflective diary, 6/1/15). Upon another participant's comment to her post on Kirogi family, she replied:

> I am so glad to hear your children are enjoying school here. I didn't know many Kirogi families personally, so I was only writing from my thoughts. Thank you for introducing me to the positive things about Kirogi situation (group discussion, 6/2/15).

In this process of learning from others in the community blog, she seemed to build a membership in this community. As time went on, she seemed to enjoy communicating with other members and she sometimes made humorous comments on others' posts, while other times she made more serious comments. Indeed, many participants remembered her name and addressed her writings in their reflective journals. She seemed to feel comfortable with talking to other participants, which was seen in her friendly comments on others' posts.

This relationship helped her voice her honest thoughts. For example, without other participants' prompt or question to her, her initiation of narrating her personal story with her honest feeling, "I can never feel comfortable saying I am proud to be an American. Is this wrong? Should I feel pride? I don't know" (5/30/15, group discussion), implies that this online space seems more than just an L2 learning context. She seemed to consider this online community as a safe space where one can candidly express ideas. She knew that she would not be blamed by the disclosure of her cultural identity, which encouraged her to talk about her feeling. This also signifies that the members of this online community had already built camaraderie. Kristine mentioned that she felt comfortable in this online community because "it is encouraging to know other people are having similar struggles, frustrations and doubts when we are learning something. It is good to have others around with whom we can work through the difficulties together" (reflective diary, 4/19/15). A sense of membership in the online community helped her establish a more confident self and feel closer to her imagined community. She also mentioned:

> I realized Koreans are all different. There is no "Korean personality trait"… this [participation in this online project] was a positive experience because it made me feel like it is not so hard to identify myself as Korean as I thought. I think I feared being rejected by Koreans for not being "Korean" enough. But I realized there is no such thing like this… I felt accepted by this Korean community and it helped me to be accepted [sic]… my Korean heritage as well (6/19/15, online interview).

Her active participation in an online community helped her demystify the stereotypes of Korean people.

5.2 Reconceptualizing what a Good L2 Learner is

Kristine's interaction with other Koreans not only helped her reconceptualize Koreanness and her Korean identity but also affected her language practices. As she had opportunities to read other L2 learners' writings in the community blog, her L2 learning encountered a new phase. The interaction with other members in the community blog gave her a lot of insight into her ideas about what makes a good L2 learner. She stated:

> I was more self-conscious to my Korean… [but it] does not have to be perfect… looking at others' Korean… even when I saw Sara's Korean… her Korean is very different from other Korean-Koreans' I think, but she puts [her writing] out there, she tried to express her ideas [in Korean] and she did not care… [whether] that is exactly right or wrong (10/19/15, face-to-face interview).

Previously, Kristine thought that she needed to post a "perfect" Korean text in the community blog, which made her "feel nervous" about writing in Korean (online interview, 4/25/2015). Her self-pressure to produce "perfect" writing" became mitigated by observing other L2 learners' writings in the blog.

Another moment that helped increase her language confidence came when she had a chance to correct her partner's English expressions in their blog. When Jin asked some questions regarding English expressions or grammar, Kristine mentioned that she had to study some English grammar to teach him. Interestingly, this teacher position gave her an opportunity to reflect on her own English skills and the sense of difficulty of the English language. "I realized – English is hard! I don't even understand some English grammar rules. So how can I correct someone when I often don't know why something sounds wrong" (online interview, 4/25/2015). Also, this experience helped her realize that native speakers do not know everything in their L1, which relieved the pressure she felt to write perfect Korean sentences in the project with Korean-speaking participants. These reflective moments as a Korean language learner and native English speaker challenged her identities and preconception of what a good L2 learner is and helped her reestablish a sense of confident self. Indeed, she mentioned that she used Korean more comfortably. She also used the Korean language in her daily life more often. She mentioned that she frequently talked to her parents in Korean.

In the last online interview, Kristine noted, "I felt accepted by this Korean community and it helped me to be accepted [sic]… my Korean heritage as well" (online interview, 6/19/15). Her feeling of being "accepted by this Korean community" seemed to enable her to see her future possible self as a *speaker* of KHL and as a legitimate member of an imagined community, all of which led her to accept who she is now.

Table 14.2. Language Choice and the Number of Posts in the Community Blog

Kristine's language choice in community blog	Number of posts during weeks 1–3	Number of posts during weeks 4–6	Number of posts during weeks 7–9
Korean writing	1	3	2
English writing	3	3	3

5.3 Re-imagining Multilingual Identity

As a native English speaker, at the beginning of the study Kristine used predominantly English in her writing. When she had chat sessions with her partner, she used Korean for at least a half hour per week, but she used English for more than a half hour. When she had a biweekly interview with the researcher, she mostly used English at the beginning of the study.

Over time, her language practices have noticeably changed. She chose Korean more often when she interacted with her partner as well as with the researcher. Interestingly, as she rebuilt her confidence level at the end of the study, her posts in the community blog became more diverse in terms of language choices. When she interacted with other English speakers (i.e., KHLs) in the community blog, she used English, which represents her multilingual abilities (Table 14.2). Through interacting with other participants, she developed a sense of camaraderie, which positively affected her development of Korean language skills and helped her accept herself as who she is. The reconstruction of her identity allowed her to embrace her multilingual abilities so that she used the Korean language with the Korean speakers and the English language with other KHLs like her. In a personal communication with the researcher at the end of the study, she stated that she became a multilingual, which made her feel great about herself. Thereby, her reconstruction of Koreanness and reconceptualization of a good Korean language learner allowed her to establish her confident identity. In the following section, I situate these findings within the theories of CoP and imagined communities.

6 Discussion

Kristine's story draws attention to the relationship between language learning and identity construction. Her story showed an evolving sense of self. At first it showed her identity struggles as a heritage language learner. Then, she realized that Koreanness is diverse and varies so that all Koreans do not fit into one category of Koreanness. She learned that cultural identity is not as simple as the sum of certain characteristics. Her realization of Koreanness also allowed her to accept her multilingual self.

6.1 Envisioning Imagined Communities

Kristine alluded to her longing for a target language community and aspired to be a legitimate member of the community, which represents her imagined communities. The envisioning of her future possible self led her to improve her Korean language skills, which strengthened her Korean heritage identity. Similar to the participants in Goble's (2016) study, at the beginning of the study, Kristine felt she did not have the "Korean personality traits," including her Korean language skills, which led her to experience low self-confidence. At first, she positioned herself at the periphery of the community since she did not fit into her pre-conception of Koreanness. She said, "I think I feared being rejected by Koreans for not being 'Korean' enough" (6/19/15, online interview). Based on her perception of Koreanness which resulted in her belief that she was not fully qualified to be Korean, she thought that she might not be accepted as a legitimate member in a Korean community. Her imagined community was not tangible to her but rather she felt that it was distant from her. However, through her active participation in the community blog, she was assisted and supported by more proficient Korean language learners and Korean speakers. Her interaction with diverse KHLs and ELLs was an opportunity for her to realize that every Korean is different and there was no one particular type of Koreanness as she had imagined before.

6.2 Establishing Communities of Practice

Kristine's active participation in this online community of practice, which is intertwined with learning about her heritage language and her identity, led her to become a *legitimate* member of the community. She developed a strong sense of membership (Lave & Wenger, 1991) and felt that this online community was a "safe space" (Yi, 2009, p. 117) to freely enact her identities since all of the participants were different in terms of their characteristics and everybody seemed to accept these differences. At the same time, she recognized the shared identities among the community members (Klimanova, 2020). As time went on, Kristine more actively participated in the community blog by commenting on most of the other participants' posts (Table 14.2). Kristine's use of increased Korean language in the community blog signals solidarity with the community, which is seen as her enactment of heritage identity. This online community appeared to highly contribute to promote her multilingual abilities since not only the Korean language but also the English language was frequently used in different contexts. As mentioned, at the end of the study she commented that she became a multilingual, which shows her multilingual identity as she developed her heritage language. Her multilingual practices in the community blog signal her different identities. Her language choices reflected her growing relationship with community members and her motivation to be perceived as a Korean speaker by others. As time went on, she interacted with other KHLs in English, revealing her English speaker identity. At the same time, when she interacted with other Korean speakers, she tried to communicate in Korean, signaling her heritage identity. Her active participation in the community helped her reconstruct her identity, which is what Wenger (1998) suggests in the theory of CoP.

Having a sense of community through the telecollaborative learning experience seemed to be beneficial for not only reconstructing her heritage identity but also securing emotional support while she was overcoming her learning struggles (Lam, 2009). Kristine's diary well represented her experience of feeling a sense of community. Indeed, there were many participants who had a similar background to Kristine's as well as Korean speakers who shared the same heritage, which helped Kristine feel more comfortable and connected to them. Kristine's case resonates with the findings of Yi's study (2009). Yi shows that an online community is a safe environment for identity construction in that one Korean-American participant, Joan, practiced her multilingual skills using various online resources to reflect her identities which she would not reveal in other places. Similarly, Black (2006) examined the identity construction and language development of one Japanese-American youth, Nanako, in an online fanfiction site. As Nanako developed intimate relationships with other participants in the fanfiction site, she was supported by them emotionally and linguistically, and was able to practice and develop her L2 skills as well as multilingual identities. Like participants in Yi (2009) and Black (2006), Kristine learned her L2 and developed her new selves through a "collaborative and participatory form of writing" (Thorne et al., 2009, p. 806) in this online community.

7 Conclusion and Future Direction

The current research examined how one heritage language speaker constructs and negotiates multiple identities in an online community and how

L2 learning is practiced in relation to identity construction. The current study has some pedagogical and theoretical significance. First, it shows a more nuanced view of the HL learner's complex construction of identity. The study presents one KHL's ambivalent feelings of identities and her struggles. Second, the study illuminates the importance of community in online spaces for second or foreign language learners. It elaborates how a sense of intimate camaraderie that the community members developed affects Kristine's heritage language practices and identity construction. Finally, this study adds a new insight to the interactions between heritage language learners and heritage language speakers. These participants' shared identities as Korean helped them develop a stronger community membership. At the same time, as Kristine realized, the participants have their own distinctive ideas and identities, which can make the community a more exciting space for learning. The interaction occurred in a telecollaborative context in this study, which is a good venue for both groups since they can learn language and culture from one another without spatial and temporal barriers.

Despite the implications mentioned above, there are some limitations of the current research. Although the current study adopts a case study method in order to collect a more thorough understanding of language learners' identity construction and language practices, the findings of this research are based on one participant in the context of a specific research design. In this sense, Kristine's story does not represent all the heritage language learners and it could be a partial view of language and identity construction of heritage language learners. The study was based on a small number of participants who had Korean and bilingual abilities to some degree. Future research may include more populations from more diverse backgrounds.

References

Black, R. W. (2005). Access and affiliation: The literacy and composition practices of English-language learners in an online fan fiction community. *Journal of Adolescent and Adult Literacy*, *49*(2), 118–128.

Black, R. W. (2006). Language, culture, and identity in online fanfiction. *E-Learning and Digital Media*, *3*(2), 170–184, 257.

Black, R. W. (2008). Just don't call them cartoons: The new literacy spaces of anime, manga and fanfiction. In J. Coiro, M. Knobel, C. Lankshear, & D. J. Leu (Eds.), *Handbook of research on new literacies*, Routledge.

Cappellini, M. (2016). Roles and scaffolding in teletandem interactions: A study of the relations between the sociocultural and the language learning dimensions in a French–Chinese teletandem. *Innovation in Language Learning and Teaching, 10*(1), 6–20.

Cheon, H. (2012). *Linguistic affordances of Korean-English tandem learning.* Unpublished doctoral dissertation. Columbia University, New York.

Cho, J. Y., & Lee, E. H. (2014). Reducing confusion about grounded theory and qualitative content analysis: Similarities and differences. *Qualitative Report, 19*(32).

Deusen-Scholl, V. (2018). The negotiation of multilingual heritage identity in a distance environment: HLA and the plurilingual turn. *CALICO Journal, 35*(3), 235–256.

Dooly, M., & Sadler, R. (2013). Filling in the gaps: Linking theory and practice through telecollaboration in teacher education. *ReCALL, 25*(1), 4–29.

Duff, P. (2008). *Case study research in applied linguistics*. Erlbaum.

Fishman, J. A. (2001). 300-plus years of heritage language education in the United States. In J. K. Peyton, D. A. Ranard, & S.McGinnis (Eds.), *Heritage languages in America. Preserving a national resource* (pp. 81–89). Center for Applied Linguistics.

Gee, J. (2003). *What video games have to teach us about learning and literacy.* Palgrave Macmillan Ltd.

Goble, R. (2016). Linguistic insecurity and lack of entitlement to Spanish among third-generation Mexican Americans in narrative accounts. *Heritage Language Journal, 13*(1). 29–52.

Goertler, S., Schenker, T., Lesoski, C., & Brunsmeier, S. (2018). Assessing language and intercultural learning during telecollaboration. In S. Link & J. Li (Eds.), *Assessment across online language education* (pp. 21–48). Equinox Publishing Ltd.

Guth, S., & Helm, F. (2010). *Telecollaboration 2.0: Languages, literacies and intercultural learning in the 21st century*. Peter Lang.

Hagley, E. (2016). Making virtual exchange/telecollaboration mainstream – large scale exchanges. In S. Jager, M. Kurek, & B O'Rourke (Eds.), *New directions in telecollaborative research and practice: Selected papers from the second conference on telecollaboration in higher education* (pp. 225–230). Research-publishing.net.

Jin, L. (2017). Digital affordances on WeChat: Learning Chinese as a second language. *Computer Assisted Language Learning, 31*(1–2), 27–52.

Kanno, Y., & Norton, B. (2003). Imagined communities and educational possibilities: Introduction. *Journal of Language, Identity, and Education, 2*(4), 241–249.

Klimanova, L. (2020). The phenomenology of experiencing oneself online: Critical dimensions of identity and language use in virtual spaces. In M. Freiermuth & N. Zarrinabadi (Eds.), *Technology and the psychology of second language learners and users* (pp. 279–308). Palgrave Macmillan.

Kondracki, N. L., Wellman, N. S., & Amundson, D. R. (2002). Content analysis: Review of methods and their applications in nutrition education. *Journal of Nutrition Education and Behavior, 34*(4), 224–230.

Lam, W. S. E. (2009). Multiliteracies on instant messaging in negotiating local, translocal, and transnational affiliations: A case of an adolescent immigrant. *Reading Research Quarterly*, *44*(4), 377–397.
Lantolf, J. P. (2007). Sociocultural source of thinking and its relevance for second language acquisition. *Bilingualism: Language and Cognition*, *10*(1), 31–33.
Lantolf, J. P., & Thorne, S. L. (2006). *Sociocultural theory and genesis of second language development*. Oxford University Press.
Lave, J., & Wenger, E. (1991). *Situated Learning: Legitimate peripheral participation*. Cambridge University Press.
Llopis-García, R., & Vinagre, M. (2014). Writing and culture in CALL: 21st century foreign language learning via email tandem exchanges. In M. Thomas (Ed.), *Pedagogical considerations and opportunities for teaching and learning on the web*. IGI Global.
Luzón, M. J. (2018). Constructing academic identities online: Identity performance in research group blogs written by multilingual scholars. *Journal of English for Academic Purposes*. *33*, 24–39.
Mullen, A., & Bortoluzzi, M. (2019). Assessing intercultural awareness: Reflection vs. interaction in telecollaboration. *Lingue e Linguaggi*, *33*.
Norton, B. (2001). Non-participation, imagined communities and the language classroom. In M. Breen (Ed.), *Learner contributions to language learning: new directions in research*. Pearson Education.
Norton, B., & Toohey, K. (2011). Identity, language learning and social change. *Language Teaching*, *44*(4), 412–446.
O'Dowd, R. (2005). Negotiating sociocultural and institutional context: The case of Spanish– American telecollaboration. *Language and Intercultural Communication*, *5*(1), 40–57.
Pavlenko, A., & Norton, B. (2007). Imagined communities, identity, and English language learning. In J. Cummins & C. Davison (Eds.), *International handbook of English language teaching* (pp. 669–680). Springer.
Reyes, S. A., & Vallone. T. (2007). Toward an expanded understanding of two-way bilingual immersion education: Constructing identity through a critical, additive bilingual/bicultural pedagogy. *Multicultural Perspectives*, *9*(3), 3–11. doi: 10.1080/15210960701443433
Rezaei, S., & Latifi, A. (2020). Iranian EFL learners' identity construction in a critical reflective course: A case of an online course. *Open Learning: The Journal of Open, Distance and e-Learning*, *35*(1), 63–81.
Sauro, S. (2017). Online fan practices and CALL. *Calico Journal*, *34*(2), 131–146.
Sung, C. C. M. (2019). Investments and identities across contexts: A case study of a Hong Kong undergraduate student's L2 learning experiences. *Journal of Language, Identity & Education*, *18*(3), 190–203.
Taskiran, A. (2019). The effect of augmented reality games on English as foreign language motivation. *E-Learning and Digital Media*, *16*(2), 122–135.
Tesch, R. (2013). *Qualitative research: Analysis types and software*. Routledge.

Thorne, S. L., Black, R. W., & Sykes, J. M. (2009). Second language use, socialization, and learning in Internet interest communities and online gaming. *The Modern Language Journal*, *93*, 802–821.

Toscu, S., & Erten, İ. H. (2020). Developing intercultural communicative competence by the means of telecollaboration. *Education and Information Technologies*, *25*(5), 4517–4534.

Turkle, S. (1995). *Life on the screen: Identity in the age of Internet*. Simon & Schuster.

Vygotsky, L. (1978). *Mind in society: The development of higher psychological processes*. Harvard University Press.

Wenger, E. (1998). *Communities of practice: Learning, meaning and identity*. Cambridge University Press.

Wenger, E., McDermott, R., & Snyder, W. (2002). *Cultivating communities of practice: A guide to managing knowledge*. Harvard Business School Press.

Yi, Y. (2009). Adolescent literacy and identity construction among 1.5 generation students: From a transnational perspective. *Journal of Asian Pacific Communication*, *19*(1), 100–129.

Yin, R. K. (2003). *Case study research: Design and methods*. Sage Publications.

About the Author

Se Jeong Yang is an assistant professor in the Department of Education, Counseling, and Leadership at Bradley University, Peoria, IL. Her main research interest is multilingual students' learning of multiple literacies and identity construction via telecollaboration.

Index

www.ingramcontent.com/pod-product-compliance
Lightning Source LLC
LaVergne TN
LVHW010443080826
844660LV00026B/1203

* 9 7 8 1 8 0 0 5 0 0 7 9 2 *